INTERMEDIATED SECURITIES

The Impact of the Geneva Securities Convention and the Future European Legislation

In today's financial markets, investors no longer hold securities physically. Instead, securities such as shares or bonds are mostly held through intermediaries and transferred by way of book-entries on securities accounts. However, there are some remarkable conceptual differences between the various jurisdictions with regard to the legal treatment of intermediated securities. It is widely agreed that this patchwork creates considerable legal risks, especially in cross-border situations. Two initiatives are well advanced to reduce these risks. In 2009, the UNIDROIT Convention on Substantive Rules for Intermediated Securities (the 'Geneva Securities Convention') was adopted, aiming at harmonisation on the international level. At the regional level, the EU Commission is running a legislative project to achieve harmonisation. This book compares both initiatives and analyses their impact on the securities laws of selected European jurisdictions.

PIERRE-HENRI CONAC is Professor of Commercial and Company Law at the University of Luxembourg.

ULRICH SEGNA is an assistant researcher at the University of Luxembourg.

LUC THÉVENOZ is Professor at the Faculty of Law, University of Geneva, Switzerland, and the director of its Centre for Banking and Finance Law.

INTERMEDIATED SECURITIES

The Impact of the Geneva Securities Convention and the Future European Legislation

Edited by

PIERRE-HENRI CONAC, ULRICH SEGNA
AND LUC THÉVENOZ

CAMBRIDGE
UNIVERSITY PRESS

CAMBRIDGE UNIVERSITY PRESS
Cambridge, New York, Melbourne, Madrid, Cape Town,
Singapore, São Paulo, Delhi, Mexico City

Cambridge University Press
The Edinburgh Building, Cambridge CB2 8RU, UK

Published in the United States of America by Cambridge University Press, New York

www.cambridge.org
Information on this title: www.cambridge.org/9781107023475

First published 2013

Printed and bound in the United Kingdom by the MPG Books Group

A catalogue record for this publication is available from the British Library

Library of Congress Cataloguing in Publication data
Intermediated securities : the impact of the Geneva Securities Convention
and the future European legislation / edited by Pierre-Henri Conac, Ulrich Segna,
and Luc Thévenoz.
pages cm
Includes bibliographical references and index.
ISBN 978-1-107-02347-5 (hardback : alk. paper)
1. Securities – Europe. 2. Intermediation (Finance) – Law and legislation – Europe.
3. Unidroit Convention on Substantive Rules for Intermediated Securities (2009)
I. Conac, Pierre-Henri, editor of compilation. II. Segna, Ulrich, editor of compilation.
III. Thévenoz, Luc, editor of compilation.
KJC2247.I58 2013
346.24′0666 – dc23 2012048505

ISBN 978-1-107-02347-5 Hardback

CONTENTS

CONTRIBUTORS

PIERRE-HENRI CONAC is Professor of Commercial and Company Law at the University of Luxembourg, where he is director of the Master 2 in European and International Financial Law, specialisation in European Banking and Financial Law (LL.M.). From 1999 to 2006, he was Associate Professor of Law at the University of Paris 1 (Panthéon-Sorbonne). He graduated from the University of Paris 1 (Panthéon-Sorbonne) in business law (1991), from HEC School of Management (1990), and from the Institute of Political Studies of Paris (1994). He also earned an LL.M. from Columbia Law School (1995).

Pierre-Henri Conac's Ph.D. thesis, 'The regulation of securities markets by the French Commission des Opérations de Bourse (COB) and the US Securities and Exchange Commission (SEC)', was awarded several prizes. His research areas deal principally with securities law, company law, and comparative law in these fields, especially with reference to the United States. He has written numerous articles on corporate, securities and comparative law, both in French and in English. He has been a member of several working groups in these areas, including the European Model Company Act (EMCA) Group. He has also been an ECGI Research Associate since 2006, and is managing editor of the *Revue des Sociétés* (Dalloz), France's oldest corporate law review, and is one of the editors of the *European Company and Financial Law Review* (ECFR).

In 2011 the Board of Supervisors of the EU's new financial markets regulator, the European Securities and Markets Authority (ESMA), appointed him to its consultative Stakeholder Group.

PHILIPPE DUPONT is a founding partner of Arendt & Medernach law firm, and is head of the firm's Banking and Insurance Industry Group. He also is a member of the firm's management board and is responsible for human resources. He specialises in banking and finance, and has considerable experience in bank regulatory matters as well as capital markets, lending securities and structured finance transactions. He has been a member of the Luxembourg Bar since 1986.

He is a member of two legal advisory committees, of the securitisation committee, of the ad hoc interpretation group of the Prospectus Directive, of the ad hoc working group on the Market Abuse Directive, of the ad hoc working group on takeover bids, and of the ad hoc working group on the Transparency Directive with the Commission de Surveillance du Secteur Financier (CSSF), the regulatory authority of the financial sector in Luxembourg.

Philippe Dupont was a member of the Luxembourg delegation and of the drafting group of the UNIDROIT Convention on substantive rules for intermediated securities, and was the Luxembourg expert at the Hague Convention on the law applicable to certain rights in respect of securities held with an intermediary. He was a member of the Luxembourg delegation and of the drafting group at the diplomatic conference leading to the Luxembourg Protocol to the Convention on international interests in mobile equipment on matters specific to railway rolling stock. He is also a member of the EU Clearing and Settlement – Legal Certainty Group set up by the European Commission. He is a visiting lecturer in securities law at the University of Luxembourg. He is a conciliator and arbitrator at the International Centre for Settlement of Investment Disputes of the International Bank for Reconstruction and Development and a member of the Permanent Court of Arbitration.

FRANCISCO GARCIMARTÍN is a Chair Professor of Private International Law at Universidad Autónoma of Madrid. His main fields of expertise are international transactions, cross-border insolvency, international litigation as well as cross-border company law. He has published in most of the leading law journals on different aspects of private international law and cross-border transactions, and is co-author of *The European Insolvency Regulation: Law and Practice* (The Hague: Kluwer, 2004). He has represented the Spanish government as national expert in different international organisations, such as UNIDROIT, UNCITRAL, the Hague Conference and the Counsel of the European Union. He is a member of the advisory body constituted by the Spanish Securities Exchange Commission to modernise the Spanish legal framework on securities markets and securities settlement systems.

HANS KUHN is a director and Head of Legal and Corporate Services of the Swiss National Bank, Switzerland's central bank. Before joining the SNB in 2001 he served as a deputy head of the Private International

Law section of the Swiss Federal Office of Justice. He has participated in a number of law reform projects, both domestic and international. He chaired the UNIDROIT Committee of Governmental Experts for the preparation of a Draft Convention on Substantive Rules Regarding Intermediated Securities from 2005 to 2007 and the Committee of the Whole of the Diplomatic Conference for the adoption of the UNIDROIT Securities Convention in 2008. From 2000 until 2002 he served as a delegate for Switzerland to the Hague Conference for Private International Law for the Hague Securities Convention; and from 1995 until 2000 to UNCITRAL for the UN-Receivables Convention. He was also involved in domestic securities law reform in Switzerland, where he chaired a committee of experts commissioned to draft a Federal Act on Intermediated Securities and prepare the ratification of the Hague Securities Convention. Since 2004 he has taught secured transactions and securities law at the University of Lucerne Law School. Hans Kuhn is a graduate of Zurich University (lic. iur. 1993, Dr. iur. 1998) and of Tulane University Law School (LL.M. 2000). He was admitted to the Zurich Bar in 1995.

PHILIPPE LANGLET is General Counsel for Global Investment Management and Services at Société Générale. He is a member of the Commission Consultative de l'Autorité des Marchés Financiers (AMF), dedicated to clearing custody and settlement, and a member of the Paris Europlace UCIT depositary working group. He is also Chairman of the Observatoire Juridique de l'Association Française des Professionals des Titres (AFTI), a member of the Legal Framework Securities working group of the European Banking Federation, and served as a member of the French delegation to UNIDROIT for the Geneva Convention on Intermediated Securities.

CHARLES W. MOONEY, JR. is the Charles A. Heimbold, Jr. Professor of Law at the University of Pennsylvania Law School, where he was previously Interim Dean (1999–2000) and Associate Dean for Academic Affairs (1998–2000, 2008–9). He graduated from the University of Oklahoma (B.A. (high honors) 1969) and the Harvard Law School (J.D. (cum laude) 1972).

His appointments have included Visiting Professor of Law, Georgetown University Law Center (1993), Visiting Professor of Law, University of Virginia School of Law (2000), Visiting Professor of Law, University of Tokyo (2009, 2010) and Visiting Professor of Law, Waseda University (2009).

Mooney was a partner of Shearman & Sterling in New York City (1981–6), and a member of Crowe & Dunlevy, Oklahoma City (1972–81).

He is a member of the American Law Institute, a fellow of the American College of Commercial Finance Attorneys, and a fellow and At-large Regent of the American College of Bankruptcy. He has been and continues to be involved in many law-reform efforts on the state, federal, and international levels. He was a member of the SEC's Federal Advisory Committee on Market Transactions (1991–7) and a co-reporter for the Drafting Committee on the Revision of UCC Article 9 (Secured Transactions).

Professor Mooney served as a US delegate and position coordinator at the UNIDROIT Convention on Security Interests in International Mobile Equipment, including the 2001 Diplomatic Conference in Cape Town which completed the Cape Town Convention and Aircraft Protocol.

He also served as a member of the US delegation to UNIDROIT for the Geneva Convention on Intermediated Securities, including the Diplomatic Conferences in Geneva in 2008 and 2009. He was a visiting scholar at the Institute for Monetary and Economic Studies, Bank of Japan, Tokyo, during the autumn 2006 term, conducting comparative research on the legal regimes of Japan, the United States, and the UNIDROIT Draft Convention on Intermediated Securities. Mooney teaches in the areas of commercial, debtor-creditor, bankruptcy, international business transactions, and real property law and he is the author of books, chapters, articles, and other materials in the commercial law and bankruptcy fields.

HABIB MOTANI is a leading international financial markets lawyer, with particular expertise in relation to derivatives, securities lending, repo, netting and collateral and clearing and settlement systems. A partner since 1986 in Clifford Chance's International Financial Markets Group, he is global head of the Derivatives Group. He specialises in OTC and securitised derivatives, Islamic derivatives, structured capital markets products including derivative linked retail and wholesale structured products, investment banking sales and trading advisory work, securities lending and repos, netting and collateral and their regulatory capital treatment, and in the infrastructure aspects of the financial markets, such as payment and settlement systems, clearing systems, prime brokerage and custody.

PHILIPP PAECH is a lecturer in financial law and financial regulation at the Law Department of the London School of Economics and Political Science. He joined LSE in 2010 after working in the Financial Markets

Directorate of the European Commission for four years. He is also a member of the Frankfurt Bar and a Research Fellow at the Institute for Law and Finance in Frankfurt. In 2008, he was a Visiting Associate Professor at Tokyo University's Graduate School for Law and Politics. He was secretary of the EU Clearing and Settlement Legal Certainty Group of the European Commission and Chairman of the G30 Clearing and Settlement Legal Committee. From 2002 to 2006, he was a member of the UNIDROIT Secretariat in Rome and co-ordinated work on what is today the Geneva Securities Convention.

ULRICH SEGNA is a research assistant at the University of Luxembourg. He holds both German state examinations in Law, a doctorate in Law (Dr. iur., University of Osnabrück, 2001) and is currently preparing a postdoctoral thesis (Habilitationsschrift) on 'Intermediated securities' under the supervision of Prof. Dr. Dr. h.c. mult. Theodor Baums. Before joining the University of Luxembourg in June 2009, he was Assistant Professor in Civil Law and German and European Corporate Law at the Goethe-University of Frankfurt am Main (2003–9). In 2008, he was Visiting Scholar at Columbia Law School, New York. His doctoral thesis, 'Vorstandskontrolle in Großvereinen', was awarded the Rasch-Förderpreis of the academic year 2001 for being the first such work to deal fundamentally with corporate governance problems in registered associations.

LUC THÉVENOZ is a professor at the Faculty of Law of the University of Geneva and the director of its Centre for Banking and Finance Law. His research and teachings include the law of obligations, contracts, trusts, as well as the law of banking and securities transactions, markets and regulation.

He is the president of the Swiss Takeover Board, the regulatory agency supervising the takeover market. He has previously served as a commissioner of the Swiss Federal Banking Commission (2001–7) and as a member of the International Arbitral Tribunal for Dormant Accounts in Switzerland (1997–2001). He has contributed to a number of legislative and regulatory projects, including in the areas of trusts, intermediated securities, takeovers and unclaimed assets. He was the main Swiss negotiator for the UNIDROIT Convention on Substantive Rules for Intermediated Securities, a member of its drafting committee, and an editor of its official commentary. After obtaining his law degree (1982) and his Ph.D. (1987), he trained and qualified as an attorney-at-law. He was admitted to the Bar of Geneva (1989), where he practised with the law firm of

Lenz & Staehelin. He was appointed full-time professor in 1993. He teaches regularly at the University of Luxembourg and has been a visiting professor or scholar at Duke Law School, Boston University and the University of California at Berkeley (Boalt Hall).

Luc Thévenoz is a member of the editorial boards of the *Swiss Business Law Review* and of *Trust Law International.* In 2007, the Society of Trust and Estate Practitioners awarded him honorary membership for his contribution to a better understanding and recognition of trusts in civil law jurisdictions and to the ratification by Switzerland of the Hague Convention on Trusts.

MICHEL TISON is a professor at the Financial Law Institute of the University of Ghent. After having obtained a law degree in Ghent (1990) and a Master of European law in Brussels (ULB, 1992), he worked as a doctoral researcher in the newly founded Financial Law Institute. He obtained his Ph.D. in 1997 with a thesis on the legal aspects of the mutual recognition principle in European banking and financial law (published in 1999). He took up a teaching assignment at the Law School of Ghent University in 1998, where he currently teaches courses on banking and capital markets law, credit law, general commercial law and insolvency.

Michel Tison was a visiting professor at Pittsburgh University Law School in 2001, at Bonn University (Germany) in 2004 and at Bond University (Australia) in 2008. In summer 2006, he taught in the law module of the 'Semester at Sea' programme. Since 2005, he has served as an assessor in the Legislative Section of the Belgian Council of State, which advises the government and parliament on draft decrees and bills.

HUBERT DE VAUPLANE Ph.D., is a partner at Kramer Levin Naftalis & Frankel LLP in Paris, and a professor at Paris II University (Assas). Prior to joining Kramer Levin, he served as Group General Counsel, Legal & Compliance for Crédit Agricole SA Group, France's largest retail banking group. Previously he served as the head of legal affairs at Crédit Agricole Corporate & Investment Bank. He is designated as an expert at the European Central Bank, the European Commission and the French Securities Commission (Autorité des marchés financiers, or AMF).

LIENTJE VAN DEN STEEN obtained her law degree at Ghent University in 2004, and immediately joined Ghent's Financial Law Institute as assistant. In May 2009, she obtained her Ph.D., which dealt with intermediated securities and securities accounts. She was then appointed as assistant professor at the Business Law Department of Tilburg University. Her fields of interest include financial law, Islamic banking and finance, company law, consumer protection, property law and civil law. Since 2011, she has been a lawyer specialising in financial regulation at Clifford Chance in Brussels.

JEAN-PIERRE YON has spent his entire career at the Crédit Agricole Group, first as a financial analyst, then successively head of an agrifood financing team, administrative organisation specialist, and since 2000, as Senior Legal Counsel in charge of Stock Exchange and Securities Issues at Crédit Agricole SA's Legal Affairs department. He holds a postgraduate diploma in public law, private law and in industrial property rights and in political science.

PREFACE

In today's financial markets, investors no longer hold their investment securities in physical form. Instead, securities such as shares or bonds are mostly held through intermediaries and transferred by way of electronic book-entries on securities accounts. In its simplest form, an intermediated holding system may be understood as a three-tier pyramid: the investors ('ultimate account holders') are at the bottom, with their securities credited to securities accounts maintained by their intermediaries. The intermediaries, in turn, hold their securities on a book-entry basis with the top-tier intermediary, normally a Central Securities Depository (CSD). Especially in cross-border relationships, this multi-tiered structure can build up to four, five or more levels. However, regardless of the number of levels, all intermediated holding systems have it in common that no certificates circulate, and that the securities are transferred only by making debits and credits to securities accounts. Increasingly, certificated securities are being replaced by fully dematerialised securities.

Nevertheless, there are remarkable conceptual differences between the various jurisdictions with regard to the legal treatment of intermediated securities, reflecting the variety of legal traditions and market practices. It is widely agreed that this patchwork of legal rules creates obstacles to the efficiency and safety of securities transactions, especially in cross-border situations. Several projects have been developed, both at the international and at the European levels, to reduce the legal risks inherent in the cross-border settlement of securities transactions by harmonising the legal framework for intermediated securities. On 9 October 2009, a Diplomatic Conference held in Geneva adopted the UNIDROIT Convention on Substantive Rules for Intermediated Securities (in short, the Geneva Securities Convention). At the same time, the European Commission was preparing a draft Directive on legal certainty of securities holding and dispositions (Securities Law Directive – SLD), which was expected to cover both substantive law and conflicts of laws.

This development was the reason for Pierre-Henri Conac and Ulrich Segna from the Faculty of Law, Economics and Finance of the University of Luxembourg, and Luc Thévenoz from the Centre for Banking and Financial Law of the University of Geneva, to organise an international conference entitled 'Intermediated Securities – The Geneva Securities Convention, the European Securities Law Directive and their Impact on Securities Laws of selected European Jurisdictions'. This conference was held in Luxembourg on 23 and 24 September 2010, at the Luxembourg Chamber of Commerce. It featured fourteen distinguished speakers, both academics and legal practitioners, and attracted 150 participants, mainly from European countries, but also from the United States and India.

The purpose of the conference was to compare the Geneva Securities Convention and the future EU Securities Law Directive, in order to analyse how and to what extent these instruments would impact on the securities laws of selected European jurisdictions. Following this concept, the first part of the conference dealt with the functional approach underlying these instruments and with several key issues of the harmonisation process, such as the rights of the account holder, the rights of the investor, the transfer of intermediated securities, intermediated securities as collateral, and the integrity of the intermediated holding system. In the second part of the conference, legal experts from various European countries gave an overview of the legal framework for intermediated securities of their respective home countries and examined whether the implementation of the Geneva Securities Convention and the future EU Directive would bring with it the necessity to amend national law, perhaps substantially.

The extremely positive response to the Luxembourg conference, and the major importance of the policy issues discussed during the conference for the smooth development and the internationalisation of securities markets, were the main motivation for the organisers to publish a conference volume. It provides additional perspectives on a number of issues, and should be read as a complement to the Official Commentary of the Geneva Securities Convention published in May 2012.

Regarding the future European legislation, no formal proposal has yet been adopted by the European Commission. As things currently stand, it is not even clear whether the instrument should be a directive, a regulation or a mere recommendation. For this reason, the authors of this book have substantially relied on the last published document, i.e. the Consultation Document of November 2010.

We believe that this book is relevant for policy makers, for legal practitioners, as well as for academics. We hope that it will contribute to a better understanding of the Geneva Securities Convention and inform the European debate about a more extensive harmonisation of the law of intermediated securities, ensuring the acceptability and the success of both initiatives.

We express our deep appreciation to all who have contributed to this book or to the conference. We want to include José Angelo Estrella Faria, Secretary-General of UNIDROIT, for his participation and support, as well as Garth Hall and Christian Deprez for their valuable assistance in preparing this publication.

Pierre-Henri Conac, Ulrich Segna and Luc Thévenoz
Luxemburg and Geneva, February 2013

TABLE OF LEGISLATION

Belgium

European Union

France

Germany

Spain

Switzerland

United Kingdom

United States of America

TABLE OF INTERNATIONAL INSTRUMENTS

PART I

The Geneva Securities Convention and the future EU legislation in comparison

1

The Geneva Securities Convention: objectives, history, and guiding principles

LUC THÉVENOZ

1.1 Money, securities and the intermediary holding system

Capital markets form the essentially virtual and increasingly global marketplace where money flows from investors to governments, companies and some international financial institutions that use these funds for their operation and growth. However, investors do not part with their money for free. They are offered future cash flows, such as interest and repayment of capital (for bonds) or dividends (for shares). The issuers of these bonds, shares, and any variation thereof sell promises of future cash flows to investors. Indeed, they issue rights to investors in exchange for their cash. Such rights are enforceable against the relevant issuer. They typically consist of monetary claims, fixed or contingent; voting and other rights to participate in certain decisions in respect of the issuer; or any combination thereof.

Investors are willing to pay good money against rights entitling them to future cash flows and some degree of decision-making power. But that is not enough. Such rights would have less value if investors did not have the ability to re-sell their rights to other investors. Absent this feature, they would be stuck with their bonds until redemption (note, however, that some bonds are perpetual), and with their shares until the issuer goes bankrupt or is otherwise liquidated, which is not usually what investors hope for.

In the capital markets, the rights issued to investors must therefore be negotiable, i.e., capable of being transferred by way of sale, or being used as collateral in a credit or other financial transaction. The problem with such rights is that they are intangible. Transferring intangible rights is fraught with risks. How can the seller or collateral provider prove that she is the legal owner of such rights? How can she prove their actual contents and extent? How will the buyer or the collateral provider be able to exercise them and, if need be, to sell or pledge them further on? Entitlement to and transfer of intangible rights raise significant evidential and legal problems. That creates a variety of risks, ranging from legal uncertainty to operational mistakes and fraud.

By contrast, physical property is much easier to trade, because the thing that is being sold or pledged has physical substance and can be delivered to the buyer or to the secured party. There are also risks in transaction over tangible property, such as legal title, authenticity and other qualities of that thing. Legal rules have evolved so as to protect against such risks to various degrees, from the protection of an innocent acquirer (*acquéreur de bonne foi*) to remedies against the seller for defective goods.

The law can never fully protect the acquirer of either tangible or intangible property, but there is no doubt that tangible, movable property is usually easier to transfer, and allows the acquirer to more easily assess its risks and protect against their occurrence.

It was therefore a great innovation of mercantile law and of the infant capital markets to start treating intangible rights against issuers *as if* they were tangible movable property. Issuing physical securities representing fungible fractions of the rights created by an issuer to a large degree allowed such rights to be treated *as if* they were movable property. The securities were not only evidence of the rights issued ('certificates'), they were also the movable vehicles whose transfer according to the law governing chattels also operated the transfer of the intangible rights 'attached to' or 'incorporated in' them. Investment securities, *valeurs mobilières*, *Wertpapiere* were a major innovation of the financial markets. In their purest form as bearer certificates, securities might actually be subject to the very rules applying to chattels and incur the same types of risk (e.g., lack of authenticity, defective title). Registered securities have retained mixed features because registration of the transfer was and still is required to effect transfer of title or to procure or allow the exercise of all or some of the rights.

Why use the past tense for most of the last paragraph? Because transferring securities as pieces of movable property has become quite exceptional. It is even impossible or prohibited in certain jurisdictions which have legally abolished the issuance of certificated securities, at least in so far as listed securities are concerned. Over the last sixty years, the great innovation of turning intangible rights into tangible, movable property has been rendered impractical, costly, and undesirable. At the risk of over-simplifying the story, issuers find it costly to issue and redeem certificates and coupons, to handle registration of investors, and to deal with lost or stolen certificates. For investors, keeping certificated securities may be quite inconvenient. For example, storing them in a safe deposit box is somewhat risky and/or costly; handling the certificates every time one wants to sell, pledge or redeem the certificates securities or simple to cash in the coupons is inconvenient. Banks, securities dealers and other financial intermediaries are willing to earn a fee for keeping those certificates in safe custody, but they would rather avoid detaching coupons and dealing with the physical delivery of certificates for every transaction. Notwithstanding economies of scale, processing costs and operational risks increase exponentially with the number of issues and with transaction speeds. Governments have taxation and anti-money laundering issues of their own, with certificated securities moving from hand to hand.

In the same way as private cars and highways allowed mass tourism and the development of sprawling suburbs, certificated securities were the vehicles that allowed the expansion of the capital markets. However, ever-more cars, moving at ever-increasing speed, created increasing traffic jams. Investors, issuers, and the intermediaries for the capital markets set about creating huge and safe parking lots where securities would be immobilised most of the time, if not for ever. Thus appeared central securities depositories (CSDs), to which banks and other financial institutions would deliver their own securities and the securities of their clients for safekeeping. At an ever-increasing scale starting from the 1960s, the physical delivery of securities was replaced by credits and debits in securities accounts maintained by CSDs for their participating financial institutions, and by financial institutions for their clients or for other financial institutions. By doing so, participants in the capital markets actually ceased to treat securities as movable property and resumed dealing with the rights attached to the securities, though not by way of assignment in the legal sense, but in a sort of a book-keeping way.

In other words, while one of the great innovations of capital markets was to load intangible rights into physical vehicles, to facilitate their circulation in the markets and among investors, the costs and risks of exponentially crowded highways connecting markets and investors resulted in the parking of the vehicles. The vehicles themselves became largely irrelevant, and sales and other transactions in respect of the rights stored in the vehicles were henceforth recorded in special accounts called 'securities accounts'.

It is interesting to note that whether vehicles of the same brand and type, or securities of the same issue, are considered as fungible bulk and their transfer recorded by a debit and a credit of a given number, or whether they are individually registered and a record is kept of every particular vehicle or security transferred in any given transaction, is a matter of national preference.[1] The huge data-handling capacities of modern information technologies accommodate either approach.

If the market can work by keeping a record of vehicles immobilised all year long, why continue manufacturing individual cars in large numbers? Might issuers instead consider creating a small truck containing all the rights comprised in a single issue? Or might they abstain from making cars completely, and use the same securities accounts for rights which could be registered somewhere, rather than manufactured in the form of cars? Both approaches would save time and cost and might help minimise risks, assuming of course that investors would accept forgoing the right to take their car out for a drive.

This is actually what happened. Once the immobilisation of securities with CSDs became generally accepted, issuers tested the market acceptance of jumbo certificates – each representing a whole issue, and fully dematerialised securities – and discovered that this was often acceptable. In most countries where full dematerialisation of listed securities has not yet been statutorily imposed, dematerialised securities and jumbo certificates are driving out certificated securities. National differences remain in this area, which are deeply linked to market usage, operational arrangements, investment costs, legal doctrines and investor preferences.

1.2 New risks, new legal issues

When bonds and shares were traded as certificated securities, risks did exist, which the laws allocated among participants to a transaction: defective title and protection of bona fide purchasers, forged certificates, effectiveness of defences and of restrictions not documented in the certificate, implied representations and warranties by the transferor, etc. But once

1 A very good example of the latter is Spain, and described by Francisco Garcimartín in Chapter 12 of this book. Whether securities are fungible or not remains controversial in English law: see Goode, 'Are Intangible Assets Fungible?', [2003] *Lloyd's Maritime and Commercial Law Quarterly*, 379, and is a core issue in the English 'Rascals' case which arose from the insolvency of Lehman Brothers; see *Pearsons & Ors as the Joint Administrators of Lehman Brothers International (Europe) (In Administration)* v. *Lehman Brothers Finance SA* [2011] EWCA Civ. 1544, and its discussion by Dilnot and Harris, 'Ownership of a Fund', 272.

such securities circulated without physical delivery, most of these rules became de facto obsolete. The acquirer could no longer rely on possession of the certificate as prima facie evidence of the transferor's title, nor could he read the fine print on the certificate.

New risks emerge when the delivery of securities is replaced by book-entries in securities accounts. The financial intermediary keeping the books may make mistakes. It may act upon instructions that were forged or not otherwise authorised by the account holder. More rights may happen to be credited to the securities accounts of clients than the intermediary itself has in custody or which are credited to its own account with the CSD or other intermediaries. In the intermediated world, mistakes and fraud do not generally affect certificates; they relate to instructions received and entries made by the intermediary.

Indeed, the immobilisation and dematerialisation of securities create huge efficiencies, at the cost of relying almost exclusively on the operational safety and financial soundness of CSDs, banks and other financial intermediaries maintaining securities accounts for their clients. In most jurisdictions, all these intermediaries are regulated and supervised, which should improve their reliability and financial soundness. But this is not a foolproof guarantee of no risk, no loss. The financial crisis that started in 2007 provides ample evidence to the contrary.

Besides the regulation and supervision of intermediaries maintaining securities account, it is clear that the commercial law principles that dealt with certificated securities needed to be supplemented, if not replaced, by new rules dealing with immobilised or dematerialised securities, or rather with securities held through the intermediary holding system. In some jurisdictions, such as Belgium,[2] Luxembourg,[3] France[4] and the United States,[5] the legislature quickly stepped in. In some others, such as

2 *Arrêté royal n° 62 du 10 novembre 1967 favourisant la circulation des instruments financiers fongibles*; see also Chapter 9 of this book by Michel Tison and Lientje Van den Steen.

3 *Règlement grand ducal du 17 février 1971 concernant la circulation de valeurs mobilières*, replaced by the *Loi du 1er août 2001 concernant la circulation de titres et d'autres instruments fongibles*. This is soon to be supplemented, according to a Bill (*Projet de loi relative aux titres dematerialises*, n°6327) of 12 September 2011 now pending before the Luxembourg Parliament.

4 *Décret n° 83–359 du 2 mai 1983 . . . relatif au régime des valeurs mobilières*. The relevant provisions are now codified in the *Code Monétaire et Financier* at Arts. L211–1 et seq.

5 An initial revision of 1977 was replaced in 1994 by the current version of Art. 8 ('Investment Securities'), which has been enacted in all fifty-one states and adopted by the Federal Reserve Board to regulate the clearing and settlement system for the federal government's bonds.

Switzerland,[6] new statutory provisions were implemented only recently, or are presently being considered.

These new provisions deal with all or some of the following issues:

- What is the legal meaning of a credit of securities to a securities account? Is it merely evidential? Or does it represent or somehow contain rights against the relevant issuer, as did certificated securities before?
- Who should enjoy the rights attached to the securities? Any account holder to whose account such securities are credited? Or only the ultimate account holder down the pyramid, i.e. one who does not act as an intermediary for a further account holder?
- What steps are required for a credit to a securities account to be effective against the bank maintaining the account? Are additional steps required for the rights to become effective against the issuer and against third parties? Are such rights also effective in case of insolvency of the bank?
- Is a credit to a securities account the only way to acquire securities held through the intermediary holding system (let us call them intermediated securities, for convenience)? Is a debit the only way to dispose of intermediated securities? Can they be pledged to the intermediary or to a third party in some other way than by having them credited to a securities account in the name of the collateral taker? Which steps are necessary for such dispositions to become effective against third parties and against the insolvency administrators of the collateral provider?
- What happens if a debit to a securities account was not authorised by the account holder? Is the acquirer in that transaction protected? Is knowledge or lack thereof (bona fide) relevant? Must one party lose whenever the other wins, or are there circumstances in which both are protected and it is for the intermediary to make up for the missing securities?
- Until what point can an instruction to transfer intermediated securities be revoked by the transferor? What if the transferor is pronounced insolvent before the transfer has been completed? For systemic reasons, can the rules of a securities settlement system modify the legal rule on that issue?
- Can transfer orders and their respective credits and debits be netted, so as to be settled on a net basis?

6 Federal Intermediated Securities Act of 3 October 2008; see Chapter 13 of this book by Hans Kuhn.

- Can credits be made conditionally, so that they can be reversed if the relevant condition is not fulfilled? Does this apply to credits made before the settlement date if the transfers are not settled?
- Can an investor's securities be attached with any intermediary other than the one maintaining that investor's securities account? What are the effects of an attachment notified to a CSD instead?

It would not be very difficult to expand that list over the next three pages, but that is not the purpose of this chapter.

Our point here is to note that these numerous issues connected with the intermediary holding system are likely to be regulated in one way or another in most jurisdictions, but unlikely to be regulated in the same way. If Canadian investors only held securities issued in Canada, and Greek securities were only in the hands of Greek residents and institutions, this would bother nobody except perhaps for a few highly specialised scholars of comparative law. But such is not the case. Bonds issued by the Greek government are held by many investors outside of Greece, and Canadian investors hold, personally or via investment funds or pension funds, significant stocks of non-Canadian securities. In short, the globalisation of the financial markets has resulted in very significant cross-border holdings. A good example is offered by Swiss banks, which traditionally hold internationally highly diversified portfolios of securities for resident and non-resident clients.[7]

In short, besides the legal (and operational) risks associated with investors holding domestic securities through domestic intermediaries, cross-border situations give rise to additional legal (and operational) risks.

1.3 The governing law issue

The first obvious risk relates to the determination of the applicable law in cross-border holdings. When a Canadian investor sells Greek bonds to a Caiman Island vulture fund, which law governs the questions listed above and some others? The same question also applies when that same Canadian investor uses US Treasury bills as security for a loan extended by a Japanese bank.

7 At the end of April 2012, securities held by all clients with Swiss banks were valued at CHF 4,281 billion, of which 58.6% were issued by foreign issuers. Non-resident (individual and institutional) clients held a higher proportion of 70.8% of foreign-issued securities. Source: Swiss National Bank, *Monthly Statistical Bulletin*, June 2012, Table D52a.

The need for a clear rule of conflict was identified and discussed abundantly in the 1990s.[8] As early as 1998, the European Community adopted the 'place of the relevant intermediary approach' (PRIMA). For example, Article 9(1) of the Financial Collateral Directive refers to 'the law of the country in which the relevant account is maintained'.[9] Similar rules are mentioned in two other directives.[10] These directives achieved a fair degree of European Union-wide harmonisation, even though their respective scopes remain partial and the national provisions implementing those directives are not identical, and may thus provide diverging answers in some cases.

But cross-border holdings are not confined to the European Union. Considering the significant legal risk created by the diversity and sometimes uncertainty of the relevant rules of conflict, the Hague Conference on Private International Law took up that very issue in an expedited project.[11] Initiated in 1999, the project resulted in a diplomatic conference held in October 2002 which adopted the Hague Convention on the Law Applicable to Certain Rights in Respect of Securities Held with an Intermediary.[12] This 'Hague Securities Convention' is dated 5 July 2006, being the day when the US and Switzerland formally signed the Convention.[13]

While the initial work of the Conference essentially followed the same lines as the then recent European directives, the approach was changed. Careful analysis showed that a purely objective test yields uncertain results when the relevant intermediary maintains securities accounts using a global platform or extensive outsourcing. In such situations, where is a

8 Guynn et al., *Modernizing Securities Ownership, Transfer and Pledging Laws*; Potok et al., *Cross Border Collateral: Legal Risk and the Conflict of Laws*.

9 Directive 2002/47/EC of the European Parliament and of the Council of 6 June 2002 on financial collateral arrangements (FCD). See also below pp. 38 et seq. and 51 et seq.

10 Art. 24 of the Directive 2001/24/EC of the European Parliament and of the Council of 4 April 2001 on the reorganisation and winding up of credit institutions (WUD); Art. 9(2) of the Directive 98/26/EC of the European Parliament and of the Council of 19 May 1998 on settlement finality in payment and securities settlement systems (SFD), as amended by Directive 2009/44/EC of the European Parliament and of the Council of 6 May 2009.

11 Bernasconi, *The Law Applicable to Dispositions of Securities Held Through Indirect Holding Systems*, Preliminary Document No 1 of November 2000, especially at 30 et seq.

12 Hague Conference on Private International Law, Proceedings of the Nineteenth Session (2002), tome II: Securities, 2006.

13 The Hague Securities Convention is not yet in force because it has been signed by three states (Mauritius, Switzerland and US) but ratified only by the first two. It nonetheless became part of Swiss statutory law on 1 January 2010.

particular securities account maintained? Is it the place of the branch where the client opened her account? Is it the place where the computers and the back-office people do the heavy work of keeping the databases and electronic accounts? Is it the branch that maintains the commercial relationship with the client, advising her and taking her securities order? Wherever is the best choice as the 'place of the relevant intermediary', is it sufficiently recognisable and stable so that the determination of the governing law is stable and predictable? Faced with these difficulties, the Conference departed from the original test and embraced a primary rule based on a designation of the governing law in the securities account agreement subject, however, to the rule that this designation is only effective if the intermediary has (or appears to have) actual securities account operations in the state whose law is designated in the account agreement.[14]

The consensus which allowed the finalisation and adoption of the text of the Hague Securities Convention during the 2002 diplomatic conference turned out to be short-lived. Important Member States of the European Union and the European Central Bank quickly raised objections against the Hague rule. Since the ratification of the Convention would need the approval of the European institutions and of the parliaments of each of the twenty-seven Member States, there is not much chance that such unanimity will be reached any time soon. Recently, the EU Commission has suggested that the present rule could be supplemented so as to clarify the result where multiple branches are concerned.[15] It has also been suggested that the expanded provision might be part of a regulation rather than a directive, noting that regulations are not implemented by national legislation, and are thus less prone to diverging interpretations.

However unfortunate the present situation, it is fair to say that the Hague rule and the European rule are likely to produce identical results in most situations.[16] This is because, for many reasons, banks and other financial intermediaries want the (money and securities) accounts they maintain for their clients to be governed by the law of the place of the establishment with which the client has his business relationship. It is

14 See Art. 4 of the Hague Securities Convention; Art. 5 contains fall-back rules.

15 'Where an account provider has branches located in jurisdictions different from the head offices' jurisdiction, the account is maintained by the branch which handles the relationship with the account holder in relation to the securities account, otherwise by the head office.' See Principle 14.2 of the EU Consultation Paper, presented below in section 1.6.

16 See also 'Legal assessment of certain aspects of the Hague Securities Convention', Commission Staff Working Document of 3 July 2006, SEC(2006) 910.

very unlikely that an intermediary would be willing to operate a securities account in one jurisdiction under the rules of another jurisdiction. There is such a deep connection between the commercial law governing the account and the regulatory framework, which is essentially territorial, that intermediaries are unlikely to take the risk of submitting the account to any other law.

Once the conflict of laws uncertainty had been sorted out – if not by a uniform rule, at least by a better understanding of the existing approaches and their respective outcome – the international focus shifted to the diversity and mismatches among the substantive laws governing intermediated securities. This project was taken up in 2002 by the Institute for the International Unification of Private Law (UNIDROIT) in Rome, and resulted in the UNIDROIT Convention on Substantive Rules for Intermediated Securities being adopted in 2009 by a diplomatic conference convened in Geneva, henceforth known as 'the Geneva Securities Convention'.

1.4 A brief history of the Geneva Securities Convention

Why should the substantive law of intermediated securities be harmonised? And to what extent? These were the first questions addressed by a restricted study group meeting for the first time in September 2002 in Rome.

The study group's provisional answer was released for public discussion in a position paper dated August 2003.[17] The following paragraphs summarise the group's thinking at the time:

> The issues at stake can be divided into two categories –
>
> - The first category is internal soundness, which comprises issues relating to the key features which any structure for the holding and transfer of securities through intermediaries must possess if it is to be regarded as sound, bearing in mind in particular the objectives of investor protection and efficiency.
> - The second category is compatibility, which comprises issues affecting the ability of different legal systems to connect successfully where securities are held or transferred across national borders.

17 'The UNIDROIT Study Group on Harmonised Substantive Rules Regarding Indirectly Held Securities', Position Paper, UNIDROIT 2003 – Study LXXVIIII – Doc. 8, August 2003. All documents relating to that project are available from the UNIDROIT website, www.unidroit.org.

> A harmonised rule should be regarded as appropriate if, but only if, it is clearly required to reduce legal or systemic risk or to promote market efficiency. This approach recognises that, desirable though it may be in principle to achieve harmonised rules, in practice this is a complex and difficult process that requires both technical and political consensus. The difficulty of achieving this, particularly within a reasonable timeframe, strongly argues in favour of a restrictive approach to the scope of harmonization. Furthermore, a functional approach should be adopted, that is, one which uses language which is as neutral as possible and which formulates rules by reference to their results.[18]

It is worth noting that the core principles set out here guided the whole process up to the adoption of the Convention. We will shortly revisit them in the next section. The position paper identifies the following issues for which harmonisation, or some degree of it, is needed:

- prohibition of attachment at an upper tier;
- legal requirements for a valid transfer;
- creation and realisation of security (collateral) interests;
- availability of non-harmonised disposition methods;
- protection of good faith acquisition;
- effectiveness of net settlement;
- finality and irrevocability;
- possibility of provisional credits;
- allocation of shortfall;
- protection in insolvency.

All those points are part of the final text of the Convention. But some other important issues were later identified in the process and are also part of the Convention.

The restricted study group had the benefit of numerous comments to the position paper and attracted the interest of the financial regulators and of the financial industry. With the support of UNIDROIT's Secretariat, its members made fact-finding visits to various countries, the results of which fed back into the thinking of the group. Altogether in four sessions over two years, the group came up with a draft instrument.[19] This draft served as the starting point for negotiations that were handled by a Committee of Governmental Experts convened by the Governing

18 *Ibid.*, at 5–6.

19 Preliminary Draft Convention on Harmonised Substantive Rules Regarding Securities Held with an Intermediary, Explanatory Notes, UNIDROIT 2004, Study LXXVIII – Doc. 19, December 2004.

Council of UNIDROIT. The Committee held four sessions, from May 2005 to September 2007. Its progress was supported by inter-sessional working groups, seminars, and consultations. Its work (drafts, working papers, comments by delegations and observers, minutes) is thoroughly documented on the UNIDROIT website.[20]

This book is not about the history of the Convention. It is nonetheless useful to recall some of the most significant issues that were only properly identified during the work of the Committee and attracted a lot of attention and concern until they could be solved.

1. So-called 'transparent systems' are intermediated holding systems where the investor accounts are maintained by the CSD or where the CSD by some other means actually identifies investors. Such systems exist in emerging markets (notably China and Brazil) and in mature markets (Spain, Nordic countries). At the second session of the Committee of Governmental Experts, serious doubts were raised whether such systems could actually fit into the draft Convention. Extensive research and dialogue followed that session, resulting in a ground-breaking working paper which allowed the Committee to give full consideration to the issues raised by transparent systems and make sure that the Convention would include them.[21]
2. In most systems, only regulated intermediaries are allowed to maintain securities accounts for clients. This legal requirement is supported by the idea that intermediaries maintaining such accounts bear a huge responsibility in respect of their clients' holdings as well as the systemic stability of the whole system. Some official supervision and review of their operation is an important support to the application of sound commercial rules. Should that disqualify clients of unlicensed intermediaries from enjoying the benefits of the Convention? A number of delegations thought that it should, a possibility now offered to Contracting States.[22]
3. The means by which the total number of securities circulating in the intermediated holding system matches the number of securities that

20 At www.unidroit.org.

21 Report of the Transparent Systems Working Group, UNIDROIT 2007, Study LXXVIII – Doc. 88, May 2007. That work resulted, inter alia, in the addition of Art. 7 (Performance of functions of intermediaries by other persons) of the Convention and by an attenuation of its Art. 22 (Prohibition of upper-tier attachment).

22 See Art. 5(b) of the Convention.

were actually issued are a topic of constant debate.[23] How it is to be achieved is linked closely with fundamental issues of property law (whether an investor actually and individually owns the securities she has bought, or whether she owns an interest in the pool of like securities held by its intermediary), corporate governance (number of voting rights that can be exercised), and protection in the insolvency of an intermediary. Articles 21 to 28 of the Convention represent a compromise solution to this issue. One side-effect of this debate is that a uniform rule confirming the validity of transfers of intermediated securities that are processed on a net basis was replaced by a neutral statement to the effect that the Convention does not stand in the way of any such national rule.[24]

4. A list of internationally harmonised methods for disposing of intermediated securities or some interest therein was present from the very start. It was clear that, while credits and debits to securities accounts are and must be universally available, other methods are optional for Contracting States. The Committee of Governmental Experts made three fundamental changes to the original proposal, the result of which is now in Article 12 of the Convention. First, the Committee expanded the list of optional methods to include control agreements.[25] Second, the menu approach, whereby each Contracting State may choose to apply one, more, or none of the optional methods, was supplemented by a declaration to be made by the relevant state so as to give some degree of international publicity to the methods available under the laws of that state. Third, and perhaps most important, the Committee recognised that each method should be available for any type of disposition, whether it is an outright transfer, a collateral transaction, or the creation of yet another type of interest (such as usufruct or a trust).

Eight weeks of meetings of the Committee of Governmental Experts, supplemented by numerous inter-sessional working groups and consultations, transformed and enriched the initial draft of December 2004. In

23 See Chapters 7 (Charles Mooney) and 8 (Hubert de Vauplane and Jean-Pierre Yon) in this book.

24 Compare Art. 11(5) of the Convention with Art. 3(4) of the Preliminary Draft Convention, UNIDROIT 2004 Study LXXVIII – Doc. 18, November 2004.

25 Control agreements and designating entries now seem to compete. Because dispositions must be effective against third parties, some states concerned with the lack of publicity toward third parties of interests perfected through control agreements obtained the possibility that their priority rule may derogate from a strict *prio tempore* principle and give preference to interests perfected by way of a designating entry. See Art. 19(7).

2007, UNIDROIT's Governing Council considered that the project was ripe for diplomatic conference. The conference was hosted by the Swiss Government in Geneva during the first two weeks of September 2008. The crisis of the financial markets was developing on a daily basis – the failure of Lehman Brothers (which filed in bankruptcy court on 15 September 2008) occurred only three days after the first session of the conference ended.

Ten days of work by delegates of fifty-two states and by observers of the European Community and eleven international organisations and groups allowed a first and a second reading of the full text of the Convention, but did not result in its adoption. Delegations were keenly aware of the unusual complexity of the instrument and of its technicality. They wanted more time to better understand the implications of the text that had been arrived at. To help them in this assessment, the conference requested that a draft Official Commentary be prepared and circulated at least three months before a second session be convened.[26]

That final session was held in Geneva in October 2009, at the end of which the Conference adopted the UNIDROIT Convention on Substantive Rules for Intermediated Securities, Resolution No 1 of which recommends that it be known as the 'Geneva Securities Convention'.[27]

The Official Commentary was subsequently supplemented, circulated for comment, finalised and published.[28] Besides an emerging literature on the subject, the Official Commentary is the main source of information on the policy discussions and drafting issues considered during the whole process leading up to the adoption of the Convention.

1.5 Objectives and guiding principles of the Convention

As far as conventions harmonising a particular topic of private law are concerned, there are hardly any as complex as the Geneva Securities

26 See the Final Act of the first session of the diplomatic Conference to Adopt a Convention on Substantive Rules regarding Intermediated Securities held under the auspices of the International Institute for the Unification of Private Law in Geneva from 1 to 12 September 2008, including Resolution No. 2 relating to the Official Commentary on the Convention.

27 Final Act of the final session of the diplomatic Conference to Adopt a Convention on Substantive Rules regarding Intermediated Securities held under the auspices of the International Institute for the Unification of Private Law in Geneva from 5 to 9 October 2009.

28 Kanda et al., *Official Commentary on the Unidroit Convention on Substantive Rules for Intermediated Securities*, also published in French as *Commentaire officiel de la Convention d'Unidroit sur les règles matérielles relatives aux titres intermédiés.*

Convention. That complexity has many reasons. The sheer technicality of the topic is one. Another is the huge diversity of legal and technical arrangements on which national systems for the intermediated holding of securities developed over time. That complexity should not however hide its objectives and guiding principles, which this section attempts to sketch out with a broad brush.

Whereas the Hague Securities Convention contains rules of conflict, the Geneva Securities Convention deals exclusively with substantive rules. It often refers to the 'non-Convention law'[29] or to 'the applicable law', but never purports to designate which law, besides its own provisions, should govern any particular issue.

The subject matter of the Convention, 'intermediated securities', is not a pre-existing concept. In fact, it is a new term of art defined in Article 1(b) as 'securities credited to a securities account or rights or interest in securities resulting from the credit of securities to a securities account'. The Convention provides substantive rules for securities when they are credited to a securities account maintained by an intermediary. How the securities were issued – certificated securities, jumbo certificate or fully dematerialised securities – is irrelevant to the operation of the Convention, as long as the securities are kept within the intermediated holding system.[30]

The Convention has three fundamental objectives: protecting the rights of investors, preserving the integrity of the intermediated holding system, and ensuring the cross-border compatibility of legal systems. However, the breadth and depth of its provisions are much more limited than these objectives would suggest. Most of its provisions read like principles, expressed in terms of a result to be achieved, rather than a prescription for how to achieve it. Why is this so?

One of the main reasons for the complexity as well as the limitations of the Convention lies with the recognition that the global intermediated holding system is actually a complex network of as many different systems as there are jurisdictions and markets. The legal, commercial and technological elements of each system are heavily dependent on how it developed

29 Defined in Art. 1(m) of the Convention. On this topic, see particularly Garcimartín Alférez, 'The Geneva Convention on Intermediated Securities: a Conflict-of-Laws Approach'.

30 Art. 9(1)(c) of the Convention states that 'to the extent permitted by the applicable law, the terms of the securities and, to the extent permitted by the non-Convention law, the account agreement or the uniform rules of a securities settlement system' decide whether securities can be held otherwise than through a securities account.

and, to an amazing extent, on the fundamental doctrines of property that underpin its design and evolution. The mixed nature of securities before their intermediation, intangible property transmuted into chattels, gave rise to very different legal characterisation of the rights arising from the immobilisation or dematerialisation of the securities and their credit to securities accounts.[31]

It was soon acknowledged in the preparatory work that no instrument harmonising the law of intermediated securities would be acceptable if it implied interfering with basic national doctrines of property law. This is why the design of the Convention follows a functional approach.[32] Rules are drafted by reference to facts and results; they avoid in so far as possible legal notions.[33] For example, while the Convention is essentially about the property of investors in respect of intermediated securities, it almost entirely omits the word itself.

In addition, it soon became apparent that in these matters, less is more. For example, it was obvious that fully harmonising the validity requirements for book entries would be impossible. As a result, the Convention requires that the intermediary acts upon an instruction authorised by the account holder or by the law, and states emphatically that no further step than a credit or a designating entry is necessary to make the acquisition effective against third parties. The harmonisation goes no further and leaves other validity requirements for 'non-Convention law', the shorthand for the applicable law besides the Convention itself.[34]

A common criticism is that the Convention defers so often to the non-Convention law that it fails to achieve any meaningful degree of harmonisation. The Official Commentary itself speaks of a 'minimalist' approach.[35] The Convention falls far short of a uniform set of rules that would apply irrespective of the law governing a given securities account. It offers many options, and for the most important ones requires that the choices be publicised by a declaration by the relevant Contracting

31 See Chapter 2 by Philipp Paech in this book; see also Thévenoz, 'Intermediated Securities', at 401 et seq.

32 See the 6th recital of the Preamble.

33 The *Official Commentary*, at Int-20, speaks of a 'a functional and neutral approach.' See particularly Than, 'Der funktionale Ansatz in der UNIDROIT Geneva Securities Convention vom 9. Oktober 2009'.

34 Kronke, 'Das Genfer UNIDROIT-Übereinkommen über materiellrechtliche Normen für intermediär-verwahrte Wertpapiere und die Reform des deutschen Depotrechts'; Deschamps, 'The Geneva Securities Convention – Selected Issues Left to Law Outside the Convention'.

35 *Official Commentary*, Int–21.

State. But this self-limiting approach to harmonisation must be seen as the only chance of its success. Any more would be outright unacceptable. This does not prevent more extensive harmonisation at a regional level.

1.6 The ongoing EU harmonisation process

An international convention designed to support enhanced harmonisation at regional level was not an abstract idea. Early on in the UNIDROIT project, the European Union set upon assessing the need, ways and means for further and deeper harmonisation.[36]

In 2005, the EU Commission appointed a group of experts, the so-called Legal Certainty Group, which embarked on an extensive and detailed review of the laws of Member States as well as of some other significant jurisdictions (Japan, Switzerland, the United States). The compiled results make for an impressive 666-page document.[37] The group also produced a number of interesting topical papers. Its main output is however a short first advice,[38] released together with the comparative compilation mentioned above, followed two years later by a second (and final) advice.[39]

Based on these advices, the Commission began preparing draft legislation. A Consultation Document was circulated in April 2009, which obtained a broad audience and numerous comments.[40] Further internal documents were then prepared. At the time of the conference in which

36 The first report of the committee chaired by Alberto Giovannini ('Cross-Border Clearing and Settlement Arrangements in the European Union', November 2001) had earlier concluded (at 54) that 'the existence of different legal rules defining the effect of the operation of a system, including different legal structures concerning securities themselves' are significant barriers to efficient cross-border clearing and settlement, and thus obstacles to the extension and deepening of the single market for securities and investment services. The report also noted that 'Barriers relating to legal certainty are of a different order to the others, as they cannot be removed without affecting basic legal concepts' (*ibid.*) As noted above when discussing the 'functional' and 'minimalist' approaches, the UNIDROIT harmonisation project relied on the tenet that harmonised rules should interfere as little as possible with such basic legal concepts.

37 Document MARKT/G2/MNCT D(2005), 26 July 2007.

38 Legal Certainty Group, 'EU Clearing and Settlement', Advice, dated 11 August 2006.

39 Second Advice of the Legal Certainty Group, 'Solutions to Legal Barriers related to Post-Trading within the EU', August 2008.

40 Directorate-General Internal Market and Services, 'Legislation on Legal Certainty of Securities Holding and Dispositions', Consultation Document G2/PP D(2009), 16 April 2009.

this book originates,[41] participants generally had access to an 'Updated Compilation of the rules and explanatory notes discussed so far', prepared in September 2010.[42] While the circulation of the document was limited to a working group of Member States, the sheer number of persons involved in the work, and the extraordinary interest that it raised, resulted in a near-public dissemination.

While this 'Updated Compilation' was certainly on the mind of the speakers in Luxembourg, their chapters in this present book can now refer explicitly to the officially published subsequent Consultation Document, released by the Services of the Directorate-General Internal Market and Services in November 2010,[43] and to the summary of responses that was made available in May 2011.[44] This is why, when referring to the ongoing legislative process, the authors of this book have generally referred to the EU Consultation Document of November 2011.

The adoption of a proposal by the EU Commission has been deferred many times. Other burning issues took priority in the legislative agenda of Mr Barnier, the Commissioner for Internal Markets, and of the Commission itself. The editors of this book decided that they should wait no longer and proceed with its publication, even though there is not yet an actual draft piece of EU legislation that can be discussed. It is hard to know whether and when such a draft will be adopted by the Commission, whether it will be a directive or a regulation (the favoured approach recently, it seems), or whether it will incorporate and supplement the Geneva Securities Convention or contain rules that would be incompatible with it and would actually prevent the European Union and its Member States from signing and ratifying the Convention.

41 'Intermediated Securities – The Geneva Securities Convention, the European Securities Law Directive and their Impact on Securities Laws of Selected European Jurisdictions', Luxembourg, 23–4 September 2010. The conference was organised by the Faculty of Law, Economics and Finance of the University of Luxembourg jointly with the Centre for Banking and Financial Law of the University of Geneva.

42 Directorate-General Internal Market and Services, 'Legislation on Legal Certainty of Securities Holding and Dispositions, Member States Working Group, Updated Compilation of the rules and explanatory notes discussed so far', G2/PhP D(2010), 17 September 2010.

43 Directorate General Internal Market and Services, 'Legislation on Legal Certainty of Securities Holding and Dispositions', Consultation Document DG Markt G2 MET/OT/acg D(2010) 768690 [November 2010], available at http://ec.europa.eu/internal_market/consultations/2010/securities_en.htm.

44 'Legislation on Legal Certainty of Securities Holding and Dispositions, Summary of Responses to the Directorate-General Internal Market and Services' Second Consultation' [May 2011].

Bibliography

Deschamps, M., 'The Geneva Securities Convention – Selected Issues Left to Law Outside the Convention' [2010] *Uniform Law Review*, 703–12.

Dilnot, A. and Harris, L., 'Ownership of a Fund' [2012] *Butterworths Journal of International Banking and Financial Law*, 272–4.

Garcimartín Alférez, F. J., 'The Geneva Convention on Intermediated Securities: a Conflict-of-Laws Approach' [2010] *Uniform Law Review*, 751–77.

Goode, R., 'Are Intangible Assets Fungible?' [2003] *Lloyd's Maritime and Commercial Law Quarterly*, 379.

Guynn, R. D. et al., *Modernizing Securities Ownership, Transfer and Pledging Laws: A Discussion Paper on the Need for International Harmonization with Responding Comments* (London: Capital Markets Forum, International Bar Association, 1996).

Kanda, H., Mooney, C., Thévenoz, L. and Béraud S., with the help of Keijser, T., *Official Commentary of the Unidroit Convention on Substantive Rules for Intermediated Securities* (Oxford University Press, 2012).

Commentaire officiel de la Convention d'UNIDROIT sur les règles matérielles relatives aux titres intermédiés (Convention de Genève sur les titres) (Zurich: Schulthess, Paris: LGDJ and Montreal: Thémis, 2012).

Keijser, T. and Parmentier, M., 'The Geneva Securities Convention: the Debates of the Diplomatic Conference' [2010] *Butterworths Journal of International Banking and Financial Law*, 230–2.

Kronke, H., 'Das Genfer UNIDROIT-Übereinkommen über materiellrechtliche Normen für intermediär-verwahrte Wertpapiere und die Reform des deutschen Depotrechts' [2010] *Zeitschrift für Wirtschafts- und Bankrecht (WM)*, 1625–35.

Mooney, C., 'The (UNIDROIT) Geneva Securities Convention on Intermediated Securities' [2009] *Butterworths Journal of International Banking and Financial Law*, 602–4.

Potok, R. (ed.), *Cross Border Collateral: Legal Risk and the Conflict of Laws* (London: Butterworths, 2002).

Than, J., 'Der funktionale Ansatz in der UNIDROIT Geneva Securities Convention vom 9. Oktober 2009', in S. Grundmann et al. (eds.), *Festschrift für Klaus Hopt* (Berlin/New York: de Gruyter, 2010), 231–46.

Thévenoz, Luc, 'Intermediated Securities, Legal Risk, and the International Harmonization of Commercial Law', 13 [2008] *Stanford Journal of Law, Business & Finance*, 384–452.

2

Market needs as paradigm – breaking up the thinking on EU securities law

PHILIPP PAECH*

2.1 Introduction

More than a decade ago, the international community realised that there was a need to harmonise certain parts of their securities laws, notably those rules regulating the holding and disposition of securities.[1] Reports on the legal framework governing the holding and disposition[2] of securities found that what had become highly internationalised markets were underpinned by purely national legal frameworks, and that this situation created legal risk, notably as acquisition of securities and security interests therein might prove unexpectedly ineffective in cross-jurisdictional situations.[3]

* The text was updated in May 2012. The author would like to thank Niamh Moloney and Peter Mülbert for their most useful comments on an earlier draft of this paper, and Martin Mojzis, research assistant at LSE, for his invaluable assistance.

1 'Securities law' is generally too broad a term, referring to the various legal aspects of securities, depending on its use the relevant jurisdictions. However, in this chapter I use the term to refer to those legal rules governing the owning, holding and disposition of securities and related aspects. Depending on the relevant jurisdiction, the relevant provisions are typically part of property law, commercial law, the law governing security interests such as pledges and charges, insolvency law, corporate law, and, in some countries, dedicated laws governing the holding of securities. Likewise, rules belonging to the sphere of 'regulation' can belong to 'securities law', as long as they have legal effects dealing with the question of 'who owns what', see the recent judgment of the UK Supreme Court in *Re Lehman Brothers International (Europe) (In Administration)* [2012] UKSC 6, addressing the question whether the client money rules set up by the UK Financial Service Authority, which require separate holding of client monies ('segregation'), impact on the insolvency analysis if the segregation requirement is not complied with.

2 'Holding' is a neutral, non-legal term that leaves open whether the holder is the owner/proprietor or only the custodian/bookkeeper; 'Disposition' is a term that covers both outright transfer and creation of a collateral or security interest over securities.

3 Since the introduction of intermediated securities, the debate has focused on the domestic legal treatment of such securities (see sections 2.2.1 and 2.4.1). Cross-border complications were identified only later; groundbreaking in particular: Einsele, *Wertpapierrecht als Schuldrecht*, 392–542; Guynn et al., *Modernizing Securities Ownership, Transfer and*

As a consequence, the EU adopted the Settlement Finality Directive in 1998 and the Financial Collateral Directive in 2002.[4] However, both were restricted in their scope, and both left conceptual questions largely untouched.[5] Subsequently, further harmonisation efforts, both in international fora and the EU, rapidly slowed to a trickle: the 2002 Hague Securities Convention[6] and the 2009 Geneva Securities Convention,[7] though unanimously adopted after years of expert discussions, faced considerable opposition from inside the EU, and to date have not been implemented[8] by a sufficient number of countries. The European Commission worked on its own proposal for a comprehensive harmonisation of securities law aimed at mitigating legal uncertainty in this area.[9] Its

Pledging Laws; Benjamin, *Interests in Securities*, 147–70. A number of legal policy papers followed: Bernasconi, *The Law Applicable to Dispositions of Securities Held through Indirect Holding Systems*; The Giovannini Group, *Cross-Border Clearing and Settlement Arrangements in the European Union* ('First Giovannini Report'), and *Second Report on EU Clearing and Settlement Arrangements* ('Second Giovannini Report'), Barriers 3, 9, 13–15. However, it should be noted that a policy paper by the CPSS-IOSCO on 'Cross Border Securities Settlement', at 30, mentioned 'the legal status of securities' as early as 1995 and concluded that 'In a cross-border context, the involvement of multiple legal jurisdictions and multiple settlement intermediaries increases the importance of custody risks and greatly complicates their analysis'.

4 Directive 98/26/EC of the European Parliament and of the Council of 19 May 1998 on settlement finality in payment and securities settlement systems (as amended by Directive 2009/44/EC); Directive 2002/47/EC of the European Parliament and of the Council of 6 June 2002 on financial collateral arrangements (as amended by Directive 2009/44/EC).

5 The Settlement Finality Directive is confined to system operators and system participants. It prescribes that (national) insolvency rules cannot reverse transfer orders once entered into the settlement system. The Financial Collateral Directive prescribes that formalities in respect of securities collateral are to be abolished and is (by and large) confined to wholesale market participants. Neither of the Directives attempts to harmonise the content of the securities holder's right, the rules on how such rights are to be transferred or encumbered, or any rules on priority or good faith acquisition. Furthermore, the two Directives, given their uncoordinated scope, contribute to creating a generally patchy framework for securities holding and disposition in the EU.

6 Convention on the Law Applicable to Certain Rights in Respect of Securities held with an Intermediary ('Hague Securities Convention'), hcch.net/index_en.php?act=conventions.text&cid=72.

7 UNIDROIT Convention on Substantive Rules for Intermediated Securities ('Geneva Securities Convention'); unidroit.org/english/conventions/2009intermediatedsecurities/main.htm.

8 The Geneva Securities Convention has been signed by Bangladesh only. The Hague Securities Convention has been ratified by Switzerland and Mauritius, and signed by the United States of America.

9 See Annex to the Commission Work Programme 2012, Brussels, 15 November 2011, (COM(2011) 777 final), 17. For the preparatory work see the European Commission 'Harmonization of Securities law', ec.europa.eu/internal_market/financial-markets/securities-law/index_en.htm and 'Legal Certainty Group, ec.europa.eu/internal_market/financial-markets/clearing/certainty_en.htm.

proposal,[10] based on a blueprint submitted by an expert group and very similar to that put forward by the Geneva Securities Convention, contains rules harmonising the core substance of the right vested in the holder of securities:

- the methods allowing for effective acquisition of securities and collateral interests therein;
- the regimes regarding good faith acquisition and priorities; and
- the regimes addressing the question of who answers for a possible shortfall in securities in the event of insolvency of an intermediary.

This proposal has now been mouldering in the Commission's drawers for two years.

The fate of both the Hague Convention and the Geneva Convention, as well as that of the European legislation, show a common pattern: the instruments (or the project, in the case of the EU) became bogged down as they passed from the stage of expert discussions into the political sphere. The proposed solutions were rejected, and even the case for harmonisation was reopened and questioned. In all three cases, the furore centred mainly on concerns that account holders' securities would be less protected if existing legal concepts governing the holding of securities, notably the concept of property, were undermined.[11]

This controversy exposed conflicts and tensions of different kinds. Some commentators were genuinely convinced that rights in securities can best be expressed in the form of proprietary positions for conceptual reasons, notably in view of the general approach which classifies securities as tangibles.[12] Others feared that harmonisation of the legal approaches in respect of securities law would inevitably lead to a proliferation of the 'Anglo-American' approach which purportedly leads to diminished protection of client securities, in the event of a bank's or broker's insolvency.[13]

10 See n. 16.

11 Here, I employ 'property' as a global term, referring to the idea of full legal title, but without paying attention to differences of detail that a comparison of the various jurisdictions' concepts of property or ownership would reveal.

12 *E.g.*, Drummond, 'Intermediated securities: reflections on a new concept', 438–440; Mülbert, 'Vom Ende allen sachenrechtlichen Denkens', at 446 et seq.

13 *E.g.*, Cremers, 'Reflexions on 'Intermediated Securities' in the Geneva Securities Convention', 93 et seq.; Scherer and Gallei, 'UNIDROIT Draft Convention and German Securities Law: Friend or Foe?', 473 et seq.; Voß, 'Die Securities Law Directive und das deutsche Depotrecht', 209 et seq. However, I submit that the distinction between an 'Anglo-American' approach to securities holding and disposition on the one hand, and a 'Continental' or 'Civilist' approach on the other hand, should *not* be made. Rather, the

Small wonder that this argument proved very effective in political terms in the wake of the financial crisis. A third type of criticism skimmed the surface of the legal debate – centring in particular on property concepts – but in substance aimed at preserving current business models in the securities markets against legal reform, as legal or regulatory changes regularly cause costs and might, in this particular case, open up certain business domains to international competitors.

It was impossible to sort the partisans into clear factions.[14] Governments, regulators, issuers, brokers, merchant banks, service providers and private and institutional investors across national boundaries could be found on both sides of the discussion. There were even divides within organisations acting globally, where the merchant bank arm argued in favour of market-focused harmonisation, while the securities service arm held out for conceptual purity.[15] Justice ministries and central banks in one and the same country might likewise be at odds over the question – and even different divisions within the ECB did not agree as to which concept was the correct basis for harmonisation.

This chapter, first, addresses the stand-off between an approach centring on the needs of the market, taking them as a paradigm for law reform and harmonisation, on the one hand, and the idea that a legal concept (in particular, that of 'property') should guide the international harmonisation of securities law, on the other hand. I will argue that the former approach offers better guidance and that the needs of the market for legal predictability are the natural and traditional driver and determining factor. However, this approach is not necessarily particularly favourable to the specific interests of banks, brokers and other financial intermediaries, since 'the market' also encompasses the interests of institutional and private investors, as well as of securities issuers and, ultimately, of society as a whole.

rift is between jurisdictions in which securities are identified *per investor* and jurisdictions where securities are held on a commingled basis in *omnibus* accounts, see below, section 2.4.3.

14 See the various replies to both public consultations on Securities Law conducted by the European Commission: http://ec.europa.eu/internal_market/consultations/2009/securities_law_en.htm and http://ec.europa.eu/internal_market_consultations/2010/securities_en.htm

15 This phenomenon can be explained by the fact that the aim of a merchant bank is to secure more and easier cross-border business, whereas the securities service arm of the same banking group will consider the protection of the status quo, i.e., market fragmentation, which is more advantageous for its business model.

Further, this paper sheds light on the legal choices which the EU will have to consider when shaping harmonised legal underpinnings for holding and disposition of intermediated securities. These include the advantages and drawbacks, in the context of securities law reform, of the two alternative legislative instruments at hand in the EU, i.e., directives or regulations. Following several years of European legislative effort, a directive emerged as the instrument of choice, i.e., an instrument that allows Member States flexibility in implementing the rules.[16] The term 'Securities Law Directive' ('SLD') became a household name even before the instrument was officially proposed.[17] Over the past three years, however, there has been a growing tendency within the European institutions to embark – as far as its financial services are concerned – on legislative projects in the form of regulations, i.e., directly applicable law, rather than directives.[18]

16 The European Commission based its initiative to harmonise securities law on the findings of the two Giovannini Reports, published in 2001 and 2003, which identified operational, legal and tax-related discrepancies ('barriers'), as set out in its Communication of 28 April 2004 (*Clearing and Settlement in the European Union – The Way Forward, Communication from the Commission to the Council and the European Parliament*, Brussels, 28 April 2004 (COM(2004) 312 final). Subsequently, an expert group was set up, the Clearing and Settlement Legal Certainty Group, to provide further analysis as to the extent of the legal problems and possible solutions (the Clearing and Settlement Legal Certainty Group, *Solutions to Legal Barriers related to Post-Trading within the EU – Second Advice of the Legal Certainty Group*, Brussels, August 2008, ec.europa.eu/internal_market/financial-markets/docs/certainty/2ndadvice_final_en.pdf). The Commission published two consultation questionnaires. As no further documents have been issued to date, this chapter refers to the intentions and thinking of the Commission as set out in its second consultation questionnaire, dated November 2010 (European Commission, *Legislation on Legal Certainty of Securities Holding and Disposition* (DG Markt G2 MET/OT/acg D(2010) 768690, see Appendix). See also the Summary of Responses to the Directorate-General Internal Market and Services' Second Consultation, ec.europa.eu/internal_market/consultations/docs/2010/securities/extended_summary_responses_en.pdf.

17 The Commission itself mentions a 'securities law directive' on the website mentioned above.

18 See some recent, major regulations: Regulation (EU) No. 236/2012 of the European Parliament and of the Council of 14 March 2012 on short selling and certain aspects of credit default swaps, and Regulation (EC) No. 1060/2009 of the European Parliament and of the Council on credit rating agencies, as amended. The planned legislation on central counterparties is equally planned to become a regulation (Proposal for a Regulation of the European Parliament and of the Council on OTC derivative transactions, central counterparties and trade repositories, Brussels, 15.9.2010 COM(2010) 484 final 2010/0250 (COD) (also known as the European Market Infrastructure Regulation (EMIR)); there is a Commission proposal to recast the Market Abuse Directive into a regulation (Proposal for a Regulation of the European Parliament and of the Council on insider dealing and market manipulation (market abuse), Brussels, 20 October 2011, (COM(2011) 651 final

Hence – and given that the Commission still seems to be looking at the fundamentals of the future securities law – it is now probably safer to refer to 'securities legislation' so as to leave the ultimate form of the future instrument open, whether it turns out to be a directive or a regulation.

I will analyse, in turn:

- the misconception that national legal concepts of securities law are a suitable starting point for securities law harmonisation – rather, the international character of the market imposes an international perspective to which national legal concepts can only submit: see section 2.2;
- whether there is a mandate for EU and international harmonisation, the presence of legal uncertainty in securities law as such not being sufficient justification – rather, the need to act must be expressed in cost incurred by the market in good times, as well as the cost of the market and society in times of market turmoil, when an ill-constructed legal framework may cause additional risk or even have systemic implications: see section 2.3;
- the different legal choices at hand regarding the fundamentals of reform, including the alternative forms of the future EU instrument: see section 2.4.

My conclusion is that there is an ever clearer need to increase legal certainty in this area, and that the advantages and drawbacks of both functional and conceptual harmonisation need to be considered very carefully.

2.2 Mind the gap – between domestic thinking and legal reality

The European System of Central Banks (ESCB) and the European Committee of Securities Regulators (CESR) describe the importance of a sound and reliable legal framework for securities holding and dispositions as follows:[19]

2011/0295 (COD))) and there is a proposal to improve securities settlement (Proposal for a regulation of the European Parliament and of the Council on improving securities settlement in the European Union and on central securities depositories (CSDs) and amending Directive 98/26/EC). The Alternative Investment Fund Managers Directive (2011/62/EU of 8 June 2011) is the only recent major directive in the area of financial markets.

19 Explanatory Memorandum on Recommendation 1, ESCB-CESR, Recommendations for Securities Settlement Systems and Recommendations for Central Counterparties in the European Union, May 2009 (Ref. CESR/09–446) www.esma.europa.eu/system/files/09_446.pdf (CESR has since been transformed into ESMA, the European Securities and

> The reliable and predictable operation of a securities settlement system depends on two factors: (1) the laws, rules and procedures that support the holding, transfer, pledging and lending of securities and related payments; and (2) how these laws, rules and procedures work in practice – that is, whether system operators, participants and their customers can enforce their rights. If the legal framework is inadequate or its application uncertain, it can give rise to credit or liquidity risks for system participants and their customers or to systemic risks for financial markets as a whole.

It is obviously the role of national laws, in particular the law of personal property, commercial law and insolvency law, to provide such a legally sound framework. In the first phase, national laws laboured for many years to digest an important change in market practice in respect of transactions involving securities. Paper certificates were transformed into 'intangible' book-entry securities which are now acquired and disposed of through credits and debits in accounts held by intermediaries (see section 2.2.1).[20] That fundamental change triggered adjustments in the underlying domestic legal regimes in all the relevant markets, including the EU Member States. However, these adjustments were made, more or less consistently, on the basis of highly diverse concepts (see section 2.2.2). Since these domestic concepts are now in place, there is little appetite for the notion that the market has *again* changed over the past twenty years, growing increasingly international (see section 2.2.3). The conflict-of-laws analysis, however, reveals that legal certainty in the area of securities law cannot be achieved without harmonisation of substantive law (see section 2.2.4).

2.2.1 Some notes on market practice

For reasons of efficiency – i.e., to avoid having to move physical security certificates whenever a change in ownership of the various banks' clients occurred – the first central securities depositories (CSD) for security certificates were established in Vienna in 1878 and in Berlin in 1882 (both probably modelled on the eighteenth-century London Clearing

Markets Authority). Similar statements have been formulated by other intergovernmental organisations or public consultative bodies, and also much earlier, see n. 3.

20 In the following, I generally use the term 'intermediary' in order to describe an institution that maintains securities accounts for an account holder. This could be a bank, a broker, a central securities depository, a settlement system, central counterparty or other type of infrastructure. An account is either maintained for another intermediary or for the 'ultimate account holder'.

House for cheques and bank notes).[21] Centralised custody of security certificates, combined with centrally organised services to keep account balances for the participating banks and settle securities transfers between these accounts, was gradually adopted in all developed financial markets. The institution of a CSD and 'clearing and settlement' of securities services is therefore nothing new. However, while the modern securities-holding structures and their legal underpinnings have been described often, and at length,[22] certain aspects are rarely highlighted, although they are important for our purpose.

First, the actual length of a 'holding chain', i.e., the number of intermediaries intervening between the investor and the issuer, depends on concrete circumstances. In some jurisdictions, there is no other intermediary besides the CSD, and investors hold their securities directly with the CSD ('transparent systems', see below). In other jurisdictions, the number of intermediaries may be limited to one. In yet other jurisdictions, the number is not limited in any way. However, as soon as securities are held across national borders, i.e., as soon as the underlying securities are located in a foreign CSD, holding chains quasi-naturally involve several intermediaries.[23] Regulation to impose a certain holding pattern (e.g., one- or two-tier holding) is only effective within its home jurisdiction. As soon as the ultimate part of an otherwise domestic holding chain is foreign, domestic regulation no longer has any control over whether this – supposedly – ultimate part is itself an intermediary for others, or an investor holding for its own account.[24]

Second, the terms 'account holder', 'account provider' and 'intermediary' are often ill-employed. The investor (or rather, the 'ultimate account holder') is, in functional terms, one of several account holders in respect of the same assets.[25] This is because its direct intermediary maintains a

21 For the historical aspects: Huang, *The Law and Regulation of Central Counterparties*, 44 et seq.

22 The most fundamental works are probably Benjamin, *Interest in Securities*; Einsele, *Wertpapierrecht als Schuldrecht*; Nizard, *Les Titres Négociables*; Rogers, 'Policy perspectives on revised UCC Article 8'; Yates and Montagu, *The Law of Global Custody*.

23 Davies, 'Using Intermediated Securities as Collateral: Equitable Interests with Inequitable Results', at 70.

24 See Thévenoz, 'Intermediated Securities, Legal Risk, and the International Harmonization of Commercial Law', at 398–401.

25 'Ultimate account holder', 'shareholder' and 'investor' are often used as synonyms. It is important, however, to make a clear distinction: (i) 'ultimate account holder' refers to a person's functional position within a holding structure; that person does not maintain a securities account for another person; (ii) 'shareholder' or 'bondholder' are terms

securities account for it and thereby acts as its account provider. However, at the same time, this first intermediary does not itself keep the securities, but holds them through its own account maintained for it by a second intermediary, which might or might not be the CSD. The first intermediary is, therefore, an account provider and, at the same time, an account holder, depending on the perspective. The same principle applies throughout the entire holding chain.[26] Only the CSD is not an account holder, since it keeps the securities itself.[27]

Third, intermediaries have to separate ('segregate') client securities from any securities they may hold for their own account.[28] In practice, own securities and client securities are often booked to distinct accounts with the intermediary's own account provider. However, in most[29] jurisdictions, client assets are not separated *per client* at the upper tier. Rather, they are pooled in an 'omnibus account', and cannot be distinguished per client as they are fungible, i.e., not individually identifiable.

2.2.2 *Insular substantive law – an ideal world*

Jurisdictions have adapted their laws in order to address the realities of intermediated securities holding, but they have done so in an insular

belonging to the sphere of corporate law, referring to those persons recognised under company law as being called upon to exercise corporate rights (dividends, vote, etc.); (iii) 'investor' is probably not a legal term, referring rather to the person bearing the economic risk of a share or bond investment. This can be a person 'standing behind' the legal shareholder and/or the ultimate account holder.

26 EU Clearing and Settlement Legal Certainty Group, *Solutions to Legal Barriers* (n. 16), 30.

27 CSDs have a relationship with the securities issuer. This relationship is not characterised as a securities account. CSDs often have a double role: first, they provide services to issuers; second, they provide services to those who hold securities. The details of the first role vary considerably, as a CSD, under the applicable law, may be part of the process of issuing securities. In that, they often have a legal role determined by the company law. For example, in the UK the CSD in legal terms maintains part of the company register, see below, section 2.2.2. In their second role, CSDs organise the clearing and settlement process by operating the 'settlement platform' (meaning: IT infrastructure) to which the accounts of all participating banks are connected.

28 See, e.g., Arts. 13(7) and 13(8) Directive 2004/39 of the European Parliament and of the Council of 21 April 2004 on Market in Financial Instruments (MiFID) and Art. 16(1)(d) of the Commission Directive 2006/37/EC of 10 August 2006 implementing MiFID; Art. 35(2) Proposal for a Regulation of the European Parliament and of the Council on improving securities settlement in the European Union and on central securities depositories (CSDs), COM(2012) 73/2 2012/0029 (COD).

29 In 'transparent systems', client securities are always kept in individual accounts, see section 2.2.2 (fifth indent).

manner. The task of these substantive legal concepts is to define the legal position of account holders (including the ultimate account holder) and account providers in respect of the securities. Additionally, the substantive law governs the way in which the securities are disposed of, i.e., transferred (for the purpose of sale) or encumbered (by way of collateral/security or 'quasi security', including transfer to the collateral taker) and related aspects such as priorities and good faith acquisition.

There are no two legal approaches wholly identical to one another. However, common lines of conceptual thinking allow us to identify five different schools of thought.

- The first method is built on the creation of a trust.[30] This approach is in place in particular in England and Wales.[31] The method of holding securities in pooled accounts has become frequent in England only relatively recently, with a significant increase in indirect holdings occurring only after uncertificated securities had been introduced in 1996.[32] Under the trust model, the issuer entrusts its securities to the CSD. The CSD ('CREST') assumes the role of the company shareholder register under corporate law, and has no legal interest whatsoever in the securities.[33] The participants in CREST are considered the legal owners of the securities which they hold, whether for their own or their customers' accounts. English securities are transferred by way of amending the shareholder register. As regards securities which the CREST participants credit to the accounts of their account holders, the former act as trustee, i.e., the CREST participant's account holder becomes trustor (beneficiary) and acquires equitable ownership in the securities. This is not quite the same as legal ownership, but encompasses similar elements and is notably protected in the event of the trustee's insolvency.[34]

30 Micheler, 'The Legal Nature of Securities', at 132.

31 Financial Markets Law Committee, *Property Interests in Investment Securities*, fmlc.org/Documents/fmlc1_3_july04.pdf (2004), 9; Benjamin, *Financial Law*, 428; Davies, 'Using Intermediated Securities as Collateral: Equitable Interests with Inequitable Results', at 72. Similar approaches are found in Ireland, Australia, and other common law countries.

32 Uncertificated Securities Regulations 1995, as replaced by the Uncertificated Securities Regulations 2001, as amended.

33 Benjamin, *Interests in Securities – A Proprietary Law Analysis of the International Securities Markets*, 205.

34 Financial Markets Law Committee, *Property Interests in Investment Securities* (n. 31), 9. It is of particular interest that English law struggled to overcome the requirement of certainty of subject matter when fungible assets are kept in bulk: see Micheler, 'The Legal Nature of Securities', at 132, referring to the decision in *Hunter* v. *Moss* [1994] 1 WLR 452

To the extent that there is another level, or 'tier', in the holding chain, this trustor/holder of an equitable interest in turn acts as trustee for its own customer (the ultimate account holder in our example). The latter, again, acquires equitable ownership in what the trustee holds for it. Thus, in a holding structure involving the CSD and two intermediaries, the ultimate account holder acquires, in legal terms, equitable ownership in an equitable ownership in the securities. In practice, however, the investor is treated as though the securities were its own.[35]

- Second, in the USA and Canada the legal concept underlying intermediated securities is the 'security entitlement'.[36] To some extent, this resembles the trust model, but there are differences. The legal owner of the securities under this model is a special legal entity, Cede & Co, which is a 100 per cent subsidiary company of the NYSE. Under US law, every account holder acquires a security entitlement against its account provider, i.e., every intermediary, acting as account holder, has a security entitlement against its own account provider. In their role as account providers, intermediaries are the addressee of their account holders' security entitlements. The legal nature of a security entitlement is not exactly the same as legal ownership, but is somewhat similar to an equitable interest under English law. In particular, security entitlements are separated from the intermediary's estate in the event of the latter's insolvency,[37] hence they are not mere claims. The difference is that security entitlements do not 'overlap' as is the case with equitable interests under English law. Every security entitlement against an account provider is distinct from the security entitlements that the account provider itself holds. Consequently, there are legally disconnected security entitlement holders at each level of the holding chain, as opposed to beneficiaries under English law. As under English law, each account holder can only turn to its immediate account provider, not to one at a higher level.[38]
- The third model operates on the basis of granting a full, undivided property interest to the investor. This applies in France. The legal framework

(CA), which cleared the question for English law. The issue was recently reopened and cleared by the Supreme Court decision [2012] UKSC 6 (see n. 65).

35 Davies, 'Using Intermediated Securities as Collateral', at 72.

36 Uniform Commercial Code ('UCC') §8–102(a)(17); See for relevant aspects, Mooney, *Law and Systems for Intermediated Securities*, 11–13.

37 UCC § 8–503(a).

38 Hakes, 'UCC Article 8: Will the Indirect Holding of Securities Survive the Light of Day', at 688–90.

recognises only 'dematerialised' securities, i.e., physical, paper certificates have been abolished though the law still refers to 'bearer securities'. The CSD is supposed to act as a mere register. Neither the CSD nor any of the intermediaries have any legal interest or right in the securities.[39] The investor has an undivided property interest in the securities which are deemed to be located directly in its account, i.e., the account maintained by its account provider. The investor can only access its securities through its account provider, not through any other intermediary at a higher level.

- Germany and Austria serve as examples for the fourth school of thought, and a similar model is in place in Japan.[40] The model of pooled holding was introduced in Germany on a large scale in 1925, when hyperinflation forced banks to find more cost-efficient ways of holding securities.[41] Under this approach, the investor acquires a property interest in a pool of domestic securities located at CSD level.[42] It is a *sui generis* type of shared property, which only exists in this precise context.[43] The intermediaries are supposed to have no interest or legal ownership; however, they can de facto dispose of the securities (in other words, this position is in some ways comparable to 'possession' or 'control', which describes a factual relationship, with factual control over the securities).[44] Acquisition and disposition, both outright and by way of creating security, strictly follow the rules of property law in relation to chattels.[45] The investor can access its securities only through its own account provider and other account providers up in the chain are unable to identify the securities since the client's securities holdings are part of a pool.

39 Drummond, 'Intermediated Securities: Reflections on a New Concept', at 439.

40 See a combined analysis for both German and Austrian law in Micheler, *Property in Securities*, 145–221. Japanese law: Mooney, *Law and Systems for Intermediated Securities*, 28–43.

41 Micheler, 'The Legal Nature of Securities', at 132.

42 *Ibid.*, at 136–43, argues that securities were originally regarded as intangibles under German and Austrian law and that the conceptual change to property law was made solely to accommodate the need of the market for bona fide acquisition and protection against adverse claims.

43 *Depotgesetz* §1 para. 3; Geier, 'Comparison of the Electronic Securities Settlement Systems for the Secondary Securities Markets in Germany and England', at 100; Scherer and Gallei, 'UNIDROIT draft Convention and German Securities Law', at 473.

44 Geier, 'Comparison of the Electronic Securities Settlement Systems for the Secondary Securities Markets in Germany and England', at 102.

45 Mülbert, 'Vom Ende allen sachenrechtlichen Denkens', at 446.

- Fifth, the Nordic countries, as well as Greece, follow the so-called transparent approach.[46] Spain has a slightly different model.[47] Outside Europe, China and Brazil have systems in place that resemble this approach.[48] The framework for purely national holdings is as follows: in a transparent system, there are no intermediaries involved, except the CSD. Every investor has its account directly in the CSD. The banks intervening in the securities business do not maintain an account for the investor but only operate the account maintained by the CSD under a special legal and operational framework. In this context, therefore, they are also called 'account operators', or something similar. The investor has a direct and unshared property interest in the securities.[49] However, the transparent system does not work for cross-jurisdictional holdings. This is because the foreign intermediaries involved are unable to 'operate' the accounts in the CSD directly, since they are not part of that highly integrated national system. In other words, the framework for cross-jurisdictional situations in a transparent system resembles the pooled property model.

These national legal concepts applied to intermediated securities are intimately entangled with other areas of national law, such as, in particular, insolvency law, corporate law, and tax law. Additionally, the operations of national CSDs and their participants are perfectly aligned with the national legal framework, and standard account agreements with customers usually mirror the particularities of each system. It comes as no surprise therefore that thinking on intermediated securities remains caught within the web of national concepts.

As a consequence, any discussion on an international framework for intermediated securities tends rapidly to deteriorate into a dialogue of the deaf. Actors and authors think inside their respective boxes of local law and local operations. However, they forget that such an approach neglects part of the source of the problem: the international character of the securities market is significant (see section 2.2.3) and represents

46 See Afrell and Wallin-Norman, 'Direct or Indirect Holdings – a Nordic Perspective', 277–284.

47 See Garcimartin Alferez, 'The UNIDROIT Project on Intermediated Securities: Direct and Indirect Holding Systems', 1–21; Gómez-Sancha Trueba, 'Indirect Holdings of Securities and Exercise of Shareholder Rights – a Spanish Perspective', 32–57.

48 Thévenoz, 'Intermediated securities', at 405.

49 Afrell and Wallin-Norman, 'Direct or Indirect Holdings – a Nordic Perspective', at 279.

a challenge to legal certainty which is even greater than that stemming from the simple fact that securities are intermediated (see section 2.2.4).

2.2.3 *The financial market is not an island unto itself*

As mentioned before, it makes little sense these days exclusively to test domestic legal frameworks against the criterion of legal soundness. Securities are held, transferred, lent and pledged across borders to a significant extent, and this market cannot be conceptually divided into domestic and international spheres. The EU market is supposed to be an 'internal' market, and there is important activity across the Atlantic as well as with Switzerland, Japan and other international financial centres.

Data shows that between 5 and 95 per cent of investments in the different European financial centres are allocated to cross-border securities; typically, in large financial centres like London, Frankfurt and Paris, between 30 and 70 per cent are allocated to cross-border holdings.[50] The share of cross-border holdings is mirrored by a correspondent percentage of cross-border trading activity.[51] No data is available indicating the percentage of securities collateral provided across borders but, going by the aforementioned figures, a significant percentage may be assumed. It is probably justified, therefore, for ease of reference, to collapse these three elements into one catchy, yet still conservatively estimated, figure: on average, about 40 per cent of all holding, trading and collateral operations by EU market participants in one way or another imply a cross-jurisdictional element.[52]

50 Data extracted from Oxera, 'Monitoring Prices, Cost and Volumes of Trading and Post-Trading Services', Report prepared for the European Commission, London and Brussels (2011), 73. Though the data itself relates to equity investments, the authors note, *ibid.*, that they have found a positive correlation between equity and debt securities in respect of cross-border holdings.

51 Oxera, 'Monitoring Prices', 73.

52 The value of cross-border securities holdings in absolute terms is equally staggering (though irrelevant for this analysis). It can be exemplified by the value of cross-border holdings of EU banks and money market funds at the end of 2011, which amounted to EUR 2069.3 billion (data extracted and compiled from European Central Bank, Cross-border positions of euro-area MFIs, February 2012, ecb.int/stats/money/aggregates/cross/html/index.en.html). This amount relates to short- and long-term debt, money market fund shares and equity. Holdings of other financial market participants (investment funds, insurance companies, other investors) are not included in this figure, i.e., the actual absolute value of cross-border holdings of the economy as a whole is significantly higher.

For these 40 per cent of cases, a purely domestic legal analysis cannot yield a comprehensive result. Yet private international law is only part of the answer, as the following section will show.

2.2.4 The problem driven beyond private international law

Understandably, the immediate reaction to cross-jurisdictional cases is to seek a solution provided by private international law which will point a given case to one or the other applicable national law. However, the case of intermediated securities is special in that more than one law applies to the same asset (see section 2.2.4.1). This leads to incompatibilities which cannot be overcome by private international law rules alone (see section 2.2.4.2).

2.2.4.1 PRIMA and tiered holding structures

As in any other matter of commercial law, when analysing a cross-jurisdictional situation involving intermediated securities, private international law has to be looked at first. Private international law rules will point to one or another applicable law. Private international law in relation to securities holding and disposition can use a variety of very different criteria capable of connecting a case to the most suitable jurisdiction.[53] Today, the criterion is that the 'connecting factor' in relation to intermediated securities is the law of the securities account to which the relevant securities are credited.[54] This approach has been termed PRIMA, which stands for 'place of the relevant intermediary approach'. However, the term is somewhat misleading, first, because it is not connected to the 'intermediary' but to the account and, second, because it subsumes two different sub-species:

- In relation to what might be termed the *factual* PRIMA, the law of the account is the law of the place where the account is actually maintained.

53 Formerly, a variety of additional approaches existed, which led to huge legal uncertainty. In particular, the law under which the securities are issued; the law of incorporation of the issuer; the law of the place where the paper securities are located; or the law of the place where the initial electronic record is made. See overview in Bernasconi, 'The Law Applicable to Dispositions of Securities Held through Indirect Holding Systems', Hague Conference on Private international Law, Collateral Securities Prel. Doc. 1 (November 2000), 27 et seq.; discussion in Ooi, 'The Choice of a Choice of Law Rule', 219–44.

54 Ooi, 'The Choice of a Choice of Law Rule', at 221.

This PRIMA subcategory is, roughly, the approach taken by the relevant EU legislation.[55]

– In relation to what might be termed the *contractual* PRIMA, the law of the account is the law agreed upon by the parties, generally supplemented by a requirement that the intermediary has a qualifying establishment in the country the law of which has been chosen. This is the approach underlying the Hague Securities Convention.[56]

The difference between both approaches is usually marginal, but it might matter in cases where the law agreed upon by the parties is not the law of the country where the account is 'maintained', as will be discussed below, section 2.4.4. However, I will disregard this difference for the moment. Both approaches follow the same basic idea, that of determining the law applicable to securities on the basis of a two-party relationship, i.e., the account holder and account provider being bound together by an account.

As a consequence, each account holder (including intermediaries in their role as account holders, see above, section 2.2.1) acquires the legal position attributed to it under the relevant legal treatment in the relevant account provider's home jurisdiction. As securities are generally pooled in omnibus accounts, the relevant law applies on each tier to the entire pool of securities credited to the relevant account, regardless of the fact that different laws may apply to ultimate account holders' accounts, as these accounts may be subject to different jurisdictions.

If, for example, a Frankfurt fund holds shares of an English issuer through Frankfurt Bank which holds them with Paris Bank, which in turn holds them with London Bank which ultimately is a member of the CREST system, German, French and English law will apply to these shares on the various tiers. Each account holder acquires the legal position as

55 Art. 9(1) Directive 2002/47/EC of the European Parliament and of the Council of 6 June 2002 on financial collateral arrangements; Art. 9(2) Directive 98/26/EC of the European Parliament and of the Council of 19 May 1998 on settlement finality in payment and securities settlement systems; Art. 24 Directive 2001/24/EC of the European Parliament and the Council of 4 April 2001 on the reorganisation and winding up of credit institutions. However, the European conflict-of-laws rules pose a difficulty in that there is no universal rule: these sectoral provisions (which, to complicate matters further, employ a slightly different connecting factor) apply in certain segments of market activity only. This leads to the coexistence of all three rules and autonomous national conflict-of-laws rules.

56 Arts. 2(1) and 4(1) Convention on the law applicable to certain rights in respect of securities held with an account provider, of 5 July 2006 (adopted in December 2002, the Convention however officially indicates the date of the first signature).

determined by the applicable law:[57] the topmost account holder, London Bank, is the legal owner under English law; Paris Bank would be the holder of an equitable interest in the shares under English law; French law cannot control the holding chain outside its territory and attributes a full property interest to Frankfurt Bank, despite the fact that Frankfurt Bank acts as intermediary; the account maintained by Frankfurt Bank for the Frankfurt fund is governed by German law which would generally, i.e., in a purely domestic holding chain, attribute a shared *sui generis* property interest in a pool of securities to the ultimate account holder.

The obvious difficulty is that different laws apply to what are, at least economically, the 'same' securities. Depending on the conceptual approach towards intermediation, domestic laws and those who apply them have more or less difficulty in accepting this fact. Where intermediated securities are strongly assimilated to tangibles, such as under French and German law, the fact that various laws apply to the proprietary aspects of the same asset is difficult to explain. Additionally, in any jurisdiction, the *nemo dat* principle would prevent any intermediary from providing its account holder with a legal position better than that which it itself has. In other words, where an intermediary receives securities as beneficiary under a trust, the question arises of whether it can pass on that economic position to its own account holder as legal ownership or property. The fact that such inconsistency arises exclusively because different laws apply does not make the result more acceptable.

Fortunately, in this concrete example, German rules *would* reflect the dilemma that it would be unreasonable to provide the investor with a 'shared property interest in a pool of securities in a cross-border situation. Instead, the investor acquires, contrary to the general approach, a *fiduciary* interest in the securities.[58] The features of this interest very much resemble the position of equitable ownership under English law. It is probably appropriate to regard this institutionalised 'legislative emergency exit' as anecdotal evidence that property concepts as such are difficult to extend across jurisdictional borders when it comes to securities holdings.

57 See the basis of domestic legal concepts in England, France and Germany in section 2.2.2.

58 Mülbert, 'Vom Ende allen sachenrechtlichen Denkens', at 446. The law is not, however, explicit on this point. Section 22 Safe-custody Act (*Depotgesetz*) assumes that ultimate account holders would not acquire property when purchasing securities located in another jurisdiction. Further, the German standard securities account agreement stipulates in Art. 12 that, instead, ultimate account holders acquire a right to delivery of securities which is insolvency-proof as intermediaries act as trustees in respect of these rights.

2.2.4.2 Incompatibility and domestic flaws

In light of the principles underlying cross-border holding of securities as described above, the legal position of ultimate and intermediary account holders in cross-jurisdictional holding chains may be unclear in respect of the relevant securities. The fact that more than one law affects their position raises a number of questions:

- What type of right does each account holder in the chain acquire? Nothing, a limited right, or a full right? Is the legal position acquired through the chain compatible with the legal concept attributed by the applicable domestic law?
- Can the right attributed to the investor be violated by any wrongdoing in other parts of the holding chain, for example, by an unauthorised pledge to an intermediary's creditor (in breach of the intermediary's duties)?
- Who can exercise voting rights and receive dividends when there is more than one 'legal owner' (or 'proprietor', respectively) in the chain? After all, only the investor (i.e., the account holder who bears the risk of the investment) should be entitled to voting rights and dividends.

Concentrating on the first and second of these issues (the third belongs rather to the sphere of corporate law), it would appear that doubts as to the nature or quality of the account holders' legal position become palpable in particular in the event of insolvency of one of the intermediaries involved or of a collateral taker. These questions typically centre on:[59]

- the validity and enforceability of an earlier outright transfer of securities;
- the validity and enforceability of security or collateral provided;[60]
- the validity of an earlier good faith acquisition;[61]
- the possibility to unwind or reverse dispositions;

59 This list reflects the thinking behind the sequence of Arts. 9, 11–28 of the Geneva Securities Convention and in Recommendations 4–11 of the EU Clearing and Settlement Legal Certainty Group, *Solutions to Legal Barriers* (n. 16). This article does not discuss inconsistencies occurring in the sphere of corporate law as a consequence of intermediation: cross-border holding chains tend to sever the link between investor and issuer, entailing questions as to whether investors can effectively exercise the participatory and other rights flowing from securities; see Arts. 10, 29–30 of the Geneva Securities Convention and Recommendations 12–14 of the EU Clearing and Settlement Legal Certainty Group.

60 See the examples in Paech, *Cross-Border Issues of Securities Law*, 26–7 and 35.

61 See the example provided in EU Clearing and Settlement Legal Certainty Group, *Solutions to legal barriers* (n. 16), 60.

- the rank and priority of interests relating to the same asset;
- the protection of client assets and the effectiveness of the acquired position against general creditors of the insolvent intermediary.

The above addresses situations in which the interaction of two or more laws in relation to the same securities leads to legal uncertainty because these laws may be incompatible. So far, I have assumed that each of the laws involved is internally sound. However, that might not always be the case. Within the EU, for some time now the official line has been that the domestic soundness of the law underlying securities holding and dispositions was not an issue,[62] since cross-border incompatibility was a sufficient argument for harmonisation as it is capable of affecting the functioning of the internal market.

UNIDROIT pointed to potential problems with 'internal soundness' back in 2003.[63] De facto, it is unlikely that all twenty-seven EU Member States have a perfectly coherent legal framework in an area as complicated and new as this one, and there have been studies and papers[64] as well as cases[65] questioning the soundness of the domestic legal framework.

62 The Commission's preparatory work (see n. 16) did not address that aspect and concentrated on cross-jurisdictional issues.

63 UNIDROIT Study Group, 'Position paper on harmonised substantive rules regarding indirectly held securities', 13.

64 See in respect of English law: Financial Markets Law Committee, *Property interests in intermediated securities* (2004), 10–14, setting out inconsistencies regarding (i) the nature of the investor's right, (ii) the treatment of a shortfall at intermediary level, (iii) the intermediaries' liability for complying with fraudulent instructions from third parties, (iv) insufficient perfection requirements, (v) the prevention of account holders trying to trace their securities beyond the level of their direct intermediary, (vi) the risk of creditors to attach account holders securities at a level above the direct intermediary, (vii) uncertainties regarding the priority of competing claims to the same securities, (viii) the absence of a clear bona fide rule under English law, (ix) uncertainty regarding whether assignment is the method of transferring book-entry securities, and (x) uncertainty regarding whether a valid trust is created at all, considering the lack of segregation of securities in omnibus accounts. See also Davies, 'Using Intermediated Securities as Collateral – Equitable Interests with Inequitable Results', at 5–6: (i) it is uncertain whether intermediated securities are within the scope of application of the UK Collateral Regulations, (ii) uncertainty regarding the possibility of bona fide acquisition. See in respect of German law: Mülbert, 'Vom Ende allen sachenrechtlichen Denkens', at 447–8, summarising the ongoing debate within German academia on the possibility of good faith acquisition of intermediated securities and the question of whether the requirement of possession can be fulfilled in the absence of any express legal rule or relevant court decisions.

65 See in the UK, two recent Supreme Court decisions in connection with the insolvency of LBIE: [2012] UKSC 6 concerned the question as to whether client monies were held on trust despite the fact that LBIE did not comply with the relevant regulatory requirements, 'CASS7', to segregate them; [2012] UKSC 6 concerned the question as to whether trusts arise validly over securities in which the trustee was allowed to deal freely (under a repo

Furthermore, the borderlines between lack of clarity of the law and its unsoundness are fluent – a fact that is particularly relevant where foreign courts are called upon to apply domestic law. If the law is unclear, there is a tangible risk of the court's interpreting the relevant rules in a manner that is incompatible with the general assumption as to the effect of these rules. Consequently, cross-jurisdictional incompatibility and lack of internal soundness are not necessarily two separate phenomena. There is a risk that any lack of internal soundness or clarity of the domestic legal framework will be perpetuated and amplified in a cross-border context.

The private international law analysis is unable to remedy these problems. As the fate of the same asset might be analysed under different laws at different tiers of the holding chain (in accordance with PRIMA), a loss of rights on the upper tier (i.e., the tier that is closer to the CSD) cannot be made up under a different law on a lower tier. The securities might simply be 'gone', regardless of the legal nature that the lower-tier law attributes to the right. As we accept the idea of PRIMA (disregarding the conceptual differences between factual and contractual approach), then logically the governing substantive laws on each tier of a holding chain must be realigned.

2.3 Risk, cost and the legislative mandate

Having established that there is legal uncertainty caused by a gap between the legal framework and market reality, the question is whether legislators – national and EU – should act to close it. In that discussion, individual scenarios of uncertainty are irrelevant. Rather, a market-wide perspective needs to be adopted and policy needs to be determined by goals such as increased competitiveness, economic growth and, very prominently indeed of late, prevention of systemic consequences. Therefore, the micro-view on legal risk has to be broadened into a macro-view on the consequences for the market as a whole. The consequences are measured by analysing the cost of uncertainty for the market and for

scheme named *Rascals*); earlier, in *Hunter v Moss*, the Court had to decide more generally whether a trust was validly created over un-segregated client assets: [1993] 1 WLR 934, and the appeal case [1994] 1 WLR 425. In France, the recent Appellate Court of Paris judgment 2008/22085 of 8 April 2009 – *RBC DEXIA Investor Services Bank France* (and two parallel cases) concerned hedge fund assets which the depositor (Dexia) had sub-deposited with Lehman Brothers International. After the securities were dragged into Lehman's insolvency, there was uncertainty as to whether the depositor (Dexia) had to make up for the loss and 'return' the securities to the hedge fund at its own cost. The Appellate Court upheld an earlier decision by the regulatory authority in that sense.

society as a whole. Logically, heightened cost systemically incurred by individual market participants translates into a decline in competitiveness throughout the market.

Most of the mechanisms by which legal risk translates into cost in the area of securities law are no different from those in other areas of commercial law. In particular, the cost of uncertainty is directly reflected in the preparatory and monitoring work[66] of the parties, notably that of their legal departments and mandated law firms. Additionally, the degree of legal risk – in particular in respect of collateral – is reflected in the conditions for obtaining credit and in risk-weighting for purposes of establishing capital requirements for financial institutions.[67] In some cases, legal risk can result in the parties abstaining from the envisaged transaction altogether ('opportunity cost').[68] Ultimately, parties might suffer a loss because of erratic legal planning that might materialise in the event of the other party's insolvency.

Any further discussion of the need to harmonise securities law requires quantifying risk-related cost, preferably in absolute figures, or at least in relative terms.

2.3.1 Difficulties in quantifying risk and cost

Data in absolute figures is extremely scarce and it appears difficult to quantify the absolute cost of legal risk inherent in the holding and disposition of securities, as described before,[69] for three reasons.

First, risk-prone situations are too varied, and the degree of risk differs. The relevant circle of market participants is highly diverse, and risk and

66 '[A] few years ago I was unable to complete a transaction for a short term secured loan by a Canadian bank to a Canadian life insurance company after a week of trying to piece together the legal advice necessary to do the deal. The security for the loan was to be bonds of a foreign issuer that had been deposited into [Clearstream] in Luxembourg. The physical certificates were actually being held in safekeeping in the Cayman Islands, for tax reasons, and could not be moved. The bonds were owned not by the Canadian life company directly, but by its French subsidiary, which had its chief executive offices in Paris. Five law firms struggled for a week to figure out how to put together the chain of opinions that would be necessary to ensure the lender that the loan was fully secured by the bonds, and could not do it. Because we were unable to advise the client as to the nature and extent of the risks involved, it could not price the transaction appropriately or get internal approval to proceed.' Crawford, 'The 'Prima Convention', at 163.

67 *Bank for International Settlements/Basel* Committee on Banking Supervision, International Convergence of Capital Measurement and Capital Standards (Comprehensive version), June 2006, www.bis.org/publ/ bcbs128.htm ('Basel II Accord'), [109.-110.], [117.-118.], [119.-138.], [145.-187.].

68 See n. 66.

69 See section 2.2.4.2, in particular nn. 64–6.

cost occur both at the level of all parties that hold securities or use them in any way, and at the level of intermediaries and market infrastructures such as settlement systems. At the same time, the circumstances that produce legal risk differ just as, for instance, holding arrangements differ, including the length of the holding chain and the involvement of foreign law.

Second, regulatory, operational and legal frameworks are heavily intertwined, and cannot be disentangled. In fact, it is fair to speak of a comprehensive legal-regulatory-operational framework governing the holding and use of securities in each jurisdiction. As a result, there would appear to be no way of extrapolating the excess cost due exclusively to legal uncertainty.[70]

Lastly, legal risk which is initially concentrated on the parties alone can develop systemic importance due to a number of transmission mechanisms.[71] Other market participants may be affected, leading to a chain reaction leaving the market dysfunctional and thereby affecting the economy as a whole. The cost involved is difficult to predict.

It may be possible to put a figure on the concrete risk-related excess cost involved in single transactions. However, such evidence must remain anecdotal. Due to the heterogeneity of the market and the variety of potential cases, as described above, we can only quantify the global cost of legal uncertainty on the basis of a model.

2.3.2 Model for splitting excess cost

A 2001 paper estimated cross-border clearing and settlement within the EU as costing up to ten times as much as domestic clearing and settlement.[72] In 2009, a price monitoring study commissioned by the European Commission found that it was still between two and seven

70 The data available in the Oxera, *Monitoring Prices*, present excess cost on an aggregate basis. The respondents to the Commission's consultation provided information on cost on an aggregate basis, though the consultation paper expressly aimed at legal excess cost.

71 There are two basic cases, legal spill-over and economic spill-over. In the former, widely held assumptions regarding the legal soundness of a given legal arrangement are disappointed; e.g. a court rules clauses in a standard contract invalid; this can lead to an entire market instantly pulling out of this specific type of financial transaction. In the second case, the solvency or liquidity problems of one financial institution which are due to a loss taken as a consequence of legal uncertainty in turn affect that institution's counterparties' solvency or liquidity.

72 First Giovannini Report, 36–43.

times as expensive.[73] An updated version of that study published in 2011 provides sufficient data to develop a clearer picture of the excess cost caused by legal uncertainty, on the basis of a model.

The cost of cross-border clearing and settlement incurred by fund managers is twice the cost of domestic clearing and settlement. For custodians, this factor is 3.4, for CSDs, 3.8 and for brokers as much as 4.1.[74] These stark differences between domestic and cross-border situations can be attributed to a variety of factors, notably (i) cross-border legal and technical discrepancies,[75] (ii) economies of scale, and (iii) variations in the cost across financial centres,[76] including variations in the types of service provided.[77]

It should be noted that the 2011 study does not identify the relative contribution of the various drivers (including legal discrepancies) to the higher cross-border cost in any precise manner. The only indication it gives is that operational and legal discrepancies can only explain some of the price differences[78] and that at least some of them are due to lower cross-border volume (i.e., lower scale effects), rather than being a specific feature of the cross-border nature of the relevant services.[79] Further, the variation in the cost across financial centres plays a role.[80]

Assuming that:

- cross-border transactions in the EU are 200 per cent (average of the indicated scale, above) more expensive than domestic ones, all across the post-trading sector, and that
- economies of scale and variations in the cost of financial centres each account for one-third of the excess cost, and that
- operational, regulatory and legal discrepancies each produce one-ninth of the extra cost,

legal discrepancies alone would drive the prices of cross-border transactions up by 22.2 per cent, as compared to purely domestic cost. As

73 Oxera, *Monitoring Prices*, 85–7.

74 Data extracted from Oxera, *Monitoring Prices*, p. 9 Figure 3 and 108 et seq., Tables 6.4 and 6.12.

75 Technical and legal discrepancies are called 'barriers' in the jargon of the Giovannini reports.

76 The last element addresses the situation in which the service buyer is located in a 'cheap' financial centre and trades in an 'expensive' financial centre. This will *per se* result in a transaction cost for the cross-border transaction which is higher than the domestic cost, without any other factors intervening, see Oxera, *Monitoring Prices*, p. x.

77 See Oxera, *Monitoring Prices*, p. ix.

78 *Ibid.*, p. ix.

79 *Ibid.*, pp. x and 109.

80 *Ibid.*, p. x.

securities custody settlement is regarded as a business with very low margins, this share in the overall cost is significant.

However, this figure cannot be taken at face value. On the one hand, there is a general or residual legal risk inherent in commercial transactions that cannot be eliminated. On the other hand, harmonising the legal framework would also allow further streamlining of operational aspects, potentially increasing scale effects. In the ideal case, domestic and cross-border settlement would happen on integrated platforms,[81] considerably dismantling the excess cost of cross-border settlement as compared to domestic settlement. However, that can only happen provided the legal environment allows for such integration.

Lastly, it needs to be stressed that these figures relate exclusively to direct transactional excess cost. It appears impossible to predict any indirect cost caused by an unsound legal framework, such as, in particular, those arising because of repercussions on the financial sector and the economy as a whole. First, the amplitude of such repercussions is pure speculation. Second, an unsound legal framework will never be the sole cause of crisis situations that have a wider significance.[82]

2.4 Functionality *vs* conceptuality – or the risk of perpetuating the problem

Whereas the preceding two sections addressed the sources and consequences of legal uncertainty flowing from intermediated securities, the following paragraphs will discuss some of the elements involved in solving the problem. The Geneva Securities Convention already offers a comprehensive functional framework for intermediated securities. The preparatory work undertaken by the European Commission[83] likewise provides insight into how legal uncertainty could be dismantled. The

81 *Cf.* the ECB's initiative to set up a pan-European settlement platform to bring down the cost of cross-border settlement ('Target-2-Securities').

82 *Cf.* the 'Dexia' example in n. 65: legal uncertainty regarding the duty to return client securities which had been lost by a sub-custodian was not the original threat to the relevant hedge funds. Rather, Lehman's insolvency and the loss of securities that resulted at depositor level was the cause. However, the unclear legal situation left the relevant hedge funds and all investors in comparable situations in the dark as to the safety of their investments, causing considerable liquidity squeezes.

83 EU Clearing and Settlement Legal Certainty Group, Solutions to Legal Barriers related to Post-Trading within the EU (n. 16), Part I (recommendations 1–11).

approach taken in both texts has been criticised, first, for seemingly turning investors' property rights into lesser rights;[84] second, for missing an opportunity, as some commentators sensed, to harmonise securities law while embracing property concepts as its centrepiece.[85]

However, it is conceptually unsound to centre the debate on legal concepts such as, in particular, property, as the better and safer solution, and it often becomes a battle of words.

- First, applying property concepts to securities is a relatively new development which occurred in response to market needs in the nineteenth and twentieth centuries, so why now argue that this approach must be preserved in the teeth of contemporary market developments that demand new adjustments (see section 2.4.1)?
- Second, attributing a property right without being able to control its content raises expectations that cannot be fulfilled (see section 2.4.2).
- Third, the divide between direct and indirect holding, which is often referred to as a benchmark for safety, is unsuitable (see section 2.4.3).
- Fourth, in that context and against common assumptions, the debate on the factual or the contractual PRIMA approach is irrelevant (see section 2.4.4).
- Lastly, harmonisation has been promoted on the basis of a functional approach. However, conceptual harmonisation is equally conceivable – be it on the basis of property or any other concept. The latter approach would require the creation of a new legal and operational framework that is both new and separate from pre-existing domestic securities law. As a consequence, Europe would need to set up a '28th regime', should it opt for conceptual harmonisation (see section 2.4.5).[86]

2.4.1 Market needs as drivers of the legal concept of securities

The concept of proprietary rights in respect of (non-intermediated) securities is itself relatively recent and was introduced in response to market

84 See Voß, 'Die Securities Law Directive und das deutsche Depotrecht', at 210–11; Cremers, 'Reflexions on 'Intermediated Securities' in the Geneva Securities Convention', at 102–3; Mülbert, 'Vom Ende allen sachenrechtlichen Denkens', at 454.

85 Cremers, 'Reflections on 'Intermediated Securities' in the Geneva Securities Convention', at 105.

86 At the time of writing, there were twenty-seven member jurisdictions, with Croatia expected to join on 1 July 2013. Therefore, in the future, this should read '29th Regime'.

needs. Both shares and bonds consist, in substance, of a relationship between the issuer and the investor. This relationship largely consists of payment obligations. The shareholder is commited to paying the capital contribution to the issuer. The issuer is commited to paying a dividend to the shareholder and to granting certain participatory rights. The bondholder is commited to lending money (the 'principal') to the bond issuer. The bond issuer is commited to paying regular interest and to repaying the principal upon maturity.

All rights in these bundles are, by their very nature, obligations and they were originally regarded as such. However, issuers conceived of the idea to create secondary markets for these obligations, in which pricing was easy and transparent, thereby increasing liquidity.[87] The idea of incorporating securities in certificates stems from that objective. Apart from the fact that the paper legitimates its bearer to receive payments or exercise participatory rights, the mechanism of delivery of the certificate allows for bona fide acquisition, protecting the disposer from adverse claims.

Although traditionally, good faith acquisition of claims was not widely accepted, the market's need for certainty as regards acquisitions of securities in good faith was paramount, and in 1853, von Savigny wrote that 'the desire was felt to create new concepts which allowed to apply the aforementioned advantages in respect of disposing of property to obligations as well'.[88]

Other alternatives existed, notably to provide for the possibility of good faith acquisition of this particular type of claims immediately.[89] However, legislators chose to take the property route, thereby coating the original set of obligations with a property hull to allow for good faith acquisition in particular.

Today, the market stands at a crossroads again. It still needs the possibility of good faith acquisition of securities – it is probably even fair to say that the modern securities markets operate on the assumption that account holders will have securities credited to their account without any need to verify whether the disposer holds good title. However, there is now a second main concern which did not exist when von Savigny promoted the assimilation of securities to tangibles, and this is connected to

87 Micheler, 'The Legal Nature of Securities', at 145.

88 von Savigny, Das Obligationenrecht als Theil des heutigen römischen Rechts, 97 (translation by the author).

89 For instance, the General German Commercial Code (1871) protected the purchaser of securities against adverse claims without classifying securities as tangibles: Micheler, 'The Legal Nature of Securities', at 142.

the phenomenon of intermediation: securities need to be protected in the event of the insolvency of a participant in the holding chain.

Nowadays, intermediation has become standard. As a result, while the legal concept of property over securities still caters for one of the main market needs (good faith), it must also cater for protection against the risks of intermediation as the second requirement. Given that the concept of coating obligations by a property hull was market-driven from the outset, there should be nothing to stand in the way of adjusting the legal approach once again, now that IT and globalisation have changed the market so radically.

2.4.2 Property, intermediation and stretched expectations

Strikingly, pure property law concepts have never been capable of solving the intermediation problem, *precisely because* their application was conceived to allow for good faith acquisition. These two goals are mutually exclusive. Even in a traditional setting, as soon as a security was delivered into custody, the owner could only trust its custodian that it (i) would comply with segregation requirements to keep the property identifiable, and (ii) that it would abstain from unauthorised dealings in the asset in its own name. As soon as the custodian breached its contractual or legal obligations in this respect, the possibility of loss of the property was always a real one.

Additionally, the ability of a (domestic) property interest as such to provide effective protection against loss is even more limited where the holding chain is international. As set out above (section 2.2.4.2), the fact that the conflict-of-laws analysis is built on a tiered approach following PRIMA leads to a situation in which the same underlying asset is governed by different laws on different tiers of the holding structure. The legal analysis on one tier of the holding chain is therefore disconnected from the analysis on the other tiers. Assuming that the right deteriorates at an upper tier – for instance, by being dragged into the insolvency of one of the intermediaries involved or by being disposed of to a third person[90] –

90 In most, if not all, jurisdictions, the law prescribes that client securities would in principle never be part of the insolvent estate and are not accessible by the intermediary's general creditors. Further, there are usually rules limiting the power of intermediaries to dispose of the securities exclusively in the interest of the relevant client. However, in case of an intermediary breaching these obligations or going beyond the power attributed to it by the law, rules on specificity or on bona fide acquisition might result in the client losing

the legal position on the lower tier, property or other, cannot make up for a loss.

The only solution is to disconnect the fate of the ultimate account holder's right from the rights of other account holders up the chain and to protect it separately. In other words, protection against insolvency on the upper tier requires that the right at account holder level should always be available regardless of what happens to the pooled rights held in different account layers up the chain. However, if we accept this approach, we can no longer maintain the pretence that the rights are property rights in relation to the same asset.

European law, somewhat ill-conceived, takes that route in the Alternative Investment Fund Managers Directive, establishing a 'strict liability' of the account provider in the event that securities become lost on the upper tier of the holding chain.[91] However, the account holder's duty to replace lost assets, even if unconditional, is at odds with the concept of a property interest which always relates to a *specific* item. Being obliged to replace something implies that it has been lost in the first place.

The fact that the security certificate has lost its function[92] over the last thirty years is only a symptom of this logic. The law has already admitted that the market cannot live with the concept of a security that is located in a specific place. Instead, the market accepts that technically, IT systems document their rights, and that the same securities are documented in different pools of securities in different accounts.

Consequently, to call a legal position 'property' does not as such provide an adequate level of protection against the insolvency of an upper-tier intermediary. Rather, the use of the term in the context of cross-jurisdictional securities holding creates unfounded expectations of certainty and safety, as the domestic legal concept cannot provide the account holder with an appropriately robust legal position. The only relevant question is whether the legal framework actually *achieves* the two main goals – good faith acquisition and protection of account holders'

its securities to the insolvent estate or to a third person. See [2012] UKSC 6 – *Rascals* (n. 65).

91 Art. 21(12) Directive 2011/61/EU of the European Parliament and of the Council of 8 June 2011 on Alternative Investment Fund Managers.

92 There are now plans to promote dematerialisation in all European jurisdictions, see Art. 3(1) and Recital (11) Proposal for a Regulation of the European Parliament and of the Council on improving securities settlement in the European Union and on central securities depositories (CSDs), COM 2012 73 final.

interests in the event of insolvency – also in a cross-border context. If it does, it does not matter how one labels the right.

2.4.3 Sense and non-sense of the direct/indirect divide

In the early discussions on this subject, the various models as set out above (see section 2.2.2) were not clearly identified. Reference was often made to 'direct' and 'indirect' holding models.[93] The general feeling was that the trust model (UK) and the security entitlement model (USA) were 'indirect', whereas the 'property-based' models (France, Germany, Nordic countries, etc.) were 'direct'.

However, it was never clear what exactly this meant. Did 'direct' mean that the investor enjoyed a 'property' right in respect of the securities? Or did it mean that there was literally *no* intermediation, i.e., that the investor had immediate control over the securities?

In my view, the watershed is located at the German and French approaches to securities holding. In both systems, the ultimate investors' rights are termed 'property' in one form or another. However, the source of the title, i.e., the securities certificate in Germany or the root entry in the French CSD, respectively, is relatively remote from the investor. In particular, intermediaries maintain accounts for their customers (investors) and pool customer securities in a separate account to be held with an upper-tier entity (CSD or other). In other words, the credit to the account maintained by the CSD is in favour not of the investor, but of an intermediary. As a consequence, the intermediary has the de facto power to dispose of the securities, even though it is generally not allowed to do so under regulatory requirements.[94]

The close link of 'property' can be established – in jurisdictions such as France and Germany – only by way of definition. In France, the law

93 See as early promoters of this terminology Bernasconi, *The Law Applicable to Dispositions of Securities Held through Indirect Holding Systems*, Hague Conference on Private international Law, Collateral Securities Prel. Doc. 1 (November 2000); Guynn et al., *Modernizing Securities Ownership, Transfer and Pledging Laws*. Further: Garcimartín Alférez, 'The Unidroit Project on Intermediated Securities: Direct and Indirect Holding Systems'; Afrell and Wallin-Norman, 'Direct and Indirect Holding – a Nordic Perspective', 277–84.

94 It is important to distinguish between the power to dispose of securities in a legally valid manner (in particular on the basis of bona fide rules) and regulatory requirements not to do so and safeguard client assets, as for example Art. 16(1) Commission Directive 2006/73/EC of 10 August 2006 implementing Directive 2004/39/EC of the European Parliament and of the Council as regards organisational requirements and operating conditions for investment firms and defined terms for the purposes of that Directive.

specifies that the ultimate account holder is the sole proprietor of 'bearer securities'. In Germany, there are neither legal rules nor court guidance on the subject. Doctrine and academic analysis explain the existence of the property concept.

Therefore, the distinction between 'direct' and 'indirect' as used in the past now seems too vague.[95] The so-called transparent systems are probably the only examples in the world of direct securities holding.[96] The US security entitlement is unambiguously 'indirect'. All other models, including that of England, are somehow in between. Yet, tested against the criterion of account structures, they must probably be classified as indirect systems as well.

In the conceptual debate, the notions of 'direct' and 'indirect' should be dropped as being too vague. Rather, a more nuanced approach should be taken, along the lines suggested above. In any case, it was always questionable whether such a rough categorisation was helpful at all, as the next section will explain.

2.4.4 PRIMA and property

The question of whether the phenomenon of intermediated securities can sensibly be addressed by resorting to property law concepts seems to reverberate on the discussion regarding the private international law aspect.

The factual PRIMA (see above, section 2.2.4.1) is strongly associated with thinking rooted in the world of property. According to that approach, the law of the place where the account is maintained (a location) is the law that applies. However, the criterion of de facto maintenance of the account may seem to be an easy approach on the surface but is in fact extremely difficult to apply when it comes to detail. First, there is a whole array of practical questions (Where is the computer located? Is it relevant whether the client steps into the branch in country A or country B? What if branches in several countries are involved in dealings in relation to the relevant account?). Second, nobody has so far been able to define what an account actually means in an international context, as

95 Garcimartín Alferez, 'The Unidroit project on intermediated securities: direct and indirect holding systems', at 3, pointing to the fact that the difference between direct and indirect did not relate to the fact that the investor did or did not physically possess the securities (in that sense all holding systems were indirect), but to the way in which the legal system prevented custody risk and facilitated the exercise of corporate rights by investors.

96 See above, section 2.2.2.

it is mostly the *national* regulatory authority which determines what an account is and who maintains it. Is an account something physical, i.e., comparable to the books traditionally kept by merchants (which would point us to the location of the computer and the outsourcing issue)? Or is an account a relationship, which raises the question of whether such a relationship can actually have a location, or is the 'location' subject to contractual agreement? Totally opaque though these issues may be, this factual PRIMA subcategory is the approach taken by Article 9 of the EU Financial Collateral Directive and Article 9(2) of the EU Settlement Finality Directive.

As to what might be termed the contractual PRIMA, the law of the account is the law agreed upon by the parties. This approach ultimately leads to a situation where the law governing proprietary aspects over securities can be chosen by the parties, an approach perceived as alien to civil law traditions even though it usually requires the intermediary to have a qualifying establishment in the country the law of which has been chosen. This is the law in Switzerland and is also the approach underlying the Hague Securities Convention.

In concrete terms, the difference between both approaches matters in cases where the law agreed upon by the parties is not the same as the law of the country where the account is 'maintained'. This might occur, in particular, where two financial institutions acting globally have securities accounts with each other. In today's computerised financial world, the account could literally be in Singapore, New York, Paris, London or Frankfurt. Therefore, most global players prefer to fix the 'location' of the account contractually, in order to be sure which law applies.

The arguments for either approach are legion.[97] It needs to be stressed, however, that the tiered approach as such and the application of different laws to the same asset that comes with it are the novelties that produce repercussions in point of substantive law. Whether the conflict-of-laws rule settles on either the factual or the contractual PRIMA is an additional complication, but it is not the core of the problem.

Accordingly, future deliberations on the connecting factor should attempt to settle on the most practicable solution that offers the highest

97 See, amongst others, Bernasconi and Sigman, 'Déterminer la loi applicable – Les facteurs de rattachement retenus par la Convention de la Haye', 53–65; Bloch and De Vauplane, 'Loi applicable et critères de localisation des titres multi-intermédiés dans la Convention de La Haye'; Einsele, 'Das Haager Übereinkommen über das auf bestimmte Rechte im Zusammenhang mit zwischenverwahrten Wertpapieren anzuwendende Recht'; Sigman and Bernasconi, 'Myths about the Hague Convention Debunked'.

degree of predictability and certainty, and then concentrate on solving the problems surrounding substantive law.

2.4.5 Stripping sheep's clothing and the 28th regime

Both the preparatory work undertaken by the EU and the Geneva Securities Convention on intermediated securities follow a functional approach. This means that the changes that must be made to the legal framework are defined by way of describing the factual effect which the domestic law should produce. Two issues arise in this context. First, the functional approach has been criticised – in relation to both initiatives – by some authors as a wolf in sheep's clothing, as its purported functionality in reality produces a steep conceptual impact on national law. Second, there is room to re-think whether further integration of the EU internal market for capital and financial services would require a greater leap beyond the functional approach in the form of a directly applicable and fully developed new concept for the entire EU securities market. Developing such a concept in the form of a separate, additional and closed legal regime ('28th regime'[98]) may prove to be the more consistent solution and might still be compatible with the Geneva Securities Convention.

2.4.5.1 The remit of the functional approach

The functional approach was introduced into the universe of securities law by a 2003 UNIDROIT discussion paper, described as 'an approach using language that is as neutral as possible and which formulates rules by reference to their results'.[99] However, there is disagreement as to whether the Convention's rules transcend the sphere of functionality by de facto venturing deeply into national legal concepts underlying securities holding.[100]

In getting to the bottom of these issues, it is worth recalling the core of legal inconsistencies in relation to intermediated securities: the incompatibility, in principle, of negotiability/bona fide on the one hand, with

98 See above, n. 86.

99 UNIDROIT Study Group, 'Position paper on harmonised substantive rules regarding indirectly held securities', p. 6; detailed: Paech, 'Explanatory Notes to the Preliminary Draft Convention on Harmonised Substantive Rules Regarding Securities Held with an Intermediary', 70 et seq.

100 Cremers, 'Reflexions on Intermediated Securities', at 102–4; Drummond, 'Intermediated Securities: Reflections on a New Concept', at 438–40; in-depth argument: Mülbert, 'Vom Ende allen sachenrechtlichen Denkens', at 454.

absolute protection of holders of intermediated securities, on the other hand.[101] Most jurisdictions provide for a viable route under domestic law to deal with this dichotomy.

However, these domestic solutions differ as to their concepts and results. Some apply the ideas of the classical property/insolvency law doctrine,[102] others go down different, *sui generis*, paths.[103] Some domestic legal frameworks place more emphasis on negotiability, while others are stronger as regards mechanisms to protect account holders.[104] The obvious consequence of this divergence is incompatibility and legal uncertainty in cross-jurisdictional situations flowing from the different answers to that dichotomy.[105] As long as this discrepancy is not eliminated, securities laws will mismatch in terms of the question of 'who owns what' in a cross-jurisdictional context.

Considering this situation from the solutions angle, it is evident that the key to overcoming this mismatch is to design a *uniform* international

101 See above, section 2.4.1.

102 Notably France, Germany and Austria: property of account holders does not, a priori, form part of the insolvent estate. The result of the English trust model – assets held on trust are not accessible to the intermediary's general creditors – is identical. See section 2.2.2.

103 Notably the USA (§8–503(a) UCC: securities held by an intermediary are a priori client securities and not accessible to its creditors) and Switzerland (Art. 17 Federal Intermediated Securities Act: client securities shall be excluded from the insolvent estate. Non-segregated securities are deemed client securities).

104 The US system is probably the paradigm of a legal framework ensuring negotiability. The fact that security entitlements are entitlements (only) against the direct intermediary (see section 2.2.2) disconnects the acquisition leg from the disposal leg in both operational and legal terms. In many other jurisdictions, the de facto disconnection cannot be denied – where an intermediary 'draws on the pool', acquisition by bona fide customers can often not be avoided – whereas *de lege* that disconnection and the entailed increase of the aggregate number of securities credited in the system is impossible. It is important to note, however, that the US system employs regulatory safeguards to avoid inflation of securities. The result is that in many countries, inflation of securities is conceptually 'impossible' but happens de facto, whereas in the US, inflation is conceptually 'possible' and happens de facto but is forbidden by law. The actual difference in terms of certainty for account holders is probably marginal.

105 For example, in a cross-jurisdictional situation of defective acquisition of securities, both jurisdictions involved might in principle protect good faith acquisition. However, if the law applicable to the acquirer's account requires a good faith acquisition to be mirrored by an equivalent loss of another account holder, whereas the law applicable to the purported disposer's account protects the disposer against the loss because the transaction was defective, the acquirer will *de lege* acquire the securities, whereas the purported disposer will *de lege* keep its securities. The two regimes on negotiability/bona fide are not compatible. See the example in EU Clearing and Settlement Legal Certainty Group, *Solutions to Legal Barriers*, 60.

solution to the core problem itself.[106] In other words, there is no getting around changing and aligning national laws in respect of issues such as irreversibility of account holder rights, bona fide acquisition and priorities. Such a uniform framework may well require changes to the existing domestic solutions.

The prospect of being compelled to change parts of the core of the domestic legal framework as regards acquisition and disposition of securities is what fuels complaints about lack of functionality and disguising as functional what is in substance conceptual harmonisation. However, this criticism is beside the point. Jurisdictions will continue to be able to organise securities holding, acquisition or disposition on the basis of *their* concept, be it trust, entitlement, full or shared property, transparent holding, etc.,[107] as long as the relevant aims are achieved. The current legal frameworks underpinning intermediated securities are generally relatively recent and were developed to accommodate intermediation.[108] They are creative to the point where the result might be called a legal fiction.[109] Consequently, that conceptual flexibility should be used again when adapting the existing frameworks in light of a new, additional and inevitable imperative, i.e., the internationalisation of the market and the widespread cross-jurisdictional holding of securities.

In summary, the rules proposed by the Geneva Securities Convention and the EU Commission are functional as to their nature, though demanding as regards their content, since they require substantial legislative changes. The idea of functionality delivers what it is intended to deliver. Therefore, it is not a wolf in sheep clothing – rather, it is still a sheep in sheep's clothing, though a pretty big one.

2.4.5.2 Functionality, uniform law and the 28th regime

Drafting directly applicable EU law in the areas of substantive private and commercial law is a delicate task. Therefore, directives – i.e., legal acts

106 See the relevant provisions of the Geneva Securities Convention: Art. 18 (acquisition by an innocent person); Art. 24(3) (buy-in in case of uncovered holdings); Art. 26 (loss sharing in case of insolvency of the intermediary).

107 See the different 'schools of thought', above, section 2.2.2.

108 See above, sections 2.4.1 and 2.2.2.

109 One prominent legal fiction is that, under German law, an account holder is supposed to have 'possession' over the securities, see the criticism by Einsele, *Wertpapierrecht als Schuldrecht*, 64–88. A second example is that French law still applies rules originally applicable to 'bearer securities' despite the fact that all French securities have been dematerialised and only exist in electronic form; see Drummond, 'Intermediated securities: reflections on a new concept', at 435.

addressed to Member States which require autonomous implementation into their laws – have in most cases been the instrument of choice. As directives are probably the paradigm of a functional legal instrument,[110] they allow Member States to adapt the EU rules to the wider architecture of their legal bodies and to honour domestic legal concepts in the process of implementation. The form of directive has generally been chosen to harmonise aspects of private and commercial law underlying financial market and securities transactions, in particular. The relevant examples are the Financial Collateral and the Settlement Finality Directives, as well as the Directive on the Winding-up of Credit Institutions.[111]

EU legislators will have to consider whether the law governing the holding and disposition of intermediated securities would be better cast into a directive or a regulation. As mentioned in the introduction, a Securities Law Directive has been in the making, so far.[112] However, both the functional, more flexible instrument of directives and the conceptual, more stringent instrument of regulation have specific advantages and drawbacks when applied to the area of intermediated securities.

These advantages and drawbacks can probably be best understood by analysing a similar case. The Financial Collateral Directive[113] governs legal matters closely related to the holding and disposition of intermediated securities.[114] To a certain extent, therefore, the process of implementing the Financial Collateral Directive is comparable to that of harmonising

110 See Art. 288 Treaty on the functioning of the European Union: 'A directive shall be binding, as to the result to be achieved, upon each member State to which it is addressed, but shall leave to the national authorities the choice of form and methods.'

111 See nn. 4 and 55. 112 See above, section 2.1.

113 My argument focuses on the Financial Collateral Directive since the second relevant instrument the Settlement Finality Directive, is very limited in its personal and material scope and as such scarcely qualifies as a wide-ranging reform of securities law. Further, the practical need for the core rule of the Directive – preventing a settlement freeze in a settlement system after its commencement – was uncontested, whereas the need for harmonisation of securities law is still queried.

114 The Financial Collateral Directive relates to the provision of collateral in the form of financial instruments, cash or credit claims provided under an arrangement either involving transfer of title or by way of security to a collateral taker (i.e., pledge, charge, lien, etc). The material aspects are the following: Formalities regarding the creation of a collateral interest are abolished (Art. 3) and procedures and formalities for the enforcement of collateral in a default situation simplified (Art. 4). Furthermore, the directive enables the parties to agree on a right of use over securities provided as collateral (Art. 5). Lastly, it institutionalises certain market practices, i.e., close-out netting (Art. 7), top-up collateral and substitution of collateral securities (Art. 8). The material scope of the Financial Collateral Directive may be regarded as a clipping from the wider project of securities law reform. However, it relates exclusively to

Member States' laws on intermediated securities. Also, this instrument takes a functional approach, i.e., its provisions are capable of being incorporated into different types of legal concepts underlying securities collateral transactions.[115] However, the process of implementing the Financial Collateral Directive into all domestic laws produced a patchwork of quite diverse national regimes governing collateral: first, the directive gave some levy to national legislators as regards the personal[116] and material[117] scope of the rules. This levy was the result of political compromise and created an EU-wide regime comprising maximalist frameworks in some Member States, and minimalist frameworks in others. Second, the (functional) drafting of the Financial Collateral Directive left room for different interpretations as to the substance of the rules, which produced mismatches between existing domestic law and harmonised EU law, ultimately creating legal uncertainty in respect of certain issues instead of removing it.[118] Third, Member States went on dragging their feet in respect of implementation for some considerable time; as a consequence, EU-wide implementation was delayed by two years. This was because of the existence of conceptual hurdles that needed to be overcome in order to be able

the creation of collateral interests and to the recognition of the aforementioned market practices. The basic question of how acquisitions and dispositions, including the creation of security, are rendered legally effective is dealt with only as regards formal requirements.

115 See, for instance, the functional definition for security financial collateral of paras. 1(c) and 2 of Art. 2 of the Financial Collateral Directive: '"security financial collateral arrangement" means an arrangement under which a collateral provider provides financial collateral by way of security to or in favour of a collateral taker, and where the full or qualified ownership of, or full entitlement to, the financial collateral remains with the collateral provider when the security right is established; . . . References in this Directive to financial collateral being "provided", or to the "provision" of financial collateral, are to the financial collateral being delivered, transferred, held, registered or otherwise designated so as to be in the possession or under the control of the collateral taker or of a person acting on the collateral taker's behalf.'

116 *Cf.* comparison in Löber and Klima, 'The Implementation of Directive 2002/47', at 207 et seq.

117 *Cf.* comparison in *ibid.*, at 208 et seq.

118 *E.g.*, as to the UK, the application of the rules of the Financial Collateral Directive to floating charges, an important means of providing security under English law, is in doubt. Under the Directive, the relevant collateral assets need to be 'in possession or under control' of the collateral-taker. This requirement might conflict with the general freedom of a provider of a fix charge to continue dealing in the relevant assets. As the need to register the charge depends on whether the charge is inside or outside the scope of the Directive, uncertainty regarding this aspect has immediate repercussions on legal certainty, see Fawcett, 'The Financial Collateral Directive', at 212.

to adapt certain areas of contractual, commercial and material insolvency law to the new standard.

Against this background of patchy and unsatisfactory implementation of the Financial Collateral Directive, difficulties are probably also in store when incorporating the harmonised rules on the holding and disposition of intermediated securities into domestic law. Indeed, the difficulties may prove significantly greater, since the material scope of the law governing intermediated securities holding and disposition is much wider and delves more deeply into the substance of material law than does the Financial Collateral Directive. Therefore, it is probably fair to predict that the securities law harmonisation as currently envisaged by the EU will resemble an exponentiated Financial Collateral Directive. With this in mind, I expect the problems encountered in implementing that instrument to be a multiple of what was experienced with the Directive. As a consequence, there seems to be little chance that a *directive* on wider securities law harmonisation could be meaningfully implemented.

A directly applicable EU *regulation* would avoid the aforementioned drawbacks. There are generally two approaches to building such a self-contained legal regime in the EU. The first model entails comprehensive replacement of domestic law. Under this approach, the entire sphere of securities holding and disposition would be governed by directly applicable EU law and national laws in this area would cease to have effect. It would also entail the introduction of a universal European definition of 'security'. This 'all in' approach would have the advantage that no doubts can arise as to whether a given transaction is covered by the regime or not. However, there are market segments on the fringes of the universe of intermediated securities where harmonisation is of no interest and where the application of rules designed for intermediated securities would not make sense.[119] Therefore, a 'rump' domestic securities law would necessarily need to remain in place.

This dilemma would be avoided by drawing on the second model, i.e., that of coexistence under which a new, supplementary legal framework for a clearly defined part of the securities market is introduced while a residual part of the market continues to be governed by national law. National law would not be displaced. Rather, the relevant transactions would be imported into an independent, separate EU regime. Here, a

119 In certain cases there seems to be no or little need for harmonisation: (a) securities which are directly held by the ultimate investor on the issuer's books; (b) non-fungible securities, like parts in private limited companies; and, (c) non-publicly traded securities.

clear distinction would have to be made between those securities subject to the EU regime and those that continue to be governed by domestic laws. It would be paramount to introduce clear-cut criteria such as (a) the type of the relevant assets, (b) the fact of being traded on regulated markets or other recognised types of market, (c) whether the securities are booked to securities accounts or settled through designated settlement systems, or (d) whether the securities have an ISIN.[120] Also, an opt-in could be created by (e) allowing issuers to issue their securities into the new regime, even though these securities would otherwise not be covered. By contrast, the involvement of an international element in the relevant situation would be too unclear a criterion.

The major drawback of creating a uniform, directly applicable regime for all EU jurisdictions resides in the need to create a fully-fledged legal, regulatory and operational set-up. The functional approach naturally relies on domestic rules and structures and would only require changes to those aspects of the law that needed to be harmonised. By contrast, any directly applicable conceptual and uniform regime would need to be comprehensive, since there would be no general provisions of national commercial law available to provide that general legal foundation of securities law. Also, the relevant market infrastructure, such as, in particular, securities settlement systems, would need to adapt to the new legal framework. Such a project would naturally require considerable effort and resources and probably meet with scepticism from academia and national policy makers. However, it might be clearer in terms of legal certainty.

In essence, the European legislator will have to choose between a directive built on a functional approach, and a regulation built on defined legal concepts. Though a regulation appears to be more intrusive, it should be borne in mind that the effect of functional harmonisation will be substantial, too.[121] Therefore, there might not be too big a difference between both alternatives in terms of 'legislative fallout'. As regards compatibility with international standards, in particular the Geneva Securities Convention, both approaches are capable of producing an instrument that will ultimately create European law which is compatible with that international benchmark.

120 The International Securities Identification Number (ISIN) identifies exchange traded shares, bonds, funds, options and futures.

121 See the preceding section.

2.5 Conclusion

After about a decade of discussing the law of intermediated securities in Europe, the time has now come to recognise that modern securities law is bound to centre around three fundamental legal challenges.

First, negotiability has been a guiding principle of securities law since von Savigny's times: acquirers and security takers need to be sure that they receive good title without being obliged to verify the origin of the relevant securities or to investigate the transferor's power to dispose of them. This principle has, in many jurisdictions, resulted in the application of property law concepts to rights which are obligations in substance. The incorporation of securities in negotiable paper certificates was the most obvious characteristic of this development. In modern securities settlement systems, where transferor and transferee remain anonymous and interconnect remotely through intermediaries, the principle of negotiability of securities is ever more essential.

Second, securities laws have also been guided by the purpose of protecting account holders against intermediary risk. Originally, that risk could be addressed by applying traditional concepts such as safe-custody of property or trust. Five different general concepts are still in use, all more or less employing elements of traditional property law. However, the development of modern multi-tier holding, which in many jurisdictions entails the pooling of securities in *omnibus* accounts, meant that these concepts needed to be modified to ensure that the ultimate account holder's remoteness from its assets would not impinge on the robustness of its legal position. However, traditional legal concepts appear to be stretched to their limits and may be unable effectively to protect against intermediary risk. This is all the more true since the aim of protecting investors against intermediary risk on the one hand, and the achievement of negotiability on the other hand, are two conflicting aims. Domestic laws do not always manage to reconcile these aims in a manner capable of withstanding severe pressure.

Third, cross-jurisdictional compatibility is needed in respect of the above because securities holding and securities dispositions now stretch across national borders, amounting to at least 40 per cent of the overall volume within the EU. Cross-jurisdictional holding and disposition are equally built on the principles of negotiability and protection against intermediary risk. In this respect, they require the same degree of legal certainty as purely domestic scenarios. In cross-jurisdictional scenarios, 'PRIMA' governs the conflict-of-laws question. Though the PRIMA-based conflict-of-laws analysis features some uncertainties of its own, the novelty consists mainly in the way it disconnects the different tiers of a holding chain from one another. This leads to the application of different laws to what is, at least economically, the *same* asset. As the applied laws differ in substance, notably as regards the mechanisms balancing negotiability and protection against intermediary risk, there is considerable risk of mismatch and resulting legal uncertainty. This arises from incompatible legal solutions to that dichotomy being forced to interconnect. As a typical result, a loss sustained on a tier closer to the source of the title cannot be made up for on the lower tier, even if the lower-tier law provides for the securities to be the account holder's property. The rules of private international law cannot remedy that situation.

With legal uncertainty rife, legislators must ponder the prospective gains of improving and harmonising the law. However, anecdotal evidence alone does not provide a sufficient case for action. The potential advantages of harmonisation should be measured in that part of the cost of legal uncertainty that can be removed. Its absolute cost in the area of intermediated holdings cannot be measured. The relative cost of legal uncertainty and a lack of clarity can be determined on the basis of a model: it increases cost by about 22.2 per cent in cross-jurisdictional transactions, as compared to purely domestic situations. The potential cost to the market and society, should market turmoil produce legal uncertainty on a wider scale is impossible to predict with any certainty.

As to the approach to be taken, settling on property concepts as understood in some continental jurisdictions cannot provide a satisfactory solution. The word 'property' alone is unable to guarantee the possibility of good faith acquisition while at the same time protecting the investor against intermediary insolvency on one of the upper tiers of the holding chain. Accordingly, harmonisation is bound to happen either on a result-based and functional approach, or on the basis of a newly created, supranational, directly applicable and 'closed' legal framework.

Functional harmonisation, on the one hand, ties in more smoothly with existing domestic securities law and with existing market infrastructure. However, its harmonising effect will be smaller. A supranational legal framework, on the other hand, in particular one built by way of EU Regulation, requires the creation of a fully fledged legal and infrastructure system that does not have recourse to national laws and national operational specificities. The definition of clear criteria determining which securities are 'inside' that framework and which are 'outside' would be of utmost importance. The legislative effort for such a project would be considerable, but the gain in legal certainty would also be more significant.

Bibliography

Books

Benjamin, J., *Financial Law* (Oxford University Press, 2007).

Interests in Securities – A proprietary Law Analysis of the International Securities Markets (Oxford University Press, 2000).

Einsele, D., *Wertpapierrecht als Schuldrecht – Funktionsverlust von Effektenurkunden im internationalen Rechtsverkehr* (Tübingen: Mohr Siebeck, 1995).

Huang, J., *The Law and Regulation of Central Counterparties* (Oxford: Hart Publishing, 2010).

Micheler, E., *Property in Securities. A Comparative Study* (Cambridge University Press, 2007).

Savigny, F. C. von, *Das Obligationenrecht als Theil des heutigen römischen Rechts* (Berlin: Veit und Comp., 1853).

Nizard, F., *Les Titres Négociables* (Paris: Economica, 2003).

Yates, M. and Montagu, G., *The Law of Global Custody*, 3rd edn (London: Tottel, 2009).

Articles

Afrell, L. and Wallin-Norman, K., 'Direct or Indirect Holdings – a Nordic Perspective' [2005] *Uniform Law Review*, 277–84.

Bernasconi, C. and Sigman, H. C., 'Déterminer la loi applicable – Les facteurs de rattachement retenus par la Convention de la Haye', in Bonomi, A., Cashin-Ritaine, E. and Volders, B. (eds.), *La loi applicable aux titres intermédiés* (Zurich: Schulthess, 2006).

Bloch, P. and de Vauplane, H., 'Loi applicable et critères de localisation des titres multi-intermédiés dans la Convention de La Haye' [2005] *Journal du droit international – Clunet*, 3–40.

Crawford, B., 'The 'Prima Convention': Choice of law to govern recognition of dispositions of book-based securities in cross border transactions', (2003) *Canadian Business Law Journal*, 157–206.

Cremers, T., 'Reflexions on "Intermediated Securities" in the Geneva Securities Convention' [2010] *European Banking and Financial Law Journal (Euredia)*, 93–7.

Davies, G., 'Using Intermediated Securities as Collateral: Equitable Interests with Inequitable Results' [2007] *Journal of International Banking and Financial Law*, 70–3.

Drummond, F., 'Intermediated Securities: Reflections on a New Concept in French Financial Markets Law' [2007] *Law and Financial Markets Review*, 435–42.

Einsele, D., 'Das Haager Übereinkommen über das auf bestimmte Rechte im Zusammenhang mit zwischenverwahrten Wertpapieren anzuwendende Recht' [2003] *Zeitschrift für Wirtschafts- und Bankrecht (WM)*, 2349–56.

Fawcett, A., 'The Financial Collateral Directive: an examination of some practical problems following its implementation in the UK' [2005] *Journal of International Banking Law and Regulation*, 295–99.

Garcimartín Alférez, F. J., 'The UNIDROIT Project on Intermediated Securities: Direct and Indirect Holding Systems' [2006] *Revista para el análisis del derecho*, 1–21.

Geier, B., 'Comparison of the Electronic Securities Settlement Systems for the Secondary Securities Markets in Germany and England' [2008] *Journal of International Banking Law and Regulation*, 97–104.

Gómez-Sancha Trueba, I., 'Indirect Holdings of Securities and Exercise of Shareholder Rights – a Spanish Perspective' [2008] *Capital Markets Law Journal*, 32–57.

Hakes, R. A., 'UCC Article 8: Will the Indirect Holding of Securities Survive the Light of Day' [2002] 35 *Loyola of Los Angeles Law Review*, 661–786.

Löber, K. and Klima, E., 'The Implementation of Directive 2002/47 on Financial Collateral Arrangements' [2006] *Journal of International Banking Law and Regulation*, 203–12.

Micheler, E., 'The Legal Nature of Securities: Inspirations from Comparative Law' in L. Gullifer and J. Payne (eds.), *Intermediated Securities. Legal Problems and Practical Issues* (Oxford: Hart Publishing, 2010), 131–49.

Mülbert, P. O., 'Vom Ende allen sachenrechtlichen Denkens im Depotrecht durch UNIDROIT und die EU' [2010] *Zeitschrift für Bankrecht und Bankwirtschaft (ZBB)*, 445–58.

Ooi, M., 'The Choice of a Choice of Law Rule', in L. Gullifer and J. Payne (eds.), *Intermediated Securities. Legal Problems and Practical Issues* (Oxford: Hart Publishing, 2010), 219–44.

Rogers, J. S., 'Policy Perspectives on Revised UCC Article 8' [1996] 43 *UCLA Law Review*, 1432–1545.

Scherer, P. and Gallei, R., 'UNIDROIT Draft Convention and German Securities Law: Friend or Foe?' [2009] *Journal of International Banking Law and Regulation (JIBLR)*, 470–6.

Sigman, H. C. and Bernasconi, C., 'Myths about the Hague Convention Debunked' [2005] *International Finance Law Review*, 31–5.

Thévenoz, L., 'Intermediated Securities, Legal Risk, and the International Harmonization of Commercial Law', 13 [2008] *Stanford Journal of Law, Business & Finance*, 384–452.

Voß, T., 'Die Securities Law Directive und das deutsche Depotrecht' [2010] *Europäisches Wirtschafts- und Steuerrecht (EWS)*, 209–11.

Other materials

Bernasconi, C., The Hague Conference on Private International Law, 'The Law Applicable to Dispositions of Securities Held Through Indirect Holding Systems, The Hague Conference on Private International Law', Report prepared for the attention of the Working Group of January 2001 (Prel. Doc. No. 1, November 2001).

Giovannini Group, 'Cross-Border Clearing and Settlement Arrangements in the European Union', Brussels, November 2001 ('First Giovannini Report').

Giovannini Group, 'Second Report on EU Clearing and Settlement Arrangements', Brussels, April 2003 ('Second Giovannini Report').

Guynn, R. D. et al., 'Modernizing Securities Ownership, Transfer and Pledging Laws', Discussion paper, Capital Markets Forum, Section on Business Law, International Bar Association, 1996.

Mooney, C. W., 'Law and Systems for Intermediated Securities and the Relationship of Private Property Law to Securities Clearance and Settlement: United States, Japan, and the Unidroit Draft Convention', Bank of Japan, Institute for Monetary and Economic Studies Discussion Paper Series (2008).

Oxera, 'Monitoring Prices, Cost and Volumes of Trading and Post-Trading Services', Report prepared for the European Commission (London and Brussels: 2011).

Paech, P., 'Cross-Border Issues of Securities Law – European Efforts to Support the Securities Market with a Coherent Legal Framework', Study prepared for the European Parliament (2011).

'Explanatory Notes to the Preliminary Draft Convention on Harmonised Substantive Rules Regarding Securities held with an Intermediary' [2005] *Uniform Law Review*, 36–115.

Unidroit Study Group, 'Position Paper on Harmonised Substantive Rules Regarding indirectly held Securities' (2003).

3

The proposed EU legislation on securities holding

HABIB MOTANI

The possibility of achieving some degree of harmonisation within Europe in the approach to holding securities with intermediaries has been under discussion for some years. The issues arising in relation to this subject are not new, and in fact were not primary concerns in the context of the problems resulting from the insolvency of Lehman Brothers International (Europe), but the increased focus on the protection of assets held with intermediaries following the Lehman collapse and other market difficulties revived the impetus to achieve some resolution for the long-standing issues regarding securities held with intermediaries, particularly cross-border. At the time of writing, the latest incarnation of the review of this subject may be seen in the European Commission's Consultation Document entitled 'Legislation on Legal Certainty of Securities Holding and Dispositions' published in November 2010 (the 'Consultation Document'),[1] together with the lengthy summary of the responses received to the Consultation Document published by the European Commission on 22 September 2011 (the 'Response Summary'). The Consultation Document contains twenty-two Principles intended to 'cover the full scope of the possible legislative approach',[2] which are expected in due course to be used as the basis for a legislative instrument (the 'Proposed Legislation') and which are an updated form of the draft Articles for a Directive as set out in the 'Updated Compilation of the rules and explanatory notes discussed so far' (the 'Updated Compilation') published by the European Commission on 17 September 2010.

The proposals in the Principles are of considerable interest, and are likely to have significant implications for the operations of both

1 EU Commission, Legislation on Legal Certainty of Securities Holding and Dispositions, Consultation Document of the Services of the Directorate-General Internal Market and Services, November 2010, DG Markt G2 MET/OT/acg D(2010) 768690. The consultation opened on 5 November 2010 and closed, after an extension due to the number of responses, on 21 January 2011.

2 Consultation Document, Preliminary Remarks, clause 4.

entities holding securities for clients and entities holding securities through intermediaries. Points of particular interest are considered in the following sections (extracts from the text of the draft Principles are taken from the Consultation Document).

For the purpose of the discussion in the following sections, for consistency with the terminology used in the draft Principles, the Consultation Document and the Response Paper, an intermediary holding securities for a client is referred to as an 'account provider' and the client of an intermediary is referred to as an 'account holder'.

3.1 Functional approach

Principle 1: Objectives

1. EU law should regulate the legal framework governing the holding and disposition of securities held through securities accounts and the processing of rights flowing from securities held through securities accounts.

2. The legislation should not harmonise the legal framework governing the question of whom an issuer has to recognise as the legal holder of its securities.

According to Principle 1, the main purpose of the Proposed Legislation, which it appears from the Response Summary is generally supported, is to specify requirements applicable to entities which carry out the function of holding securities for others, but not to impose a general rule regarding the legal nature of the relationship between such an entity and the person for whom the securities are held. This is a sensible practical approach, given that the legal analysis of the holding of securities through an account provider in different jurisdictions may vary considerably (for example, some jurisdictions recognise the concept of a trust, whereas others do not), therefore trying to achieve or impose a common legal analysis would involve significant difficulties. However, by focusing on the functions of an account provider, it is still possible to work towards some consensus on the rights which different jurisdictions would expect a person holding securities through an account provider to have.

Principle 14: Determination of the applicable law

1. The national law should provide that any question with respect to any of the matters specified in paragraph 3 arising in relation to account-held securities should be governed by the national law of the country where the relevant securities account is maintained by the account provider. Where an account provider has branches located in jurisdictions different from

the head office's jurisdiction, the account is maintained by the branch which handles the relationship with the account holder in relation to the securities account, otherwise by the head office.

2. An account provider is responsible for communicating in writing to the account holder whether the head office or a branch and, if applicable, which branch, handles the relationship with the account holder. The communication itself does not alter the determination of the applicable law under paragraph 1. The communication should be standardised.

3. The matters referred to in paragraph 1 are:

(a) the legal nature of account-held securities;
(b) the legal nature and the requirements of an acquisition or disposition of account-held securities as well as its effects between the parties and against third parties;
(c) whether a disposition of account-held securities extends to entitlements to dividends or other distributions, or redemption, sale or other proceeds;
(d) the effectiveness of an acquisition or disposition and whether it can be invalidated, reversed or otherwise be undone;
(e) whether a person's interest in account-held securities extinguishes or has priority over another person's interest;
(f) the duties, if any, of an account provider to a person other than the account holder who asserts in competition with the account holder or another person an interest in account-held securities;
(g) the requirements, if any, for the realisation of an interest in account-held securities.

4. Paragraph 1 determines the applicable law regardless of the legal nature of the rights conferred upon the account holder upon crediting of account-held securities to his securities account.

Consistently with the European Commission's main objective, Principle 14 aims to refer certain questions for determination according to the national law of a particular jurisdiction, rather than attempting to produce answers to such questions which must then be applied in all Member States. The major challenge is in creating a rule which identifies a particular jurisdiction with sufficient certainty, and is generally acceptable. As may be seen from the Response Summary, there is broad support for draft Principle 14, but there is also considerable concern as to whether the test of 'the law of the country where the relevant securities account is maintained by the account provider' gives sufficient certainty. The second sentence is helpful in identifying the securities account as maintained by 'the branch which handles the relationship with the account holder in relation to the securities account', and otherwise 'the head office'. However, the most obvious difficulty with this is where there is a transfer between accounts of different account holders with different account providers, and the laws applicable in each case conflict in their approach to, for example, the effectiveness of the transfer and whether it can be invalidated, reversed or otherwise be undone. There is also the question of the extent to which this method of identifying where a securities account is maintained could result in conflicting analysis in a situation where the Financial Collateral Directive (Directive 2002/47/EC) applies, since such Directive also uses the concept of the jurisdiction where an account is maintained in order to determine the relevant law for certain purposes.

3.2 Regulatory context and scope of application

Principle 21: Account provider status

All securities account providers should be regulated on a European level. To this end, 'safekeeping of securities [etc.]', Annex I Section B(1) of the MiFID, should be upgraded to become an investment service (under Section A(9) of Annex I) and those which provide this service should be authorised and supervised under MiFID.

Principle 2: Shared functions

1. It should be possible for Member States to provide that a person other than the account provider is responsible for the performance of certain, but not all, functions of an account provider. In such a case, references made in EU law to an account provider aim at the person responsible for performing the function to which the relevant provision applies.

2. The Commission would need to be notified accordingly and could specify the exact content of the notification. The Commission should publish on its website a list of Member States allowing for the sharing of account-provider functions, including all relevant specifications.

3.2.1

As may be seen from the text of Principle 21, it is proposed that MiFID should be amended so that the provision of safekeeping and administration services in respect of financial instruments (as defined in MiFID) becomes one of the 'investment services and activities' listed in MiFID Annex I Section A, rather than an ancillary service in MiFID Annex I

Section B.[3] The effect of this amendment is likely to be considerable, because at present an entity which provides safekeeping and administration services but no 'investment services and activities' within MiFID Annex I Section A is not subject to MiFID, and therefore the extent of the regulation applicable to such an entity depends only on the regulatory regime in the jurisdiction where it provides such services. Potential issues arising from the amendment which will require consideration include the following:

1. An entity providing only safekeeping and administration services will become an investment firm for the purposes of MiFID, and will be subject to all regulatory requirements implementing MiFID and the MiFID implementing directive.[4]
2. An entity providing only safekeeping and administration services will as a result of the MiFID passport arrangement be able to apply to provide such services in an EEA (European Economic Area) state other than the EEA state in which it is authorised and regulated, without the need for a second authorisation in the host state (at present, because the provision of safekeeping and administration services is an ancillary service, such service can only take advantage of the MiFID passport if provided together with a service or activity within MiFID Annex I Section A).
3. An entity which provides safekeeping and administration services and certain other services may currently be able to rely on one of the MiFID exemptions specified in MiFID Article 2(1) because the provision of safekeeping and administration services is an ancillary service, but following the amendment to MiFID the relevant exemptions will no longer apply. Examples are the exemptions which apply to:
   - 'persons who do not provide any investment services or activities other than dealing on own account unless they are market makers or deal on own account outside a regulated market or an MTF on an organised, frequent and systematic basis by providing a system accessible to third parties in order to engage in dealings with them' (MiFID Article 2(1)(d));
   - 'persons dealing on own account in financial instruments, or providing investment services in commodity derivatives or derivative

3 Directive 2004/39/EC of 21 April 2004 on Markets in Financial Instruments (MiFID).
4 Commission Directive 2006/73/EC of 10 August 2006 implementing MiFID.

contracts included in Annex I, Section C 10 to the clients of their main business, provided this is an ancillary activity to their main business, when considered on a group basis, and that main business is not the provision of investment services within the meaning of this Directive or banking services under Directive 2000/12/EC' (MiFID Article 2(1)(i)).

4. Some entities which provide safeguarding and administration services will, even if MiFID Annex I is amended as proposed by Principle 21, still be outside the scope of MiFID due to the existing exemptions in MiFID Article 2, for example:
   - entities which provide safekeeping and administration services (and any other investment services) 'exclusively for their parent undertakings, for their subsidiaries or for other subsidiaries of their parent undertakings' (MiFID Article 2(1)(b));
   - entities which provide safekeeping and administration services (and other investment services) 'consisting exclusively in the administration of employee-participation schemes' or 'which only involve both administration of employee-participation schemes and the provision of investment services exclusively for their parent undertakings, for their subsidiaries or for other subsidiaries of their parent undertakings' (MiFID Article 2(1)(e) and (f));
   - entities which are depositaries for collective investment undertakings or pension funds.

3.2.2

The main obligations under the Proposed Legislation will apply to any entity which is an 'account provider'. The definition of this term is therefore of fundamental importance to the application of regulatory requirements which implement the Proposed Legislation. As currently drafted, it would benefit from clarification to ensure it will achieve the intended result. In Principle 22 (Glossary), the term 'account provider' is defined as follows:

(c) 'account provider' means a person who:
   - maintains securities accounts for account holders and is authorised in accordance with Article 5 of Directive 2004/39/EC to provide services listed in Annex I Section A indent (9) of Directive 2004/39/EC

or is a Central Securities Depository as defined in . . . and, in either case, is acting in that capacity;

- [in relation to Principles 3 to 13, if not subject to a national law, in the course of a business or other regular activity maintains securities accounts for others or both for others and for its own account and is acting in that capacity].

There are various aspects of this definition which raise questions.

1. In the first bullet point, the term is defined primarily by reference to whether the entity is authorised under MiFID, rather than by reference to whether the entity is performing the function of holding assets on behalf of another person. This is not consistent with the apparent intention of adopting a functional approach for the purposes of the Proposed Legislation, and the underlying aim of clarifying the position for all persons holding securities through another person.
2. The cross-reference to an account holder means that the definitions are circular, because an account holder is taken to mean 'a person for whom an account provider maintains a securities account'.
3. The first bullet point of the definition will not catch depositories or trustees of funds which are 'collective investment undertakings' for the purposes of MiFID, or depositories or trustees of pension schemes, since these are exempt under MiFID Article 2 as discussed above, but will potentially apply to the following (if such entities hold financial instruments as defined for the purposes of MiFID and maintain securities accounts):
   - any custodian;
   - any escrow agent;
   - any trustee (whether a bond trustee, or other type of trustee);
   - any nominee;
   - any issuer of depositary receipts.

   To the extent that the Proposed Legislation imposes specific obligations, rather than simply identifying the relevant applicable law, it will create an additional compliance burden for these entities. For custodians which are already regulated under MiFID when providing services within both Sections A and B of MiFID Annex I, and for entities such as trustees which are subject to substantial existing duties under general law, this will mean coordinating overlapping compliance obligations, and will mean additional complexity in transaction structures for custodians and trustees, as well as nominees, escrow agents and issuers of depositary receipts.

4. It is not clear how 'Central Securities Depositary' will be defined, but if the final definition captures not only central securities depositaries that hold assets for participants (such as the systems operated by, respectively, Euroclear Bank, SA/NV and Clearstream Banking, SA) but also central securities depositaries that operate central records but do not hold any assets (such as the CREST system operated by Euroclear UK & Ireland Ltd, and the system operated by Euroclear France SA), this would produce odd results and would not be consistent with the purpose of the Proposed Legislation, which is intended to cover the account providers holding assets, not registrars. (In the Consultation Document, the European Commission acknowledges that 'EU law should not cover the functions of creation, recording or reconciliation of securities, against the issuer of those securities, by a person such as a central securities depository, central bank, transfer agent or registrar'.)
5. The purpose of the second bullet point in the definition needs clarification. It refers to persons not subject to national law (presumably the national law of the implementing Member State), but it is not clear if this is intended to extend the application of the Proposed Legislation to entities not incorporated in an EEA state, or to entities within an EEA state but otherwise exempt (for example, persons exempt from authorisation under MiFID).

3.2.3

The rationale of Principle 2 in relation to shared functions is very hard to understand, and seems to result from confusion produced by the proposed definition of 'account provider'. Since the Principles contain a draft definition of 'account provider' which is based on the concept of the maintenance of securities accounts, and such concept is itself difficult to define, this inevitably leads to concern regarding the way in which an account may be maintained, and whether maintenance of an account may involve several persons. Arguably, when deciding who is an account provider, the functional approach should be followed, with a focus on identifying the person holding securities for another person, not the person who may be acting as registrar or performing other administration functions. The concept of shared responsibility is likely to create uncertainty, and cannot be correct if it will result in imposing the obligations of an account provider on entities such as registrars (see comments in section 3.2.2.4 above).

3.3 Acquisitions and disposals

Principle 4: Methods for acquisition and disposition

1. The national law should provide for acquisitions and dispositions of account-held securities and limited interests therein to be effected by crediting an account and debiting an account respectively.

...

5. The applicable national law may in addition allow for acquisitions and dispositions being effected under one or more of the following methods:

(a) earmarking account-held securities in an account, or earmarking a securities account, and the removing of such earmarking;
(b) concluding a control agreement; or
(c) concluding an agreement with and in favour of an account provider.

Principle 5: Legal effectiveness of acquisitions and dispositions

1. The legal nature of dispositions over account-held securities effected under one of the methods listed in Principle 4 would be determined by the national law, as far as the legal nature does not contravene the principles.

2. No further steps than those set out in Principle 4 paragraphs 1 and 5 should be required to render an acquisition or disposition effective between the account holder and the account provider and against third parties. . . .

3. Acquisitions and dispositions arising by mandatory operation of the national law are effective and have the legal attributes, in particular rank, attributed by that law.

4. Effectiveness in the above sense does not determine whom an issuer has to recognise as legal holder of its securities.

5. The effectiveness can be made subject to a condition in accordance with national law.

6. The national law prescribes whether the credit is legally ineffective, liable to be reversed or subject to a condition, and the consequences thereof if the terms of issue of the relevant securities, in accordance with the national law under which the securities are constituted, require the agreement of the issuer for an acquisition to be legally effective.

7. The national law may provide for reasons which trigger ineffectiveness of acquisitions and dispositions effected under a control agreement or an

agreement with and in favour of the account provider and regulate the consequences of such ineffectiveness.

Principle 9: Priority

1. The national law should provide that Priority rules prescribe that:

(a) interests in the same account-held securities which are acquired by earmarking rank amongst themselves in chronological order;
(b) interests in the same account-held securities which are acquired by control agreement or an agreement with and in favour of the account provider rank amongst themselves in chronological order;
(c) interests in account-held securities which are acquired by earmarking have priority over interests acquired in the same account-held securities by means of a control agreement or an agreement with and in favour of the account provider.

2. An acquisition of securities, account-held securities or interests therein effected under Articles 5 should prevail over any other method permitted by the national law.

3. Parties should be able to deviate from the above rules by agreement. Such agreement cannot affect the rights of third parties.

4. Security interests or other limited interests created by mandatory operation of the applicable law should have the priority attributed by that law.

3.3.1

It seems unarguable that the main way in which an account holder acquires securities held through an account provider is by the credit of securities to the account holder's account with the account provider. However, the term 'acquisition' is defined to mean not receipt of securities in an account, but 'the receiving of account-held securities or of a security interest or other limited interest therein'. As a result of this wide definition of acquisition, various terms of the draft Principles may have unintended consequences or may conflict with other Principles. For example, given the requirements of Principle 4(1), it appears that the acquisition of any interest in account-held securities (such as a security interest or some other form of interest) must be 'effected by crediting an account', but this is not consistent with Principle 4(5), which permits acquisitions to be effected by concluding appropriate agreements, as well as earmarking securities in the account. (Similar issues arise in relation to dispositions.)

3.3.2

A different problem arises with Principle 9. Principle 4(5) permits national law to allow interests in account-held securities to be acquired and disposed of by earmarking such account-held securities, or earmarking the securities account (presumably the one in which the securities are held), or by a control agreement, or an agreement with and in favour of an account provider. Principle 9 requires that interests acquired by earmarking of securities at any time should take priority over interests acquired by a control agreement or similar agreement (even if such interest were acquired earlier in time than the interests acquired by earmarking). The Response Summary shows that many have argued that it is sensible if an interest resulting from earmarking always takes priority, because such interest is more visible to third parties, since it is recorded in the relevant account, and an obvious interest is easier to deal with, particularly in the event of insolvency. However, it is difficult to see the logic of this, given that the account records are unlikely to be publicly available, and by creating such a priority rule, prior interests in securities created by any other means are significantly weakened. Not only does this constitute a fundamental change to current practices, certainly under English law, but it could significantly disrupt existing security interests. Indeed it creates uncertainty, the very thing the Proposed Legislation is intended to eliminate. Moreover, here the stated intention, to operate functionally and not change substantive law, fails. Surely, the better approach would be for all interests to rank in chronological order of creation, regardless of the manner in which they are created.

3.4 Securities in books of intermediary to match securities held

Principle 4: Methods for acquisition and disposition

2. The national law should provide that an account provider may credit the accounts of its account holders, for each description of securities, only if it holds a corresponding number of securities of the same description by:

(a) having available account-held securities in a securities account maintained for the account provider by another account provider;
(b) arranging for securities to be held on the register of the issuer in the name, or for the account, of its account holders;
(c) holding securities as the registered holder on the register of the issuer;

(d) possessing relevant securities certificates or other documents of title; or

(e) creating the initial electronic record of securities for the issuer in accordance with the applicable law.

and that an account provider continuously holds that corresponding number.

3. If the applicable law allows crediting and debiting to be made conditional it should also define the extent to which such conditional crediting or debiting is taken into account in determining the number of securities referred to in the preceding paragraphs. Credits to a securities account the effectiveness of which is subject to a condition must be identifiable as such in the account.

Principle 5: Legal effectiveness of acquisitions and dispositions

7. The national law prescribes whether the credit is legally ineffective, liable to be reversed or subject to a condition, and the consequences thereof if the terms of issue of the relevant securities, in accordance with the national law under which the securities are constituted, require the agreement of the issuer for an acquisition to be legally effective.

3.4.1

The commentary in the Consultation Document indicates that Principle 4 is intended to cover 'the *methods* for acquisition and dispositions and the corresponding duties of the account provider', whereas 'the requirements for the legal effectiveness of acquisitions and dispositions' are to be dealt with in other Principles.

3.4.2

While it would seem not unreasonable that an account provider can only credit the account of an account holder with securities if the account provider holds the appropriate number of securities itself (broadly, either directly or through a delegate), there are circumstances where a more flexible approach is helpful in facilitating various market processes, and therefore a rigid rule could create difficulties. As regards both the drafting of this Principle and its implications, the following are some particular issues:

1. It is not clear why Principle 4(2)(b) is relevant in this context at all, because if an account provider arranges for securities to be recorded on the register of title in the name of the account holder, the account

holder is the direct holder of the relevant securities and the account provider is not holding such securities on behalf of the account holder, therefore such an arrangement is outside the scope of the Proposed Legislation.

2. Principle 4(2)(e) should not be included in this list, because it refers to a registrar function, rather than the function of holding securities on behalf of another person.
3. As a result of the rigid requirement in Principle 4(2):
   (a) Securities normally credited to a client account on the due date for receipt, rather than on actual receipt, could not be so credited until actual receipt.
   (b) Securities transferred to a third party pursuant to a stock loan or repo entered into by the client could not be recorded in the client account while the stock loan or repo was outstanding (even though generally for accounting purposes the assets transferred pursuant to a stock loan or repo are regarded as remaining on the balance sheet of the transferor).
   (c) An issuer of depositary receipts could not issue depositary receipts in advance of receipt of shares (this process, known as pre-release, is common in the depositary receipt market to facilitate compliance with standard settlement timing requirements).

It is difficult to predict the effect such changes would have on the business of account providers generally, but on the basis that the arrangements described in section 3.4.2.3 above are generally accepted to be important facilitative measures for both account providers and account holders, a requirement which prohibits such arrangements may have considerable market impact. Both Principle 4(3) and Principle 5(7) appear to contemplate the possibility that EEA states may allow credits to an account to be made on a conditional basis, provided that conditional credits are identified in the client account, but it is unclear whether this provides sufficient scope to permit the arrangements described in section 3.4.2.3, particularly as Principle 5(7) could be interpreted as meaning that the only relevant condition for this purpose is a condition in the form of a requirement for issuer consent to an acquisition of securities.

3.5 Variation by contract

The draft Principles indicate various approaches to the question of whether contractual arrangements between account provider and account holder should be permitted to override the provisions implementing the

Proposed Legislation. While in principle it may be argued that the consistency of maximum harmonisation achieved by mandatory terms is beneficial, it is difficult to see the benefit of imposing on parties particular arrangements which they do not wish to have and where only they are impacted.

3.5.1 Rights conferred by securities

Principle 3: Account-held securities

1. The national law should clarify that securities standing to the credit of a securities account confer upon the account holder at least the following rights:

(a) the right to exercise and receive the rights attached to the securities if the account holder is the ultimate account holder or if, in any other case, the applicable law confers the right to that account holder;
(b) the right to effect a disposition under one of the harmonised methods (see below);
(c) the right to instruct the account provider to arrange for holding the securities with another account provider or otherwise than with an account provider, as far as permitted under the applicable law, the terms of the securities and, to the extent permitted by the national law, the account agreement and the rules of a securities settlement system.

2. The national law should make sure that account holders which act in the capacity of account provider for a third person exercise the rights (b) and (c), above, in accordance with the instructions of that person (see below).

3. In case of acquisition of a security interest or other limited interest in account-held securities the national law should be able to restrict the rights (a)-(c), above.

Principle 3 requires jurisdictions implementing the Proposed Legislation to ensure certain rights are conferred upon an account holder, but it must surely be the case that the account holder is able to agree not to exercise such rights, or to waive such rights, in circumstances where the nature of a particular structure so requires. For example, a waiver of such rights may be important when deciding whether an account holder granting a security interest over securities held with an account provider has sufficiently dispossessed itself of control over such securities. It is not clear whether this would be permitted by Principle 3, and it is important that the possibility of contractual variation should be clarified.

3.5.2 Legal effectiveness and conditions

Principle 5: Legal effectiveness of acquisitions and dispositions

3. To the extent that the requirements of Principle 4 paragraph 2 are not met, and until measures under Principle 4 paragraph 4 are successfully applied, the national law, or the rules of a settlement system in accordance with the applicable law, should determine, subject to Principle 8 below, whether and in what circumstances a credit is legally ineffective, liable to be reversed or subject to a condition, and the consequences thereof.

...

6. The effectiveness can be made subject to a condition in accordance with national law.

7. The national law prescribes whether the credit is legally ineffective, liable to be reversed or subject to a condition, and the consequences thereof if the terms of issue of the relevant securities, in accordance with the national law under which the securities are constituted, require the agreement of the issuer for an acquisition to be legally effective.

8. The national law may provide for reasons which trigger ineffectiveness of acquisitions and dispositions effected under a control agreement or an agreement with and in favour of the account provider and regulate the consequences of such ineffectiveness.

It is not clear whether the above provisions of Principle 5 would permit individual jurisdictions to allow the effectiveness or otherwise of acquisitions or dispositions to be subject to terms agreed between the account provider and the account holder.

3.5.3 Priority of interests

Principle 9: Priority

1. The national law should provide that Priority rules prescribe that:

(a) interests in the same account-held securities which are acquired by earmarking rank amongst themselves in chronological order;
(b) interests in the same account-held securities which are acquired by control agreement or an agreement with and in favour of the account provider rank amongst themselves in chronological order;
(c) interests in account-held securities which are acquired by earmarking have priority over interests acquired in the same account-held securities by means of a control agreement or an agreement with and in favour of the account provider.

2. An acquisition of securities, account-held securities or interests therein effected under Article 5 should prevail over any other method permitted by the national law.

3. Parties should be able to deviate from the above rules by agreement. Such agreement cannot affect the rights of third parties.

While it is helpful that, as a result of Principle 9(3), parties can agree to deviate from the priority rules in Principle 9, in practice this is of minimal assistance if one party then agrees a different arrangement which complies with Principle 9 with a third party, to the detriment of the party to the earlier agreement. Principle 9 presents considerable problems, as discussed in section 3.3 above.

3.5.4 Facilitating exercise of rights

Principle 17: Facilitation of the ultimate account holder's position

1. The national law should require that the account provider of the ultimate account holder should be bound to facilitate the determination of the exercise of rights attached to securities by the ultimate account holder against the issuer or a third party as requested by the ultimate account holder.

2. Such facilitation must at least consist in the account provider of the ultimate account holder:

(a) arranging for the ultimate account holder or a third person nominated by the ultimate account holder being the representative of the legal holder with respect to the exercise of the relevant rights, if the account provider or a third person is the legal holder of securities, in which case Article 11 of the Shareholders' Rights Directive applies correspondingly; or,

(b) exercising the rights attached to the securities upon authorisation and instruction and for the benefit of the ultimate account holder, if the account provider or a third person is the legal holder of the securities; or,

(c) providing the ultimate account holder, regardless of whether it is the legal holder of the securities or not, with evidence confirming its holdings and it being enabled to exercise the rights attached to the securities against the issuer or a third party, under a general framework guaranteeing the integrity of the number of available rights and the position of the legal holder of the securities in respect of lit. (c) of paragraph 2. The content and form of the evidence to be provided should be specified and standard forms should be developed, in particular to

> define under which conditions issuers should recognise such evidence for purposes of exercising rights attached to securities.
>
> 3. The extent to which the obligations following paragraphs 1 and 2 can be made subject to a contractual agreement between the ultimate account holder and its account provider as well as the formal requirements to be met by such agreement should be subject to restrictions for purposes of client protection.

Although Principle 17(3) seems to contemplate that the facilitation of the exercise of rights pursuant to this Principle can be made subject to a contractual agreement, it is not clear whether this would permit Member States to allow an account provider and account holder to agree that no facilitation services will be provided, or only permits Member States to specify 'the manner of the facilitation may be as agreed between the account provider and account holder'.

3.5.5 *Exercise of rights by the account provider*

Principle 20: Exercise by account provider on the basis of contract

> Where an ultimate account holder is able to exercise itself the rights flowing from securities but does not want to do so, its account provider exercises these rights upon its authorisation and instruction and in accordance with the contractually agreed level of services. There should be an EU-wide standard regarding the formal requirements to be met by such an agreement as far as it provides for general authorisation of the account provider to exercise the rights flowing from the securities.

This Principle acknowledges that an account holder may not want to exercise rights arising under securities, and refers to the 'contractually agreed level of services', but it is not clear whether in the relevant contract it may be agreed that the rights will not be exercised at all. This may be an important issue for structures where there is no realistic way in which the exercise of rights can be directed by the entity (for example, a special purpose vehicle) which is technically the account holder.

3.6 Risk allocation

Principle 4: Methods for acquisition and disposition

> 4. If a corresponding number (paragraph 2) is not held, the account provider should promptly apply either or both of the following mechanisms in order to re-establish compliance:

(a) reverse erroneous credits;
(b) provide additional securities of the relevant description, to be held by one of the methods provided for in paragraph 2.

3.6.1

The sharing of any cost entailed by the provision of additional securities pursuant to subparagraph (b) can be subject to a contractual agreement between the account provider and those account holders holding securities of the relevant description at the time of the occurrence of the loss in non-segregated accounts only in cases where the account provider held securities of the relevant description with another account provider pursuant to Article 17(3) subparagraphs (a) and (b) of the MiFID.

Principle 7: Reversal

1. The national law should ensure that Book entries can only be reversed under the following circumstances:

(a) in the case of crediting provided that the account holder consents to the reversal;
(b) in the case of erroneous crediting which was not authorised by the account holder, subject to Article 9;
(c) in the case of debiting which was not authorised by the account holder, or a third person who has acquired an interest in the relevant account-held securities;
(d) in case of earmarking which was not authorised by the account holder, subject to Article 9;
(e) in case of removal of an earmarking which was not authorised by the person in whose favour it was made.

2. Paragraph 1 should be, to the extent permitted by the applicable law, subject to any rule of a securities settlement system.

3. The national law should specify the extent to which consent in the sense of paragraph 1(a) can be given in a general manner and any formal requirements for giving such consent.

Principle 8: Protection of acquirers against reversal

The national law should ensure that:

(a) an account holder is protected against reversal of a crediting;
(b) a person in whose favour an earmarking has been made is protected against reversal of this earmarking unless it knew or ought to have known that the crediting or earmarking should not have been made.

3.6.2

The question of reversals is related to the requirement (discussed in section 3.4 above) that an account provider only credits an account with securities if it actually holds such securities. Such a requirement immediately raises the question of what happens if after making a credit to an account the account provider discovers that it does not in fact hold the relevant number of securities. The Consultation Document acknowledges that the possibility of error and fraud cannot be ignored, and that therefore Principle 4(4) sets out the requirements where there is an inconsistency between securities recorded in an account and securities actually held, namely that the account provider must either reverse erroneous credits or provide additional securities.

3.6.3

Reversal of a credit entry is the usual way of remedying the situation where an account provider concludes that it does not hold the number of securities credited to the account. Such a situation may arise for various reasons, including a simple error when inputting details or a reversal by a settlement system or other third party with whom the account provider holds securities (such third party or settlement system will not necessarily be subject to the Proposed Legislation), as well as more serious matters such as where there has been fraud or theft.

3.6.4

Although it is not stated specifically in Principle 4, reversal of erroneous credits is presumably subject to Principles 7 and 8. This severely limits the situation in which reversals can be made. Principle 7 permits reversals in various circumstances, including where there has been an 'erroneous crediting', but reversals are dependent on consent from the client or the fact that the original entry was not authorised by the client. This appears to mean that provided an erroneous credit was authorised by the account holder, the account provider cannot reverse the erroneous credit without the client's consent. This could create considerable difficulties in the event of fraud by a third party or by the client itself. Moreover, it is not clear whether Principle 7 would permit the inclusion in an agreement between the account holder and the account provider of a general consent from the account holder to reversals (particularly as Principle 7(3) requires national law to specify 'the extent to which consent in the sense of paragraph 1(a) can be given in a general manner and any formal requirements for giving such consent'), and it would appear that Principle 8 takes priority over Principle 7.

3.6.5

Under Principle 8, the national law of Member States must 'ensure' that an account holder is protected against reversal of crediting (and a person with the benefit of an earmarking of securities in the account is protected against its reversal) unless such person knew or ought to have known that the relevant credit or earmarking should not have been made.

3.6.6

This is apparently intended to protect account holders who receive a credit of securities or earmarking without notice of a problem, but is arguably a significant change to most existing law, since there is no exception for reversals required by insolvency rules or where there has been fraud. Principle 8 also appears to override Principle 7(2) which states that the conditions for reversal in Principle 7(1) 'should be, to the extent permitted by the applicable law, subject to any rule of a securities settlement system'. As a result, by prohibiting reversals in certain circumstances, the current Proposed Legislation exposes the account provider to the risk of having to provide additional securities at its own expense in such circumstances, including where a reversal is made by any third party through which the account provider holds securities and such reversal does not result from any fault of the account provider.

3.6.7

Under Principle 4(4), if reversal of erroneous credits is not possible, the account provider must acquire replacement securities. The account provider can agree with the account holder how to share the cost, but this is subject to a significant restriction if the securities were held in 'non-segregated accounts' at the time of the loss, since in such case agreement regarding cost-sharing is only permitted if the account provider held the securities with 'another account provider' in a jurisdiction which does not regulate the holding and safekeeping of financial instruments, in the circumstances permitted by Article 17(3), subparagraphs (a) and (b), of the MiFID implementing directive (broadly, where the nature of the securities means the securities have to be held in the relevant jurisdiction, or the client is a professional client for MiFID purposes and has requested that the securities are held in the relevant jurisdiction). As a result, an account provider cannot agree with the account holder to share costs for replacement of securities in relation to securities which are held by the account provider in a 'non-segregated account' within the EEA. The important question is therefore what is meant by a 'non-segregated account'. This term is not defined in the Updated Compilation, and the Consultation Document provides no explanation. However, in the context of discussion of Principle 13, the Consultation Document makes reference to the requirement in Article 16(1)(d) of the MiFID implementing directive which requires investment firms holding client assets with a third party to 'take the necessary steps to ensure' that the client assets 'are identifiable separately from the financial instruments belonging to the investment firm and from financial instruments belonging to that third party, by means of differently titled accounts on the books of the third party or other equivalent measures that achieve the same level of protection'. The European Commission appears to regard an account with a third party which satisfies Article 16(1)(d) as a 'segregated client account', and therefore presumably an account with a third party which does not satisfy such requirement is a 'non-segregated account'. This suggests that this provision of the Proposed Legislation is intended to take effect as the introduction of a penalty for entities failing to comply with Article 16(1)(d) of the MiFID implementing directive (as implemented in the relevant jurisdiction). If this is the intention, this should be clarified, and a definition of 'non-segregated account' should be inserted in the Proposed Legislation, since this point will have a significant impact on risk analysis by account providers and therefore it is important that the purpose and effect of the proposed Principle is clear.

3.7 Insolvency

Principle 6 – Effectiveness in insolvency

1. Acquisitions and dispositions that have become effective under the methods described in Principles 4 and 5 should be equally effective against the insolvency administrator and creditors in any insolvency proceeding.

2. The principle contained in Paragraph 1 does not affect the application of any substantive or procedural rule of law applicable by virtue of an insolvency proceeding, such as any rule relating to:

(a) the ranking of categories of claims [in the case of violation of the methods described in Principles 4 and 5];
(b) the avoidance of a transaction as a preference or a transfer in fraud of creditors; or
(c) the enforcement of rights to property that is under the control or supervision of the insolvency administrator.

Principle 10: Protection of account holders in case of insolvency of account provider

1. The national law should ensure that in the event of insolvency of the account provider securities and account-held securities held by the account provider for its account holders should be unavailable for distribution among or realisation for the benefit of creditors of the account provider.

2. The national law applicable in the insolvency of an account provider should provide for a mechanism governing the distribution of the shortage in the event of an insufficient number of securities or account-held securities in the sense of Principle 4 paragraph 2 being held by an insolvent account provider.'

3.7.1

Under Principle 6, acquisitions and dispositions under Principles 4 and 5 are required to be 'equally effective against the insolvency administrator and creditors in any insolvency proceeding'. This seems to mean that whether the insolvency proceeding relates to the account holder, the account provider, or any other person, the acquisition or disposition cannot be challenged by the insolvency official or creditors. One obvious problem with this is that it is difficult to see how this would be binding on an insolvency official outside the EEA.

3.7.2

There are specific exceptions to this rule for any 'substantive or procedural rule of law applicable by virtue of an insolvency proceeding', such as rules regarding ranking of categories of claims and avoidance of transfers due to a preference or fraud, and the enforcement of rights to property that is under the control or supervision of the insolvency administrator. The existence of insolvency exceptions is not surprising, given that provisions which override existing insolvency laws would constitute a major change under the laws of each EEA Member State, but the result is of course that as at present account providers and account holders will need to check the situation carefully when party to cross-border arrangements.

3.7.3

Principle 10(1) is extremely helpful if it results in clear statutory protection for all securities held by an account holder with an account provider in the event of the insolvency of the account provider.

3.7.4

Principle 10(2) is interesting in that it leaves it to national law to 'provide a mechanism' for deciding how to allocate loss where the insolvent account provider holds fewer securities than are recorded in the accounts maintained for account holders. It is frequently assumed that loss in such case will be shared pro rata by the relevant account holders, but this is not necessarily the case. The Response Summary shows roughly equal support for leaving the allocation to be determined by national law and having a harmonised rule based on a pro rata principle (or other mechanism), although the total number of responses to this question was exceeded by the number of respondents who provided no response to this question. Deference to national law is perhaps the logical answer, given that the allocation of loss in such circumstances is closely linked to national approaches to appropriate procedures on insolvency.

3.8 Prohibition of cross-border discrimination

Principle 15: Cross-border recognition of rights attached to securities

1. The national law governing a securities issue as well as the national law governing the holding of securities should not discriminate against the exercise of rights attached to securities held in another jurisdiction on the sole grounds that the relevant securities are held in a specific manner, in particular:

- through one or more account providers,
- through an account provider acting in its own name but for the account of its account holders,

- through accounts in which securities of two or more account holders are held in an indistinguishable manner.

2. The national law should remain free to prescribe which holding methods account providers should offer to their account holders.

Principle 18: Non-discriminatory charges

The national law should ensure that Charges [this term is not defined] levied by an account provider on its account holders for any service relating to the compliance with any of the duties established in Principles 16 and 17 in respect of cross-border holdings of securities should be the same as the charges levied by that account provider on its account holders in respect of comparable domestic holdings of securities.

3.8.1

Principle 15 requires Member States to ensure that neither the law governing a securities issue nor the law governing the holding of securities 'discriminate against' the exercise of rights in respect of the securities where the securities are held by persons in other jurisdictions through an intermediary. It seems from the comments in the Consultation Document that the intention underlying this Principle is that national law should not prescribe procedures in relation to the exercise of rights attached to securities which by their nature (perhaps as a result of the time in which instructions to exercise rights must be received by the issuer, or the manner on which such instructions should be given) would make it particularly difficult or impossible for the exercise of such rights by persons who hold interests in such securities who are located in jurisdictions other than the jurisdiction of the issuer. This seems not unreasonable, although may necessitate some careful consideration of existing procedures currently required by relevant law, since there may be concerns regarding matters such as security and reliability of procedures, or the impact of amendment to time periods on other corporate procedures.

3.8.2

However, if the Proposed Legislation incorporated the wording in its current broad form, this would cause difficulties, if interpreted to mean that there could be no difference in the process for the exercise of rights by persons holding interests in securities directly, and persons holding interest in securities through an intermediary. It is not immediately clear how such an approach could be achieved, since there will inevitably be differences in the way a person holding securities through an intermediary exercises its rights. For example, a person holding securities through an intermediary which is the direct holder will inevitably receive information regarding the exercise of rights more slowly than a person who is a direct holder, since such information must be forwarded by the intermediary, and a person who holds securities through an intermediary which itself holds through an intermediary will receive the relevant information with an even greater delay, and similar time delays will apply to the transmission of information back to the issuer. Further such problems arise where the various parties are operating in different time zones.

3.8.3

A similar point arises in relation to Principle 18 which requires fees charged in respect of cross-border holdings of securities to be 'the same' as charges in relation to 'comparable domestic holdings'. This will only be achievable if the same external system resources are available for both types of holding. If in practice the intermediary incurs extra expense in relation to cross-border holdings, the intermediary's only option is to increase charges to all clients so that all clients are subject to the same charges. This is a somewhat awkward result of a requirement intended to benefit investors.

3.9 Conclusion

In general, any legislation which manages to achieve some degree of harmonisation across EEA states regarding securities held with intermediaries would be a very welcome development, but as may be seen from the issues discussed above, there is still some way to go in order to produce legislation in a form which achieves the level of certainty that is the ideal goal.

4

Rights of the account holder relating to securities credited to its securities account

PHILIPPE DUPONT

4.1 Introduction

The UNIDROIT Convention on Substantive Rules for Intermediated Securities, or Geneva Securities Convention ('the Convention'), and the Commission Consultation Document of the Services of the Directorate-General Internal Markets and Services of November 2010 on Legislation on Legal Certainty of Securities Holding and Dispositions ('the Commission Consultation Document') aim at protecting the rights of securities account holders by enhancing legal certainty as to the rights acquired by each account holder in a holding chain of intermediaries. In conferring upon each account holder in such a chain an equivalent set of rights, they attempt to devise the minimum compatibility between national legal systems that is necessary to ensure that all parties in an intermediated holding chain of securities can connect successfully.[1]

This chapter does not purport to describe in detail all rights acquired by account holders under the Convention or the Commission Consultation Document, but will focus on the rights of the account holders as set out in Article 9 of the Convention, and the corresponding rights set out in various provisions of the Commission Consultation Document. The rights conferred on the account holder pursuant to Article 9(1) of the Convention are a minimum set of rights that each account holder must acquire at each level of the intermediated holding chain, and some rights that may only accrue to the ultimate account holder. Neither the Convention nor the Commission Consultation Document strive to fully harmonise national securities laws, but rather to introduce the set of rights

1 The UNIDROIT Study Group on Harmonised Substantive Rules Regarding Indirectly Held Securities, 'Second Advice of the Legal Certainty Group, Solutions to Legal Barriers related to Post-Trading within the EU', Position Paper, August 2008.

that are indispensable for reducing legal and systemic risks promoting market efficiency and ensuring connectivity in a cross-border holding chain of securities.

Recognising the vast diversity in terms of the nature of the rights acquired by account holders in various jurisdictions ranging from full ownership, co-ownership, equitable interest, contractual rights, securities entitlement to *sui generis* rights[2] and the intimate link such rights have with national civil, commercial and corporate law, neither the Convention nor the Commission Consultation Document attempts to characterise the nature of such rights, but instead leave this to national law.[3] Therefore the Convention and the Commission Consultation Document take a 'functional approach', meaning that they use neutral language and merely formulate rules by reference to their result.

The Convention and the Commission Consultation Document impose upon states the obligation to ensure that the account holder acquires at least the rights listed below. Any provisions of national law that would disallow or not fully allow the acquisition or exercise of such rights by the account holder will need to be changed.

As a result, account holders, irrespective of their level in the holding chain, will have certainty that the basic rights they have acquired are identical.[4] Ultimate account holders will enjoy additional rights from which other account holders in the holding chain may not benefit.

In addition to the rights that national law[5] confers on the account holder, the Convention requires that the account holder be granted at least the following three rights:

1. the right to receive and exercise any rights attached to the securities;[6]
2. the right to effect a disposition of or grant an interest in the securities held in its securities account;

2 See particularly Paech, *Cross-Border Issues of Securities Law*, 13 et seq.; Thévenoz, 'Intermediated Securities', at 401 et seq.; Micheler, 'The Legal Nature of Securities'.

3 Unlike the Convention, which is silent on this issue (see however Official Commentary, 9–3 and 9–4), Art. 3(4) of the Commission Consultation Document refers expressly to national law to characterise the legal nature of the rights acquired by the account holder upon a credit of securities to its securities account.

4 With the exception of some rights which may only accrue to the ultimate account holder.

5 This chapter does not deal with private international law aspects, and uses the term 'national law' as a substitute for the terms 'non-Convention law' and 'applicable law' used in the Convention. On this distinction made by the Convention, see Kanda et al., *Official Commentary*, s. 1–55 et seq.

6 This right will accrue to ultimate account holders and, depending on national law, also to other account holders in the chain (see section 4.3.2).

3. the right, by instructions to the relevant intermediary, to cause the securities to be held otherwise than through a securities account.

The above rights are acquired by the account holder upon the credit of the securities to its securities account. It is that credit that confers the right on the account holder without the need for any further formalities.[7] Such rights are enforceable against the intermediary and against third parties.[8]

Conversely, Article 10(1) of the Convention imposes on the intermediary the duty to take 'appropriate measures' to enable its account holders to exercise the above three rights. The content of these 'appropriate measures' is not defined in the Convention. Article 28(1) of the Convention merely provides that the obligations of the intermediary are those that are imposed by national law, the account agreement or the uniform rules of a securities settlement system. In ratifying the Convention, States will need to adapt their national laws so as to ensure that intermediaries will perform those duties that are indispensable to ensure that account holders can exercise the rights conferred on them in Article 9(1) of the Convention.

Before moving to the heart of the subject it is important to clarify the meaning of three key terms, namely 'account holder', 'intermediary'[9] and 'ultimate account holder.'[10]

4.2 Account holders and intermediaries

The Convention defines the 'account holder' in its Article 1(e) as 'a person in whose name an intermediary maintains a securities account, whether that person is acting for its own account or for others (including in the capacity of intermediary)'. The definition given to such term in the Glossary of the Commission Consultation Document is in substance identical, albeit with an unfortunate minor terminological difference.[11]

7 Art. 11(1) of the Convention; Arts. 4(1) and 5(2) of the Commission Consultation Document.

8 Art. 9(2) of the Convention The effect against third parties is not dealt with in the Commission Consultation Document.

9 The Commission Consultation Document uses the term 'account provider' instead of 'intermediary'.

10 The Convention refers to the same concept by using the phrase 'account holder [which] is not an intermediary or is an intermediary acting for its own account' at Art. 9(1)(a)(i).

11 Glossary point (d) of the Commission Consultation Document: '"account holder" means a person for whom an account provider maintains a securities account, whether that

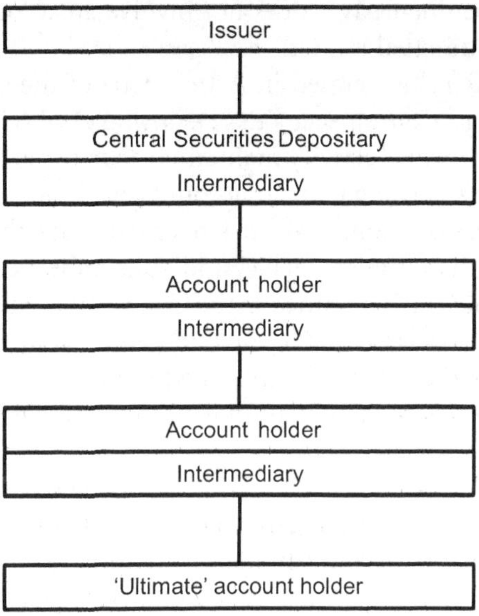

Figure 4.1 Simplified holding chain

An account holder is not necessarily the investor in the securities credited to its securities account. In a holding chain where more than one intermediary intervenes, middle-tier intermediaries act both as intermediaries vis-à-vis their account holders and as account holders vis-à-vis their own intermediary.

Figure 4.1 illustrates a simplified holding chain which may involve several jurisdictions and evidences the dual role of intermediary and account holder played by a number of actors.

The ultimate account holder is merely the last holder of a securities account in the chain of intermediaries. It may hold the securities on its own account, in which case it will also be the investor, but it might also hold the securities in its name, for example as an agent for a third-party investor. The relationship between the ultimate account holder and the investor is not covered by the Convention or the Commission

person is acting for its own account or for others, including in the capacity of account provider'. In using the term 'for whom' rather than 'in whose name', the Commission Consultation Document seems to be characterising the legal nature of the relationship between the intermediary and the account holder, characterisation which is not made by the more neutral wording used in the Convention.

Consultation Document, as it does not involve an account relationship, and is a mere contractual matter.

The 'intermediary' is defined in Article 1(d) of the Convention as 'a person (including a Central Securities Depositary) who in the course of a business or other regular activity maintains securities accounts for others or both for others and for its own account and is acting in that capacity'. The Commission Consultation Document uses the term 'account provider' rather than 'intermediary', and adds an important element to the definition that is not contained in the Convention, that is, to the extent that the intermediary is located in the European Union, the intermediary must be a regulated entity.[12] The intermediary will typically be a bank, a broker or a Central Securities Depositary, but not a registrar or a transfer agent.[13]

As Figure 4.1 illustrates, not each account holder in the chain bears the same economic risk with regard to the securities held in its securities account. The rights of account holders may thus vary, depending upon their position in the holding chain. The rights of account holders will also be impacted by various laws such as the law applicable in the State of the relevant intermediary and the law governing the issuer[14] or the issue.[15]

4.3 Rights attached to the securities

4.3.1 Nature of the rights

Pursuant to Article 9(1)(a) of the Convention and Article 3(1)(a) of the Commission Consultation Document, the credit of securities to a securities account confers on the account holder the right to receive and exercise the rights 'attached' to the securities. These are typically the right to receive a distribution under the securities or to exercise voting rights.

These rights are not created by the Convention or the Commission Consultation Document – they result in general from the law applicable to the securities or the issuer thereof or from their contractual terms applicable to the securities. The rights 'attached' to the securities are defined in particular by the terms of the securities, by the law governing the issuer and/or by the articles of association of the issuer.

12 See point 2.4.2 of the Second Advice of the Legal Certainty Group (*op. cit.* n. 1) on the issue of 'regulated' versus 'unregulated' intermediary. Such limitation is not required by the Convention, but it is nonetheless compatible with, see Art. 5(a) of the Convention.

13 See Art. 6 of the Convention.

14 Typically for equity financial instruments.

15 Typically for debt financial instruments.

With the objective of inter alia fostering a proper connectivity in a cross-border holding chain of intermediaries, the Convention and of the Commission Consultation Document only intend to ensure that the rights attached to the securities can properly flow through the holding chain of intermediaries and that at no level of the holding chain will an obstacle arise that would prevent the account holder from obtaining what is due to it.

4.3.2 Beneficiary

Since in a holding chain of securities not each holder of the securities has the same position concerning such securities, the Convention differentiates as to who can receive and exercise the rights attached to the securities.

Pursuant to Article 9(1)(a)(i) of the Convention, the rights attached to the securities must at least accrue to the ultimate account holder. Any national legislation that denies all or part of the rights attached to the securities of the ultimate account holder will need to be amended.

National laws vary considerably in the characterisation of the right to the securities. Transparent systems[16] and those systems that consider the ultimate account holder to be the 'owner' of the securities, and intermediaries mere account keepers,[17] will typically limit the exercise of the rights attached to the securities to the ultimate account holder. Systems characterising the right of the account holder pertaining to the securities as an entitlement will conceptually grant the exercise and receipt of the rights attached to the securities to all account holders in the holding chain, albeit with certain restrictions so as to avoid the multiple exercise of rights with respect to the same securities.[18]

Both the Convention and the Commission Consultation Document are drafted to avoid encroaching upon the characterisation of the nature of the rights acquired by each account holder; both provide that an account holder which is not the ultimate account holder may exercise the rights attached to the securities, if national law so provides. In the latter case

16 Transparent systems are intermediated holding systems where the central securities depository is the (only) intermediary maintaining accounts directly in the name of the ultimate account holders or can otherwise identify them. Brokers and banks are responsible for performing certain functions of an intermediary, such as operating the accounts maintained by the CSD on behalf of their clients. See Art. 7 of the Convention.

17 So-called 'direct ownership systems', see Thévenoz, 'Intermediated Securities', at 404–6.

18 See *ibid.*, at 406–8.

the account holder/intermediary should however, pursuant to Article 10(2)(f) of the Convention, pass down the distributions received to its own account holders. For the same reason, neither the Convention nor the Commission Consultation Document makes the passing down of distributions a mandatory rule, leaving it instead to national law to decide upon this point. Further, neither of these instruments requires that the rights be exercised by the intermediary in accordance with the instructions of its account holder although, at least with respect to voting rights, the Commission Consultation Document seems to give some indications in that sense.

4.3.3 *Exercise of rights*

The Convention provides in its Article 9(2)(b) that the rights attached to the securities may be exercised by the account holder against its intermediary or the issuer of the securities, or both, in accordance with the Convention, the terms of the securities and national law.

In order for account holders to be able to exercise the rights attached to the securities (e.g. voting rights, conversion rights), they must be informed of the event ('corporate action') pursuant to which they must or may exercise a right.

The Convention is cautious on this point, and leaves it to national law to decide whether an intermediary must pass on to notify the account holder information on regarding corporate actions.[19]

The Commission Consultation Document fills this gap in its Article 16. It imposes upon each intermediary in the holding chain an obligation to pass on information to its account holders without undue delay under three cumulative conditions:

1. It must have received the information from the issuer or its intermediary, i.e. it does not have to look at all possible sources of information to find out about possible corporate actions, but it may rely on the information received from its intermediary or the issuer.
2. The information received must be 'necessary' in order to exercise a right attached to the securities which exists against the issuer. The term 'necessary' is interpreted by the Commission's services as information

19 See Art. 10(2)(e) of the Convention.

which is a *conditio sine qua non* for the exercise of rights attached to securities.[20]

3. The information must be directed at all legal holders of securities of that description.

Whilst the Convention requires that the ultimate account holder has the right to exercise the voting rights attached to the securities it does not specify how this result should be achieved in practice. National systems vary considerably in this respect on the one hand because of the doctrinal approach to the nature of the rights acquired by the account holder in the securities and because of corporate law requirements.

4.3.4 *Obligations of intermediaries*

The Convention requires intermediaries to 'take appropriate measures' in order to enable the account holder to exercise its voting rights, without however specifying these measures.

The Commission Consultation Document goes a step further in its Article 17, in imposing on intermediaries the obligation to facilitate the exercise of voting rights by the ultimate account holder. The Commission Consultation Document contains a non-exhaustive list of ways in which the above duty can be satisfied by an intermediary:

1. by designating the ultimate account holder as the legal representative of the person entitled to exercise the voting rights pursuant to corporate law or the terms of the issue;
2. by granting the ultimate account holder the right to give voting instructions to the person entitled to vote;
3. by issuing certificates evidencing the holding of securities of a given designation by the ultimate account holder, certificate on the basis of which the ultimate account holder may participate in a general meeting and exercise its voting rights.

The above methods are very difficult for an intermediary to implement if voting procedures are not standardised throughout the entire holding chain. It might therefore be wise if future EU legislation were to grant authority to the Commission to enact harmonised secondary legislation on this issue. A harmonisation of voting procedures at European level

20 Second Advice of the Legal Certainty Group (*op. cit.* n. 1) n° 97.

would be an important step forward, and might trigger a larger drive towards universal harmonisation.

Because its scope covers the European Union, Article 20 of the Commission Consultation Document imposes upon intermediaries a duty to make reasonable arrangements with intermediaries in third countries to facilitate the exercise of the rights attached to the securities in accordance with the Commission Consultation Document.

4.3.5 Relationship with corporate law

The above requirements must be nuanced by the fact that neither the Convention nor the Commission Consultation Document covers corporate law aspects.[21] The interaction between the rights conferred upon account holders pursuant to Article 9(1) of the Convention and corporate law is defined in Article 8 of the Convention.[22]

Pursuant to Article 8(1), the Convention does not affect any right of the account holder against the issuer of the securities. This means in substance that, where an account holder has acquired rights attached to securities pursuant to the Convention, the issuer cannot hold that the account holder has not acquired such rights. However, local corporate law will determine, for example, under which circumstances dividends may be paid by the issuer or the voting procedures at a general meeting of securities holders. These aspects are not covered by the Convention.

Article 8(2) of the Convention provides that the Convention 'does not determine whom the issuer is required to recognise as the shareholder, bondholder or other person entitled to receive and exercise the rights attached to the securities or to recognise for any other purpose'.

This article is not an exception to Article 9(1)(a) of the Convention, but applies in a sense 'next to' Article 9(1)(a) of the Convention.

The Convention determines who has the rights attached to the securities, and the issuer cannot refuse this. This however does not necessarily mean that the account holder who has rights attached to

21 For a general discussion of this issue, see de Vauplane, 'Droit des sociétés et Convention de Genève', and Thévenoz, 'Who Holds (Intermediated) Securities?' Except for the fact that the Convention requires in its Art. 29(2) that states must recognise nominee holdings and split voting, and that the Commission Consultation Document imposes in its Art. 15 a general non-discrimination duty against the exercise of rights attached to the securities held in another jurisdiction for the sole reason that the securities are held in a holding chain of intermediaries, through a nominee or in an omnibus account.

22 See Art. 5(5) of the Commission Consultation Document for a corresponding provision to Art. 8(2) of the Convention.

securities pursuant to the Convention can necessarily exercise such rights directly against the issuer. The question as to who can exercise rights attached to securities against the issuer will be determined by corporate law, the articles of association of the issuer and the terms of the securities or the law applicable to the securities. If, for example, local corporate law provides that only the person who is recorded in the shareholders' register may exercise voting rights, then such person will be entitled to exercise the voting rights and not the person who has the rights attached to the securities pursuant to the Convention.

According to the Convention and the Commission Consultation Document or national laws the person exercising the voting rights may however be bound to exercise the voting rights only in accordance with the instructions received from its account holder.

4.4 Right to dispose of the securities

4.4.1 Right

Pursuant to Article 9(1)(b) of the Convention the account holder, at whatever level of the holding chain, may dispose of the securities credited to its securities account or grant an interest in such securities.

A disposition is performed by debiting the securities from the securities account of the account holder pursuant to an instruction of the latter to its intermediary. This instruction will frequently be part of the execution of a securities sales agreement implying a transfer against or free of payment. The way in which dispositions are performed is specified in Articles 5, 11 and 12 of the Convention.[23]

The account holder may also grant an interest in the securities to a third party, which may be the intermediary or any other person. Such interest will either be a security interest (e.g. a pledge or charge) or a limited interest (e.g. a usufruct). Articles 11 and 12 of the Convention define the granting of interests in securities, and Chapter V of the Convention contains special provisions on collateral transactions.

4.4.2 Exercise restrictions

The Commission Consultation Document provides in substance for the same rights, but restricts the exercise of the rights of the account holders depending on their position in the holding chain. Ultimate

23 See Ch. 6 in this book; Kanda et al., *Official Commentary*, s. III-1 et seq.

account holders may exercise such rights without restrictions, but account holders who act, with respect to the relevant securities, as intermediaries, may only exercise the rights in accordance with the instructions of their account holder.

Whilst one can understand the reasoning leading to this addition to the Commission Consultation Document, this provision may have unintended consequences. Indeed the provision raises the question as to whether the intermediary whose account holder also acts as intermediary will have to check whether its account holder has been duly instructed by the latter's account holder. A positive answer to this question would seriously jeopardise the proper and smooth functioning of the intermediated securities holding system. In the final version of the Commission Consultation Document it must imperatively be specified that the intermediary does not have to concern itself with the question of whether its account holder has received the necessary instructions from its own account holder.

The right to dispose of securities or to grant an interest in them may, pursuant to Article 9(2)(c) of the Convention, be exercised by the account holder only against its intermediary. This is true for each account holder in the chain, including the ultimate account holder. This provision, which is probably inadvertently missing from the Commission Consultation Document, is of fundamental importance for avoiding possible disruptions in the chain of intermediaries. Each intermediary should only have to abide by the instructions of its account holder, which is typically the only account holder it will actually know, and not by those of any other account holder even if the latter is the ultimate account holder.

This restriction also illustrates the difference between the rights of the account holder 'to' the securities, which may only be exercised against its intermediary, and the rights 'attached' to the securities, which may be exercised against the intermediary and the issuer.

4.5 Right to hold securities other than through a securities account

4.5.1 Principle

Article 9(1)(c) of the Convention grants to the account holder the right to request from its intermediary the retrieval of the securities which the account holder maintains in its securities account in order to hold them in certificated form.[24] This is a typical feature of a 'property' right. The

24 See also Art. 3(1)(c) of the Commission Consultation Document for the corresponding provision to Art. 9(1)(c) of the Convention.

securities that are retrieved will be withdrawn from the intermediated holding system and will thereafter fall outside the scope of the Convention and the Commission Consultation Document, since both instruments deal exclusively with account-held securities.

The Commission Consultation Document grants in Article 3(1)(c) the additional right to the account holder to instruct the intermediary to arrange for the securities to be held with another intermediary. The objective of this provision seems to be to grant to each account holder the freedom to choose, at its discretion, its intermediary and to avoid the creation of monopolies. The necessity of this additional provision is however doubtful since the Commission Consultation Document contains a whole set of provisions allowing the account holder to dispose of the securities held in its securities account and thus the right to have the securities transferred to a securities account with another intermediary.

Whilst the above rights appear clear and straightforward in principle, they will in actual practice often either be impossible or very difficult to realise.

4.5.2 Exception

Because of these difficulties, the Convention and the Commission Consultation Document provide for a large number of limitations to this right in subjecting the latter to possible restrictions imposed by national law, the terms of the securities, the account agreement and the uniform rules of a securities settlement system.

A number of states[25] have made the dematerialisation of securities mandatory. In such states, securities issued by local issuers or subject to local laws can only be held in book-entry form. The law will thus be an obstacle to the right to retrieve certificated securities from the intermediated holding system.

To avoid the expensive, cumbersome and insecure process of printing certificated securities, and to be able to monitor compliance with certain national selling restrictions,[26] the market has created so-called 'global notes' i.e. a single certificate which represents an entire issue of securities.

25 Examples are France and Belgium.

26 Such as the US Regulation S on the Rules governing offers and sales made outside the United States without registration under the Securities Act of 1933.

The terms of these global notes vary, but can be divided essentially into three categories:

1. the global note may be replaced in full or in part by individual certificated securities after the lapse of a certain period of time following the issuance of the note;
2. same as above, but only in case of the occurrence of a limited number of events, such as the insolvency of the issuer;
3. the global note may never be replaced by individual certificated securities.

For global notes the terms of the issue will thus restrict to varying degrees the right of the account holder to retrieve the underlying securities from the intermediated holding system.

To ensure the integrity of a securities issue, all securities of that issue are typically held at the upper-tier level of the intermediated holding chain by a Central Securities Depositary. Retrievals of securities from such a depositary may be precluded by law, or be subject to stringent conditions.

Because the retrieval of certificated securities is in practice an expensive (especially in a cross-border context) and risky process (e.g. risk of theft during transportation from the storage area to the place of the account holder), a number of intermediaries provide in their account agreements that they do not accept requests for retrieval or subject such requests to strict requirements. It may thus be that neither the applicable law nor the terms of the issue preclude the retrieval of the securities, but that one intermediary in the chain has contracted out the right to retrieve the securities, with the consequence that account holders at a lower tier may be unable to exercise their right of retrieval.

The general trend towards dematerialisation of securities, for cost, security and tax reasons, will certainly affect the right conferred on the account holder in Article 9(1)(c) of the Convention. In the context of anti-money laundering and terrorist financing, the Financial Action Task Force also supports the generalisation of the dematerialisation of securities.[27]

As in the case of the right to dispose of the securities, the account holder may only exercise its right of retrieval against its own intermediary which will in turn need to exercise the same against its own intermediary (and so forth).

27 FATF Recommendations, International Standards on Combating Money Laundering and the Financing of Terrorism Proliferation, February 2012.

4.6 Restrictions on the rights of the account holder

The account holder may not enjoy the full benefit of the rights set out in Article 9(1) of the Convention. This may be the case where a person, albeit an account holder, has only a limited interest in the securities credited to its securities account. National law will, in such a case, determine the limits imposed on the rights of the account holder.

Taking as an example the beneficiary of a pledge, the laws of many states deny the pledgee the right to vote, and leave that right with the pledgor. Some laws provide that distributions will accrue to the pledgor, at least until an event of default occurs and not to the pledge (i.e. the account holder). The intermediary will have to abide by such limitations but only to the extent it is aware thereof.

Similar restrictions apply with respect to limited interests such as a usufruct. The beneficiary of the usufruct will typically be entitled to receive the distributions but will not be entitled to dispose of the securities or grant an interest therein.

4.7 Conclusion

Article 9(1) of the Convention and its corresponding provisions in Article 3(1) of the Commission Consultation Document grant the account holders the minimum set of rights which, together with other rights set out in the Convention and the Commission Consultation Document, should ensure proper connectivity between national securities holding systems. The provisions of Article 9(1) of the Convention are, however, not self-executory, but will require detailed national implementation measures. These measures will need to be designed in such way that they fully allow the result set out in Article 9.

The discussions leading to the Convention and the work on the Commission Consultation Document have shown the urgent need to standardise a number of procedures, such as voting procedures, at a global scale to ensure an efficient and cost effective exercise of voting rights. This process will hopefully be driven by the market and international bodies operating on a worldwide scale.

Bibliography

Dubertret, M., 'Droit des sociétés et Convention de Genève: pomme de discorde?' [2010] *Uniform Law Review*, 693–702.

Micheler, E., 'The Legal Nature of Securities: Inspirations from Comparative Law', in L. Gullifer and J. Payne (eds.), *Intermediated Securities: Legal Problems and Practical Issues* (Oxford: Hart Publishing, 2010), 131–49.

Paech, P., 'Cross-Border Issues of Securities Law: European Efforts to Support Securities Markets with a Coherent Legal Framework', EU Parliament, Directorate-General for Internal Policies, May 2011.

Thévenoz, L., 'Intermediated Securities, Legal Risk, and the International Harmonization of Commercial Law' [2008] 13 *Stanford Journal of Law, Business & Finance*, 384–452.

'Who holds (Intermediated) Securities? Shareholders, Account holders, and Nominees' [2010] *Uniform Law Review*, 845–59.

5

Rights of the investor

PIERRE-HENRI CONAC

5.1 Introduction

The objective of the UNIDROIT Convention on Substantive Rules for Intermediated Securities of 9 October 2009 ('the Convention') and the proposal of a European Securities Law (hereafter 'the EU legislation', or EL) is not to regulate the status of the 'investor'.[1]

The investor is the person who bears the risk of the investment and who purchased or received the securities. He is the natural or legal person who should be entitled to exercise the rights and receive the benefits in relation to the issuer. He is either the 'legal holder' of the securities according to national law, or he derives his rights from the 'legal holder' if national law distinguishes the latter from the 'investor'. Therefore, clarifying the concept of 'legal holder' is the first step to identifying the 'investor'.

However, there are at least two valid reasons for ignoring the 'investor' and the 'legal holder' in international or European legislation dealing with intermediated securities. First, regulating the relationship between the issuer and the investor is not necessary to reach the goal of such legislation, and second, it would be too difficult to reach an agreement.

The first and main reason is that it is not needed. The objective of the Convention and of the EU legislation is to harmonise, at the international level and at the European level, the legal framework governing securities credited to a securities account and not to regulate the relationship between the issuer and the investor. In the nineteenth century, securities were represented by paper certificates, which were usually held in safes

1 The EU legislation could be a Securities Law Directive or a Regulation. In 2010, the Services of the Directorate-General Internal Market and Services of the European Commission published an Updated Compilation of the rules and explanatory notes discussed so far on Legislation on Legal Certainty of Securities Holding and Dispositions (Brussels, 17/09/2010, G2/PhP D(2010)) and a Consultation Document (hereafter the 'Commission Consultation Document') of the Services of the Directorate-General Internal Markets and Services of November 2010 on Legislation on Legal Certainty of Securities Holding and Dispositions (DG Markt G2 MET/OT/acg D(2010) 768690).

in a bank or at home. With the development of the banking systems and technology, most securities are now held in securities accounts at financial institutions. This is the case even when they are not legally dematerialised, which is still the situation in most countries.[2] However, most countries have adopted different views as to the legal regime of intermediated securities. Therefore, the objective of the Convention and the EU legislation is to bring legal certainty to the regime of securities held in the intermediary chain.

Both texts are only concerned with the chain of intermediaries between the issuer and the holder of the account. They deal with the rights of the 'account holder' (Convention) or of the 'ultimate account holder' (EL), who is the person holding the intermediated securities in a 'securities account' (Convention and EL). Those concepts are specific to intermediated securities, which is the concept which both texts deal with. Their scope is limited to determining the rights within the intermediary chain. As a consequence, the Convention and the EU legislation do not deal with issues of company law, unless an exception applies.

A second reason for not dealing with the 'investor' is that issues of company law have proven to be very difficult to harmonise between countries. In this area, national traditions are diverse, strong and alive. In the international area, some de facto harmonisation has been realised through the influence of one model on other countries.[3] However, this is an effect of voluntary legal transplants or influence, and not of a forced harmonisation resulting from an international binding agreement. The Convention does not even use the term 'company law' to limit its scope of application, as it would be difficult to define. In addition, the scope of company law varies from one country to another. Despite these differences, it usually covers the internal organisation of the company and the rules applicable to the relationship between the company and the holder of securities, be it a shareholder or a bondholder or the holder of any type of securities issued by the company. Therefore, company law covers the issue of who an issuer is required to recognise as the securities holder, across the

2 In the European Union, only France, Denmark and Italy have a system of compulsory dematerialisation.

3 For instance, the British Companies Act of 1846 served as a model for the French Act on Companies in 1867, which then served as a model for Belgian law in 1872. German company law served as a model for France when it adopted the two-tier structure for boards of directors in 1966. Since the 1990s, the American model of the business corporation, based on a contractual rather than an institutional approach, has been influential in many countries.

intermediary chain, for the purpose of exercising its rights, whether political or financial. The determination of who is the shareholder or the bondholder or the securities holder is left to each country.

The same approach has been adopted in the EU legislation. This is not surprising because Member States themselves also hold very different views as to who should be recognised as a shareholder or the securities holder. The directive of 11 July 2007 on the exercise of certain rights of shareholders in listed companies (hereafter the Shareholders' Rights Directive, or SRD)[4] leaves to the law of the Member State where the company has its registered office to determine who is recognised as a shareholder.[5] Even at the European level, agreeing on who is the shareholder of a listed company, in the very directive designed to enhance their rights, proved too difficult and had to be left to national Member State law.

Therefore, the issue of who should be recognised as the 'investor' by the issuer is outside the scope of the Convention and of the EU legislation. As indicated by the Official Commentary of the UNIDROIT Convention, the decision to put aside issues of company law was taken at the outset of the work.[6] This exclusion is provided for in Article 8 of the Convention, 'Relationship with issuers', with an important exception provided in Article 29(2), 'Position of issuers of securities'. This exclusion is all the more important in that the Convention and the EU legislation are not limited to listed companies. They cover both listed and non-listed companies.

Because of the importance of the issue, the drafting of the exclusion of company law matters led to extensive discussions, with opposition particularly from France and from EuropeanIssuers, a European association representing listed issuers.[7] As mentioned by Luc Thévenoz, the interface 'with company law was one of the difficult questions tackled during the preparation and negotiation of the Convention. It remains a controversial issue, fuelling resolute opposition from certain corners.'[8] The main point of concern was that the 'issuer law should be the only SOURCE when it

4 Directive 2007/36/EC of the European Parliament and of the Council of 11 July 2007 on the exercise of certain rights of shareholders in listed companies, OJ L184/17, 14.7.2007.

5 Art. 2(b) '"shareholder" means the natural or legal person that is recognized as a shareholder under the applicable law'.

6 Kanda et al., *Official Commentary*, ss. 8–3 and 29–4.

7 EuropeanIssuers (www.europeanissuers.eu) is a pan-European organisation created to promote the interests of issuing companies. It represents the vast majority of publicly quoted companies in Europe. It is the successor to EALIC (European Association for Listed Companies) and UNIQUE (Union of Issuers Quoted in Europe) in 2008.

8 Thévenoz, 'Who Holds (Intermediated) Securities?', at 845.

comes to granting so-called corporate law rights to shareholders'.[9] The same concern has been raised for the EU legislation. The issue is most sensitive for listed issuers, as it could affect their relations with their shareholders and has an impact on corporate governance, although non-listed companies and bondholders are also covered by the Convention. EuropeanIssuers raised this issue constantly from the start of the negotiation of the Geneva Securities Convention, without much effect on the final draft, which seems to show that the drafting was acceptable to the overwhelming number of delegations.

The Convention and the EU legislation do not determine who is the 'investor', and leave this issue outside of their scope (see section 5.2). However, the exercise of the rights of the investor is facilitated by the Convention, and the EU legislation provides rights to 'investors' holding intermediated securities (see section 5.3).

5.2 Determination of the 'investor': beyond the scope of the Convention and the EU legislation

The principle adopted by the Convention and the EU legislation is that the determination of who is the 'investor' is outside their scope (section 5.2.1). This is all the clearer in that the term 'investor' is also different from the concepts used in the Convention and in the EU legislation (section 5.2.2).

5.2.1 The lack of 'investor' determination by the Convention and the EU legislation

The term 'investor' appears only once in the Convention. Paragraph 8 of the Preamble reads, 'EMPHASISING the importance of the integrity of a securities issue in a global environment for intermediated holding in order to ensure the exercise of investors' rights and enhance their protection'. In the EU legislation, the term investor does not even appear. However, it appears indirectly, through another name, in provisions which exclude company law from the scope of the Convention and the EU legislation (section 5.2.1.1). In both texts, the relationship between the 'investor' and the issuer is clearly governed by national law (section 5.2.1.2).

9 Diplomatic Conference to Adopt a Convention on Substantive Rules Regarding Intermediated Securities, Final session, Geneva, 5 to 7/9 October 2009, UNIDROIT 2009 CONF. 11/2 – Doc. 7, Original: English, Comments *(submitted by EuropeanIssuers)*, 6 August 2009.

5.2.1.1 The limited scope of the Convention and the EU legislation

The relationship between the 'investor' and the issuer is left outside of both the Convention and the EU legislation.

5.2.1.1.1 The Convention The title of Article 8 of the Convention is 'Relationship with issuers' and is included in Chapter I of the Convention on 'Definitions, sphere of application and interpretation'. The very position of the article at the beginning of the Convention, and as the last article of Chapter I, indicates that it includes a fundamental principle. Initially, Article 8(1) was part of the current Article 10, 'Measures to enable the exercise of rights', which is part of Chapter II 'Rights of the Account Holder'. It was moved to Chapter I, which increases its status. Article 8 contains two paragraphs which state the same rule, but from a different perspective.

Article 8(1) provides that 'Subject to Article 29(2), this Convention does not affect any right of the account holder against the issuer of the securities'. This provision indicates that the relationship between the issuer and the 'account holder' is outside the scope of the Convention and is left to the national law of the Contracting States. As mentioned in a comment during the Fourth session (2007), 'the intention is that neither the form nor the country of custody is to have any influence on the rights arising from the instrument in favour of the security holder against the issuer'.[10] This solution is logical, since the Convention deals only with the intermediation chain. Article 29(2) of the Convention constitutes the exception and allows the 'nominee' to exercise rights of the 'account holder'. This paragraph could have been considered sufficient, but it is complemented by a second paragraph.

Article 8(2) provides that the Convention 'does not determine whom the issuer is required to recognize as the shareholder, bondholder or other person entitled to receive and exercise the rights attached to the securities or to recognize for any other purpose'.[11] Therefore, the Convention makes clear that the relationship between the issuer, the legal holder and the

10 UNIDROIT Committee of Government Experts for the Preparation of a Draft Convention on Substantive Rules Regarding Intermediated Securities, UNIDROIT 2007, Study LXXVIII – Doc. 95, Original: English, August 2007, Fourth session, Rome, 21/25 May 2007, report, 81.

11 Art. 8(2) of the Convention.

'investor' is not governed by the Convention. Article 8(2) reinforces the exclusion provided already by Article 8(1).

From a logical point of view, Article 8(2) should have been placed before Article 8(1). The reason is that Article 8(2) states the basic premise of the Convention that issues of company law are governed by non-Convention law. As the principle, it should have appeared in the first paragraph, all the more so since Article 8(1), as it stands now, refers to an important exception to the principle.

Article 8(1) states in another way the same principle as Article 8(2). However, the perspective adopted by Article 8(1) is somewhat different from the one of Article 8(2) which might explain the existence of two provisions. Article 8(2) deals with the 'account holder', which is a core concept used by the Convention and refers to financial intermediation. It does not deal with the company law concept of shareholder or bondholder as Article 8(1). Therefore, there is a strong logic for using the first paragraph to address the relationship between the issuer and the account holder, a concept related to intermediated securities, and mention the traditional company law concept in the second paragraph.

Article 8(2) does not exclude company law issues as such but relies on the functional approach adopted throughout the Convention.[12] The Official Commentary states that 'This Convention follows the functional approach, and delineates the coverage of the subject matter not by using the notion "corporate law" but by directly spelling out (in functional terms) what is not covered by the Convention.'[13] The main reason is that, as mentioned in the Official Commentary, 'It is not easy to draw a line in precise language between what is covered and what is not covered by this Convention. In particular, it is obvious that using the notion "corporate law" would not work, because the coverage of corporate law varies from jurisdiction to jurisdiction.'[14] For instance, insolvency law is usually not considered to be part of company law, but can be considered so in some countries.

5.2.1.1.2 The EU legislation The Commission Consultation Document on a European Legislation of November 2010 does not mention the 'investor' even once, but also provides in Article 1 'Scope' that the relationship between the issuer and the holder of securities is governed by national Member States' law.

12 On the functional approach, see Mooney and Kanda, 'Core Issues', at 74.

13 Kanda et al., *Official Commentary*, s. 8–2.

14 *Ibid.*, s. 8–2.

To this effect, Article 1(2) of the EU legislation provides that 'This Directive does not harmonize the legal framework governing the question of whom an issuer has to recognize as the legal holder of its securities'. The EU legislation uses the term 'legal holder', which is not used by the Convention, although this is close to what Article 8(2) implicitly designates. It is all the clearer that Article 2(f) of the EU legislation states that the '"legal holder" means the shareholder, bondholder or holder of other financial instruments, as defined by the law under which the relevant securities are constituted'.

The EU legislation adopts the same cautious approach of not determining who is the shareholder or the bondholder as in the Convention. This is consistent with the approach adopted in the directive of 11 July 2007 on the exercise of certain rights of shareholders in listed companies which left this issue of company law to national Member States. Article 2(b) of the SRD simply states that the '"shareholder" means the natural or legal person that is recognized as a shareholder under the applicable law'. Like the Convention, the EU legislation does not even use the term 'company law' to identify matters which are outside its scope. This is a more cautious approach than the one adopted by the Takeover Directive of 21 April 2004 to identify the applicable law and the competent authority in case of a cross-border takeover.[15] Article 4(2)(e) of this directive indicates, alongside a list of examples, that 'in matters of company law . . . the applicable rules and the competent authority shall be those of the Member State in which the offeree company has its registered office'.

Finally, like the Convention, the EU legislation provides an exception for securities held through nominees (Article 16). A similar provision exists in the SRD,[16] but only 'regarding voting rights and general meetings in respect of publicly traded shares but not in relation to other types of securities (in particular bonds) or other types of rights attached to securities, as for instance the acceptance of a takeover-bid or the exercise of a subscription or exchange right'.

Since the determination of the 'legal holder' and ultimately of the 'investor' is left outside of the Convention and the EU legislation, this issue needs to be addressed by the non-Convention law or by Member States' law.

15 Directive 2004/25/EC of the European Parliament and of the Council of 21 April 2004 on takeover bids, OJ L142/12, 30.04.2004.

16 Arts. 13(4), (5) and 10(1), (3) of the SRD.

5.2.1.2 Determination of the 'investor' decided by national law

The determination of who is the 'legal holder' and who is the 'investor' is decided by national law both in the Convention and the EU legislation.

5.2.1.2.1 The Convention The Convention does not contain conflict-of-laws arrangements to determine which law applies to the issuer in order to ascertain who he should recognise as the shareholder, bondholder or other person entitled to receive and exercise the rights attached to the securities, or to recognise for any other purpose.

Therefore, each signatory of the Convention can continue to apply its national approach. The traditional rule is that the law applicable to the relationship of the issuer with the shareholder is the *lex societatis*. Some countries apply as a connecting factor the registered seat (*siège social*) of the issuer, while others retain the real seat (*siège réel*) of the issuer. The connecting factor is left for each *lex societatis* to decide.

The rights which are to be decided by the *lex societatis* are at least those mentioned in Article 9(1)(a) of the Convention. They include in particular 'dividends, other distributions and voting rights'. The *lex societatis* applies whether the shares are registered shares or bearer shares. The point was raised by EuropeanIssuers in a commentary before the final diplomatic conference that 'the examples given in the draft Official Commentary seem to suggest that this provision would only hold for registered shares and that for bearer shares the rights attached to the securities, including voting rights, will definitely go to the account holder, whatever the issuer law says, according to Article 9'.[17] However, Article 8(2) does not distinguish between registered and bearer shares. Therefore, the determination of who is the legal holder of bearer shares is certainly also left to non-Convention law.

This solution also applies to the relationship between the issuer and the bondholder, and to the question of who should be recognised as the bondholder by the issuer. As to issues of voting and organisation, especially in order to modify the rights to interest of bondholders in case of financial trouble of the issuer, they are also subject to the *lex societatis* of the issuer. However, bonds are also subject to a contract whose provisions

17 UNIDROIT Convention on Substantive Rules Regarding Intermediated Securities, EuropeanIssuers Comments on the Draft UNIDROIT Convention 2009 Conf. 11/2, 5 August 2009, at 3.

are outside the scope of the Convention. Therefore, the bondholders are not usually subject only to the *lex societatis*, but also to the *lex contractus*, which is often of a third jurisdiction, such as the UK or New York.

As to the 'other person entitled to receive and exercise the rights attached to the securities or to recognize for any other purpose', she is also subject to the *lex societatis* and to the law designed by the contract for aspects not covered by company law.

5.2.1.2.2 The EU legislation The EU legislation adopts the same approach. There is no conflict-of-laws arrangement to determine which law applies to the issuer in order to determine who he should recognise as the shareholder, bondholder or other person entitled to receive and exercise the rights attached to the securities or to recognise for any other purpose. Therefore, Member States can still define who is the shareholder or the bondholder according to their *lex societatis.*

The term 'investor' is different from the terms used in the Convention and in the EU legislation, ensuring that the right of the issuer to decide who is the shareholder or the bondholder cannot be impeded even unintentionally.

5.2.2 Distinction between the 'investor' and the terms used in the Convention and the EU legislation

The Convention and the EU legislation define and identify both the 'account holder' and the 'nominee'. None of them can be assimilated to the 'investor' or the 'legal holder' – terms that are covered by company law.

5.2.2.1 Distinction between 'investor' and 'account holder'

The distinction between the 'investor' and the 'account holder' is clearly made in both the Convention and in the EU legislation.

5.2.2.1.1 The Convention Article 1(e) of the Convention defines the 'account holder' as a 'person in whose name an intermediary maintains a securities account, whether that person is acting for its own account or for others (including in the capacity of intermediary)'. However, only the ultimate account holder can be close to the investor. The ultimate account holder is identified in Article 9, 'Intermediated securities', as the account holder who 'is not an intermediary or is an intermediary acting for its own account' (Article 9(1)(a)). The Convention does not use the term 'ultimate', but this is what it designates. She is the person entitled 'to receive and exercise any rights attached to the securities, including dividends, other distributions and voting rights'. Therefore, the ultimate account holder is the closest possible to the 'investor'. This reference to the ultimate account holder 'results from the refusal, on the part of certain negotiating States, to see those rights attributed to any account holder in the chain'.[18] The ultimate account holder cannot also be confused with the investor. An 'ultimate' account holder can hold the securities serving as an agent, trustee or in another capacity on behalf and for the benefit of one or more other persons.

Article 9 recognises rights which are equivalent to those exercised by a shareholder or a bondholder. This recognition led to three related criticisms: the Convention does not sufficiently distinguish the investor from the account holder, which leads to the favouring of intermediaries rather than issuers; it favours the US approach, and thus it provides the account holder with rights which should be enjoyed only by the shareholder.

– The first criticism, by a French author, is that 'by creating a legal concept of "intermediated securities" and not defining in any manner, which rights investors and shareholders have in securities; not even clearly distinguishing the shareholder from an account holder, the Convention does express a preference for market liquidity, intermediary benefit and protection, over maintaining the direct relationship between the issuer and the shareholder and over one of the primary functions of capital markets, which is to provide liquidity to securities issuing companies'.[19] However, as mentioned by Luc Thévenoz, 'Proposals to distinguish the legal position of the investor (or ultimate account holder) from that of any other account holder, who is but an intermediary, were not accepted during the negotiations', and this 'may be the one most potent explanation for the perception that the Convention gives intermediaries rights that should only be enjoyed by the shareholders themselves'.[20] This criticism is also somewhat contradictory, since it accuses the Convention of affecting company law, and at the same time regrets that it does not

18 See Cremers, 'Reflexions on "intermediated securities" in the Geneva Securities Convention', at 101.

19 See *ibid.*, at 101. See also Dubertret, 'Droit des sociétés et Convention de Genève: pomme de discorde?', 693–702.

20 See Thévenoz, 'Who holds (Intermediated) Securities?', at 851.

define the notion of 'shareholder', which certainly belongs to company law. In addition, such a decision is logical since it was not necessary to reach the goal of the Convention, and agreeing on a common definition would have certainly proved impossible. The European legislator, although placed in a more favourable situation, did not succeed either in defining the shareholder in the SRD, and this has been identified by EuropeanIssuers as a failure on a crucial matter.[21]

- A second criticism, by the same author, is that 'the Convention is essentially inspired by Article 8 of the Uniform Commercial Code and by the U.S. experience and is strongly biased against direct holding systems where investors have property rights over the securities themselves and enjoy a direct legal relationship with issuers while intermediaries are mere custodians of their clients' assets'.[22] Another author, in an article which deals more generally with the concept of 'intermediated securities', considers that the 'account holder would not have the property of the share but the property of a security created by the intermediary, economically linked to the share, but legally distinct'.[23] This security would only provide a bundle of rights that he could exercise solely against the intermediary.[24] Therefore, could the account holder still be qualified as a shareholder, and upon what basis should the account holder be granted a voting right? The criticism assumes that the Convention favours the US approach and that the nature of the rights of the investor on intermediated securities affects the direct relationship between the issuer and the shareholder.

  First, the drafting of Article 1(b) of the Convention makes it clear that both systems are recognised by the Convention, as it defines 'intermediated securities' as securities credited to a securities account 'or' rights or interests in securities resulting from the credit of securities to a securities account.

  Second, even if the Convention had promoted the US approach, which is not the case, this would not affect as much as dispute the relationship between the issuer and the investor. The choice to adopt a

21 Second Advice of the Legal Certainty Group, Solutions to Legal Barries related to Post Trading within the EU, EuropeanIssuers Comments, 13 November 2008, at 2.

22 See Thévenoz, 'Who holds (Intermediated) Securities?', at 850.

23 Drummond, 'Les titres intermédiés', at 159–60.

24 Some French authors argue that shares are, under French law, not subject to property rights but are only rights against the issuer. See Le Nabasque, 'Les actions sont des droits de créance négociables', 671–95.

bundle of rights instead of recognising full ownership affects the protection of the investor in case of insolvency of the intermediary. From this point of view, the recognition of full ownership would rather have our preference for reason of protection of the investor, of cultural tradition in those countries which have adopted this system, and because it tends to limit the possibility of unlimited collateralisation of the same economic value which should be strongly discouraged since it is a factor of systemic risk. However, the relationship between the issuer and the investor can remain identical, regardless of the legal status of the investor in relation to the intermediated security. The challenge to the relationship between the issuer and the investor lies in the intermediation itself, not in the nature of the intermediated securities. Therefore, it is for the national company law to organise this relationship. The idea that the recognition of a bundle of rights would weaken this relationship is not justified. It might originate from the fact that shareholders in the United States enjoy fewer rights and less influence over the management of listed companies than in Europe. However, this is not because of the nature of the right of the investor on the intermediated securities, but because of the limited rights recognised by state law. Who would seriously claim that shareholders are not considered as such in the US or the UK because they do not legally own the share ?

– A third, closely related, critique is that, as a consequence, 'the Geneva Securities Convention confers (those rights) to certain account holders, and not to shareholders and bondholders, to whom the issuer intends to confer them and whom the Geneva Securities Convention recognizes', and that 'the Convention designates a beneficiary of the corporate rights, flowing from the securities, who is different from the beneficiary pursuant to company law'.[25] In order to understand whether Article 9 really provides rights that should be enjoyed only by the shareholder or the bondholder, it is necessary to analyse the relationship between Article 8 and Article 9.

The Official Commentary notes that 'While Article 8(1) uses the phrase "does not affect any right", it is not an exception to Article 9(1)(a). In other words, Article 8(1) is not intended to deny or otherwise limit the right resulting from the credit under Article 9(1)(a).'[26] Therefore,

25 See Cremers, 'Reflexions on "Intermediated Securities" in the Geneva Securities Convention', at 101.

26 Kanda et al., *Official Commentary*, s. 8–12.

> Article 9 and Article 8 deal with the same situation, but from two different perspectives. The first is the perspective of the account holder and the second is the perspective of the shareholder or the bondholder. They are not in the same domain or at the same level; as stated by Philippe Dupont, Article 8 is 'next to' Article 9(1)(a).[27] This leaves the exclusion in Article 8 unaffected by the rights granted in Article 9.
>
> The fact that Article 8 is not an exception to Article 9 underlines also that company law issues are left unaffected by Article 9. If Article 8 had been presented as an exception to Article 9, this would have meant that Article 9 dealt with issues of company law. The argument would have been validated.
>
> Finally, if Article 8 had been considered to be an exception to Article 9, this would have made Article 9 an empty shell. The investor, pursuant to company law, can only benefit from the rights flowing from the issuer through his status as the ultimate 'account holder', a fact which needs to be recognised first. As noted, 'the Convention does not prescribe who the issuer must recognize as the holder of securities. This person may be an account holder, an intermediary, or possibly some other person. The Convention is only concerned with how the rights attached to the securities flow down through the intermediary chain to whoever is entitled to receive and exercise them.'[28]

The 'account holder' cannot also be confused with the 'investor', because the Convention does not create a presumption that the ultimate 'account holder' is the shareholder or the bondholder. Articles 8 and 9 are independent of one another and Article 8 is not an exception to Article 9. The Official Commentary gives a clear example that the relationship with the issuer is outside the scope of the Convention.[29] Therefore, the issuer can and should refuse to allow a shareholder to vote if he is not the 'legal holder' or the 'investor' entitled to vote.

5.2.2.1.2 The EU legislation The EU legislation adopts the same approach as the Convention, but in addition affects company law since it makes sure that the investor will receive the rights from the securities in preference to the 'legal holder'. Article 2(e) of the EU legislation uses the term 'ultimate account holder' for 'an account holder which is not acting in the capacity of account provider for another person'. The 'ultimate

27 Dupont, Ch. 4 of this book, at p. 98.

28 See Thévenoz, 'Who holds (Intermediated) Securities?', 845 at 849.

29 See Example 8–1 in Kanda et al., *Official Commentary*, s. 8–15.

account holder' is entitled to 'receive and exercise the rights flowing from securities, regardless whether it is either itself identified by the applicable law as the legal holder of the securities, or its account provider or a third person is identified by the applicable law as the legal holder of the securities' (Article 15).

Despite the different wording, the Convention reaches the same result since Article 9 implies that certain rights are granted to the account holder, which implicitly means whoever the 'legal holder' is. However, the EU legislation includes a specific provision in order to facilitate the exercise of the rights of the 'ultimate account holder'. It should be provided with a 'certificate confirming its holdings', regardless of whether he is the legal holder of the securities or not (Article 16(a)).

The 22 June 2010 version of the Legislation on Legal Certainty of Securities Holding and Dispositions, a previous version of the EU legislation, provided that the 'ultimate account holder' should be considered as the representative of the legal holder with respect to the receipt or exercise of the relevant rights ('proxy'), where an account provider or a third person is the legal holder of securities. In such case, Article 11 of Directive 2007/36/EC should have applied correspondingly for shareholders in listed companies (Article 16(b)). This reference disappeared from the 17 September 2010 draft which is a clear indication of the willingness of the services of the Commission to leave matters of company law as much as possible outside the scope of the draft.

Therefore, the 'account holder' cannot be assimilated to the 'investor' or the 'legal holder' in terms of company law.

5.2.2.2 The 'nominee'

The Convention and the EU legislation also deal with the issue of the 'nominee', which is essential in cross-border situations. However, the nominee is not confused in both texts with the 'investor' or the 'legal holder'.

5.2.2.2.1 The Convention Article 29 deals with the position of the issuer of securities. It covers only 'securities that are permitted to be traded on an exchange or regulated market'. Article 29(2) of the Convention provides that:

> In particular, the law of a Contracting State shall recognize the holding of such securities by a person acting in its own name on behalf of another person or other persons and shall permit such a person to exercise voting or other rights in different ways in respect of different parts of a holding of

> securities of the same description; but this Convention does not determine the conditions under which such a person is authorized to exercise such rights.

Therefore, the Convention, and this is an exception to Article 8(1), forces the *lex societatis* to recognise the holding of securities through nominees, although the term nominee is not even used. This is due to the functional approach adopted by the Convention.[30]

However, the drafting of Article 29(2) makes it clear that, despite the fact that it deals with the relationship between the issuer and an intermediary, it does not hold the nominee to be the shareholder or the bondholder.

A first reason is that Article 29(2) holds that a nominee is 'a person acting in its own name on behalf of another person or other persons'. This definition implies per se that the nominee cannot be considered as the shareholder or the bondholder, since he is acting on behalf of another person. The term 'holding' (*détention*, in the French version of the Convention) itself also clearly indicates that the 'nominee' is not the legal owner of the securities.

Another reason, which also makes clear that the nominee is not considered as the shareholder or the bondholder, is that Article 29(2) allows for the splitting of votes. This should not be possible, although theoretically some company laws could allow such splitting, since voting rights are attached to shares but the vote is expressed by the shareholder who should have only one will.

A final reason why the investor cannot be confused with the shareholder or the bondholder is that Article 29(2) is not an exception to Article 8(2), which directly addresses the issue of who the issuer is obliged to recognise as the shareholder or the bondholder, but is an exception to Article 8(1), which only deals with the rights of the account holder against the issuer of the securities. Therefore, Article 29(2) is clearly outside the scope of company law issues.

5.2.2.2.2 The EU legislation The EU legislation recognises the existence of the nominee, although it also does not name it. The recognition of the nominee, for the purpose of allowing the investor to exercise its rights, had already been addressed in the SRD, but only regarding voting rights and general meetings in respect of publicly traded shares. Article 13 of

30 'Art. 29(2) does not use the notion "nominee" or "beneficiaries", and rather uses more generic terminology to maintain the Convention's functional and neutral approach'. GSC draft Official Commentary, 135.

the SRD directly addresses the issue of the nominee and allows it to cast votes 'on behalf of another natural or legal person (the client)'. The term 'client', as used by the directive, designates the person who is the investor in the Convention. This right to cast a vote can be subject only to limited conditions. Articles 10(1) and (3) complement this by allowing the right to vote by proxy.

As mentioned in the November 2010 Consultation, it is:

> appropriate to require national law not to discriminate the exercise of rights attached to securities on the sole grounds that they are held under a holding pattern which differs from the holding pattern in the issuer's jurisdiction, as for instance the holding through more than one account providers in general, or through so called nominee or omnibus accounts which might exist in a number of jurisdictions.[31]

The EU legislation provides in Article 16, 'Cross-border recognition of rights attached to securities', that:

> 1. Member States shall ensure that the law governing a securities issue as well as the law governing the holding of securities do not discriminate against the exercise of rights attached to securities held in another jurisdiction on the sole grounds that the relevant securities are held in a specific manner, in particular
>
> – through one or more account providers,
> – through an account provider acting in its own name but for the account of its account holders,
> – through accounts in which securities of two or more account holders are held in an indistinguishable manner.
>
> 2. Paragraph 1 does not determine which holding methods account providers should offer to their account holders.

This provision is the logical extension of Article 13 of the SRD to non-listed companies, to bonds and to other rights than voting rights. To the same extent as the Convention, it does not force the issuer to recognise the nominee as the shareholder or the bondholder. It only holds that the issuer should not refuse to recognise the rights of the investor when there is a nominee between him and the issuer.

The Convention and the EU legislation make great efforts to distinguish the rights of investors in the intermediary chain from those arising from company law. They do so by, on the one hand, allowing the law of the issuer

31 Commission Consultation Document on a European Legislation of November 2010, at 26.

to decide who is the shareholder or the bondholder and by recognising rights to 'account holder' or 'nominee', who are defined in a way that they cannot be assimilated to the shareholder, or the bondholder, or the securities holder.

Despite this cautious approach, critics of the Convention and the EU legislation still argue that both texts affect the relationship between the issuer and its shareholders or bondholders, which should only be governed by the *lex societatis* or the *lex contractus*. It is true that both texts have a practical impact on the relationship between the issuer and its shareholders or bondholders, either through the recognition of the nominee or through the attribution of rights to the 'account holder'. However, the direct relationship between the issuer and its shareholders or bondholders still remains legally and ultimately governed by national law. Therefore, this criticism is unfounded and somewhat self-defeating, since the Convention and the EU legislation facilitates the exercise of their rights by the investors.

5.3 The exercise of rights of the 'investor' under the Convention and the EU legislation

The Convention and the EU legislation provide rights to the 'investor', in an indirect way, through his status as an 'account holder' (see section 5.3.1) or through the use of a nominee (see section 5.3.2). This recognition does not legally affect the relationship between the issuer and his shareholders, since company law remains outside the scope of both texts. On the contrary, they facilitate such a relationship, providing a better flow of the rights in the intermediary chain, either downstream or upstream. This makes the arguments of the critics of both texts somewhat self-defeating since the Convention and the EU legislation facilitate the exercise of their rights as investor which is exactly what those critics request. However, it is obviously much easier to do it through an international or European legal instrument, than to rely on national law to achieve such result. Therefore, critics should embrace those texts if they really want to empower shareholders.

5.3.1 The rights of an investor as an 'account holder'

As mentioned, critics of the Convention and the EU legislation argue that provisions in both texts give to the ultimate 'account holder' rights that should be enjoyed only by the shareholders themselves. Article 9 on intermediated securities states that:

> 1. The credit of securities to a securities account confers on the account holder: (a) the right to receive and exercise any rights attached to the securities, including dividends, other distributions and voting rights: (i) if the account holder is not an intermediary or is an intermediary acting for its own account; and (ii) in any other case, if so provided by the non-Convention law.

Article 4 of the EU legislation on account-held securities similarly provides that:

> 1. Member States shall ensure that securities standing to the credit of a securities account confer upon the account holder at least the following rights: (a) the right to exercise and receive the rights attached to the securities if the account holder is the ultimate account holder or if, in any other case, the applicable law confers the right to that account holder.

Some other articles of the EU legislation intend to facilitate the exercise of those rights, especially Articles 17, 'Passing on information', and 18, 'Facilitation of the ultimate account holder's position'. As seen in section 5.1.2, the perception that those articles confer company law rights to the account holders is legally not founded. However, there is a need to distinguish carefully between (1) the rights flowing downstream from the issuer to the account holder, and (2) the rights exercised upstream by the account holder in relation to the issuer.

5.3.1.1 Rights flowing downstream from the issuer to the account holder

Under Article 9 of the Convention and Article 4 of the EU legislation, issuers are forced to recognise rights downstream to the ultimate account holder. Therefore, they should communicate information to the financial intermediaries who appear on their share register, in order that they may relay it to the ultimate account holder. The issuers are forced to consider the ultimate account holder as the 'investor' when it comes to sending rights downstream in order to inform or empower him to exercise his rights. As long as the 'ultimate account holder' remains passive, and only receives rights as an 'account holder', he is de facto treated as the shareholder. This includes for instance a very important right such as the payment of the dividend, since the account holder does not need to take any positive action but may remain passive. He will still receive the dividend, whether he is the shareholder or not, according to the company law of the issuer.

This situation might be considered as an infringement on the realm of national company law, but it is not. In addition, this solution is logical as it corresponds to the already existing situation, and is positive.

First, the flow of rights downstream is not an infringement on the realm of national company law because, as mentioned above, the *lex societatis* decides ultimately who is entitled to a dividend or not.

Second, the recognition of rights to the ultimate 'account holder' is the logical consequence of texts which aim to regulate the intermediary chain. Luc Thévenoz mentions that 'the Convention recognizes and requires that the rights attached to the securities must flow all the way down through the intermediary chain'.[32] As a matter of fact, it would not make any sense to regulate the intermediary chain while at the same time not recognising any right to the account holder regarding his securities. One cannot go without the other. The Convention would otherwise be an empty shell.

Third, the flow of rights to the account holder already corresponds to the current situation. The Convention and the EU legislation would impose a legal duty, where before only a market practice existed. Currently, listed issuers who have financial intermediaries, whether foreign or national, which appear on the share register treat them as an apparent shareholder, when it comes to sending information for the general shareholders' meeting, paying dividends and other types of corporate actions such as increase in capital. It is expected that this information will be transmitted down the intermediary chain to the ultimate account holder. For instance, they will pay them the amount of the dividend, so that they can distribute it to the ultimate account holder. Issuers do not subject these financial intermediaries to a test as to whether or not they are the 'investor', but treat them as if they were nominees. This is exactly what the Market Standards on General Meetings (MSGM) of 2010 provides for. The standards are part of a set of measures to remove the obstacles identified as Barrier 3 on corporate actions in the Reports from the Giovannini Group of November 2001, 'Cross-Border Clearing and Settlement Arrangements in the European Union', and April 2003, 'Second Report on EU Clearing and Settlement Arrangements'. As presented in the MSGM, the aim is:

32 See Thévenoz, 'Who holds (Intermediated) Securities?', 845 at 852.

> introducing streamlined communication and operational processes, based on a best practices approach, so as to ensure that information from the Issuer can reach the End Investor and vice versa in a timely and cost efficient manner. To ensure that all be reached the communication model proposed by the MSGM follows the holding pattern. It starts with the Issuer, goes via the Issuer CSD, through the entire Chain of Intermediaries (securities account providers), until the End Investor is reached – and vice versa.[33]

If one goes further into history, in the nineteenth century, when bearer shares were often held in private safes, the issuer would know neither the name of the shareholder nor if he was really the legal holder. The bank, if authorised by the issuer, would pay the dividend, on presentation of the physical coupon by the investor, and would then be reimbursed by the issuer itself. The amount of the dividend would flow through from the issuer to the investor. At no point would the issuer have exercised an ex ante control on who was entitled to receive the dividend, as long as the investor presented the coupon at the bank. According to the Convention and the EU legislation, account holders are to be treated exactly as holders of physical bearer shares have always been treated. The holder of the account receives the dividend, just as the holder of the coupon received it. As to the flowing of rights downstream to bearer shares, issuers have always dealt with apparent shareholders. The Convention merely recognises the reality that securities are held in an intermediary chain and are no longer held physically.

Finally, the recognition of a duty to pass through rights flowing from the securities to the investor should be considered as an improvement from the perspective of the investor and of legal certainty. It can only be efficiently done through a European or international legal instrument.

However, as recognised by Luc Thévenoz, there may be two situations where 'an account holder other than the ultimate account holder (i.e., an intermediary not acting for its own account) may also receive and exercise the rights attached to the securities. However, both are determined by the non-Convention law reserved in Article 9(1)(a)(ii)'.[34] In the first case, the intermediary holds the legal title or a property interest in the securities but is obliged to pass down the rights to the ultimate account holder.

33 Private Sector Response to the Giovannini Reports. Barries 3 – Corporate Actions – Market Standards for General Meetings, 3.

34 See Thévenoz, 'Who holds (Intermediated) Securities?', at 852.

This should not be a cause of concern since the intermediary is not the investor and, therefore, should not be treated like one. In addition, this exception has more to do with the intermediary chain itself than with the relationship between the issuer and the shareholder of the investor. The second case, when an intermediary is acting as collateral lender and has obtained a security interest from its account holder, is not really an exception.

As to the rights exercised upstream by the account holder towards the issuer, which arguably matters more for the issuer, this is subject exclusively to the *lex societatis* and to the full control of the issuer.

5.3.1.2 Rights exercised upstream by the account holder towards the issuer

Several rights can be exercised upstream by the account holder in the direction of the issuer. These are especially information rights, investigation rights, and voting rights. The rights exercised in relation to a general shareholders' meeting are arguably the most important for the issuer. In this area, the issuer has absolute control over who is entitled to vote as a consequence of Article 8 of the Convention and Article 4 of the EU legislation. Issuers can refuse the right to vote to any account holder if they consider that he is not the shareholder in application of the *lex societatis.*

Because of the rights conferred on him as an 'account holder', this latter might be considered to be a shadow shareholder. However, this is already the situation and it should be recognised as such. This would help investors to exercise their rights even if the Convention and the EU legislation do not force any recognition by the issuer which can always apply the *lex societatis.* Therefore, the texts do not substitute national company law, but are complementary to them.

The real evolution, for countries who have not done so already and especially for countries outside the EU, would be the recognition of the right for an account holder to vote through a foreign nominee.

5.3.2 The rights of an investor through a 'nominee'

The Convention and the EU legislation oblige the issuers to recognise the possibility for the investor to exercise its upstream rights through a nominee. However, the exercise of rights through a nominee can be subject to conditions determined by national company law.

5.3.2.1 The recognition of the nominee

The recognition of the nominee is done both by the Convention and by the EU legislation.

5.3.2.1.1 The Convention Article 29(2) of the Convention states that:

> In particular, the law of a Contracting State shall recognize the holding of such securities by a person acting in its own name on behalf of another person or other persons and shall permit such a person to exercise voting or other rights in different ways in respect of different parts of a holding of securities of the same description; but this Convention does not determine the conditions under which such a person is authorized to exercise such rights.

This provision constitutes the main exception to the exclusion of company law matters in the Convention. The Official Commentary explains it by the fact that 'it was felt that Article 29 and Article 30 are necessary minimum provisions in order to ensure the integrity and obtain compatibility of the securities holding systems around the world'[35] and that 'the recognition of so-called nominee holding and split voting (or split exercise of rights) is desirable for promoting cross-border holding and trading of securities'.[36] The nominee system is so widespread, especially in Common law countries, that allowing the issuer not to recognise its validity would have amounted to depriving a significant number of investors, institutional and retail, of their upstream rights.

The scope of Article 29(2) needs to be fleshed out as well as the rights which can be exercised through the nominee.

5.3.2.1.1.1 The scope of Article 29(2) The scope of Article 29(2) needs to be fleshed out first as to the type of securities covered.

The scope of application of Article 29(2), as to the type of securities, is the same as for Article 29(1). This can be deducted from the use of the term 'such securities' in Article 29(2), which refers to the securities mentioned in Article 29(1). Therefore, the obligation to 'recognise' nominees, provided for in Article 29(2), can only apply to 'securities that are permitted to be traded on an exchange or regulated market'. The offical commentary notes that 'The notion of "exchange or regulated market" is broad and includes traditional exchanges, over-the counter trading systems, multilateral trading facilities, alternative trading systems, and other

35 Kanda et al., *Official Commentary*, s. 29–12. 36 *Ibid.*, s. 29–20.

electronic communication networks.' This definition is very broad. In addition, these securities must be permitted to be held in an intermediated holding system. The Contracting State is not obliged to impose such a holding method, since Article 29(1) only requests that it 'shall permit the holding through one or more intermediary', which leaves the decision to the discretion of the company itself. More precisely, Article 29(2) only applies to those securities which are both listed and intermediated securities and not just those which are 'permitted' to be listed and intermediated.

As to the conclusion that the security must be effectively intermediated, this can be deduced from the fact that Article 29(2) refers to 'such securities'. This can only logically designate 'securities which are so held' (intermediated), rather than securities which could be so held because the objective of Article 29(1) is to allow securities to be intermediated. In addition, a nominee can only be recognised for securities which are held in an intermediated holding system. As to the fact that the security must be listed, the offical commentary notes that 'Article 29(1) does not apply to non-publicly traded securities'. This conclusion is not so obvious from the reading of Article 29(2), as the term 'such securities' could only designate 'securities that are permitted to be traded on an exchange or regulated market', but it is a logical limitation.

Second, the obligation to recognise the holding of securities through a nominee, when it applies, covers both intermediated listed shares and bonds, although in practice it will apply mostly to shareholders, since the exercise of voting rights through a nominee is more frequent for them.

Third, a Contracting State is obliged to 'recognise' the holding of listed securities by a nominee regardless of whether the securities are subject to its own company law (domestic securities) or to the company law of a foreign state (foreign securities). There is no distinction to be made because Article 29(1) does not distinguish between domestic and foreign securities and therefore should apply to both types. For instance, a Contracting State is forced to recognise the holding of domestic securities by a foreign nominee, even though it would not authorise nominees in its own jurisdiction. (See Example 29–4 in the Official Commentary for domestic securities but the Official Commentary applies the same solution also for foreign securities.)[37] The solution imposed by Article 29(2) is logical because otherwise it could allow a Contracting State to prevent foreign shareholders from voting through nominees in the case

37 *Ibid.*, s. 29–25.

of securities issued by domestic companies. For the same reason that Article 29(1) does not distinguish between securities, the obligation to recognise the holding of securities by a nominee applies regardless of whether the securities are listed in the country of origin of the issuer or in a foreign country.

The scope of the duty to 'recognise' nominees of Article 29(2) also needs to be fleshed out. There is no obligation for a Contracting State to allow nominees in its own country for domestic or foreign securities. Article 29(2) only obliges the Contracting State to 'recognize the holding of such securities by a person acting in its own name on behalf of another person or other persons'. The use of the term 'recognize' implies that the status of the nominee already exists in another Contracting State. Therefore, it does not imply that the Contracting State must create such status itself. Here there is a difference between Article 29(1) which obliges all Contracting States to allow the intermediated holding system in their jurisdiction and Article 29(2) which does not force such recognition for nominees. There is no duty for a Contracting State to allow nominees in its jurisdiction for securities which are subject to its national or foreign legislation. This is so because Article 29(2) applies to 'such securities' which can be both national and foreign securities since Article 29(1) does not distinguish between both. However, if the domestic or foreign securities are held by a nominee in a foreign country, this holding must be recognised by the Contracting State.

Although the obligation to recognise a nominee affects company law in an important way, in practice foreign nominees were already taken into account by many countries in order to remain attractive to foreign institutional investors. Therefore, the impact on company law is not as major as it might seem. The Convention only recognises what is already the de facto situation. For instance, in France, before a 2002 reform which recognised the existence of nominees, French listed issuers would in practice already allow a financial intermediary, although they would be only an apparent shareholder, to cast votes in the name of the real shareholders, without verifying ex ante whether or not they really were the shareholder. This flexibility was due to a desire to attract foreign investment in French companies.[38] This practice was made legal and regulated

38 'These practices (inscription on the registrar of nominees which are then allowed to vote) are widespread in the world, such as in France, and it is not conceivable that the Paris financial centre, which longs to become one of the major financial centres could be the only one to prohibit them, whereas and especially those practices are not in themselves

in 2002 when the French Commercial Code was amended to provide that such votes could only be cast if the financial intermediary would agree to provide the identity of the ultimate account holder if so requested by the issuer.[39]

5.3.2.1.1.2 Rights recognised by Article 29(2) Article 29(2) requests the Contracting State to allow the nominee 'to exercise voting or other rights in different ways in respect of different parts of a holding of securities of the same description'. This is a logical rule, since the nominee represents in practice many and sometimes thousands of shareholders. However, the Convention itself does not require the nominee to exercise split voting. The Official Commentary notes that this issue 'is dealt with by the applicable law, not Article 29'.[40] In practice, it would probably be illegal in many countries that the nominee does not exercise split voting if the shareholders that he represents split their votes.

Article 29(2) mentions that the Contracting State shall permit such a nominee 'to exercise . . . other rights'. Neither the article nor the Official Commentary mentions what these 'other rights' might be.

These 'other rights' include at least the other political rights that a shareholder may exercise in relation to a general shareholders' meeting, since this is when the voting rights are exercised. Such rights could be, for instance, the right to attend the general shareholders' meeting, even if the nominee is not a shareholder itself, since the right to attend the general shareholders' meeting is a fundamental right in company law. This is not obvious from the reading of Article 29(2), since it mentions that these rights should be able to be exercised in 'different ways', but the Convention should not be read too restrictively. A restrictive interpretation would weaken, without any valid reason, the obligation of a Contracting State to 'recognize the holding of such securities by a [nominee]' and would be contrary to a teleological interpretation. The 'other rights' should also include the right to ask oral questions as well as, for instance, the right to request a resolution to the agenda of the general shareholders' meeting, provided that the shareholders acting through the nominee represent the amount of capital usually required by national company law.

illegitimate.' ANSA, *Propositions pour l'identification des actionnaires dans les sociétés cotées (2ème partie du projet de rapport)*, January–February 1996, n° 2 813, C.J. of 8 Novembre 1995, 3.

39 Art. L. 228–1 of the French Commercial code.

40 See example 29–4 in Kanda et al., *Official Commentary*, s. 29–25.

Rights not attached to the general shareholders' meeting should also be covered by the notion of 'other rights'. For instance, the nominee should be able to exercise rights related to corporate actions such as subscription or exchange rights in the name of the investor.

In practice, the interpretation of the scope of these 'other rights', which could be fleshed out by the national legislator, will be subject to interpretation of national courts, so that the influence of national company law tradition should remain predominant.

The EU legislation provides for a similar provision.

5.3.2.1.2 The EU legislation The EU legislation (17/09/2010) provides in Article 16, 'Cross-border recognition of rights attached to securities', that:

> 1. Member States shall ensure that the law governing a securities issue as well as the law governing the holding of securities do not discriminate against the exercise of rights attached to securities held in another jurisdiction on the sole grounds that the relevant securities are held in a specific manner, in particular
>
> - through one or more account providers,
> - through an account provider acting in its own name but for the account of its account holders,
> - through accounts in which securities of two or more account holders are held in an indistinguishable manner.
>
> 2. Paragraph 1 does not determine which holding methods account providers should offer to their account holders.

Article 16 imposes a principle of non-discrimination. It refers implicitly to nominees ('through an account provider acting in its own name but for the account of its account holders') and omnibus accounts ('through an account provider acting in its own name but for the account of its account holders'). Article 16 is more explicit than Article 29(2) of the Convention in not forcing a jurisdiction to introduce nominees in its national system since it prohibits the discrimination 'against the exercise of rights attached to securities held in another jurisdiction'. The Shareholders' Rights Directive already addresses the issue of voting rights by nominees in general meetings, but only in respect to companies which have their registered office in a Member State and whose shares are admitted to trading on a regulated market situated or operating within a Member State.

The scope of the EU legislation is wider since it covers other types of securities, such as bonds, and other types of rights attached to securities, such as, for instance, the acceptance of a takeover bid.

These rights can be subject to conditions.

5.3.2.2 The possibility of conditions set up by national laws

The possibility of conditions set up by national laws is recognised both by the Convention and by the EU legislation.

5.3.2.2.1 The Convention The last part of Article 29(2) states: 'but this Convention does not determine the conditions under which such a person is authorized to exercise such rights'. Therefore, non-Convention law can impose requirements to allow the exercise of these rights by nominees. This provides national company law with great freedom to organise this exercise. Such requirements can be disclosure- or substantive-based.

As to disclosure-based requirements, national company law could impose that the nominee first discloses his status as a nominee. It could also be compelled to disclose the name of the investor for whom he is acting. It could request the disclosure of specific facts as to the investor, such as the number of shares held, or his contact details in order for the issuer to be able to contact him. The French reform of 2002 provides an example of such requirements. For instance, French law requires the nominee to identify itself to the company as soon as the account is opened with the issuer.[41] The nominee can attend the shareholder meeting if requested.[42] The issuer can request, at any moment, that the nominee disclose the identity of the shareholders.[43]

As to substantive-based requirements, national company law could impose for instance a requirement to hold a specific voting instruction for each resolution. It could request, as suggested by EuropeanIssuers for instance, that 'The representative should be authorized to exercise the voting rights only in accordance with the instructions by the shareholder and be able to provide evidence of these instructions.'[44] It could also impose that the shareholder, who is voting through a nominee, has disclosed a crossing of a threshold of voting rights such as, for instance,

41 Art. R. 228–1 of the French Commercial code.

42 Art. L. 225–107–1 of the French Commercial code.

43 Art. L. 228–2 II of the French Commercial code.

44 UNIDROIT Convention on Substantive Rules Regarding Intermediated Securities, EuropeanIssuers Comments on the Draft UNIDROIT Convention 2009 Conf. 11/2, 5 August 2009, at 7.

a 5 per cent threshold. National company law could also recognise the right of the investor to vote directly, in any circumstances, even when the intermediary is a nominee.

These requirements could be provided by national company law. However, the wording of Article 29(2) of the Convention does not prevent national company law from granting the articles of association of a company the right to require those disclosure or specific disclosures.

5.3.2.2.2 The EU legislation The EU legislation does not mention the possibility for a Member State to determine the conditions under which a nominee is authorised to exercise such rights. However, this is not prohibited by Article 16 of the EU legislation. It only states that Member States should not 'discriminate'. Therefore, as long as no discrimination occurs, a Member State should be allowed to establish conditions for the exercise of rights by nominees.

5.4 Conclusion

The fact that the Convention and the EU legislation would affect the issuer–shareholder relationship and would encroach on national company law, creating a shadow company law and substituting the investor with the account holder, is a major issue raised by critics of both texts, but which is unfounded. According to those critics, the question of who the issuer should recognise as the securities holder should be left only to national company law to decide. However, the Convention and the EU legislation have obviously taken this concern into account, with the exception of the recognition of nominees. The refusal to recognise foreign nominees, which is a widespread holding method, would have made the recognition of rights of the 'account holder' legally pointless, as their exercise could have been refused by national company laws and/or practices.

More generally, the opposition raised in the name of company law is not convincing.

First, such a claim is contradictory to the very recognition of the intermediated holding system as such. It is not possible to recognise the existence of intermediated securities without affecting de facto the relationship between the issuer and the investor. They belong together. For instance, as mentioned, the recognition of the holding by 'nominees' is a necessary and inescapable consequence of recognising the existence of intermediated securities themselves. The same can be said of the downstream rights that 'investors' are entitled to receive as ultimate account holders. The Convention and the EU legislation only recognise this reality. To allow the issuer not to recognise the flowing of those rights downstream would be tantamount to negating the existence of the intermediation of the securities themselves. This is not the universal practice, even from an historical perspective, and there is, quite to the contrary, a de facto recognition of the account holder. The real issue is for the *upstream* rights of the investor. However, in this case, both the Convention and the EU legislation make clear that the *lex societatis* and the law of the issue chosen by the issuer govern the relationship with the investor. Therefore, the issuer is entitled to recognise or not to recognise any shareholder willing to exercise upstream his rights against the issuer.

In addition, to complain that the Convention and the EU legislation affect national company law is somewhat misguided. The Convention and the EU legislation realise company law by facilitating the exercise of rights of the 'investor'. The current situation is characterised by major difficulties by foreign shareholders and investors to exercise their rights upstream cross-border. This is also true in Europe because the SRD has realised only a very limited improvement. Therefore, any international or European legal instrument which would facilitate the exercise of these rights, even at the price of affecting national company law, should be encouraged rather than opposed. It would be surprising to be willing to encourage cross-border shareholder participation in general shareholders' meetings, and in general investors' participation with the issuer, but at the same time to refuse any modification of national law which might facilitate the achievement of this goal. If a major goal of company law is to regulate the relationship between investors and the issuer, some harmonisation should be welcome. Rather than oppose it, critics should embrace it.

The real issue left untouched by the Convention and by the EU legislation is that the recognition of the existence of intermediated securities should be accompanied by a right to easily identify the investors. It is missing from the Convention, either because it was considered to be a company law issue, or because it would have been difficult to adopt an international regime. Unfortunately, the EU legislation does not provide for such a regime either, although the European Commission has jurisdiction in company law, especially on cross-border issues. Such a regime is missing and should be introduced in the EL or in another European legal instrument, as suggested also by the report of the Reflection Group on the Future of European Company Law who argued for the introduction of 'mechanisms that facilitate companies to identify who the shareholders are and make it easier to communicate with [their] shareholders, especially in multilayered depositary systems'.[45] At least, as requested by EuropeanIssuers, EU legislation should ensure that existing national identification mechanisms be enforced effectively across borders. It is therefore a very positive development that the Action Plan of the Commission on European company law and corporate governance of December 2012 provides that the Commission will propose, in 2013, an initiative to improve the visibility of shareholdings in Europe as part of its legislative work programme in the field of securities law.[46]

Bibliography

Cremers, T., 'Reflexions on "Intermediated Securities" in the Geneva Securities Convention' [2010] *European Banking and Financial Law Journal (Euredia)*, 93–106.

Drummond, F., 'Les titres intermédiés. Regards sur un nouveau concept du droit financier', *Etudes de droit privé, Mélanges offerts à Paul Didier* (Paris: Economica, 2008), 147–60.

Dubertret, M., 'Droit des sociétés et Convention de Genève: pomme de discorde?' [2010] *Uniform Law Review*, 693–702.

Kanda, H., Mooney, C., Thévenoz, L. and Béraud, S., with the assistance of T. Keijser, *Official Commentary on the UNIDROIT Convention on Substantive Rules for Intermediated Securities* (Oxford University Press, 2012).

Mooney, C. W. and Kanda, Hi., 'Core Issues under the UNIDROIT (Geneva) Convention on Intermediated Securities: Views from the United States and Japan', in L. Gullifer and J. Payne (eds.), *Intermediated Securities. Legal Problems and Practical Issues* (Oxford: Hart Publishing, 2010), 69–130.

Le Nabasque, H., 'Les actions sont des droits de créance négociables', in *Aspects actuels du droit des affaires, Mélanges en l'honneur de Yves Guyon* (Paris: Economica, 2003), 671–95.

Thévenoz, L., 'Who Holds (Intermediated) Securities? Shareholders, Account Holders, and Nominees?' [2010] *Uniform Law Review*, 845–59.

45 Report of The *Reflection Group* on the future of *EU* company law, 5 April 2011, at 50.

46 Communication from the Commission to the European Parliament, the Council, the European Economic and Social Committee and the Committee of the Regions, Action Plan: European company law and corporate governance – a modern legal framework for more engaged shareholders and sustainable companies, Brussels, 12 December 2012, COM (2012) 740 final, at 7.

6

Transfer of intermediated securities

LUC THÉVENOZ

6.1 Introduction

The ability to sell or charge financial assets is inherent to financial markets and essential to most investors. Assets that cannot be realised may lose all or most of their value. Most financial assets are issued as securities. In times when securities were transferred as certificates or negotiable instruments (*valeurs mobilières, papiers-valeurs, Wertpapiere*), the rules providing the methods and the effects of such transfers were critical to the safety of the securities markets. They were taught at law schools, and were not deemed to be an easy subject. In most cases, financial market securities are no longer sold or pledged by way of certificates. In many legal systems and markets, certificates have been displaced altogether. Nowadays, securities traded in the financial markets are held through intermediaries such as banks, securities dealers and other financial intermediaries. The rules governing the full or partial transfer of such intermediated securities, the methods available and their effects, are as important as the corresponding rules were to certificated securities. They form a core component of any statutory or case law governing intermediated securities. Their efficiency and predictability is essential to the proper functioning and stability of the financial markets.

The provisions regarding the transfer of intermediated securities thus constitute a very important chapter of the international harmonisation of the law of intermediated securities, from the 2006 Hague Securities Convention to the 2009 Geneva Securities Convention and the future EU Securities Law Directive.

From a legal viewpoint, 'transfer' is a non-technical term. In its two authentic languages, the Hague Securities Convention uses '*transfert*' in French, but 'disposition' in English, to mean 'any transfer of title whether outright or by way of security and any grant of a security interest, whether possessory or non-possessory'.[1] The Geneva Securities Convention also uses the French '*transfert*', and the English 'transfer' in its heading for Chapter III 'Transfer of intermediated securities', but refrains from further use of that concept in respect of acquisition and disposition of intermediated securities.[2] The EU Consultation Document of January 2011 uses acquisition and disposition consistently.

This chapter examines the main provisions of the Geneva Securities Convention concerning the acquisition and disposition of intermediated securities, and of any limited interest (such as security interests) in the same. Wherever it is useful, we compare the provisions of the Convention with the principles discussed in the EU Consultation Document. As we shall see, the latter is in line with the Convention on most issues:

- both deal only with voluntary acquisitions and dispositions; the existence, requirements for, and priority of, interests arising automatically from the operation of the law (non-consensual interests) are exclusively determined by the applicable national law, or the 'non-Convention law' for the purposes of the Convention;[3]
- both make one method (credit and debit) available generally for transferring full title to intermediated securities or any limited interest therein;
- both offer a choice of three other methods (designating entry or earmarking, control agreement, agreement with and in favour of the relevant intermediary), of which Contracting or Member States[4] may elect to make one or more available to account holders, or none at all;
- both include key provisions on the effectiveness of acquisitions and dispositions against third parties and in insolvency;

1 Convention on the Law Applicable to Certain Rights in Respect of Securities Held with an Intermediary, concluded in The Hague on 5 July 2006 (Hague Securities Convention), Art. 1(e).

2 The word 'transfer' is further used in set phrases such as 'fraudulent transfer' or 'title transfer.'

3 Many provisions of the Convention defer to additional or different provisions of the applicable law governing a particular issue falling within the scope of the Convention. As defined in Art. 1(m) in connection with Art. 2, those provisions are referred to as 'the non-Convention law'. The EU Consultation Document merely refers to 'the applicable law'. In this chapter, both have the same meaning.

4 Treaties and legal instruments of the European Union speak of Member States while the Convention refers to Contracting States.

- none interferes with the contents and characterisation of the interests that are created, transferred, or extinguished; these questions are entirely left to the applicable law;
- both protect an innocent acquirer (*acquisition de bonne foi*) when certain circumstances affect the transaction;
- both determine the priority of competing interests in (i.e. successive dispositions over) the same intermediated securities;
- both explicitly state that the rules on acquisitions and dispositions do not determine who the issuer of the securities must recognise as shareholder or bondholder.

While covering the same ground, the EU Consultation Document differs from the Convention by closely connecting debits and credits with concerns about the integrity of the intermediated holding system and the avoidance of so-called excess securities. Where the Convention deals with these concerns in a separate Chapter IV, Principle 4(2) of the EU Consultation Document requires an intermediary to make a credit 'only if it holds a corresponding number of securities of the same description', and Principle 4(4) mandates the intermediary to 'reverse erroneous credits' or to buy in additional securities if the requirement is not satisfied.

This difference of emphasis highlights the concern of significant European jurisdictions with the integrity of securities issues. Principles 4(2) and 4(4) remain nonetheless well within the framework set out by the Convention. Subject to the protection of an innocent acquirer, Article 16 of the Convention defers entirely to the non-Convention law to determine when a credit may or must be reversed. Article 24, which requires the intermediary to hold or have available enough securities to cover the credits made to the securities accounts it maintains, also defers to the non-Convention law to determine the methods of complying with that requirement. This chapter does not deal further with these issues, which are extensively discussed in Chapters 7 (Mooney) and 8 (de Vauplane) of this book.

This chapter examines the methods available for acquiring and disposing of intermediated securities (section 6.2), the rights and interests that may be created or transferred according to these methods (section 6.3), and the effectiveness of such acquisitions and dispositions (section 6.4). It will then examine and compare the provisions on innocent acquisition (section 6.5) and priority (section 6.6).

6.2 Methods for acquisition and disposition

6.2.1 Debits and credits

Intermediated securities exist as book-entries in securities accounts maintained by financial institutions. The form of their recording is reflected in synonyms such as account-held securities,[5] or book-entry securities.[6] As a result, credits to the transferee's account and debits to the transferor's securities account are quintessential to the dematerialised world of intermediated securities. As far as we know, they are available in all jurisdictions where securities are held through intermediaries. Credits and debits are therefore the one method that must be available to all account holders under the Convention and the EU Principles alike.

When the intermediated holding system developed (in the 1960s), and before it was supported by statutory provisions, entries made in accounts recording the securities holdings of clients generally received evidential value. They were deemed to evidence the acquisition of certain rights by the account holder, not to effectuate that acquisition. The acquisition relied on traditional legal rules dealing, for example, with certificated securities. The key legal requirements were, for example, the delivery of the securities to the acquirer or the acquirer's bank, the endorsement of the certificate, or the registration of the new securities holder in the company registry. The book entries in the accounts of the transferor and the transferees were not legally decisive. Book entries in securities accounts operated essentially like entries in a company account: they recorded assets or claims, but did not create or transfer them.

The development of the intermediary holding system has placed tremendous importance on credits and debits. Book entries have become the 'gold standard' of the holding pattern worldwide. This is why in many jurisdictions statutes were enacted that changed the legal doctrines applicable to dematerialised or immobilised (intermediated) securities, retaining credits and debits as a transfer's decisive elements.

Debits and credits do not occur in a void. They rely on transactions concluded on an exchange or directly between the parties and generally result from instructions issued by the parties to their respective intermediaries. National legal doctrines have therefore connected credits

5 As in the EU Consultation Document.

6 As in the German version (*Bucheffekten*) of the Swiss Intermediated Securities Act of 2008, which uses '*titres intermédiés*' in its French version. On this Act, see further Chapter 13 (Kuhn).

and debits with other relevant circumstances, such as (valid) instructions from the transferor. Many jurisdictions also require – with varying degrees of stringency – that there be no credit to the transferee's account without a matching debit in the transferor's account. The circumstances under which a credit or a debit may be deemed invalid or liable to be reversed differ significantly among legal systems.

It seems however that all or most legal systems consider that the time of the acquisition is the time when the credit is made to the acquirer's securities account. This is the time when the acquisition becomes effective against third parties and effective in the insolvency of the acquirer and in the insolvency of the relevant intermediary. Even though a credit might be subsequently reversed for a number of reasons, it is also the trigger for the protection of an innocent acquirer.

What constitutes a credit (or a debit) to a securities account has various definitions, depending on the operational arrangements and on the legal rules applicable to a given system or jurisdiction.

Given the universality of credits and debits, on one hand, and the diversity of legal rules and operational systems on the other, the Geneva Securities Convention sets out a limited set of harmonised rules:

- Intermediated securities are acquired when a credit is entered in the account of the acquirer, and they are disposed of when a debit is made to that account.
- What constitutes a credit or a debit is not determined by the Convention.
- Except that a debit must be authorised by the account holder,[7] the Convention does not determine which other requirements must be satisfied for a credit or a debit to be valid; non-Convention law determines those requirements and the effects of an invalid or reversed book entry.
- The Convention neither precludes nor includes a 'no credit without debit' rule, which is left entirely to the non-Convention law.
- The non-Convention law determines when a credit or a debit is or can be made conditional.
- On all these questions, the non-Convention law may defer to the account agreement or to the uniform rules of a securities settlement system.

The connection between debits and credits is an area of significant differences between national legal and regulatory regimes. Many jurisdictions of the civil law tradition (including France, Germany, Switzerland and Japan) consider the intermediated securities debited from the transferor's

7 Art. 15(1)(a) of the Convention.

account to be the very same as the ones that are credited to the account of the transferee.[8] It is the same property that is relinquished by the transferor and acquired by the transferee. The book-entries should occur at the same moment, as far as operationally possible, though it is rarely the case in fact, but legal doctrines ensure that there is a single conceptual and legal moment for the acquisition/disposition and that any mismatch between the relevant accounts are corrected as soon as possible.

Because the Convention deals in separate paragraphs of Article 11 with credits (paragraphs 1 and 2) and with debits (paragraphs 3 and 4), some observers have suggested that the Convention favours the Anglo-American approach to intermediated securities. Under the English law of trusts, which is the conceptual framework for securities held in 'street name' by banks and broker-dealers for their clients, account holders acquire an equitable interest in the assets held by the intermediary; they are the beneficiaries of a trust.[9] When an account holder sells shares, she is not legally transferring her equitable interest to the acquirer. Rather, her beneficial interest, derived from her bank's holding, is extinguished, while a comparable interest is created by the buyer's bank for the buyer. Although a securities entitlement under Article 8 of the Uniform Commercial Code is not identical with a beneficial interest under English trust law, the same analysis applies to the creation of the acquirer's entitlement and to the extinguishment of the seller's entitlement in the United States. In these and similar legal systems, a seller is not technically transferring her interest to the buyer of intermediated securities, but is causing the acquisition of the buyer's interest, usually at the cost of relinquishing her own.

While the structure of Article 11 of the Convention would appear to favour the English and American approach by treating credits and debits separately, and does not require that they are necessarily connected or inter-dependent, Article 16 allows Contracting States to thoroughly interconnect debits and credits so that they become two sides of the same coin. The Official Commentary to the Convention has put to rest any concern about full deference to the non-Convention law on these issues.[10]

8 I have discussed this conceptual differences in Thévenoz, 'Intermediated Securities', at 401 et seq.; see also Paech, *Cross-Border Issues*, at 13.

9 See Benjamin, *Interests in Securities*, 10; [UK] Financial Markets Committee, *Issue 3*, at 36–59; Micheler, 'The Legal Nature', at 131.

10 Kanda et al., *Official Commentary*, s. 11–4 and s. 11–12 and example 11–1 at s. 11–13.

The EU Consultation Document, which is drafted in the form of a set of principles rather than legal rules, takes those things in its stride and deals with credits and debits in Principle 4(1). However, other principles deal separately with credits or debits, wherever appropriate.[11] In substance, however, the Consultation Document does not propose to push any further the limits of harmonisation in the area of credits and debits. While it requires that the account provider (intermediary) crediting securities to the transferee's account may only do so if it holds 'a corresponding number of securities of the same description', the breach of this requirement does not result in the invalidity of the credit, but imposes on the account provider to remedy the situation by either reversing the erroneous credit or by obtaining additional securities of the same description.[12]

6.2.2 Choice among other methods

Other methods for the acquisition and disposition of intermediated securities, or interests therein, are available in most jurisdictions but have not reached the same level of universal acceptance as credits and debits. While it is unnecessary for international harmonisation to impose them, it is important to recognise them wherever they exist as methods capable of transferring intermediated securities or limited interests therein. Uniform rules then apply to the protection of an innocent acquirer and to the priority of interests created in the same intermediated securities.

Article 12 of the Convention, followed on that matter by Principle 4(5) of the EU Consultation Document, lists the three most common methods and sets out their basic features. Each state may choose one, several, or none of them. For the sake of international transparency, the Convention requires that this choice should be specified in a declaration, and may be varied any time with the declaration modified accordingly.

All these methods have in common that the intermediated securities over which rights are transferred remain credited to the transferor's securities account. As stated in Article 12(1) of the Convention, each method requires two steps:

1. the account holder and the acquirer enter into an agreement in respect of the rights to be created or transferred; and
2. the specific condition of the relevant method is satisfied.

11 See the EU Consultation Document, Principles 4(2), 4(4), 5(3), 5(7), 7(1), and 8(1).
12 Principles 4(2) and 4(4).

6.2.3 Designating entry (or earmarking)

A designating entry (*identification*), called earmarking in the EU Consultation Document, is a book entry in favour of the acquirer, authorised by the account holder and made by the intermediary into that account holder's securities account.[13] As a book entry, it evidences the fact that someone other than the account holder has an interest in the whole account, or in certain intermediated securities. This form of publicity is somewhat limited by the nature of securities accounts. Securities accounts are not public registries and they may not be consulted by anyone who is not authorised by law or by the account holder. Moreover, limited reliance can be placed in an account statement or in a printout of an electronic access to a securities account, which may be modified within a minute after printing the statement or accessing the account. Unencumbered intermediated securities may be earmarked (or debited) within a minute after the statement has been printed or the account electronically inspected. But designating entries, like debits and credits, are book entries and, in that respect, they conform to the 'gold standard' of intermediated securities. The symmetry between those methods appeals to many jurisdictions.

When the account holder grants an interest in intermediated securities which remain credited to her securities account, it is not enough that an entry be made to record the existence of that interest; it is also necessary that the entry has certain effects protecting the acquirer against further unauthorised dispositions of the same intermediated securities by the account holder. These questions are not dealt with extensively.

It is for the non-Convention law to determine whether a designating entry provides the acquirer with 'positive' or 'negative control', or possibly both, over the designated securities. By positive control, we mean that the intermediary maintaining the account is required to comply with any instructions given by the acquirer in relation to those intermediated securities 'in such circumstances and as to such matters as may be provided by the account agreement, a control agreement or the uniform rules of a securities settlement system, without any further consent of the account holder'.[14] By negative control, we mean that the intermediary 'is not permitted to comply with any instructions given by the account holder in relation to the intermediated securities as to which the entry is made without the consent of that person'.[15] While the non-Convention

13 Art. 15(1)(b) of the Convention. 14 *Ibid.*, Art. 1(l)(ii). 15 *Ibid.*, Art. 1(l)(i).

law determines the issue, the Convention requires the Contracting State to make a declaration stating that its non-Convention law provides for designating entries as a method available to grant an interest in intermediated securities and specifies the type of control resulting from the designating entry.[16]

Book entries rely on the authority of the person whose rights are affected. Like debits, designating entries must be authorised by the account holder.[17] Conversely, the removal of a designating entry must be authorised by the person in whose favour it was made.[18]

6.2.4 *Control agreement*

While certain jurisdictions prefer the formalism of designating entries, others favour the flexibility of control agreements. Essentially, both methods may have the same effects over the relevant intermediated securities and provide the acquirer with positive or negative control, or both, as determined by the non-Convention law.[19] The one significant difference is that control agreements do not require a book entry in the account of the transferor; they open a wide space for contractual provisions regulating the various circumstances under which the account holder and the acquirer may respectively issue instructions to the intermediary and thus effect dispositions over the assets.

Like a designating entry, a control agreement imposes additional obligations on the intermediary for the benefit of the acquirer. The difference is that the exact extent of those obligations is typically determined between all three parties involved. Technically, control agreements may be tripartite or bipartite.[20] Two-party control agreements are typically negotiated between the account holder and the intermediary, obviously on the basis of what has been agreed upon between the account holder and the acquirer. Such a two-party agreement is a contract for the benefit of a third party, and creates contractual rights for the acquirer. In certain jurisdictions, control agreements may be executed by the account holder and the acquirer and merely notified to the intermediary. The binding effect of a control agreement imposing obligations on a person, the intermediary, who is not a party to it seems to contradict the doctrine of privity of contracts and must probably rely on some specific statutory provision.

16 *Ibid.*, Art. 11(5) and (6). 17 *Ibid.*, Art. 15(1)(b).
18 *Ibid.*, Art. 15(1)(c). 19 *Ibid.*, Art. 1(k). 20 *Ibid.*, Art. 1(k).

Since interests granted by any method are meant to be effective against third parties, it is often questioned whether it is safe to create such interests without the limited form of publicity effected by a designating entry, i.e., a book entry. As a matter of fact, the whole intermediary holding system relies on the reliability and integrity of intermediaries. An interest granted by any of the Article 12 methods is only as good as the capacity and willingness of the relevant intermediary to apply the limitations resulting from designating entries or control agreements. For the potential acquirer of, say, a security interest, the only safe way to ensure that it will enjoy a priority over any other subsequent interest is to have this fact confirmed by the relevant intermediary. It is all the more important that intermediaries often enjoy a first interest in the intermediated securities credited to their client securities accounts, either as a statutory lien (an area not harmonised by the Convention or by the contemplated Securities Law Directive), or as a contractual interest created in accordance with the last of the Article 12 methods (see below section 6.2.5). In that respect, an interest granted by a designating entry made into a securities account is more transparent than the same interest granted by way of a control agreement, but it is not safer against fraud or error on the intermediary's side.

6.2.5 Agreement with and for the benefit of the relevant intermediary

The last optional method – actually the first listed in Article 12(3) of the Convention – may only be used to grant an interest to the intermediary maintaining the account where the intermediated securities are credited. Where provided for by the non-Convention law, the agreement between the account holder and her intermediary suffices to create that interest and make it effective against third parties. It is sometimes referred to as a 'self-perfecting' agreement, because the first step required (an agreement between the transferor-account holder and the transferee about the grant of an interest in intermediated securities) is enough to 'perfect' that interest, i.e., to make it effective against third parties.

The justification for this method is obvious for jurisdictions where control agreements are used: the collateral agreement (or other transaction concluded between the account holder and the intermediary) binds the very same parties as the ones required for a valid control agreement. There is no need for an additional contract. The position of the intermediary as the beneficiary of the interest is secured by the control it exercises over the securities account it itself maintains.

In jurisdictions where self-perfecting collateral agreements and statutory liens coexist for the benefit of the intermediary, the difference between both interests may be blurred. Typically, the terms of a custody account will confer on the intermediary a broader security interest over the intermediated securities it holds for its clients in respect of the securities which are pledged, the obligations that are guaranteed, and the realisation of the securities by private sale.

6.3 Rights and interests transferred

While the Convention and the EU Consultation Document deal with *how* intermediated securities can be acquired and disposed of, they say precious little on *what* – i.e., on the rights and interest that may thus be transferred or granted. This issue deserves a closer examination in the light of the provisions of the Convention.

Article 11(1) and (3) speak of 'intermediated securities' being 'acquired' or 'disposed of', implicitly referring to the full title to these intermediated securities, or in other words to the complete set of the rights arising from the credit of these securities to a securities account.[21] However, Article 11(4) broadens the subject matter of dispositions made by credits and debits by providing that '[a] security interest, or a limited interest other than a security interest, in intermediated securities may be acquired' by the same method. Further, Article 9(3) confirms that a credit can be made to grant a security or other limited interest, in which case 'the non-Convention determines any limits on the rights' resulting from that credit.[22]

In many jurisdictions, Article 12 methods are typically used to transfer limited interests in intermediated securities, most often security interests, but Article 12 itself contains no such limitation. Its paragraph 1 refers to the grant of 'an interest in intermediated securities, including a security interest or a limited interest other that a security interest.' Indeed, if 'an interest . . . *includ[es]* . . . a limited interest', then it is not *restricted* to it; otherwise, the first part of the phrase and the term 'including' would have no meaning. In other words, Article 12 may also be employed to transfer the full, unlimited interest in the intermediated securities which

21 Under the heading 'Intermediated Securities', Art. 9 describes the rights conferred upon an account holder by the credit of securities to her securities account.

22 The same rule is expressed in different terms in Principle 3(4) of the EU Consultation Document.

remain credited to the securities account of the transferor.[23] The possibility of transferring the full title to intermediated securities by one of the Article 12 methods may seem counter-intuitive, but it was a deliberate choice made during the preparation and negotiation of the Convention and is necessary to its correct implementation.

The first reason is legal and it is related to the limited purpose and scope of the harmonisation envisioned by the Convention. It has been said earlier (see Chapter 1 at page 8) that the Convention refrains from interfering with the legal characterisation, under national property laws, of the rights of an account holder. Notions of property, limited interests (*droits réels limités, beschränkte dingliche Rechte*) and security interests (*sûretés ou garanties, Sicherheiten*) differ very significantly among jurisdictions. The purpose and scope of the Convention is not to harmonise the substantive notions of property law among jurisdictions, but to create legal certainty regarding, inter alia, how and when proprietary rights (or non-proprietary rights, as the case may be) in respect of intermediated securities are acquired, charged, transferred or otherwise disposed of. This is why Chapter II of the Convention deals with these methods; the effectiveness of the rights so created or transferred; their respective priority, and the protection, of innocent acquirers. The Convention does not prescribe or describe what these rights are. This is also true of the (optional) Chapter V on 'Special provisions in relation to collateral transactions',[24] which does not interfere with existing legal doctrines regarding the legal characterisation of interests created either by a 'security collateral agreement' or by a 'title transfer collateral agreement'.[25]

In this self-limitation of the Convention lies the fundamental reason why the methods in Articles 11 and 12 apply to whatever full or partial interest the parties want to create or transfer in accordance with the non-Convention law. If Article 12 was confined to limited interests, or security interests, or collateral interests, legal certainty in cross-border legal situations would require that these concepts are defined by the Convention, implying that the Convention characterises (or re-characterises) notions of the non-Convention law. This would defeat the functional approach underlying the Convention and interfere with the property notions of national law deterring states from adopting harmonised rules, thereby thwarting the whole process.

23 Kanda et al., *Official Commentary*, s. 12-14.

24 See Zaccaroli, 'Taking Security', at 169.

25 These terms are defined in Art. 13(3)(b) and (c) of the Convention.

This fundamental reason is buttressed by a practical consideration. It is a matter of fact that in some markets, both title transfer and non-title transfer collateral transactions are effected by some Article 12 method. For example, some central banks take intermediated securities from qualifying intermediaries in repos transactions (repurchase operations) without debiting the relevant securities from the participants' securities account. This flexibility is important and the negotiations revealed no reason why Article 12 methods should be restricted to non-title transfer transactions.

6.4 Effectiveness

It is good to know that A has acquired certain intermediated securities from B, or that B has granted a security interest in some other intermediated securities to A. But the property acquired by A is only good to the extent that it is effective against third parties, including:

- against the creditors of B if B becomes bankrupt;
- against subsequent acquirers of an interest in the same intermediated securities, over which A's interest may have priority (see below section 6.6);
- against holders of prior interest in the same intermediated securities, if and to the extent that A must be protected as an innocent acquirer (see below section 6.5);
- as well indeed as in the insolvency of the intermediary maintaining the relevant securities account.

The Geneva Securities Convention does that in two identical paragraphs in Articles 11 and 12 respectively, paragraph 2 of both of which read:

> No further step is necessary, or may be required by the non-Convention law or any other rule of law applicable in an insolvency proceeding, to render the acquisition of intermediated securities effective against third parties.[26]

What are these further steps that are unnecessary to the effectiveness of an interest? The rule mostly addresses formalities, filings, registrations, and other publicity requirements that certain jurisdictions impose to make third parties aware of security interests. For example, the general rule in a

26 Para. 2 of Arts. 11 and 12 of the Convention. The same rule is contained in the EU Consultation Document, Principle 5(2). However, we will see below that the EU Consultation Document has a broader notion of effectiveness.

jurisdiction may require that a security interest be registered or filed with some public agency or registry. Another jurisdiction may require notice of the security interest to be given to holders of earlier security interests in the same assets. Such formalities may be required for the interest to be effective and enforceable against third parties, or they may be optional but would afford the (new) interest priority over earlier, unpublicised interests.

The 'no further step' rule applies to the non-Convention law as much as to the law applicable in an insolvency proceeding. It does not displace validity requirements set out by the non-Convention law, such as the no-debit-without-credit rules discussed earlier. Validity requirements are reserved by Article 16. Articles 11(2) and 12(2) provide for the *erga omnes* effectiveness of valid dispositions and only disable additional formalities and publicity requirements.

In the Convention, validity of the acquisition and effectiveness against third parties coincide in time. Effectiveness is an additional characteristic of an interest that has been validly acquired. An interest becomes effective against third parties only if, and as soon as, it has been acquired. If the interest is or becomes invalid, it does not become or cease to be effective. When the non-Convention law provides for the invalidity of an interest or the reversal of a book-entry, it must also provide for the *inter partes* and *erga omnes* effects of such invalidity or reversal.[27]

Effectiveness is the premise or precondition of several other provisions of the Convention:[28]

- Article 14: Within limits set out in subsequent paragraphs, paragraph 1 states that: 'Rights and interests that have become effective against third parties under Article 11 or Article 12 are effective against the insolvency administrator and creditors in any insolvency proceeding.'
- Article 21: Within (narrower) limits set out in subsequent paragraphs, paragraph 1 states: 'Rights and interests of account holders of a relevant intermediary that have become effective against third parties under Article 11 and interests granted by such account holders that have become effective under Article 12 are effective against the insolvency administrator and creditors in any insolvency proceeding in relation to the relevant intermediary . . . '.

27 Art. 16 of the Convention; see also Art. 15(2) leaving for the non-Convention law to determine the consequences of an unauthorised book entry.

28 See also Arts. 18, 20, 22, 23(2)(b), 39.

- Article 19 'determines priority between interests in the same intermediated securities which become effective against third parties under Article 12 or Article 13'.
- Articles 17 and 18 do not explicitly connect the protection of an innocent acquirer with the effectiveness of her acquisition, but the relevant time for the 'know or ought to know' test refers to the identical facts that trigger the effectiveness of the interest against third parties.[29]

The EU Consultation Document uses effectiveness in a broader sense. Principle 4 ('Methods for acquisition and disposition') deals with 'the operational side of acquiring and disposing through accounts'.[30] Principle 5 ('Legal effectiveness of acquisitions and dispositions') regulates effectiveness 'between the account holder *and* the account provider and against third parties'.[31] The same Principle 5 deals with questions of validity and reversal as well as with conditional entries.[32] In other words, where the Convention neatly distinguishes validity from effectiveness against third parties, the EU Consultation Document subsumes the latter in the former.

Principle 5(5) clarifies that 'Effectiveness . . . does not determine whom an issuer has to recognize as legal holder of its securities.' The point is well taken, and echoes Article 8(2) of the Convention stating that the Convention 'does not determine whom the issuer is required to recognise as the shareholder, bondholder or other person entitled to receive and exercise the rights attached to the securities or to recognise for any other purpose'.

Notwithstanding the different uses of 'effectiveness' in the two instruments, their respective rules are essentially compatible, except on one significant issue. Unlike Articles 14 and 21 of the Convention, Principle 6 ('Effectiveness in insolvency') does not differentiate between insolvency of the relevant intermediary and insolvency of any other party. Extensive and sometimes difficult negotiations in the UNIDROIT process have demonstrated the need to better protect account holders in the insolvency of the relevant intermediary, which Article 21(2) does by allowing narrower exceptions to that protection than Article 14.[33] For example, it is hard

29 Namely, when the credit is made, Art. 17(e), or when the interest becomes effective against third parties under Art. 12, see Art. 19(3).

30 Consultation Document, at 10 (first paragraph under sub-section 4.2).

31 Principle 5(2), emphasis added.

32 Reversal of book-entries is further addressed in Principle 7.

33 In Art. 14(1), the Convention reserves the application 'of any substantive or procedural rule of law applicable by virtue of an insolvency proceeding' and only provides an

to see why the protection of intermediated securities in the insolvency of the relevant intermediary should be subject to the superior ranking of some claims, such as claims of the tax or revenue authorities or from employees of the relevant intermediary. The whole notion is that intermediated (or account-held) securities are the property of account holders in the custody of the relevant intermediary and the intermediary system at large. They are not transformed into mere contractual claims against the insolvent intermediary. In most systems, property not belonging to the insolvent party is not subject to the claims of that party's creditors; it must be set aside from the insolvency and delivered to the persons having proprietary rights. It would have been useful if that distinction had been made in Principle 6.

6.5 Innocent acquisition

The protection of 'bona fide' or 'innocent' acquirers from the seller's defective title and adverse claims of other persons retaining an interest in the asset is an important aspect of any property transaction. Such '*protection de l'acquéreur de bonne foi*' originates with tangible property, specifically with movables (chattels). The possessor of a particular movable thing is presumed to be its owner, or at least to have the power to fully dispose of title to that thing *('en matière de meubles, possession vaut titre')*, unless particular circumstances require that a diligent buyer should enquire about the possessor's title. In jurisdictions where land and other assets are registered in public registries, the same doctrine often protects acquirers who have relied on the information publicised in the registry. Protection of innocent acquirers against hidden title defects is essential to the value and marketability of assets. Rules setting out the protection of purchasers of certificated securities, and the limits thereof, are an important chapter of the law governing negotiable instruments and certificated securities. The same need arises for intermediated securities. But several jurisdictions struggled with these issues because, whether the securities held through intermediaries are fully dematerialised or merely immobilised, the acquirer cannot rely on the seller's physical possession

illustrative listing of such rules. In connection with an insolvent intermediary, Art. 21(2) only reserves two narrow exceptions. For an explanation of these two provisions and the underlying policies, see the Official Commentary, under Arts. 14 and 21 respectively, with reference to the preparatory documents.

of the securities nor on a public registry.[34] Securities accounts are not open for public inspection.

Traditional rules on movable or immovable property may be helpless to protect innocent acquirers of intermediated securities or of any security or other limited interest therein. But there is an undisputed need to protect market participants and the securities markets against such problems which have the potential to disrupt transactions.

Unlike the EU Consultation Document, to which we revert later, Articles 17 and 18 of the Convention set out an extensive protection. An innocent acquirer (or '*acquéreur de bonne foi*') of intermediated securities, or of any interest in intermediated securities, is protected against two types of defective situation:

- a person other than the transferor ('another person') has an interest in securities or intermediated securities *and* the rights of that other person are violated by the acquisition; or
- there is a defective entry prior to the acquisition, such as an invalid, conditional or reversible credit or designating entry, which may invalidate the acquisition.

The Convention thus protects acquirers from two types of defect: the infringement of the rights of another person and earlier defective entries which, for any reason that may have nothing to do with the rights of another person, might invalidate the acquisition.

Such protection requires the acquirer to be '*de bonne foi*', innocent of these problems. The innocence test raised many dogmatic debates during the negotiations of the Convention,[35] but the final outcome seems essentially uncontroversial. A person is innocent unless she 'actually knows or ought to know, at the relevant time, of' the interest of the other person or of the earlier defective entry. The protection does not apply to donations and other gratuitous acquisitions. The relevant time is when the acquisition becomes effective against third parties.

What happens when an innocent acquirer is protected under Article 18(1) or (2)? Essentially, his acquisition and the book entry on which it relies, if any, are valid; he takes his interest free from the claims

34 See particularly Nizard, *Les titres négociables*, at 253 et seq.; Einsele, *Wertpapier als Schuldrecht*, at 97 et seq.

35 See inter alia the Summary report of the Informal Working Group on Art. 14 of the draft Convention, UNIDROIT 2008 CONF. 11–Doc. 8, of March 2008.

of the person whose rights are infringed upon or who would benefit from the invalidation of the acquisition; furthermore, he is not liable to that person.[36]

Conversely, the applicable law determines the consequence when an acquirer is not protected under Article 18(1) or (2). These consequences may result from various types of provisions, including the rules of the non-Convention law regarding who retains which rights and interests, which book entries are invalid or must be reversed, and the possible liability of the transferor, acquirer and intermediaries involved. Article 18(4) refers to 'the applicable law' in respect of the rights and liabilities of the acquirer because other doctrines and remedies may apply, such as unjust enrichment, breach of contract, tort, for which the relevant rules of conflicts designate applicable laws which may be different from the non-Convention law.

The protection of innocent acquirers under Article 18(1) and (2) is a minimum rule. The non-Convention law may expand it, as was discussed and accepted during the negotiations.[37]

For unexplained reasons, the protection of an innocent acquirer is the chapter where the EU Consultation Document differs most strikingly from the Geneva Securities Convention. Principle 8 is markedly different on several major issues:

- Its scope is significantly narrower than the Convention, as Principle 8 only protects 'against the reversal of a crediting' or 'an earmarking'. It does not address other remedies against the innocent acquirer, such as claims for restitution or damages. And it does not afford any protection to the other two acquisition methods offered in Principle 4.
- Despite textual differences,[38] the innocence test does not seem to depart significantly from the Convention. However, it applies to a less defined set of facts, i.e., 'that the crediting or earmarking should not have been made'.

The comments to the Principles in the EU Consultation Document do not provide an explanation for these differences. The broader description of the facts subject to the innocent test may be explained by the nature of

36 Arts. 15(2) and 16 of the Convention, dealing with the consequences of invalid dispositions or book entries, are 'subject to Art. 18'.

37 Art. 18(4) refers to 'the rights and liability, *if any*, of the acquirer' (emphasis added). See Kanda et al., *Official Commentary*, s. 18–16 and s. 18–17.

38 Compare 'unless it actually knows or ought to know, at the relevant time' and 'unless it knew or ought to have known.'

the document, which on most issues is expressed in broad principles for the purpose of the consultation, obviously to be later turned into precise and minute legal drafting.

However, it is difficult to understand why an innocent acquirer under a control agreement should not enjoy the same protection as an innocent acquirer taking his interest through a designating entry. All methods are deemed equivalent by the Principles, which leave the choice to EU Member States. The manner in which the acquirer takes his interest does not change anything regarding its knowledge (or lack thereof), nor regarding the need for protection when other conditions are satisfied.

Additionally, the protection afforded by Principle 8 in the EU Consultation Document is insufficient. Not only should an innocent acquirer be protected against the reversal of the book entry through which he takes his interest, but he should be protected also against other types of claim resulting from his acquisition. Damages and restitution are the most obvious ones. What good is it to have a credit maintained if one has to retransfer intermediated securities to an aggrieved party or pay damages to compensate their loss?

The protection of innocent acquirers, i.e. acquirers acting in good faith, must be broader. It cannot be limited to the validity and irreversibility of the book entries, and must extend to the validity of the rights that have been acquired innocently. The impact of that protection on the party who holds a previous interest in the same intermediated securities is a different issue. It will be illustrated below when comparing the respective scopes of the innocent acquisition rule and the priority rule.

6.6 Priority

The ability of an account holder to grant successive interests in intermediated securities, for example through multiple collateral transactions, is an important feature of the intermediary holding system. It must be supported by clear priority rules. Traditionally, an interest typically takes precedence over subsequent interests in the same property. *Prior tempore potior iure* encapsulates the basic, first-in-time principle governing the ranking of successive partial dispositions of the same intermediated securities. But policy reasons may dictate otherwise, and the parties may agree to multiple transactions.

Article 19 of the Convention determines the priority between interests that become effective under one of the Article 12 methods or under another method which is provided by the non-Convention law, but not by the Convention itself (non-harmonised method, see Article 13). While the provision may look complex, its three main rules are easily explained.

The first rule is absolute: any interest which became effective against third parties according to an Article 12 method has priority over any interest which became effective by any other method provided by the non-Convention law.[39] The priority of internationally harmonised methods over non-Convention methods does not apply to statutory liens and other non-consensual interests, which arise automatically under the non-Convention law and enjoy the priority determined by it.

The second rule determines the priority between Article 12 dispositions. Article 19(3) sets out a strict first-in-time priority among all dispositions made under Article 12, whichever method was employed. This rule, however, can be modified. Under Article 19(7), a Contracting State may declare that an interest granted by a designating entry has priority over any interest granted by another Article 12 method.[40] This option was introduced at the request of members of the European Union; it reflects a policy choice that designating entries should enjoy a preferential treatment over other Article 12 methods which are not based on book entries. This preferential treatment of designating entries over other methods is presently reflected in Principle 9(1)(c) of the EU Consultation Document.

The third rule allows holders of Article 12 interests to contractually modify their respective ranking as between themselves, obviously without affecting the interests of third parties.[41]

The reader will have noted that Article 19 does not apply to interests granted by way of a credit.[42] It is important to note as well that Article 18, the provision on innocent acquisition, does not modify the priorities determined by Article 19.[43] This suggests a complex interaction between the two provisions, on one hand, and debits, credits, and Article 12 methods, on the other. The issue was identified early in the processing leading to the Convention, and was very carefully examined. It arises

39 Art. 19(2) of the Convention. Under Art. 13, the Convention does not preclude any method, other than those in Arts. 11 and 12, that may be provided by the non-Convention law. Contracting States may therefore continue to allow non-harmonised methods for the transfer of intermediated securities or the creation of an interest therein, but such methods enjoy a lower priority than the harmonised methods in Art.11 and 12 of the Convention.

40 Art. 19(7).

41 EU Consultation Document, Principle 19(6).

42 Art. 19(1) of the Convention only refers to interests made effective under Arts. 12 or 13.

43 Art. 18(6).

from the fact that the innocent acquisition rule and the priority rule are typically antagonistic. Priorities are essentially based on a first-in-time principle (*prior tempore, potio iure*): earlier dispositions have priority over subsequent ones. The protection of an innocent acquirer is definitely a last-in-time rule: innocence protects the last acquirer against holders of previous interests. It is impossible to apply both rules at the same time. In every situation, it must be clear whether the confrontation between two interests (or two dispositions) is governed by one or the other rule.

The Convention achieves this by giving a broad scope to the innocent acquisition provision, only carving out all priority contests between competing interests in the same intermediated securities credited to the same securities account, which are exclusively governed by Article 19, the priority provision.

This is best explained by two examples. In both examples, we assume that A has €1 million worth of bonds credited to his securities account with Bank 1. The applicable law is that of Ruritania, which is a party to the Geneva Securities Convention and has made a declaration that its non-Convention law allows an interest in intermediated securities to become effective against third parties by a designating entry. A has granted to B a pledge over all the bonds credited to A's securities account to secure a loan of €500,000. Upon A's instruction, Bank 1 has made the relevant designating entry. A then takes from C a second loan of €800,000 to be secured by a further pledge over €800,000 worth of bonds.[44]

Example 1. A has instructed Bank 1 to make a designating entry in his securities account in favour of C. Article 19(3) applies to that situation: B's interest has priority over C's interest. If both loans are not paid back, the bonds will be realised, with the first €500,000 paid to B and whatever remains paid to C. The priority of B's interest over C's interest does not hinge upon whether C knew or ought to know at any time that the bonds were subject to a senior interest.

Example 2. A has instructed Bank 1 to transfer certain bonds worth €800,000 to the securities account of C with Bank 2. Depending on the effects of a designating entry under Ruritanian law,[45] Bank 1 must, may

44 Art. 12(4) provides that an interest made effective under Art. 12 may apply to 'all intermediated securities from time to time standing to the credit of a particular securities account', or to 'a specified category, quantity, proportion or value of such intermediated securities.'

45 Arts. 1(l) and 12(6).

or may not reject the instruction, as unauthorised by B.[46] Whether or not it was authorised to do so, or whether by mistake, Bank 1 has executed the instruction and the bonds have been debited from A's securities accounts with Bank 1 and credited to C's securities with Bank 2. Please note that, because A and C have so agreed, the credit of bonds made to C's securities account provides C with a pledge (and no more) over these bonds.[47] Article 19 does not apply to Example 2 because C's interest has not become effective under Article 12. Whether C's interest is junior to B's interest depends here on whether C is protected as an innocent person. C is protected under Article 18(1)[48] unless she knows or ought to know, at the time of the credit to her account, that B has a prior interest. If C is not protected under Article 18(1), then her situation will depend on the non-Convention law. Supposing that C is protected, what happens to B, to whom all intermediated securities standing to the credit of A's account Bank 1 are pledged, now that bonds worth only €200,000 remain credited to that account? Unless A was allowed by B or by the non-Convention law to dispose of the intermediated securities transferred to C,[49] B is protected because the debit was not authorised in the meaning of Article 15(1)(a). The non-Convention law – and to the extent it permits, the account agreement or the uniform rules of a securities settlement system – determines the consequences of that unauthorised debit. It may result in the obligation of Bank 1 to buy in the missing securities.

These examples illustrate three important features of the Convention. First, Articles 18 and 19 never apply to the same situation; their respective scopes are set out in Articles 18(6) and 19(1), and they are mutually exclusive. Second, unless the acquirer of a security interest (or any interest for that purpose) knows or ought to know of a prior (senior) interest, she is protected against that prior interest when she takes her own interest by way of a credit to her securities account, a protection that is not afforded when she takes her interest by way of any other method. This is the (intended) result of the unique role of credits and debits in the intermediary holding system. In that respect at least, a credit is stronger than a designating entry or a collateral agreement. Third, the protection of an innocent acquirer does not necessarily create a loss for the person whose rights have been violated. The non-Convention law determines

46 Art. 15(1)(a) and (e). 47 Art. 11(4).

48 Art. 18(2) does not apply because the unauthorised debit to A's account is not a 'defective entry' as defined in Art. 17(d).

49 Art. 15.

the consequences for that person.[50] If the debit must be annulled or reversed, then the interest is safeguarded as long as the intermediary is not insolvent and can buy in the missing securities. If the debit stands, then the intermediary is most probably liable to that person for having wrongfully executed the transfer instruction; that liability is governed by the non-Convention law and the intermediary may not exclude liability for its gross negligence or wilful misconduct.[51]

6.7 Harmonisation and the non-Convention law

Chapter III of the Convention, 'Transfer of intermediated securities', definitely belongs to the core of the harmonisation of the law pursued by the Convention. Nonetheless the present chapter, like most others in this book, evidences the very significant role that non-harmonised provisions, typically referred to as 'the non-Convention law', will and must retain. This is a unique feature of the Geneva Securities Convention as compared with other conventions concluded under the aegis of UNIDROIT or the United Commission on International Trade Law (UNCITRAL). It makes one wonder what the value is of a harmonisation convention that leaves so much space to national laws. Interestingly, the extent of the harmonisation contemplated by the EU Consultation Document is not significantly greater. Few of the policy choices that the Convention leaves for the non-Convention law would actually be made at the European Union level,[52] and most of them would remain (as is now the case) with EU Member States.

The reasons for such self-limitation have been made clear all along the harmonisation process, from early preparatory documents to formal negotiations in the formal setting of a diplomatic conference. Legal and operational systems for the intermediary holding of securities are very similar in some core features, but remain hugely different as to how those core features are obtained. The legal nature of a credit to a securities

50 When a credit cannot be reversed because the acquirer is protected, legal systems which put a great emphasis on the no-credit-without-debit rule tend to maintain the debit and protect the innocent loser through liability claims.

51 Art. 28(3) and (4).

52 Besides the issues discussed in the text of this chapter, see also EU Consultation Document, Principle 4(3) (if allowed at all, conditional credits 'must be identifiable as such in the account'; Principle 7(1) (book entries can only be reversed in listed circumstances); Principle 9(1)(c) (interests granted by way of earmarking have priority over interests granted by other methods).

account maintained by a French bank is very different from the same credit made to a securities account maintained by a German bank. But they serve the same function and are broadly used in the same contexts and for the same purposes. This similarity of functions resulting from such dissimilar legal systems is not special to the intermediary holding system; it is a very general feature of the law of financial markets, where national legal doctrines and national regulation retain a pre-eminent role. In this context, harmonisation must be limited to the core, functional issues, if it is to be successful at all.

Looking at the results in Chapter III of the Convention only, is there still enough value in the limited uniform provisions resulting from the negotiations between fifty states, which began in Rome and were completed in Geneva? We submit there is indeed, and more than meets the eye. This includes the effectiveness in insolvency proceedings of rights in intermediated securities when they have been made effective against third parties in accordance with the provisions of the Convention. It includes the recognition of a universal method (credits and debits), with the clear recognition that matching debits and credits may be required by law, or may not be required, subject always to the protection of an innocent acquirer. It also includes the three-pronged menu of additional methods that are internationally recognised as strict functional equivalents, even though they are not available in every state, with the corresponding priority rule. Additionally, it prominently recognises that legal provisions, account agreements, and the rules of securities settlement systems, vary hugely as to when book entries are valid or invalid, conditional, or must be reversed, but that such rules cannot defeat the protection of an innocent acquirer.

Diversity and harmonisation are in a dynamic equilibrium. Legal harmonisation contributes to financial stability by improving the internal soundness of and the international compatibility between legal systems. The legal certainty it promotes is valuable to the proper functioning of the financial markets, and ultimately to the financial stability. The two major recent financial crises, the first triggered by the US real estate market, the second by the sovereign debt crises in Europe, suggest that every contribution to the resilience of the financial infrastructure counts.

Bibliography

Benjamin, J., *Interests in Securities – A Proprietary Law Analysis of the International Securities Markets* (Oxford University Press, 2000).

Einsele, D., *Wertpapier als Schuldrecht: Funktionsverlust von Effektenurkunden, internationale Rechtsverkehr* (Tübingen: Mohr Siebeck, 1995).

[UK] Financial Markets Committee, *Issue 3:, Property Interests in Investment Securities*, July 2004.

Kanda, H., Mooney, C., Thévenoz, L. and Béraud, S., with the help of Keijser, T., *Official Commentary of the Unidroit Convention on Substantive Rules for Intermediated Securities* (Oxford University Press, 2012).

Micheler, E., 'The Legal Nature of Securities: Inspirations from Comparative Law' in L. Gullifer and J. Payne (eds.), *Intermediated Securities. Legal Problems and Practical Issues* (Oxford: Hart Publishing, 2010), 131–49.

Nizard, F., *Les titres négociables* (Paris: Economica, 2003).

Paech, P., '*Cross-border Issues of Securities Law: European Efforts to Support Securities Markets with a Coherent Legal Framework*', Briefing Paper to the European Parliament's Committee on Economic and Monetary Affairs, IPA/ECON/NT/2011–09, May 2011.

Summary report of the Informal Working Group on Article 14 of the draft Convention, UNIDROIT 2008 CONF. 11–Doc. 8, March 2008.

Thévenoz, L., 'Intermediated Securities, Legal Risk, and the International Harmonization of Commercial Law' [2008] 13 *Stanford Journal of Law, Business & Finance*, 384–452.

Zaccaroli, A., 'Taking Security over Intermediated Securities: Chapter V of the UNIDROIT (Geneva) Convention on Intermediated Securities' in L. Gullifer and J. Payne (eds.), *Intermediated Securities. Legal Problems and Practical Issues* (Oxford: Hart Publishing, 2010), 167–86.

7

The truth about shortfall of intermediated securities – perspectives under the Geneva Securities Convention, United States law, and the future EU legislation

CHARLES W. MOONEY, JR.*

7.1 Introduction

The Geneva Securities Convention[1] ('the Convention') was adopted in 2009 under the auspices of Rome's International Institute for the Unification of Private Law ('UNIDROIT') at a diplomatic conference in Geneva hosted by the Swiss government.[2] Its adoption was a remarkable achievement, for several reasons. It was adopted with a strong consensus among the participating states notwithstanding the wide variety of attitudes and positions on core issues that were, and are, held by those states.[3] These

* I thank Meredith Louis, JD 2011, University of Pennsylvania Law School, for outstanding research assistance. I also wish to thank David Aman, Mark Attar, Joseph D'Auria, Michael Jamroz, Sharmini Mahendran, and Hemant Sharma for very helpful discussions or other input. Finally, I thank the University of Pennsylvania Law School and Waseda University Law School for generous research support. Any errors, of course, are mine.

1 UNIDROIT Convention on Substantive Rules for Intermediated Securities of 9 October 2009, see Appendix. For background on the Convention, see Mooney and Kanda, 'Core Issues'; Mooney, *Law and Systems for Intermediated Securities*. In connection with the Convention I served as a member of the United States (US) delegation at the four meetings of experts in Rome (May 2005, March 2006, November 2006, and May 2007) and at the 2008 and 2009 first and second sessions of the diplomatic conference in Geneva. Also, I served as a member of the drafting committee (representing the US) at each of the experts' meetings and at both sessions of the diplomatic conference. However, the views expressed in this paper do not necessarily reflect the position of the United States or any other member of the United States' delegation.

2 Final Act of the final session of the diplomatic conference to Adopt a Convention on Substantive Rules Regarding Intermediated Securities, UNIDROIT 2009, CONF 11/2 – Doc 41, available at www.unidroit.org/english/workprogramme/study078/item1/conference2009/main.htm.

3 The negotiation and drafting process also overcame what in my view was the outright hostility to and obstruction of the project on the part of one influential state participant,

differing normative positions in some respects parallel (and, perhaps, have resulted in) vast differences in the legal doctrine affecting intermediated securities holding systems among the various states. In addition to these normative and doctrinal variations, there also are differences in market structures among the states.[4] These differences were overcome in large part through the 'functional approach' employed in the Convention.[5]

This chapter addresses one of the core issues on which widely differing views are reflected by the regulatory policies of the various states – the duty of an intermediary to have on hand sufficient securities to cover the credits that the intermediary has made to the securities accounts of its account holders.[6] To be sure, no state took the position that no such duty should exist. Rather, the principal differences lie at the margin, primarily concerning the degree of flexibility that should be afforded intermediaries and their account holders and the degree to which (and the manner in which) extensions of credit and other transactions should be accommodated.

Section 7.2 briefly surveys a variety of causes of so-called 'shortfalls' in securities credited to securities accounts. For present purposes, a shortfall exists when the number or value of a given issue of a security credited

namely France. Rather than belabour the point with a listing of examples, I think it is quite appropriate simply to take judicial notice of that behaviour. See *Black's Law Dictionary* (9th edn., 2009) (defining 'judicial notice' as '[a] court's acceptance, for purposes of convenience and without requiring a party's proof, of a well-known and indisputable fact').

4 A political economy basis for some of these structural differences may exist. For example, a top-down revamping of the securities holding system would probably not find support in the US because of the various vested interests of market participants which would be adversely affected. See, e.g., Mooney, 'Property, Credit, and Regulation Meet Information Technology', 131 at 155 (suggesting that proposals for directly connecting investors with the registration books of issuers would be successfully resisted by entrenched interests who pass on costs to investors, even if the proposed system would enhance efficiency). In Japan, on the other hand, a more or less top-down restructuring was achieved. See Mooney and Kanda, 'Core Issues' at 81–2 (discussing Japan's Book-Entry Transfer Act, Act No. 75 of 2001, as amended in 2002 (Act No. 65 of 2002) and 2004 (Act No. 88 of 2004)).

5 See Mooney and Kanda, 'Core Issues' at 75: 'This functional approach is based on the idea that the Convention should specify the operative results that arise in transactions and settings within its scope, but should not attempt to override (and harmonize among states) the whole of the underlying domestic legal doctrine that is the vehicle for producing those results. For example, Art. 9 of the Convention . . . spells out the rights that are conferred on an account holder by the credit of securities to a securities account. However, it leaves the legal characterization of those rights – such as the nature of any property interest acquired by the account holder – to the non-Convention law.'

6 In this chapter I generally adopt the terminology used in the Convention. See Convention Art. 1(a) (defining 'securities'), 1(b) (defining 'intermediated securities'), 1(c) (defining 'securities account'), 1(d) (defining 'intermediary'), 1(e) (defining 'account holder').

to an intermediary's account holders exceeds the number or amount that the intermediary holds. These causes run from the administrative error or mistake, to the nefarious. Some causes also are inherent in market structures and the processes for clearance and settlement. Section 7.3 examines the approach toward the intermediary's duties concerning shortfalls, in turn, under the Convention, under US law, and under the emerging principles for potential European legislation on securities holding. The discussion in section 7.3 recognises that it is in an insolvency proceeding of an intermediary that shortfalls have a material impact on the recoveries of the intermediary's account holders. For that reason, section 7.3 also, and necessarily, examines the treatment of shortfalls in the event of an intermediary insolvency under the Convention, US law, and the draft European principles. Finally, section 7.4 concludes the chapter.

7.2 Causes of shortfall: the good, the bad, and the ugly

Before turning to the legal frameworks for dealing with shortfalls in securities credited to securities accounts, it is useful to provide a brief description of some of the causes and contexts of such shortfalls. Two significant contributors to shortfalls are discussed in more detail in section 7.3.[7] First, an intermediary may fail to receive from a securities settlement system securities that it is entitled to receive on behalf of its account holders (a 'fail to receive', or simply a 'fail').[8] Typically, a fail to receive is caused by another settlement system participant's 'fail to deliver'.[9] In this situation it is the practice of broker-dealers in the United States to credit the securities accounts of account holders entitled to receive such securities on a settlement date, notwithstanding the creation of a shortfall arising out of a fail.[10]

Second, intermediaries, such as broker-dealers in the United States, may (subject to certain legal and regulatory restrictions and limitations) 'use' securities of their account holders. This use may consist of the 'repledge' of account holder securities to secure a loan made to an intermediary or the lending of account holder securities to a securities

7 See below pp. 169–71, 179 (discussing fails to receive securities); below pp. 170, 172–7, 179, 181, 185, 187 (discussing pledge, repledge, and lending and borrowing of securities).

8 See Mooney, *Law and Systems for Intermediated Securities*, at 104–20 (discussing clearance and settlement in the United States and Japanese securities markets).

9 For a more detailed treatment of fails to receive and fails to deliver in the United States and Japanese markets, *ibid.* at 110–16.

10 *Ibid.*

borrower.[11] As a result of such use the relevant securities may be entirely unavailable to the intermediary, although the relevant account holders' accounts are not correspondingly debited.[12]

Finally, shortfalls may result from a myriad of possible errors and omissions. These would include clerical and administrative errors, accounting errors arising from technology failures, and even fraud.

7.3 Shortfall under the Geneva Securities Convention, US law (as the non-Convention law), and the draft European principles

7.3.1 Past as prologue

In 1988 I arrived in Tokyo for a four-month stay as a visiting scholar at the Bank of Japan's Institute for Monetary and Economic Studies. I had one central question to investigate under Japanese law: 'If a Japanese securities firm or bank fails and there are insufficient securities on hand to satisfy the claims to securities credited to securities accounts of its account holders, what result?'[13] I received essentially the same answer from lawyers, bankers, central bankers, and academics alike: 'Japanese firms do not fail.' Perhaps this was an understandable response at (what later turned out to be) the peak of the Japanese bubble economy. Perhaps it also was a polite manner of making the point that my research seemed to be irrelevant.

Within a few years it became clear that my question was important and that the responses I received were inadequate.[14] This section and also section 7.4 focus on one significant aspect of the question that I raised in Japan many years ago – the nature and durability of the property rights conferred by a credit of securities to a securities account.

11 See below pp. 170, 172–7, 179, 181, 185, 187 (discussing repledge and securities lending).

12 *Ibid.*

13 Two products of this research (and my research immediately before and after my time in Japan) were Mooney, 'Beyond Negotiability'and Mooney and Kinami, 'Transfer, Pledge, Clearance and Settlement in the Japanese and United States Government Securities Markets'. A somewhat broader variation of my question would be: 'Just what is it that an account holder receives upon a credit of securities to its securities account?'

14 See Bank for International Settlements, *Bank Failures in Mature Economies*, at 7–14 (describing the Japanese banking crisis of the 1990s and various failures of banks and securities firms). More recently, Japan has thoroughly revamped its legal regime for intermediated securities. Mooney and Kanda, 'Core Issues' at 81–2.

7.3.2 The Convention approach

The Convention specifies the rights of account holders and the corresponding duties of intermediaries.[15] Article 9(1) specifies the rights conferred on an account holder by a credit made to the account holder's securities account. In general Article 9(1) describes the package of economic benefits, including voting rights, that one acquiring an interest in securities would expect to receive.[16] The Convention places various duties on intermediaries that correspond to the account holder rights specified in Article 9(1). Article 10(1) imposes a general duty; it requires an intermediary, with certain exceptions, to 'take appropriate measures to enable its account holders to receive and exercise the rights specified in Article 9(1)'.[17] The Convention also imposes additional, more specific obligations on intermediaries. For example, Article 23 addresses an intermediary's duty to act on instructions of its account holder.[18]

Of particular interest here is Article 24(1), which requires an intermediary to hold or have available securities and intermediated securities sufficient to cover securities credited to its account holders' accounts.[19] More specifically, under that provision '[a]n intermediary must, for each description of securities, hold or have available securities and

15 Section 7.3.2 draws substantially on Mooney, 'Private Law and the Regulation of Securities Intermediaries'.

16 Art. 9(1) provides: 'The credit of securities to a securities account confers on the account holder: (a) the right to receive and exercise any rights attached to the securities, including dividends, other distributions and voting rights: (i) if the account holder is not an intermediary or is an intermediary acting for its own account; and (ii) in any other case, if so provided by the non-Convention law; (b) the right to effect a disposition under Art. 11 or grant an interest under Art. 12; (c) the right, by instructions to the relevant intermediary, to cause the securities to be held otherwise than through a securities account, to the extent permitted by the applicable law, the terms of the securities and, to the extent permitted by the non-Convention law, the account agreement or the uniform rules of a securities settlement system; (d) unless otherwise provided in this Convention, such other rights, including rights and interests in securities, as may be conferred by the non-Convention law.' Art. 9(2) provides (implicitly) that the account holder may exercise the Art. 9(1) rights (subject to specified limitations) against the 'relevant intermediary'. Convention Art. 9(2)(b), (c). The account holder's rights under Art. 9(1) 'are effective against third parties'. Convention Art. 9(2)(a).

17 Convention Art. 10(1). There are exceptions to the intermediary's obligations under Art. 10(1). For example, an intermediary is not required to take any action that is not within its power or to establish a securities account with another intermediary. Convention Art. 10(3).

18 Convention Art. 23.

19 Convention Art. 24(1). Under Art. 25 an intermediary must allocate securities and intermediated securities to its account holders so as to comply with Art. 24(1). Convention Art. 25(1).

intermediated securities' sufficient to cover securities of each such description credited to the accounts of its account holders.[20] Article 24(1) speaks in absolute terms: it requires a strict and inflexible matching by an intermediary of securities credited to its account holders' accounts and securities and intermediated securities that it must hold or have available for its account holders. On its face, the provision is unforgiving.

Notwithstanding the facially absolute requirement to hold sufficient securities, imposed by Article 24(1), by virtue of the operation of Article 28 the requirement achieves necessary flexibility and harmony with the non-Convention law. As I have explained in some detail elsewhere,[21] the Convention offers considerable deference to the non-Convention law in connection with the duties of an intermediary and an intermediary's compliance with analogous duties under the non-Convention law.[22] Section 7.3.3.2 explains that an intermediary's compliance with the SEC's customer protection rules under United States law results in compliance with Article 24(1), even if a shortfall exists.[23]

7.3.3 The US approach: application of the Convention with US law as the non-Convention law

7.3.3.1 Protection of account holders from shortfall under US law

US law dealing with intermediated securities is both federal law and state law. The principal state law is the Uniform Commercial Code ('UCC'),

20 Convention Art. 24(1). Under United States law, complex 'customer protection' rules applicable to broker-dealers address the same concerns that Art. 24(1) addresses – the availability of sufficient securities to cover account holder ('customer') claims to securities credited to securities accounts. See generally Hazen and Markham, *Broker-Dealer Operations*, §§ 5.2–5.7 (updated 2010) (discussing protection of customers' free credit balances, securities possession and control requirements, restrictions on hypothecation of customer securities, and segregation requirements). These rules are discussed below, pp. 166–75 (discussing US customer protection rules). For a more detailed treatment, see Jamroz, 'The Customer Protection Rule'.

21 See Mooney, *Private Law*, at 807–13 (explaining the operation of Art. 28 in the context of conflicts between intermediary duties under the Convention and those under the non-Convention law).

22 See Art. 28(1), which provides: 'The obligations of an intermediary under this Convention, including the manner in which an intermediary complies with its obligations, may be specified by the non-Convention law and, to the extent permitted by the non-Convention law, the account agreement or the uniform rules of a securities settlement system.'

23 See Art. 28(2), which provides: 'If the substance of any such obligation is specified by the non-Convention law or, to the extent permitted by the non-Convention law, the account agreement or the uniform rules of a securities settlement system, compliance with it satisfies that obligation.'

Articles 8 (Investment Securities) and 9 (Secured Transactions).[24] Under UCC section 8–504, an intermediary has a general obligation to maintain sufficient securities to cover the credits made to the securities accounts of its account holders.[25] This obligation is not absolute, however. If an intermediary's duty under UCC Article 8 (such as that under section 8–504) is the subject of another statute or regulation, then compliance with that other law is compliance with the UCC duty.[26] The relevant regulatory regime for a registered broker-dealer[27] in the US is the Securities Exchange Act of 1934 and regulations issued by the Securities and Exchange Commission ('SEC') under that Act.[28] In particular, the applicable 'customer protection' rule is SEC Rule 15c3–3 ('Customer protection – reserves and custody of securities').[29] An intermediary's compliance with that rule, then, would constitute compliance with UCC section 8–504.[30] Indeed,

24 The UCC is a 'uniform law'. Its sponsors are the National Conference of Commissioners on Uniform State Laws and The American Law Institute. To be precise, a uniform law such as the UCC is not a 'law'; it is a model promulgated with the expectation that the various states will enact it. It actually becomes a law only when and if adopted by a state. UCC Arts. 8 and 9 have been enacted in every state in substantially uniform form.

25 UCC § 8–504(a). Section 8–504(a) provides: 'A securities intermediary shall promptly obtain and thereafter maintain a financial asset in a quantity corresponding to the aggregate of all security entitlements it has established in favor of its entitlement holders with respect to that financial asset. The securities intermediary may maintain those financial assets directly or through one or more other securities intermediaries.' Defined terms in Article 8 include (with their rough equivalents in the Convention terminology mentioned parenthetically): 'financial assets,' UCC § 8–102(a)(9) (securities); 'security entitlement,' UCC § 8–102(a)(17) (intermediated securities); 'securities account,' UCC § 8–501(a) (securities account); 'securities intermediary,' UCC § 8–102(a)(14) (intermediary); 'entitlement holder,' UCC § 8–102(a)(8) (account holder). For convenience, however, this discussion of US law uses the Convention terminology. For a broader discussion of intermediary duties under the Convention, see Mooney and Kanda, 'Core Issues' at 87–94.

26 UCC § 9–509(a). That subsection provides: 'If the substance of a duty imposed upon a securities intermediary by Sections 8–504 through 8–508 is the subject of other statute, regulation, or rule, compliance with that statute, regulation, or rule satisfies the duty.'

27 See 15 USC § 78c(a)(4) (defining 'broker'), (a)(5) (defining 'dealer'); 15 USC § 78o(a)(1 (requirement for broker or dealer to register).

28 15 USC § 78A *et seq.* See generally Guttman, *Modern Securities Transfers* § 4.10.

29 17 CFR § 240.15c3–3.

30 UCC § 8–509(a); see UCC § 8–504, Comment 5: 'This section [8–504] necessarily states the duty of a securities intermediary to obtain and maintain financial assets only at the very general and abstract level. For the most part, these matters are specified in great detail by regulatory law. Broker-dealers registered under the federal securities laws are subject to detailed regulation concerning the safeguarding of customer securities. See 17 C.F.R. § 240.15c3–3. Section 8–509(a) provides explicitly that if a securities intermediary complies with such regulatory law, its compliance also constitutes compliance with Section 8–504.'

UCC section 8–509 was the model on which the US based its proposal for what became Article 28(2) of the Convention.[31]

The basic operative rule on maintaining securities for a broker-dealer's account holders is found in subsection (b), paragraph (1) of Rule 15c3–3, which provides: 'Physical possession or control of securities. A broker or dealer shall promptly obtain and shall thereafter maintain the physical possession or control of all fully-paid securities and excess margin securities carried by a broker or dealer for the account of customers.'[32] Although seemingly straightforward, the devil is in the rule's details and definitions.

'Fully paid securities' are securities credited to a securities account for which the account holder has made full payment and in which the broker-dealer does not have a security interest.[33] The definition of 'excess margin securities' is a bit more complicated. First, 'margin securities' are securities other than fully paid securities and which are credited to a securities account (a 'margin account').[34] Unlike the case of fully paid securities, the broker-dealer does have a security interest in margin securities to secure the account holder's debt obligations to the broker-dealer. Fully paid securities may be credited to a 'cash account', as to which the broker-dealer does not have a security interest.[35] Securities credited to a margin account also may be fully paid securities if there is no secured obligation outstanding. 'Excess margin securities', then, are

31 Art. 28(2) follows closely a draft provision proposed by the United States delegation at the fourth session of the committee on governmental experts. See UNIDROIT 2007, Study LXXVIII – Doc. 91 (May 2007); see above, p. 165; below, pp. 182–5, 188–9, 191 (discussing Art. 28).

32 17 CFR § 240.15C3–3(b)(1). Rule 15c3–3(b)(1) applies only to 'securities carried by a broker or dealer for the account of *customers*.' *Ibid.* (emphasis added). '[C]ustomer' is a defined term and the securities carried for customers are 'customer securities', also a defined term. 17 CFR § 240.15C3–3(a)(1) (defining 'customer'), (2) (defining 'customer securities'). Note however, that the text generally embraces the Convention's terminology by referring to 'account holders'. In the context of Rule 15c3–3, however, 'account holder' should be read to mean 'customer'.

33 17 CFR § 240.15C3–3(a)(3) (defining 'fully paid securities'). This discussion of the customer protection rules omits some detail for convenience of explanation, but without detracting from the points made.

34 17 CFR § 240.15C3–3(a)(4) (defining 'margin securities').

35 An exception to the statement in the text exists in the case of an automatic, statutory security interest in favour of an intermediary when it credits an account holder's account before payment is made by the account holder. Such a security interest secures the account holder's obligation to pay for the securities that have been so credited. UCC § 9–206.

Table 7.1 *A Co. margin securities – calculation of excess margin securities*

Market value	= $200.
Secured debt	= $100.
140% × $100	= $140.
MV in excess of $140 ($200 – $140)	= $ 60.

margin securities with 'a market value in excess of 140 percent of' the account holder's secured obligation to the broker dealer.[36]

An example will aid in the explanation of the concept and the treatment of excess margin securities. Assume that Account Holder (AH) has credited to its margin account with Broker-Dealer (B-D) securities of A Co. with a market value of $200.[37] The debt that AH owes to B-D secured by the A securities is $100. Assume further that AH has credited to its cash account with B-D fully paid securities of D Co. with a market value of $100. The excess margin securities are those with a market value in excess of 140 per cent of the $100 secured debt, or those with a value in excess of $140. It follows that AH's excess margin securities are A securities valued at $60. This calculation of excess margin securities is presented in Table 7.1.

It is the $100 value of the D securities (fully paid securities) and the $60 in value of the A securities (excess margin securities) that B-D must have in its physical possession or control under Rule 15c3–3(b)(1). B-D has satisfied its possession or control obligation because the $100 value of the D securities and the $60 value of the A securities (and the securities of B-D's other account holders who hold fully paid and excess margin D securities and A securities in their accounts with B-D) are credited to B-D's account with the Depositary Trust Company ('DTC'), the principal central securities depository in the United States.[38]

36 17 CFR § 240.15C3–3(a)(4) (defining 'excess margin securities'). Actually, the definition refers to 'a market value in excess of 140 per cent of the total of the debit balances in the customer's' margin accounts. For ease of explanation this discussion assumes that the only component of the relevant customers' debit balances are the secured obligations owed to the broker dealer.

37 To simplify the discussion the example assumes that the securities retain the same market value at all relevant times.

38 An account with a central securities depository is a permissible control location for securities that are not in a broker-dealer's physical possession. 17 CFR § 15c3–3(c)(1).

On each business day a broker-dealer must calculate whether, as of the previous business day, it was in compliance with the possession or control requirement of Rule 15c3–3(b)(1).[39] However, there are some exceptions to the possession or control requirement for fully paid and excess margin securities. For example, a broker-dealer is not in violation of Rule 15c3–3(b) if there are 'temporary lags' between the time that the broker-dealer is required to obtain possession or control and the time that possession or control is achieved.[40] However, this exception is available only if the lags occur 'solely as a result of normal business operations' and the broker-dealer 'takes timely steps in good faith to' obtain 'prompt' possession or control.[41] A broker-dealer's failure to receive securities at settlement because of another person's failure to deliver is an example of a qualifying 'temporary lag'. A broker-dealer also does not violate the possession or control requirement if it borrows fully paid or excess margin securities from its account holders, subject to stringent protections.[42]

Rule 15c3–3 also imposes some specific curative obligations that apply when a broker-dealer is not in compliance with the possession or control requirement. If the broker-dealer has securities of the issue and class (i.e., same type or kind) for which any shortfall exists and such securities are not in qualified control locations, the broker must take certain steps to obtain control or possession within specified times. For example, if the relevant securities are subject to a security interest securing a loan of

Examples of other permissible control locations are a broker-dealer's omnibus account with another broker dealer, 17 CFR § 240.15c3–3(c)(2), the custody of a foreign depository or custodian bank, 17 CFR § 240.15c3–3(c)(4), or the custody of a bank, 17 CFR § 240.15c3–3(c)(5). DTC is a wholly owned subsidiary of the Depository Trust and Clearing Corporation ('DTCC').

39 17 CFR § 240.15c3–3(d). The calculation may be made not less than weekly for inactive margin accounts.

40 17 CFR § 240.15c3–3(b)(2).

41 *Ibid.* The broker-dealer has the burden of proof to show that its failure to obtain possession or control is 'merely temporary and solely the result of normal business operations' and that it 'has taken timely steps in good faith to' obtain possession or control. *Ibid.* As discussed below, compliance with Rule 15c3–3 is also compliance with Art. 24 of the Convention, notwithstanding such temporary shortfalls. See below, pp. 21–2.

42 17 CFR § 240.15c3–3(b)(3). The borrowing must be supported by high-grade collateral and must be marked to market at least daily. The broker-dealer also must notify a lending account holder that as a result of the borrowing the account holder may not be entitled to investor insurance protection under the Securities Investor Protection Act (SIPA), 15 USC §§ 78aaa–111. *Ibid.* SIPA is briefly discussed below at pp. 171, 176–7, 180–1, 185–8, 191. While a qualifying borrowing allows the broker-dealer to deviate from the possession or control requirement, it normally does not represent a 'shortfall' inasmuch as the account holder's securities account normally is debited for the borrowed securities.

funds to the broker-dealer or if the securities have been loaned by the broker-dealer to another broker-dealer or a clearing corporation,[43] the broker-dealer must obtain the release of the securities from the security interest or the return of the loaned securities. The broker-dealer must give instruction for such a release or return on the business day following its determination of noncompliance.[44] The broker-dealer then must obtain possession or control of the securities within two business days following the instructions in the case of a security interest or within five business days in the case of securities loaned.[45] In the case of relevant securities that are fails to receive for more than thirty calendar days, the broker dealer must 'take prompt steps' to obtain possession or control 'through a buy-in procedure or otherwise.'[46] The same obligation applies if the relevant securities are 'securities receivable' as a result of a securities dividend or the like.[47]

In all of these cases of shortfall, whether the broker-dealer is in compliance with Rule 15c3–3(b)(1) (as in the case of temporary lags, for example[48]) or not, the broker dealer either enters a credit in favour of an account holder or does not debit an account holder's account, notwithstanding the shortfall that is created or that exists. Consider the example of fails to deliver. Assume that as a result of another clearing organisation participant's failure to deliver A Co. securities at settlement, a broker dealer (B-D) fails to receive all of the A Co. securities to which it is entitled on a settlement date. Meanwhile, B-D's account holder (AH) had placed a buy order to be settled on the same settlement date. By crediting AH's account with the A Co. securities, B-D will create a shortfall in A Co. securities. In the US the credit would be made and the shortfall created.[49] Moreover, even if the credit book-entry were not made, because

43 In a securities lending transaction the lender transfers outright ownership of securities to the borrower and the borrower agrees to redeliver like securities to the lender at an agreed time in the future. For discussions of various issues concerning securities lending, see Securities and Exchange Commission, Securities Lending and Short Sale Roundtable (20 September 2009), available at www.sec.gov/news/openmeetings/2009/roundtable-transcript-092909.pdf.

44 17 CFR § 240.15c3–3(d)(1).

45 *Ibid.*

46 17 CFR § 240.15c3–3(d)(2).

47 17 CFR § 240.15c3–3(d)(3).

48 See above p. 169 (discussing lags).

49 As DTCC has explained: '[T]he broker for the buyer does not pay the contractual value for the trade to the clearing system until the stock is delivered, although the broker's customer may be given a security entitlement on the broker's records immediately. That security entitlement is what makes it possible for the markets and investors to buy and sell securities freely throughout the day or over several days. If an investor had to wait until stock was delivered and paid for, they'd have to wait several days to trade that stock again.

AH is entitled to the credit it would have account holder status in B-D's insolvency proceeding.[50] From the normative perspective of treating similarly situated persons in similar fashion in insolvency, this is a desirable result. It is purely fortuitous that the A securities did not arrive in timely fashion. In all other respects the position of AH is no different than other account holders of B-D. As discussed in more detail below, this is a central insight in the treatment of account holders in a broker-dealer insolvency proceeding under US law.[51]

The treatment of AH under the law of some other jurisdictions would be much less generous while providing only slightly better treatment to B-D's other account holders with A Co. securities credited to their accounts.[52] For example, in Japan the credit to AH would not be made in the face of the shortfall that would be created.[53] AH would be a general unsecured creditor in B-D's insolvency proceeding.[54] From the standpoint

Imagine an investor buying a stock in the morning, then finding market information being announced mid-day that might adversely impact that stock and then being told you can't sell out your position to minimize the potential loss. Freedom to trade is a cornerstone of our equity markets and a fundamental principle in the regulatory schemes that govern the markets. The SEC has flatly rejected the argument that there are such things as phantom shares or credits being created in the market.' Press Release, DTCC, *DTCC Responds to The Wall Street Journal Article, 'Blame the "Stock Vault"'* (6 July 2007) [hereinafter, 'DTCC Press Release'].

Stated otherwise, the investor must be in a position to sell, even if, by virtue of a shortfall arising out of a fail to deliver, the investor has not acquired full ownership. The last quoted sentence of the DTCC press release seems difficult to square with the following statement of the SEC staff (depending on the meaning one might give to 'phantom shares or credits'): 'Naked short selling has no effect on an issuer's total shares outstanding. There is significant confusion relating to the fact that *the aggregate number of positions reflected in customer accounts at broker-dealers may in fact be greater than the number of securities issued and outstanding.* This is due in part to the fact that securities intermediaries, such as broker-dealers and banks, credit customer accounts prior to delivery of the securities.For most securities trading in the US market, delivery subsequently occurs as expected. However, fails to deliver can occur for a variety of legitimate reasons, and flexibility is necessary in order to ensure an orderly market and to facilitate liquidity.' SEC, Division of Market Regulation, *Responses to Frequently Asked Questions Concerning Regulation SHO*, Answer to Question 7.1, available at www.sec.gov/divisions/marketreg/mrfaqregsho1204.htm (emphasis added).

50 See SIPA § 78lll(2) (defining 'customer'); see Don and Wang, 'Stockbroker Liquidations'.

51 See below p. 177.

52 The treatment would be only 'slightly better' because the other account holders would not be required to share with AH in the face of any shortfall.

53 See Mooney and Kanda, 'Core Issues' at 86 (explaining that under Japanese law an interest in securities may be acquired only by a credit and that credits are made only if the intermediary has sufficient securities on hand for a perfectly 'matched book').

54 *Ibid.*

of the unlucky, hapless AH, the other account holders avoided a *short*fall, but AH experienced what we might call a '*no*fall' through pure bad luck and fortuity. Explaining persuasively to AH that the idea of avoiding all shortfalls in such a regime is for the protection of account holders would present a substantial challenge.

In addition to the possession or control requirement for fully paid and excess margin securities, there is also a roughly analogous requirement for customer cash balances. A broker-dealer must maintain with a bank or banks a 'Special Reserve Bank Account for the Exclusive Benefit of Customers' ('Reserve Bank Account').[55] A broker-dealer must deposit cash or securities issued by or guaranteed by the US government in amounts calculated from time to time in accordance with a reserve formula.[56] Among the required deposits are 'free credit balances' – funds owed by the broker-dealer to its account holders and payable on demand.[57] As explained in one treatise: 'Rule 15c3–3 permits customer free credit balances to be deployed only in areas of the broker-dealer's business that are related to the servicing of customers. If customer funds are not so employed, they must be deposited in a segregated, specially designated bank account [i.e., the Reserve Bank Account].'[58]

Next consider AH's margin securities that are *not* in excess of 140 per cent of the secured debt – i.e., the *non*-excess margin securities – with a market value of $140. The non-excess margin securities are not subject to the possession or control requirement. It follows that B-D is free to use these securities to generate the funds necessary to fund its extensions of credit to its account holders, such as AH.

One means for a broker-dealer to raise funds by using account holders' securities is a so-called 'repledge' transaction in which the broker-dealer borrows funds from a lender and pledges (i.e., grants a security interest in) the securities as collateral to secure the loan.[59] In the context of the

55 17 CFR § 240.15c3–3(e)(1). A broker-dealer must maintain its Reserve Bank Account 'separate from any other bank account' of the broker-dealer. *Ibid.* In addition, a broker-dealer must obtain from each Reserve Bank Account bank a written notification from the bank stating that the bank was informed that all cash or securities are held in the account for the exclusive benefit of customers of the broker-dealer in accordance with SEC regulations. 17 CFR § 240.15c3–3(f).

56 *Ibid.* The formula is set out at 17 CFR § 240.15c3–3a.

57 '[F]ree credit balances' is defined, in part, as 'liabilities of a broker or dealer to customers which are subject to immediate cash payment to customers on demand.' 17 CFR § 240.15c3–3(a)(8).

58 Hazen and Markham, *Broker-Dealer Operations*, § 5.5.

59 A secured party such as the broker dealer is entitled to create a security interest in collateral that it possesses or controls in favour of a third party (i.e. another secured party). UCC

example, the funds lender-pledgee (secured party) typically would perfect its security interest in the pledged securities by requiring B-D to transfer the securities to the pledgee's account with the pledgee's custodian bank. This might involve a debit (of the A Co. securities) to the DTC account of B-D and a credit to the custodian bank's DTC account, followed by a corresponding credit to the pledgee's account with the custodian bank.[60]

Subsequent to B-D's pledge of the A Co. securities the pledgee might then lend the securities to a third party in a securities lending transaction.[61] At that point B-D would have lost all connection to the A Co. securities. Those securities simply would be 'gone' as far as B-D is concerned. In exchange for these pledged securities B-D would receive a bundle of contractual rights against its pledgee. These would include the right to the return of A Co. securities upon discharge of B-D's secured indebtedness, including the return of any excess A Co. securities after the pledgee satisfied B-D's indebtedness by enforcing its security interest against the securities. In effect, B-D has acquired a derivative contract issued by the pledgee measured by the value of the A Co. securities to be redelivered by the pledgee. But note once again that although the A Co. securities are gone, B-D does not debit AH's account (or those of other account holders); the account continues to reflect a credit balance for all of AH's A Co. securities with a market value of $200. Because the A Co. securities have been removed from B-D's account at DTC, however, a shortfall has been created.

The foregoing repledge example contemplates a shortfall in respect of the pledged customer securities, which are no longer on hand. But the customer protection rules compensate for the shortfall in two respects. First, B-D's borrowings must be entered as a credit in the formula for calculating of B-D's Reserve Bank Account for the direct benefit of its account holders.[62] Second, there is a significant limitation on B-D's ability

§ 9–207(c)(3). See generally Kettering, 'Repledge Deconstructed'; Kettering, 'Repledge and Pre-Default Sale of Securities Collateral Under Revised Art. 9'.

60 Of course, the lender itself might be B-D's custodian bank, in which case all entries would be on the books of DTC. Alternatively, but less common, B-D's DEC account might be debited for the A securities and credited to the lender's DTC 'pledge account' on the books of DTC, although B-D would continue to be identified in the DTC records as the pledgor. See the Depository Trust Company, Rules, By-Laws and Organization Certificate, at 48–55, available at www.dtcc.com/legal/rules_proc/dtc_rules.pdf; the Depository Trust Company, Procedures (Service Guide on Settlement) at 8–10 available at www.dtcc.com/downloads/products/learning/Settlement.pdf.

61 See above, p. 170, below pp. 173–5, 185, 187 (discussing securities lending).

62 17 CFR § 240.15c3–3a (Exhibit A-Formula for Determination of Reserve Requirement of Brokers and Dealers Under Rule 15c3–3), Item 2. ('Monies borrowed collateralized by

to repledge account holders' margin securities which also ameliorates the risks of such a shortfall to account holders. Under SEC regulations, B-D is not permitted to pledge its account holders' securities to secure indebtedness in an amount 'which exceeds the aggregate indebtedness of all customers in respect of securities carried for their accounts' (the 'hypothecation restriction').[63] While B-D is permitted to pledge *all* of its account holders' non-excess margin securities (i.e., with a value of 140 per cent of each account holder's secured obligations), the pledged margin securities may not secure more than the sum of all of the account holders' secured obligations. But note what the hypothecation restriction does not provide. It does not restrict B-D from pledging AH's margin securities to secure more than AH's individual secured obligation.

There is another, more typical, method by which B-D may raise funds by using its account holders' margin securities – securities lending. In a typical transaction the borrower of securities might use the securities to make a delivery under a short sale.[64] As a lender of its account holders' securities, a broker-dealer would normally receive cash collateral from the securities borrower to secure the borrower's obligation to redeliver like securities to the broker-dealer.[65] Securities lending, unlike a repledge transaction, is not subject to the hypothecation restriction.[66] However,

securities carried for the accounts of customers'); see Jamroz, 'The customer protection rule' at 1100 ('the broker-dealer includes [as a credit] the amount of customer securities pledged to banks for loans'). Debit and credit amounts used in calculating the required balance in the Reserve Bank Account should not be confounded with debit and credit entries to *securities accounts* of an intermediary's account holders.

63 17 CFR § 240.8c-1(a)(3). This rule applies to members of a national securities exchange and broker-dealers that transact securities business through such members. A rule that is identical in substance applies to all other registered broker-dealers. 17 CFR § 240.15c2–1(a)(3). Note that the definitions of 'customer' for purposes of the hypothecation restriction is broader than the corresponding definition in Rule 15c3–3. The latter excludes from its definition a 'broker or dealer, a municipal securities dealer, or a government securities broker or government securities dealer.' 17 CFR § 240.15c3–3(a)(1).

64 In a short sale, a seller is betting that the value of the subject securities will fall and the seller sells securities that it does not own. In order to make delivery of the securities to the buyer, the seller typically 'borrows' the securities from a securities lender. The seller hopes to acquire the same securities at a lower price in the future in order to return them to the lender.

65 Securities lending transaction in the US typically are documented using the standard Master Securities Loan Agreement developed by the Securities Industry and Financial Markets Association (SIFMA). See www.sifma.org/Services/Standard-Forms-and-Documentation/MRA,-GMRA,-MSLA-and-MSFTAs/.

66 See Jamroz, 'The customer protection rule' at 1100 n.197 ('The application of the hypothecation rules, however, have been interpreted by the Commission to be limited to funds

the cash collateral received must be entered as a credit in the formula for calculating of B-D's Reserve Bank Account.[67] As Jamroz has explained: '[T]he broker-dealer includes the greater of the amount of cash collateral the broker-dealer has received (and is required to return) for customer securities it has loaned and the market value of the customer securities loaned.'[68] In effect this means that funds received from lending account holders' securities may be used only to fund financing for account holders or otherwise in connection with account holder transactions.

The operation of the hypothecation restriction can be illustrated best with an example. But it is first necessary to take account of the role of the distributional rules that would be applicable in the case of B-D's insolvency. On any given day, the nature of an account holder's interest (and the effects of any shortfalls) can be assessed meaningfully *only* by determining the treatment that would be afforded the account holder in its intermediary's insolvency proceeding. As I observed more than twenty years ago:

> If the intermediary remains financially viable, the claimant [i.e., account holder] obtains the indirect benefits of ownership of the securities. If the intermediary fails, the claimant has a priority claim, shared ratably with other similarly situated claimants and measured by a fungible bulk of securities that may or may not be sufficient to satisfy those claims.[69]

Stated otherwise, if the intermediary does not fail, the account holder will receive the economic benefits of the securities credited to its account, *regardless* of any past, existing, or future shortfall. If the intermediary fails, the account holder will receive its distributional entitlement applicable in the insolvency proceeding. There are two and only two possibilities for the intermediary. It will fail or it will not fail.

obtained by the firm by pledging securities as collateral under a loan. It does not cover funds obtained by the firm by lending customer securities, through repurchase agreements or other uses that do not involve loans.').

67 17 CFR § 240.15c3–3a (Exhibit A – Formula for Determination of Reserve Requirement of Brokers and Dealers Under Rule 15c3–3), Item 3 ('Monies payable against customers' securities loaned').

68 Jamroz, 'The customer protection rule' at 1100. A broker-dealer's transfer of margin securities in a repo transaction and receipt of collateral (such as cash or cash equivalents) would receive the same treatment as its lending of securities against collateral. *Ibid.* fn.197. In a repo transaction a seller (in this context, the broker-dealer) transfers securities to a buyer and the buyer promises to repurchase the securities a specified time in the future. See generally Weiss, *After the Trade is Made*, 345–52 (discussing repos as financing devices).

69 Mooney, 'Beyond Negotiability' at 311.

Table 7.2 *Holdings of BD's account holders*

	AH-1	AH-2	AH-3	AH-4
Fully paid sec.	D Co. $100	E Co. $100	F Co. $100	G Co. $100
Margin sec.	A Co. 200	B Co. 200	C Co. 200	None
Secured debt	100	100	100	None
Excess marg. sec.	60	60	60	None
Non-excess mar. sec.	140	140	140	None

Assume that B-D has only four account holders, AH-1, AH-2, AH-3, and AH-4. AH-1 has the same holdings and secured indebtedness as AH in the earlier example: $200 market value of A Co. margin securities, $100 secured indebtedness, and $100 market value of D Co. fully paid securities. AH-2 and AH-3 have B Co. and C Co. margin securities, respectively, each with a $200 value. Like AH-1, AH-2 and AH-3 each has a $100 secured debt obligation to B-D. AH-2 has fully paid E Co. securities with a $100 value and AH-3 has fully paid F Co. securities also with a $100 value. AH-4 has only fully paid G Co. securities with a value of $100. These account holdings are illustrated in Table 7.2.

Assume further that B-D has borrowed $300 from Bank. This is the aggregate amount of all of B-D's account holders' secured debt, and the maximum that the hypothecation restriction allows B-D to secure with its account holders' margin securities. B-D has pledged to Bank all of the B Co. and C Co. non-excess margin securities, a value of $280, and A Co. securities valued at $50, for a total collateral value of $330. Finally, assume that B-D becomes subject to an insolvency proceeding under SIPA and (for simplification) that distributions are instantly and costlessly made to its account holders.

Before turning to the distributions to B-D's account holders under SIPA, it is useful to consider first their positions outside of the SIPA scheme. (This analysis assumes that Bank immediately applied the $280 of value of the B Co. and C Co. and $20 of the value of the A Co. securities to discharge the $300 B-D indebtedness,[70] returning to B-D the additional $30 in value of A Co.) AH-1 has credited to its account $200 in value of A Co. and $100 in value of D Co. B-D has on hand the $100 value of D Co.

70 For simplicity, these calculations and the calculations below concerning B-D's secured loans to AH-1, AH-2, and AH-3 ignore interest on the loans.

but has only $180 value of A Co. (the $60 excess margin, the $90 that was not pledged to Bank, and the $30 that Bank returned). This would appear to leave AH-1 with a $20 shortfall as to the A Co. AH-2 has credited to its account the $200 in value of B Co. and the $100 in value of the E Co. B-D has on hand the $100 value of E Co. but only the $60 excess margin of B Co., as Bank enforced against the $140 of B Co. that was pledged. That would seem to present AH-2 with a $140 shortfall for the B Co. AH-3 is in the same position as AH-2 with respect to the F Co. and C Co – the F Co. is on hand but there is a $140 shortfall in the C Co. What this analysis does not consider, however, is the $100 of secured debt that each of the three margin account holders owe to B-D. AH-4 has no shortfall as all $100 in value of G Co. is on hand.

While B-D is obliged to provide its account holders with the securities credited to their accounts, its account holders are obliged to repay their secured debt. Consider the arithmetic. If B-D offsets against the $200 value of A Co. the $100 of AH-1 debt, then B-D must provide to AH-1 only $100 value of A Co. – and B-D has available $180 of A Co. Similarly as to AH-2 and AH-3, when each $100 debt is offset against the $200 value of B Co. and C Co., B-D must provide those account holders $100 value each. That reduces the AH-2 and AH-3 $140 shortfalls to a $40 shortfall each – and the additional $80 value of A Co. is available to satisfy those shortfalls. In the simplest terms, this is the insight that underlies the SIPA distributional scheme. Account holders' securities are treated as fungible generally, not just on an issue-by-issue basis.

Assume now that B-D is a debtor in a SIPA liquidation proceeding and that its four account holders each file valid claims in the proceeding for all of the securities credited to their respective securities accounts.[71] With the exception of 'customer name securities', which are returned by the trustee to the relevant account holders,[72] all securities that B-D held for its

71 I have simplified the hypothetical in order to focus solely on the allocation of the value of assets to the account holders' claims. Consequently, the hypothetical ignores the Reserve Bank Account, assumes that there are no cash balances in the accounts and that the Securities Investor Protection Corporation ('SIPC') has not made any advances to purchase securities for the benefit of account holders. 15 USC § 78fff-3 (SIPC advances). It also does not take into account SIPC investor insurance coverage, which is available for each account holder for losses up to $500,000 ($250,000 for cash balances). 15 USC § 78fff-3(a). As to these matters, see generally Don and Wang, 'Stockbroker Liquidations'.

72 15 USC § 78*lll*(3) (defining 'customer name securities' to include those registered in or in the process of being registered in the name of a customer, except those in negotiable form, as by way of endorsement). 15 USC § 78fff-2(c)(2) (delivery of customer name securities).

Table 7.3 *B-D's account holders' net equities*

	Filing date			
Name	Value of securities	Cash	Debt	Net equity
AH-1	$300	None	$100	$200
AH-2	$300	None	$100	$200
AH-3	$300	None	$100	$200
AH-4	$100	None	None	$100
Aggregate total net equities:				$700

Table 7.4 *FOCP and pro rata distribution to BD's account holders*

Fund of customer property (FOCP)		Calculation of pro rata shares	
A Co.	$180	Value of FOCP	$700
B Co.	60	Aggregate net equities:	$700 = 100%
C Co.	60		
D Co.	100		
E Co.	100		
F Co.	100		
G Co.	100		
Total value	$700		

account holders become the fund of 'customer property' (FOCP) and are valued as of the filing date of the petition.[73] Each of B-D's account holders will share pro-rata in the FOCP based on its respective 'net equity'.[74] An account holder's net equity is the value of the securities and cash credited to its securities account (whether or not the securities are on hand) less the amount of debt, if any, owed to the broker-dealer.[75]

Calculation of B-D's account holders' net equities is presented in Table 7.3.

Calculation of the FOCP for B-D's account holders and the resulting pro rata distributional share for the account holders is presented in Table 7.4.

73 15 USC § 78*lll*(4) (defining 'customer property').
74 15 USC § 78fff-2(c)(2) (allocation of customer property).
75 15 USC § 78*lll*(11) (defining 'net equity').

In this simple example there are $700 of claims (net equities) and $700 in the FOCP, so each account holder is satisfied in full. This is the case notwithstanding the substantial shortfalls in B Co. and C Co. as a result of the pledge of margin securities to Bank and Bank's recovery on that collateral for B-D's loan. The hypothecation restriction served to protect AH-2 and AH-3 from loss by limiting the amount of secured debt that B-D could collateralise with the account holder securities. And the FOCC approach of pooling all account holder securities allowed those two account holders to recover value from the excess A Co. securities remaining after the deduction of AH-1's secured debt.

Now consider a variation on the example. Assume that because of a fail to receive, B-D has on hand only $100 in value of A Co. securities (the $60 excess margin, the $30 returned by Bank, and $10 that was not pledged to Bank), instead of the $180 value previously assumed.[76] The calculation of net equities would not be affected by this variation inasmuch as only the values credited to account holder accounts and the account holder debt to B-D are taken into account – not the securities that are or are not on hand. A revised calculation of the FOCP for B-D's account holders, the resulting revised *pro rata* distributional share for the account holders, and the distributions of value to each is presented in Table 7.5.

Each of the three margin account holders would receive $177 in value under the revised assumptions. Note that if each margin account holder were to receive only the value of the securities on hand of the types credited to their accounts, AH-2 and AH-3 would receive only $160 each in value, AH-1 would receive $200 in value, and AH-4 would receive $100 in value.[77] That would reflect the fact that AH-2 and AH-3 fell victim to greater shortfalls than AH-1 in their non-excess margin securities.[78]

76 The example implicitly assumes that B-D wholly failed to comply with its obligation in respect of its Reserve Bank Account arising out of the fails to deliver. The reserve formula mandates a credit for the funds that a broker-dealer is required to remit when the deliveries of customer securities are made by other broker-dealers after the settlement date. 17 CFR § 240.15c3–3a (Exhibit A-Formula for Determination of Reserve Requirement of Brokers and Dealers Under Rule 15c3–3), Item 4 ('Customers' securities failed to receive'). Note D to Item 4 also requires an increase to the credit by 'the amount by which the market value of securities failed to receive and outstanding more than thirty calendar days exceeds their contract value.' *Ibid.*, fn. 4.

77 This assumes that the $100 secured debt owed by each account holder to B-D would be set off against $100 in value of their shortfalls in securities that B-D owes to the account holders.

78 This would be the allocation under the UCC's proportionate property interest formulation and under the Convention's insolvency distribution rule. UCC § 8–503(1), (2); Convention Art. 26(2).

Table 7.5 *FOCP and pro rata distribution to BD's account holders (revised)*

Fund of customer property (FOCP)		Calculation of pro rata shares	
A Co.	$100	Value of FOCP	$620
B Co.	60	Aggregate net equities	$700 = 88.571%
C Co.	60		
D Co.	100		
E Co.	100		
F Co.	100		
G Co.	100		
Total value	$620		
Distributions of value			
AH-1	$177		
AH-2	177		
AH-3	177		
AH-4	89		
Total distributions	$620		

Notably, AH-4 would receive $89, although all $100 in value of G Co. is on hand in a permissible control location as required for fully paid securities by Rule 15c3–3(2).[79]

These results illustrate both the admirable aspects of the SIPA distributional scheme as well as a dark side. The concept of all account holders sharing in the value of the fund of customer securities is distinctly egalitarian. The account holders have no control over shortfalls and whether a shortfall occurs as to any particular issue of securities. Fortuity and luck are the determinants from the account holder perspective. Moreover, under the SIPA scheme if there is any shortfall then it bites all of the account holders on the same, pro rata basis. This means that a shortfall will affect all of the account holders. But it also means that it is much less likely that any account holder will experience a large haircut on its claim. The risk is spread among those who have selected the same intermediary and who undertook the same risks.

The dark side is illustrated by the haircut to AH-4's claim to fully paid and properly 'segregated' securities.[80] Account holders who choose

79 See above, pp. 168–9.

80 I use the term 'segregated' with some scepticism. It is true that fully paid securities must be in a broker-dealer's possession or control. But as the example illustrates, in an insolvency

to have margin accounts necessarily embrace the idea that under their account agreements and under the SEC's customer protection rules their non-excess margin securities may be pledged, repledged and loaned, that shortfalls may occur in that connection, and that the broker-dealer is not required to maintain possession of control of those securities. Account holders who choose a cash account (and perhaps those who choose a margin account but also choose not to borrow funds from their broker dealer), arguably should receive different treatment.[81] While their securities cannot be pledged under the customer protection rules, nonetheless they share the burden of any shortfalls in the fund of customer securities under the SIPA distributional scheme.

To put this discussion in perspective, it is necessary to identify the subset of account holders who are exposed to this shortfall risk. Most retail customers are protected against losses up to $500,000 by SIPC ($250,000 for losses as to cash balances).[82] This means that only a *loss resulting from a shortfall* in excess of that amount would expose an account holder to a loss under the SIPA formula. Most institutional investors, on the other hand, employ a commercial bank 'custodian' (translation: a bank 'intermediary') instead of a broker-dealer for maintaining their securities accounts, and the SIPA distributional scheme does not apply to bank insolvencies. However, in recent years, hedge funds have typically used 'prime brokerage' accounts with broker-dealers to facilitate extensions of credit by broker-dealers under the prime brokerage arrangements.[83]

To sum up on the broker-dealer customer protection rules: the combined effect of the possession or control requirement, the hypothecation restriction, and the Reserve Bank Account requirement serves to ensure that a broker-dealer will maintain assets of a value sufficient to protect account holders against any material losses in the case of the broker-dealer insolvency. Although shortfalls are ubiquitous in fact, the Reserve Bank Account addresses the gaps in terms of *value*, though not in terms

proceeding (the only time that possession or control will be relevant for the protection of an account holder), such fully paid securities become a part of the fund of customer securities and are *not* segregated *for* the account holders to whose accounts the securities have been credited.

81 See above, p. 166 and n. 25 (discussing treatment under UCC Art. 8 of account holders who consent to their intermediary's use of account holder securities).

82 15 USC § 78fff-3(a), (d).

83 For information on prime brokerage and hedge funds, see primebrokerageguide.com/2008/10/prime-brokerage-fees-hedge-fund-prime.html.

of strict matching of securities on an issue-by-issue basis.[84] As Jamroz explained:

> Although the specific Reserve Formula allocation practices may vary substantially from firm to firm, the Commission and other self-regulatory examiners appear to have grown comfortable with industry practices as a whole. This comfort may be in part due to the interaction between the possession or control requirement and the Reserve Formula. The examiners are aware that whenever the firm does not obtain possession or control of a customer security, the firm is generally required to set aside funds in the Reserve Formula. In contrast, as mentioned earlier, the Division does not generally allow broker-dealers the option of accepting a higher Reserve Formula deposit requirement in lieu of maintaining possession or control of customer fully-paid and excess margin securities.[85]

7.3.3.2 Compliance with US law as compliance with the Convention

The approach of the US broker-dealer customer protection rules differs significantly from the approach of Convention Article 24(1), which imposes strict issue-by-issue matching of securities and intermediated securities held for account holders with those credited to the accounts of account holders. Given that, does compliance with the US rules constitute compliance with Article 24(1) pursuant to the operation of Article 28(2)? Clearly, the answer is affirmative.[86]

Article 28 reconciles the duties that the Convention imposes on intermediaries with the relevant provisions of the non-Convention law. Article 28(1) generally defers to the non-Convention law with respect to intermediary obligations and compliance.[87] Article 28(1) provides

84 SIPC does not normally make cash distributions on account of customer claims. Instead, it normally acquires securities in the market for distribution in kind on account of these claims. 15 USC § 78fff-2(d).

85 Jamroz, 'The Customer Protection Rule' at 1122. The reference to 'allocation practices' in the quoted passage is to the allocation formulas that are applied to determine which cash and securities transactions relate to customers and which do not. 'The Reserve Formula Allocation is an operationally practical way to address the fact that because money and securities are fungible, it is difficult to determine which balances and transactions are customer-related and which are not. The Reserve Formula Allocation allows the broker-dealer to make assumptions on a conservative basis.' *Ibid.* at 1109.

86 This was the unequivocal answer that I have supplied elsewhere, but with only the briefest of explanation and analysis. See Mooney, 'Private Law', at 811–13. A more detailed explanation follows.

87 Convention Art. 28(1). The initial predecessor provision to Art. 28(1) was proposed by the United States delegation in the course of the drafting process. See UNIDROIT 2006, Study LXXVIII – Doc. 29 (January 2006). The result was Art. 18 of the draft

a safety-valve of sorts for the obligations imposed by the Convention on intermediaries.[88] Article 28(2) both complements and supplements Article 28(1).[89] A principal goal of paragraphs 1 and 2 of Article 28 is to protect an intermediary from the necessity of complying with two different rules or standards. In particular, Article 28(2) recognises that intermediaries are normally regulated entities and it removes the spectre of double regulation – having to comply with two sets of rules that are generally aimed at the same result and which are substantially similar but differ in details.[90] When an intermediary is in compliance with its duties under the non-Convention law (including regulatory constraints), the analogous Convention rules defer to that law pursuant to Article 28(2).

Application of Article 28(2) requires a determination of the circumstances in which 'the substance of any such [Convention] obligation is specified by any provision of the non-Convention law'.[91] When, then, does Article 28(2) apply? Or, when does Article 28(2) *not* apply because a provision of the non-Convention law sufficiently deviates from the Convention standard so that it does not 'specif[y]' the 'substance' of a Convention obligation? A provision of the non-Convention law specifies the substance of a Convention obligation if it meets two criteria. First, the

Convention produced at the second meeting of the committee of governmental experts. See UNIDROIT 2006, Study LXXVIII – Doc. 42 (March 2006).

88 As the Official Commentary explains: 'Art. 28(1) provides that the non-Convention law may specify the content of, and manner of compliance with, an intermediary's Convention obligations. This is consistent with the Convention's functional approach which identifies the results that an intermediary is to achieve but does not specify the details of how an intermediary is to accomplish those results.' Kanda, et. al., Official Commentary on the UNIDROIT Convention on Substantive Rules for Intermediated Securities [hereinafter, Official Commentary], s. 28–11.

89 Convention Art. 28(2). Art. 28(2) follows closely a draft provision proposed by the United States delegation at the fourth session of the committee on governmental experts. See UNIDROIT 2007, Study LXXVIII – Doc. 91 (May 2007), proposing, inter alia, a new Art. 20(1*bis*): 'If the substance of an obligation of an intermediary under this Convention is the subject of any provision of the non-Convention law or, to the extent permitted by the non-Convention law, the account agreement or the uniform rules of a securities settlement system, compliance with that provision satisfies that obligation.'

90 The Official Commentary notes that Art. 28(2) 'relieves intermediaries from the prospect of being subjected to a double standard: a treaty standard and the standard provided or permitted under the non-Convention law.' Kanda et al., Official Commentary, s. 28–12.

91 Convention Art. 28(2). Obviously, the non-Convention law may specify the substance of a Convention obligation even though that law *is not the same as the Convention obligation itself.* Otherwise Art. 28(2) would be meaningless. Stated otherwise, if Art. 28(2) were applicable only when a provision of the non-Convention law is substantively *identical* to a provision in the Convention that imposes an obligation on intermediaries, then Art. 28(2) would accomplish nothing.

provision should require intermediary *conduct* or a *result* that is substantially similar to that required by the Convention obligation. Second, the provision should be aimed at a substantially similar *purpose* and *function* as the Convention obligation.[92]

Clearly the Convention provides broad deference to non-Convention law concerning important aspects of the intermediary-account holder relationships and rejects a one-size-fits-all set of obligations that would override any conflicting rules under the non-Convention law. This is because adoption of harmonised rules on intermediary obligations and duties was not feasible.[93] The legal and regulatory regimes for intermediated securities vary substantially from state to state. Moreover, several states have overhauled and modernised their legal systems for intermediated securities in recent years and these states have little interest in abandoning their reforms for a harmonised international standard. On the other hand, there is considerable value in the Convention's 'default' rules, especially for states without clear, specific laws addressing intermediary obligations.

It would be a great and disingenuous distortion to characterise the operation of Article 28(2) as permitting a 'violation' of the Convention's otherwise absolute obligations imposed on intermediaries.[94] Article 28(2) is the Convention's method of tempering and reconciling those obligations with the applicable law and regulatory framework. Were it not for the approach of Article 28(2), I believe that the Convention's intermediary obligations would look quite different – and no doubt they would be laden with qualifications and exceptions.[95]

92 These are essentially the criteria that Professor Kanda and I speculated might be included as a part of the Official Commentary. See Mooney and Kanda, 'Core Issues' at 90–1, fn. 108: 'Discussions during the final session [of the diplomatic conference] suggest that the discussion in the Draft Official Commentary should be expanded to explain that such a provision would specify the substance of a Convention obligation only if the provision (i) requires intermediary conduct or a result that is substantially similar to that required by the Convention obligation and (ii) is aimed at a substantially similar purpose and function as the Convention obligation. Properly interpreted and applied, Art 28(2) would not permit the non-Convention law, account agreement, or uniform rule to expose account holders to materially greater risks.'

93 *Ibid.* at 91.

94 But see French Comments on the Draft Final Version of the Official Commentary (undated, but provided to me by UNIDROIT in December 2010) at 2 ('However, example 28–2 seems to allow a violation of the Convention, in this case a temporary violation of Art. 24.'); see below, n. 96 (quoting *Official Commentary* Example 28–2).

95 I am confident that the United States would not have supported any such absolute obligations. Or, perhaps more likely, it might have proved impossible to reach any agreement on harmonised standards for intermediary conduct.

As explained above, the US customer protection rules applicable to broker-dealers serve to ensure that in the event of a broker-dealer insolvency there will be sufficient value on hand to satisfy claims of account holders. This is so even in the face of persistent shortfalls. Compliance with these rules obtains results functionally similar to the obligations imposed by Article 24(1) and are aimed at the same purpose, namely the prevention of account holder losses. It follows that compliance with those rules constitutes compliance with Article 24(1) by virtue of Article 28(2).

Notwithstanding mismatches between credits to securities accounts and the securities that are (and are not) on hand, when fairly understood it is highly unlikely that these mismatches create the sort of shortfalls that Article 24(1) is designed to protect against. Keep in mind that the fully paid securities as well as the non-excess margin securities are required to be in the possession or control of a broker-dealer.[96] The excess margin securities, of course, may be the subject of repledge or securities lending transactions discussed in the examples in section 7.3.3.1. But such 'use' of excess margin securities necessarily occurs with the knowledge, permission, and consent of the margin account holders.[97] Obviously, if debits were made to the margin accounts to reflect securities that are no longer available to the broker-dealer, it would be clear enough that no mismatch or shortfall would exist. But what sense would that make (other than satisfying someone's compulsive and rigid matching fetish)? Such debits would not impair the broker-dealer's obligation to return the securities to an account holder on demand (after first satisfying the account holder's secured debt, of course).[98] Moreover, such debits would not affect the entitlements of margin account holders under the SIPA distributional

96 The temporary shortfalls permitted by Rule 15c3–3 are of the sort clearly contemplated by Example 28–2 in the *Official Commentary*: 'EXAMPLE 28–2: IM is located in State B. The non-Convention law and applicable regulations of State B generally require IM to hold and have available sufficient securities to match the aggregate number or amount of securities credited to its account holders' accounts. However, that law and those regulations also permit temporary shortfalls (including in connection with settlement procedures) in the securities that IM must hold and have available and provide adequate and appropriate protections for account holders (e.g., by way of collateral requirements and mark-to-market rules). Notwithstanding the existence of these shortfalls, IM's compliance with the law of State B constitutes compliance with its obligations under Art. 24.'

97 Broker-dealers are not permitted to hypothecate commingled customer securities except with the written consent of the relevant customers. 17 CFR § 240.8c-1(a); 17 CFR § 240.15c2–1(a).

98 17 CFR § 240.15c3–3(*l*) (requiring delivery of fully paid securities, and margin securities upon full payment of indebtedness, on demand of customer).

formula.[99] Indeed, the Convention's distributional rule applicable in the insolvency proceeding of a relevant intermediary explicitly contemplates that account holders will *not* necessarily share *pro-rata* on an issue-by-issue basis – which is the baseline paradigm underlying an intermediary's obligations under Articles 24(1) and 25(1).[100] This is so because Article 26 applies 'unless otherwise provided by any conflicting rule applicable in' an insolvency proceeding and the SIPA distributional scheme *does* conflict with the Convention's baseline distributional rule found in Article 26(2).[101] The Convention clearly contemplates a method of risk sharing among account holders in their relevant intermediary's insolvency proceeding which is not consistent with the assumption underpinning Article 24(1).

7.3.3.3 Epilogue: US law on banks and voting rights

The foregoing discussion of shortfall under US law has passed over two important subjects – securities accounts maintained by bank intermediaries, as opposed to broker dealers, and voting and related rights of account holders. While the details of these matters are beyond the scope of this chapter, a brief acknowledgment is in order.

The SEC's customer protection rules apply only to intermediaries that are registered broker-dealers. For commercial banks in the US, the baseline rules pertaining to the rights of account holders in case of a bank intermediary insolvency are provided by UCC Article 8[102] and the Federal Deposit Insurance Act.[103] Banks generally are required to maintain sufficient securities to cover all of the credits made to their account holders' securities accounts.[104] This is so whether the account holder securities are formally administered by a bank's trust department in a fiduciary

99 The margin account holders would continue to fall within the broad SIPA definition of 'customer' and would be entitled to share as customer claimants under the SIPA distributional scheme. 15 USC §§ 78*lll*(2) (defining 'customer'); 78fff-2(c)(1) (allocation of customer property).

100 Convention Art. 26(2).

101 Convention Art. 26(1), (2); see above pp. 177–81 (discussing the SIPA distributional scheme).

102 See UCC Art. 8, Part 5, Security Entitlements, §§ 8–501 to 8–511.

103 Federal Deposit Insurance Act, 12 USC §§1811 *et seq.*

104 See *Comptroller's Handbook* at 14: 'A custodial bank is responsible for maintaining the safety of custody assets held in physical form at one of the custodian's premises, a sub-custodian facility, or an outside depository. A custodian's accounting records and internal controls should ensure that assets of each custody account are kept separate from the assets of the custodian and maintained under joint control. National banks may hold assets off-premises if they maintain adequate safeguards and controls and if such care is consistent with applicable law.'

capacity or are held in custody for account holders outside of the trust capacity.[105] So long as securities held in custody by a bank acting as a securities intermediary are identified as being so held, the account holders' interests will be respected in the bank's insolvency proceeding.[106] In the event of a shortfall in any issue of securities held for account holders, unlike the SIPA distributional scheme, an insolvent bank's account holders would share pro-rata on an issue-by-issue basis.[107]

There is no formal statutory or regulatory flexibility that affords banks the right to use their account holders' securities that is analogous to the rights of broker-dealers with respect to non-excess margin securities. A bank intermediary's use (such as for securities lending) of an account holder's securities must be based solely on the consent of the account holder.[108] The terms of use are dictated by contract, not by regulation. For example, bank custodians frequently administer the securities lending programmes of their institutional investor account holders.[109] However, to the extent that a shortfall arises by virtue of the consent given by account holders to the bank intermediary's use of securities, a court should conclude that non-consenting account holders should be protected from such a shortfall, and should not be required to share pro rata with the consenting account holders in the bank's insolvency proceeding. Stated otherwise, if securities are missing because some account holders gave the bank intermediary permission to use them, those account holders would have waived their status as such.[110]

United States law does not impose on a securities broker-dealer an absolute obligation to ensure that its account holders can vote securities

Citations made in this discussion relate to federally chartered US national banks. However, the discussion is generally accurate as well for federally insured state-charted banks.

105 Traditional banking activities that are exempt from broker-dealer registration include both trust and fiduciary services and safekeeping and custody. 7 Fed. Banking L. Rep. (CCH) ¶¶ 69–554 (trust and fiduciary services), 69–560 (safekeeping and custody).

106 See, e.g., *Marchant* v. *Summers*, 79 F.2d 877 (4th Cir. 1935); Federal Deposit Insurance Corporation [FDIC], Advisory Opinion FDIC – 93 – 61 (25 August 1993).

107 See UCC § 8–503(1), (2) (an entitlement holder has a pro rata property interest in financial assets of a type credited to its account, together with other entitlement holders as to such assets).

108 See *Comptroller's Handbook* at 1 ('Services provided by a bank custodian are typically the settlement, safekeeping, and reporting of customers' marketable securities and cash. A custody relationship is contractual, and services performed for a customer may vary.').

109 *Ibid.* at 28 (discussing agreement between bank and account holder concerning lending of account holder securities).

110 I am aware of no direct authority for the statements made in the text, but they are consistent with independent advice that I have given.

(or exercise other rights attached to securities) credited to the account holders' accounts. Complex rules applicable to securities broker-dealers regulate the delivery and collection of proxies from 'ultimate' shareholders (i.e., the beneficial owners) in the intermediated holding system.[111] As I have explained elsewhere, if the broker-dealer complies with these rules, the application of Article 28(2) results in the broker-dealer's compliance with Article 10(1) in respect of account holder voting rights.[112]

Unlike the matter of protecting account holders against loss in an intermediary's insolvency – as to which the customer protection rules work well in the SIPA distributional scheme – the mismatches and shortfalls present in the US markets are potentially problematic in the context of voting and other rights.[113] The principal problem is that broker-dealers provide proxy materials to all account holders based on the credit balances in their accounts, but frequently there are insufficient securities available to the broker-dealer; secondly, account holders may believe that they are entitled to vote more shares, for example, than the broker-dealer has available.[114] But this situation in no way 'inflates' an issue of securities, inasmuch as *only* the registered owner on the books of the issuer (typically, DTC's nominee) is entitled to vote and even then it can vote *only* the number of shares reflected on those books.

7.3.4 The draft European legislation approach

Efforts are underway in Europe to develop European legislation that would have a scope roughly along the lines of the Convention.[115] Unfortunately,

111 See Hazen and Markham, *Broker-Dealer Operations*, § 13.13 (discussing Securities and Exchange Commission ('SEC') Rule 14a-13[4], which requires issuers to obtain the number of beneficial owners from record holders of securities, SEC Rule 14b-1[5], which requires broker-dealers to solicit proxies from and deliver proxy materials to beneficial owners, and New York Stock Exchange Rules 451 and 452, which require members to forward proxy materials to beneficial owners). Bank intermediaries are subject to the same rules. See *Comptroller's Handbook* at 53 (discussing compliance with SEC Rules 14 – 17, 17 CFR §§ 240.14–17).

112 Mooney, 'Private Law' at 811.

113 For a trenchant critique of various aspects of the corporate voting structure for intermediated securities in the United States, see Kahan and Rock, 'The Hanging Chads of Corporate Voting'.

114 The SEC has taken note of various problems in the current system of proxy distribution and voting and currently is studying these issues. See SEC, Concept Release on the US Proxy System, Release Nos. 34–62495, IA-3052, IC-29340, File No. S7–14–10 (July 14, 2010).

115 See European Commission, *Legislation on Legal Certainty of Securities Holding and Dispositions, Consultation Document of the Services of The Directorate-General Internal*

the principles currently proposed in the draft European legislation reject the flexibility and rationale of Article 28(2) of the Convention. Principle 4.1(2) provides:

> The national law should provide that an account provider [i.e., intermediary] may credit the accounts of its account holders, for each description of securities, *only if it holds a corresponding number of securities of the same description* by
>
> (a) having available account-held securities in a securities account maintained for the account provider by another account provider;
> (b) arranging for securities to be held on the register of the issuer in the name, or for the account, of its account holders;
> (c) holding securities as the registered holder on the register of the issuer;
> (d) possessing relevant securities certificates or other documents of title; or
> (e) creating the initial electronic record of securities for the issuer in accordance with the applicable law;
>
> and that *an account provider continuously holds that corresponding number.*[116]

Neither the draft European legislation nor more recent European Commission submissions[117] have made any mention of this stark difference

Market And Services (2010) at 9 [hereinafter, 'draft European legislation']. Both the process leading to the final text of the Convention and the text itself have had considerable influence on the European project relating to securities holdings and dispositions: 'The Geneva Securities Convention . . . provides for a global harmonised instrument regarding the substantive law (= content of the law) of holding and disposition of securities, covering the same scope as those parts of the present outline dealing this subject. Most EU Member States and the EU itself have participated in the negotiations of this Convention. Both the present approach and the Convention are compatible with each other.' See draft European legislation at 9. See also Legal Certainty Group, *Second Advice of the Legal Certainty Group (Solutions to Legal Barriers related to Post-Trading with the EU)* (August 2008) [hereinafter, 'Second Advice']. The principles enunciated in the draft European legislation are quite similar in many respects to the substance of the Convention. Also, the recommendations made in the *Second Advice* were similar in substance to the draft Convention text that was submitted to the first session of the diplomatic conference in September 2008.

116 Draft European legislation, above n. 115, at 9–10 (emphasis added).

117 See 'Legislation on Legal Certainty of Securities Holding and Dispositions, Summary of Responses to the Directorate-General Internal Market and Services' Second Consultation (5 June 2011), available at http://ec.europa.eu/internal_market/consultations/2010/securities_en.htm [hereinafter, 'Summary of Responses'] last consulted 16 May 2012; Legislation on Legal Certainty of Securities Holding and Dispositions, Member States Working Group 9th Discussion Paper (15 February 2011).

between the draft European legislation and the Convention on a matter that was a key factor resulting in agreement on the Convention text in Geneva. Moreover, it appears that an intermediary and its account holders would be unable to contract around or limit the intermediary's responsibilities under the proposed rule.

Several speakers at the Luxembourg Conference decried this rigidity. They emphasised that strict liability would impose costs that ultimately would be borne by all who participate in the intermediated securities holding systems.[118] The absence of flexibility would also result in reducing some putative claims to intermediated securities to mere unsecured claims against an intermediary.[119] Significantly, it would stifle any future efforts to develop creative and innovative approaches that could provide needed flexibility for market participants, while nonetheless providing adequate protection for account holders.

One hopes that further thought would be given to the draft European legislation's significant deviation from the policy of the Convention. The Summary of Responses to the Commission's second consultation on the draft European legislation reflects some significant disagreements among stakeholders of Principle 4.1(2). For example, Belgium noted that it may be necessary to tolerate some shortfalls arising out of rehypothecation transactions.[120] On the other hand, some responders clung to the notion that the so-called 'integrity of the issue' could be preserved only with a strict, matching 'no credit without debit' rule.[121] Based on the Summary of Responses, it is safe to note that there does not appear to be a consensus as to the details surrounding Principle 4.1(2). But it is also the case that there does appear to be any substantial movement toward appropriate flexibility.

7.4 Conclusion

In this chapter I have shown that the SEC's customer protection rules and the SIPA distributional scheme, working in tandem, serve to protect the

118 In this respect, the concerns were reminiscent of those expressed about the high level of liability imposed on depositories by the Directive on Alternative Investment Fund Managers ('AIFM Directive') Directive 2011/61/EU of the European Parliament and of the Council. See Comments on the AIFM Directive submitted by The Association of Global Custodians, the British Bankers' Association, and the Association for Financial Markets in Europe (17 March 2009), on file with author (commenting on 1 March 2010 draft of the AIFM Directive).

119 See above, pp. 171–2 (discussing 'nofall' issue).

120 See Summary of Responses, above n. 117, at 37–8.

121 *Ibid.* at 35.

interests of account holders in achieving the economic benefits of their securities while providing account holders as well as broker-dealers with important flexibility.[122] In particular, the customer protection rules permit account holders to have ready access to credit from broker-dealers on the strength of collateral consisting of margin securities. The Convention wisely provides, in Article 28(2), that a broker-dealer's compliance with the customer protection rules, in the shadow of the SIPA distributional scheme in case of insolvency, likewise achieves compliance with the intermediary's duties under Article 24(1). Unfortunately, the draft European legislation is taking a different path. Ultimately, one can only hope that Europe will find its way by following the trail that the Convention has already illuminated. Hoping aside, however, I am sceptical.

Bibliography

Bank for International Settlements, Basel Committee on Banking Supervision, 'Bank Failures in Mature Economies', Working Paper No. 13, April 2004.

Comptroller of the Currency, Administrator of National Banks, US Department of the Treasury, *Comptroller's Handbook, Custody Services*, January 2002.

Don, M. E. and Wang, J., 'Stockbroker Liquidations under the Securities Investor Protection Act and their Impact on Securities Transfers' [1990] 12 *Cardozo L. Rev.*, 509

Facciolo, F. J., 'Father Knows Best: Revised Article 8 and the Individual Investor' [2000] 27 *Fla. St. U. L. Rev.*, 615.

Guttman, E., *Modern Securities Transfers*, 3rd edn (Thomson West, 2010).

Hazen, T. L. and Markham, J. W., *Broker-Dealer Operations under Securities and Commodities Law* (updated 2010).

Jamroz, M. P., 'The Customer Protection Rule' [2002] 57 *Bus. Law.*, 1069.

Joo, T. W., 'Who Watches the Watchers? The Securities Investor Protection Act, Investor Confidence, and the Subsidization of Failure' [1999] 72 *So. Cal. L. Rev.*, 1072.

Kahan, M. and Rock, E. B., 'The Hanging Chads of Corporate Voting' [2008] 96 *Georgetown L. J.* , 1227.

Kanda, H., Mooney, C., Thévenoz, L. and Béraud, S., *Official Commentary on the UNIDROIT Convention on Substantive Rules for Intermediated Securities* (Oxford University Press, 2012).

Kettering, K. C., 'Repledge Deconstructed' [1999] 61 *U. Pitt. L. Rev.*, 45.

122 I do not intend to suggest, however, that either the customer protection rules or SIPA is perfect, could not be improved, or has not been subjected to thoughtful criticism. See, e.g., Facciolo, 'Father Knows Best' at 675–98 (criticising both the customer protection rules and SIPA); Joo, 'Who Watches the Watchers?' *passim*.

'Repledge and Pre-Default Sale of Securities Collateral Under Revised Article 9' [1999] 74 *Chi.-Kent L. Rev.*, 1109.

Mooney, C. W., Jr., 'Beyond Negotiability: A New Model for Transfer and Pledge of Interests in Securities Controlled by Intermediaries' [1990] 12 *Cardozo L.Rev.*, 305.

'Property, Credit, and Regulation Meet Information Technology: Clearance and Settlement in the Securities Markets' [1992] 55 *L. and Contemp. Probs.*, 131.

'Law and Systems for Intermediated Securities and the Relationship of Private Property Law to Securities Clearance and Settlement: US, Japan, and the UNIDROIT Draft Convention', IMES Discussion Paper Series 2008-E-7, available at www.imes.boj.or.jp/english/publication/edps/fedps2008_index.html.

'Private Law and the Regulation of Securities Intermediaries: Perspectives under the GSC and United States Law' [2010] *Unif. L. Rev.*, 801.

Mooney, C. W., Jr. and Kinami, A., 'Transfer, Pledge Clearance and Settlement in the Japanese and United States Government Securities Markets' [1991] 12 *U. Pa. J. Int'l Bus. L.* , 517.

Mooney, C. W. and Kanda, H., 'Core Issues under the UNIDROIT (Geneva) Securities Convention on Intermediated Securities: Views from the United States and Japan', in L. Gullifer and J. Payne (eds.), *Intermediated Securities. Legal Problems and Practical Issues* (Oxford: Hart Publishing, 2010), 69–130.

Weiss, D. M., *After the Trade is Made: Processing Securities Transactions*, 3rd edn. (New York: Portfolio/Penguin Group, 2006).

8

The concept of integrity in securities holding systems

HUBERT DE VAUPLANE AND JEAN-PIERRE YON*

8.1 Introduction

In 2010 and early 2011, the public consultation on Legislation on Legal Certainty of Securities Holding and Dispositions[1] refuelled an already old debate on the harmonisation not only of the law[2] but also of the technical standards governing the issuance, disposition and holding of securities.

Much work has been done on this important issue, which dates back more than ten years now, including the two Giovannini reports on clearing and settlement,[3] various CESR reports,[4] several working groups,[5] advice of the Legal Certainty Group[6] and, of course, the two international conventions, the 2006 Hague Convention on conflicts of law with regard to intermediated securities[7] and the 2009 Geneva UNIDROIT Convention,[8] both of which are struggling to win any broad support, for often very similar reasons. In another vein, in France there was also the conference

* The authors' opinions are not necessarily those of the institutions for which they work.

1 Legislation on Legal Certainty of Securities Holding and Dispositions, DG Markt G2 MET/OT/acg D(2010) 768690, 5 November 2010.

2 de Vauplane, H., 'Encadrement des activités Post Marchés: les enjeux pour les banques françaises', *Revue Banque* no. 723, April 2010, 82.

3 First report of the Giovannini Group on Cross Border Clearing and Settlement Arrangements in the European Union, December 2001; Second report of the Giovannini Group on EU Clearing and Settlement Arrangements, April 2003.

4 Standards for Securities Clearing and Settlement Systems in the European Union, CESR, September 2004.

5 Clearing and Settlement Advisory and Monitoring Expert group (CESAME).

6 Second Advice of the Legal Certainty Group, Solutions to Legal Barriers related to Post-Trading within the EU, August 2008; EU Clearing and Settlement Legal Certainty Group, Advice August 2006.

7 Hague Convention of 5 July 2006 on the Law Applicable to Certain Rights in Respect of Securities Held with an Intermediary.

8 Geneva UNIDROIT Convention on Substantive Rules for Intermediated Securities 2009.

on the law related to securities organised jointly by the AFTI (Association Française des Professionnels des Titres) and the French universities.[9]

The European Commission claims that the SLD, which has recently been the subject of a European public consultation, aims to reduce the uncertainty caused by the absence of an EU-wide framework for the treatment of interests in securities, to reduce the impacts of differences between national legal systems that affect the cross-border exercise of holders' rights and to lift barriers as to the choice of where to issue securities in Europe. The difficulty here is really one of how relevant these objectives are, particularly in the post 2008 crisis environment.

The latest European work shows us just how important it still is to make the right choices as regards the principles that should apply. The key issue is that of the integrity of securities holding systems, which involves (at least) two very different concepts. To simplify or maybe oversimplify, the first concept arises primarily out of US federal law whilst the second is found in most European countries and sometimes other regions of the world.[10] The question is whether we can find a response that is compatible with both approaches or whether, on the contrary, the ontological differences between them are so great that the problem is essentially insoluble. Before attempting to explain the differences between the concepts of integrity in the two main securities holding systems, we will start with a brief overview of their underlying principles.

The two concepts differ first and foremost in their underlying objectives and logically, therefore, in their resulting mechanisms. This is a highly oversimplified summary of extremely complex systems, but in order to understand the issues arising from these differences, we must take as holistic an approach as possible. The legal position in the United States and other countries with a similar system is the one that has broadly prevailed in the various international legal initiatives in the matter. One of the key objectives of the Hague Convention, the Geneva UNIDROIT Convention, sometimes the work of the European Commission's Legal Certainty Group (LCG) and the first consultation on the proposed SLD is to simplify collateralisation at international level and realisation of the collateral in the event of counterparty default in order to facilitate the circulation of securities, which most of the time are immobilised in strong rooms or securities accounts held by central depositories or other

9 AEDBF/AFTI/FBF Conference, November 2004.

10 French law in this field is the same as the law in Belgium, Germany, Italy, Austria, Spain, Portugal, Poland and, beyond Europe, Brazil, China and Japan.

registrars. The circulation of securities or security entitlements – and therein lies the difference – meets an essentially economic approach to the issue of international securities holding systems, which is predominantly, but not exclusively, to meet the growing needs of financial intermediaries to provide collateral for their transactions in derivatives instruments. We know that open derivative positions are aggregated from an accounting point of view until expiry of the contract (which can be up to ten, twenty, thirty or even fifty years!), despite prudential netting on a counterparty by counterparty basis in the balance sheets of financial institutions governed by Basel Committee rules. Holdings of derivatives are literally exploding, and with them the corresponding collateralisation needs in the form of securities or cash. Consequently, to avoid a total collapse of the system, we have to find new ways for operators to meet their collateral needs. This means giving priority to liquidity, or taking a 'dynamic' approach.

On the other hand, from the traditional European and particularly French viewpoint, it is less a question of facilitating the circulation of securities than of providing legal certainty throughout the intermediation chain, in other words, a 'static' approach.

In theory, the two concepts are not irreconcilable or incompatible. In addition, they both attempt to meet liquidity and certainty needs at the same time, although one places more emphasis on liquidity and the other on certainty. At this stage, it is essential to remember that it is perfectly possible to pursue both of these objectives, but if the worst comes to the worst (i.e. an intermediary defaults in the holding chain, or a counterparty defaults on a securities-backed transaction), we have to determine priority rankings in exactly the same way as in a bankruptcy. Who should bear the loss when a link of the chain is broken? The question is as old as bankruptcy law itself, but never in any of the debates on this issue has it been suggested that this should be the cornerstone of the law on holding intermediated securities. And this logical fallacy is undoubtedly the reason why most of the difficulties are arising today.

The question of integrity in securities holding systems is at the heart of these debates. But what does it mean?

8.2 What is integrity?

Integrity in a securities holding system is a set of provisions assuring the certainty of securities held in the global environment of an intermediation chain. The Geneva UNIDROIT Convention on securities devotes an entire chapter to integrity, and the concept appears in the recitals to the Convention.[11] But there are at least two possible approaches to integrity.

In Europe, when we speak of integrity, we mean the integrity of the securities issue. In the second report of the Legal Certainty Group, for example, the term 'integrity' refers to the integrity of the issue. This is what we might call the traditional approach to integrity. Thus, in recommendation 9 of the LCG's Second Advice, we read:

> The term 'integrity of the issue' describes an important function of the model of holding and settlement through account providers: as the issuer has issued a certain number of securities, the chain of account providers must ensure the total number of securities belonging to a specific issue does not exceed the number of securities originally issued.

Under a second approach, such as the one developed in the Geneva UNIDROIT Convention, integrity does not refer to the integrity of the issue, but to the integrity of the holding system itself.

This difference is quite important as, when we speak of integrity, we do not necessarily mean the same thing, which could lead to misunderstandings. However, despite the differences, integrity is at first sight a simple concept.

8.2.1 Integrity is based on arithmetic equality . . .

In other words, as the issuer has issued a certain number of securities, the chain of account providers (i.e. intermediaries) must therefore ensure (the key issues being *how* and *when*) that the total number of securities credited to the accounts at each level of the chain does not exceed the number originally issued. The number of securities issued is finite and invariable. The Geneva Securities Convention contains a rule that is very similar in formulation, but not in definition. Article 24 states that an intermediary must hold or have available securities and intermediated securities of an aggregate number or amount equal to the aggregate number or amount of securities credited to securities accounts that it maintains for its account holders other than itself, and if applicable, securities accounts that it maintains for itself. However this differs from the principle stated earlier in that here the intermediary is required to have an aggregate number

11 'Emphasising the importance of the integrity of a securities issue in a global environment for intermediated holding in order to ensure the exercise of investors' rights and enhance their protection.'

of securities *or intermediated securities,* meaning security entitlements, which is not the same thing as the securities themselves.

8.2.2 . . . and an exclusive right

In France, as in many other countries, this integrity is more or less taken for granted. A security *corresponds* to a single owner. There is a legal equivalence relationship between security and ownership. The security only *belongs* to one person, i.e. the end investor (unless title has been split) who has a *property* interest in it. The end investor is the only person who benefits from all the interests in the security. This is the very meaning of the world 'ownership' with its three traditional components (*usus, fructus* and *abusus*). This exclusivity is in a way consubstantial, ontological.

In practice, since dematerialisation, securities issued in France and governed by French law are, from the outset, booked to a securities account held by a financial intermediary (investment firm) or by the issuer. Ownership of the securities is evidenced by their book entry on the owner's account and the owner is therefore the only person who can benefit from the property interest in the securities.

What is the nature (and therefore the effect) of such a book entry? It is the triggering event that gives life to the security. In other words, an investor who has deposited the security with a financial intermediary has a property interest in it. This property interest cannot be turned into a personal right by a simple wave of a financial magician's wand in the higher interests of Liquidity (with a capital L). In the French concept, there is only one owner of the securities and that is the end client who holds an account with the intermediary on which the securities are held, confirmed by a corresponding entry made by the intermediary with the central depository.

This choice will have a determining influence in the event of the intermediary's failure.

In the French system, the effect of this book entry is determining. It presumes that the account holder is the owner of the securities. This is a non-rebuttable presumption with regard to third parties. Some observers go even further in their definition of the effect of book entry and say that the book entry *is* the security. In this understanding, the book entry and the security are one and the same thing. This is much too absolute a definition of book entry. At any rate, the important thing is that in French law the intermediary does not create a new interest for the benefit of the owner or anyone else. This is a fundamental difference compared with the

American system: in the French concept, the book entry and the security are inseparable (although we would not go as far as to say that the book entry *is the security*: they are separate but inseparable). The book entry is not a financial asset created by the intermediary.

8.2.3 ... *but is not a universal concept*

Unlike the French system (and many other legal systems in Europe), in the US system there is a dichotomy between the initial security and the financial asset booked to the account held by the intermediary. At each level of the intermediation chain, the system allows entitlements to be created for the benefit of each account holder. Thus, in this so-called 'indirect holding' system, the book entry only confers a hybrid set of rights on the account holder (the 'security entitlement').[12] This is a mix between personal rights vis-à-vis the intermediary and a property interest.

Unlike the French legal concept, in the US, the book entry is a distinct financial asset, a security entitlement created by the intermediary and independent of the original security itself. These intermediated securities are distinct from the securities originally issued and arise from duplication at each level of the intermediation chain. Consequently, under this arrangement, the account holder only owns the intermediated asset which gives him, as we have seen, a personal right against the intermediary and a property interest in the underlying securities.

In this case, integrity is not an equivalence relationship as referred to above. Thus, when Lehman Brothers failed, there were some major differences in the estimates of the number of shares in circulation. The result is that the 'holder's' (end investor's) entitlement is challenged by that of other people in the chain. The investor does not have a property interest but a set of hybrid rights. The security entitlement is the same, whether one is an end investor or simply an intermediary. Its content varies depending on the set of securities of the same description held by the intermediary. The benefit of this duplication is to increase market liquidity by allowing each intermediary to dispose of the economic value of the duplicated securities. This facilitates the use of securities held by a broker for collateral purposes.

12 Art. 8 of the UCC establishes the rights of an entitlement holder in the security entitlements credited to its securities account. In § 8–102(17), security entitlement is defined broadly as the 'rights' and 'property interests' of an 'entitlement holder' with respect to a 'financial asset' specified in Part 5.

8.2.4 Integrity according to the Geneva Securities Convention

The Convention deals with the question of integrity in several articles. Point 8 of the Recitals, which refers to the concept of integrity, was added during the final session of the Diplomatic Conference and it emphasises the importance of integrity in a global environment for intermediated holdings in order to ensure the exercise of investors' rights and enhance their protection: investors' rights and their protection must be guaranteed. But the integrity referred to here is not the integrity of the securities alone but the integrity of the securities *and* the security entitlements. The draft Commentary on the Convention regarding Article 24 ('Holding or availability of sufficient securities') states that Article 24 constitutes a core rule for the protection of account holders.[13] The general rule in Article 24 is that an intermediary must, for each description of securities, hold or have available securities and intermediated securities of an aggregate number or amount equal to the aggregate number or amount of securities of that description credited to securities accounts that it maintains for its account holders other than itself and if applicable, securities accounts that it maintains for itself. The Commentary states:

> Paragraph 1 states a general rule by providing that an intermediary must hold or have available securities or intermediated securities corresponding to the credits it has made to the securities accounts of its account holders other than itself, and where applicable, to the credits it has made to a securities account of itself. This means, in general, that the total amount thus held or available is at least equal to the total amount of the securities credited to the securities accounts of its account holders.[14]

This wording calls for a few comments. First of all, this provision does not deal with the integrity of the issue but the integrity of the intermediated holding, which is not at all the same thing! Article 24 states that the two amounts must be equal whilst the Commentary says that they must be 'at least' equal. The nuance is important. However, some elements lean more towards a traditional concept of integrity, seen as the equality between the amount of securities credited to the securities accounts and the amount of securities originally issued by the issuer. Thus on page 155:

13 Kanda, H., Mooney, C., Thévenoz, L. and Béraud, S., with the assistance of T. Keijser, *Official Commentary on the UNIDROIT Convention on Substantive Rules for Intermediated Securities* (Oxford University Press, 2012), s. 24–1.

14 Kanda et al., *Official Commentary*, s. 24–1.

> 24–11: The purpose of this rule is to provide a minimum duty of an intermediary to its account holders. The rule applies at any level of the chain of intermediation, and thus applies to a CSD where it acts as an intermediary. In that situation, the CSD must hold or have available securities registered on the register of the issuer which correspond to the credits it has made to the securities accounts of its account holders.

The example that follows supposes that if an issuer has issued one million shares, the CSD must not credit to the securities accounts of its participants (or itself if applicable) an amount of shares greater than one million. More troubling is the explanation that the obligation imposed on the intermediary 'to hold or have available' sufficient securities is intended to cover the fact that 'in some jurisdictions, intermediaries hold securities (or intermediated securities)'.[15] Based on this nuance, we could consider that integrity does not simply cover the securities owned by the account holders but also the intermediaries' property interests when they are recognised. This is moving away from the traditional concept of integrity.

8.2.5 Integrity in European law

During the preparatory work for what was to become the Legal Certainty Group, the concept of integrity very quickly became the main focus of debate. The concept of integrity can be found in the LCG's Ninth Recommendation which specifically deals with the 'Integrity of the issue'. Recommendation 9a provides that:

> EU legislation should provide that an account provider has to maintain a number of book-entry securities that corresponds to the aggregate number of book-entry securities credited to the accounts of its account holders or held for its own account.

Recommendation 9b provides for corrective measures in case of imbalance. The definition itself is in 9.1 (Background), which states that:

> The term 'integrity of the issue' describes an important function of the model of holding and settlement through account providers: as the issuer has issued a certain number of securities, the chain of account providers must ensure the total number of securities belonging to a specific issue does not exceed the number of securities originally issued. To this end, a

15 *Ibid.*, s. 24–14.

mechanism should be in place designed to avoid imbalances at the level of account providers.[16]

The ninth discussion paper on the draft SLD directive addresses the issue of integrity through two possible options, 'dynamic' or 'static' integrity:

> As concerns the integrity of the issue, some stakeholders argued that the best way to avoid a multiplication of securities would be to introduce the 'no debit without credit rule'. Some favoured applying the 'ex ante' exhaustive approach provided by Article 24 of the GSC, which consists in listing 5 holding methods of securities. Others favoured reducing the number of holding methods to 3 (credit of securities, holding of certificates or immobilisation with a CSD). The main rationale for this would be to enable the constitution of a regular 'dynamic reconciliation' system, which only works if the perimeter of reconciliation is limited to regular account providers and does not cover issuers (the two other types of holding methods). Many stakeholders considered that the equation between 'securities maintained' and 'securities held' does not answer the question under which timeframe a shortfall should be resolved. In this respect, they supported that the SLD or another piece of legislation (such as future CSD legislation) addressed the periodicity of reconciliation between securities 'maintained' and securities 'held'. Should it be a permanent reconciliation? A daily reconciliation (allowing intraday shortfalls)? Or a less frequent reconciliation (allowing overnight shortfalls)? Obviously the answer would depend on the type of settlement system used at the top level of the holding chain (real time or not). Furthermore, of the two corrective measures (reversal and/or buy ins), little support was given to buy-in procedures. One of the main arguments against buy-in was that the securities are not necessarily available on the market. Also, the use of the obligation to 'buy-in' in other legislative contexts raised concern. Hence, a simple reversal was preferred by most stakeholders. As concerns the share of the costs (of reversal and of buy in), several variations were proposed based either on a reversal of the charge of the proof of fault between the account holder and the account provider, or by referring to the solutions provided under Article 21 and following of the AIFM directive.

The draft directive on Central Securities Depositories deals with this question of reconciliation in a section entitled 'Integrity of the issue', stating that it should be at least daily:

> CSDs should reconcile the initial entry accounts with accounts of participants at least once a day according to best accounting practices. If other entities are involved in this reconciliation process (such as the issuer, other

16 Second Advice of the Legal Certainty Group, Solutions to Legal Barriers related to Post-Trading within the EU, August 2008, 68.

> CSDs or other entities), the CSD should seek to put in place adequate cooperation and information exchange with those entities in order to ensure the integrity of the issue. In no case should securities debit balances or securities creation be allowed by a CSD.[17]

8.2.6 What purpose does integrity serve?

First of all certainty. As we have seen, the book entry constitutes the security. The corollary to this is that the book entry can only be made once. It determines who has the property interest in the security. Integrity avoids confusion between the various parties involved in the intermediation chain. This principle is essential as it ensures the protection of each party: investor, creditor, intermediary.

Integrity protects the *end investor* who, in the continental system, is the sole owner of the securities: he has an exclusive right that is not challenged by other parties in the chain. This is logical: investors do not play the same role as intermediaries and do not have the same interests, and as such must be protected. Otherwise, their contribution through their investment will be compromised in spite of the fact that it is the cornerstone of any financial system.

What the Americans call 'legal certainty' is a prerequisite of investor confidence, but it is only possible if investors know exactly what their rights are when they buy the securities. The continental concept of integrity is the only one that provides such certainty. In the French system, it is not possible for the end investor's securities to disappear in the chain of intermediaries due to the fact that they hold intermediated securities.[18]

In an indirect holding system such as the US system, where a series of entitlements are created by each intermediary for the benefit of its client, only the central custodian holds the assets; all the other intermediaries hold merely an intermediated entitlement covering their respective accounts with the central custodian. So in countries that practise this system, clients do not have a higher entitlement or even a specific entitlement, they only have an entitlement with regard to their intermediary for the amount of securities held with that intermediary.

17 Consultation on central securities depositories (CSDs) and on the harmonisation of certain aspects of securities settlement in the European Union, DG Markt G2 D(201)8641, 13 January 2011.

18 Remember that the expression 'intermediated securities' does not mean 'securities that have been intermediated' but 'securities, distinct from the original securities issued by the issuer, created to the benefit of each intermediary'.

Integrity protects the *investor's creditor*, as the collateral is based on a real asset. If the collateral is realised, the creditor will own securities, not a security entitlement.

It also protects the *intermediary*, who cannot therefore be confused with the holder of the securities and only has obligations, not rights. The continental system provides intermediaries with real protection, especially if a client or counterparty defaults. This also ensures that there is no conflict between certainty and liquidity as this protection actively contributes to liquidity.

If we wanted to be controversial, we could say that the US system puts liquidity before certainty, and the European system manages both objectives, whilst its effect on liquidity is less spectacular (but also less uncertain).

Last but not least, the continental system also protects the *issuer* by giving it control over the issue and the ability to clearly determine its ownership structure. The US system on the other hand lacks clarity as there is no clear distinction between the intermediaries and the end investor. There is a risk of confusion between the parties involved in the intermediation chain and the end investor, who is in fact treated as a simple account holder when he should enjoy a specific entitlement and protection. Other account holders in the chain should not be able to acquire the entitlement belonging to the end investor.

8.2.7 (Over-)abundance of securities

The indirect holding system creates a specific entitlement for each account holder in the intermediation chain which they are free to dispose of. These security entitlements automatically 'inflate the securities', in other words there are more entitlements to the securities than there are securities themselves. Multiple use of the same security will automatically create a shortage in the event of a liquidity crisis. This is one of the weaknesses of the US system. Recent events have proved that this is not just a theoretical hypothesis. One of the perverse effects of the indirect holding system is the phenomenon known as over-voting.

This problem is caused by artificial inflation of securities, i.e. the decoupling of the capital issued from the capital in circulation amongst the financial intermediaries. By an inevitable arithmetic effect, the number of votes cast systematically exceeds the number of actual securities issued. To resolve this inconsistency, issuers must adopt methods that might look somewhat unorthodox. They may scale back the voting rights proportionately or adopt a lottery system to determine which votes will be retained and which will be rejected. This confusion in voting rights benefits neither the investor nor the issuer. There have been instances in some general meetings in the United States of voting rates reaching as much as 140 percent.

8.3 How to implement this integrity?

Integrity presumes that the investor's rights are not challenged either by his own intermediary or any other intermediary in the intermediation chain. There are two ways of ensuring respect for this integrity: segregation of assets and double entry accounting.

8.3.1 Segregation of assets

This ensures that assets belonging to a client cannot be mixed up with those of another client or an intermediary. This is integrity. It exists in various forms in the main countries whether they have direct or indirect holding systems. Segregation provides additional protection should an intermediary account holder fail. It means that in the securities world, the intermediary must fully segregate its clients' assets from its own assets.

8.3.1.1 French law

Several provisions of French law cover this principle.

The *Code monétaire et financier* requires investment firms to safeguard their clients' rights to financial instruments belonging to them and prevents them from using them for their own account unless expressly authorised to do so by the client.[19] In a sub-section entitled Safeguarding of Client Assets,[20] the General Regulation of the *Autorité des Marchés Financiers* (AMF) requires investment firms to take measures to protect clients' rights over financial instruments belonging to them (their title is absolute, it is not shared with other parties in the chain). A body of rules requires segregation of assets, reconciliation between its books and registers and those of third parties, and measures to avoid the loss of

19 Art. 533–10–6° of the *Code monétaire et financier* provides that investment firms must: 'safeguard the rights of clients to financial instruments belonging to them and not use them for own account without the express consent of the client'.

20 From Book III, Title 1 (Investment Services Providers).

integrity of rights over securities or their value. Investment firms are not allowed to temporarily sell securities held on behalf of clients.

Sub-section 5 'Safeguarding of Client Assets' of AMF General Regulation, Article 313–13 obliges the account providers to comply with various requirements, including the principle of segregation of assets. The means that intermediaries must be able to identify and distinguish immediately at all times securities held for one client from securities held for another client, and of course from securities held for its own account. Article 313–13–4 also requires investment services providers to take the necessary steps to ensure that any client financial instruments deposited with a third party can be identified separately from the financial instruments belonging to the investment services provider by means of differently titled accounts on the books of the third party or other equivalent measures that achieve the same level of protection.

The principle of segregation is one of the core principles in the protection of investors in Europe not just for securities but also for cash, as shown in the JP Morgan case, in which JP Morgan was fined by the FSA, the UK regulator, a record £33.32 million. This penalty sends out a strong message to firms of all sizes that they must ensure that client money is kept in segregated accounts with trust status in order to protect it in the event of the firm's insolvency.[21]

This segregation principle leads to certain advantages in terms of legal certainty and security for the investors. For example, under this the use of the securities of its account holder by the account provider may be forbidden. Thus, according to Article 313–17 RG AMF (Article 322–4 for the custody account-keeper):

> Investment services providers may not enter into arrangements for securities financing in respect of financial instruments held by them on behalf of a client or otherwise use such financial instruments for their own account for the account of one of their other clients, unless the client has given his prior express consent for the use of the instruments on specified terms, as evidenced, in the case of a retail client, by his signature or an equivalent alternative mechanism. The use of that client's financial instruments must be restricted to the specified terms to which the client has consented.

21 'FSA levies largest ever fine of £33.32m on JP Morgan Securities Ltd for client money breaches', 3 June 2010, www.fsa.gov.uk/pubs/final/jpmsl.pdf. In another case, the FSA fined the broker ActivTrades Plc for failing to protect clients' assets adequately. The FSA found that, between April 2009 and September 2010, ActivTrades was in breach of client money rules in the FSA's Client Assets sourcebook (CASS). ActivTrades failed to segregate client money appropriately and ensure that it did not hold client money in its own bank accounts or perform client money calculations.

Without the segregation principle, these different mechanisms of protection of the investor rights to securities would not be possible. Yet, this segregation principle has no actual significance in an intermediated securities system like the Geneva Convention. Each investment service provider is an account holder who has an account which holds securities which is a distinct asset from the securities and on which he has a proprietary right. Thus, all these mechanisms of protection cannot exist. In an intermediated system which prioitises liquidity over security, the use of the intermediated securities is consubstantial with the logical structure of the multi-tiered intermediated system.

8.3.1.2 Convention

Article 25 of the Convention, entitled 'Allocation of securities to account holders' rights', provides that 'Securities and intermediated securities of each description held by an intermediary as described in Article 24(2) shall be allocated to the rights of the account holders of that intermediary, other than itself, to the extent necessary to ensure compliance with Article 24(1)(a).' Article 24 on 'Holding or availability of sufficient securities' provides that an

> intermediary must, for each description of securities, hold or have available securities and intermediated securities of an aggregate number or amount equal to the aggregate number or amount of securities of that description credited to:
>
> a) securities accounts that it maintains for its account holders other than itself; and
> b) if applicable, securities accounts that it maintains for itself.

As regards the securities referred to in Article 25(1), Article 25(2) states that 'securities and intermediated securities allocated under paragraph 1 shall not form part of the property of the intermediary available for distribution among or realisation for the benefit of creditors of the intermediary'. This provision, as noted in the Commentary, will be 'particularly useful' in the event of the intermediary's insolvency. But the Convention does not say what method should be used to implement the allocation rule.

Article 25(4) states that the arrangements referred to in Article 25(3) *may* (not *must*) include arrangements under which an intermediary holds securities in segregated form for the benefit of its account holders generally or particular account holders or groups of account holders. The Commentary notes that the various legal systems in the Member States use different techniques to protect account holders in the event of the intermediary's insolvency. Consequently, 'the Convention respects this diversity and remains neutral on this issue' and logically 'segregation is not imposed by the Convention. Contracting States remain free to provide for it, either as a regulatory requirement or as a legal mechanism by which the allocation rule is satisfied, or may design other methods.'[22] This is a deliberate consequence of the Convention's neutral approach.

8.3.1.3 Position of the Legal Certainty Group (LCG)

In Recommendation 9, the LGC states:

> Segregation is a pure means to distinguish clients' assets from the account provider's assets in order to assist allocation of the segregated book-entry securities to account holders, in particular in the event of insolvency of the account provider, and to make clear that they are not part of the insolvency estate of the account provider. Segregation has only a further substantive meaning only if specifically attributed to it in particular by way of a rebuttable presumption that segregated book-entry securities cover holdings in clients' accounts and can therefore not be attached by an account provider's creditors. Consequently, it is not an appropriate means to address the issue of rectifying imbalances.

In Recommendation 11 on Attachments, the LCG recognises the goal of a rule on the

> prohibition of attachments of segregated client accounts by creditors of the account provider . . . to enhance investor protection and to allow for an efficient functioning of holding through securities account in structures using multiple tiers and omnibus accounts.

But the Group also notes that whilst the MiFID provides for segregation,[23] it does not draw the consequences of this requirement:

22 Kanda et al., *Official Commentary*, ss. 25–15 and 25–18.

23 Second Advice of the Legal Certainty Group, Solutions to Legal Barriers related to Post-Trading within the EU, August 2008, 76–7: 'Art. 13(7) and 13(8) of the MiFID and Art. 16(1)(d) of the MiFID Implementing Directive require that credit institutions and investment firms "must take the necessary steps to ensure that any client financial instruments deposited with a third party . . . are identifiable separately from the financial instruments belonging to the investment firm and from financial instruments belonging to that third party, by means of differently titled accounts on the books of the third party or other equivalent measures that achieve the same level of protection". This segregation rule is designed to safeguard client securities in case of insolvency of the direct account provider and to prevent the use by the account provider of client securities for own account.'

> A problem arises because . . . the MiFID . . . does not draw any legal consequences from such requirement. Therefore, the idea is to provide that creditors of an account provider may not attach accounts which are identified as 'client accounts' with a higher-tier account provider.

This observation should be seen in parallel with a comment made by the Member States Experts Working Group on the Security Law Directive (SLD) in September 2010:

> Whereas the MiFID provides for a segregation requirement, the Securities Law Directive should draw legal consequences from such requirement, capable of enhancing investor protection even further. The idea is to provide that creditors of an account provider may not attach accounts which are identified as 'client account' with a higher-tier account provider and the creditors might argue that the securities credited to this account therefore 'belong' to the first account provider.[24]

The LCG experts and the Member States Working Group on SLD go further and in almost identical terms:

> It is worth noting that in some Member States there is a rebuttable presumption that an account which an account provider opens with an upper-tier account provider always contains clients' assets, which is probably the strongest protection possible.

And the SLD experts add a clear recommendation:

> Such national rules should be maintained and respected by the future Directive.[25]

Such a recommendation is nowhere near enough to protect investors. Furthermore, it leads to a variety of inconsistent situations where the investor is more or less protected depending on the applicable law.

24 EU Commission, Legislation on Legal Certainty of Securities Holding and Dispositions, Member States Working Group, Updated Compilation of the rules and explanatory notes discussed so far of 17 September 2010, G2/PhP D(2010).

25 EU Commission, Legislation on Legal Certainty of Securities Holding and Dispositions, Member States Working Group, Updated Compilation of the rules and explanatory notes discussed so far of 17 September 2010, G2/PhP D(2010).

8.3.2 The principle of double entry accounting or 'no credit without debit'

8.3.2.1 Key features

Another way to ensure integrity is through the double entry accounting principle, which is as much a matter of good sense as accounting doctrine. Double entry accounting means that there cannot be a credit without a corresponding debit. The corollary to this rule is the requirement to reconcile daily movements and holdings of securities. In this way, the capital issued by the issuer is the same as the capital booked with the intermediaries in the chain. And, therefore, voting capital is the same as capital issued. This rule protects the investor, whose securities cannot disappear or be compromised by artificial duplication and therefore multiplication of collateral taken against the securities. It means that the amount of securities credited can never be more than the amount issued: no purchase is valid unless there is a corresponding sale. This is an effective means of avoiding systemic risk.

However, the various proposals under discussion seem to suggest that this rule is not as absolute as one might expect. In some competing systems, for example in the USA, intermediaries practise single entry accounting, which as we have seen on several occasions, leads to confusion due to the fact that several people can simultaneously be identified as owners of the same securities.

Thus, in the United States, a stock lender does not have to debit his securities account with the securities lent, yet the borrower credits his account. This necessarily inflates the securities. By delivering the securities without removing them from the lender's portfolio, the intermediary is in a way using the actual securities held in custody. Further, the phenomenon can be duplicated: the securities transferred can be transferred again to one or more new borrowers. This single entry system generates a structural risk; it is unstable by nature because there is no systematic reconciliation between movements and holdings. This is why we need to clearly distinguish acquisition and disposition methods (account debit and credit) from simple collateral transactions.[26]

8.3.2.2 Convention

In Article 11, the Convention enshrines the universally recognised method of acquisition and disposition of intermediated securities or any other

26 Earmarking, control agreement or agreement with and in favour of an account provider.

intermediated security entitlement: they are acquired by credit to and disposed of by debit to the holder's securities account. Whilst Contracting States may, via non-Convention law, specify what constitutes a credit to a securities account, they may not require any further step for the acquisition to be effective against third parties.[27] Paragraph 4 provides that a credit to a securities account does not necessarily convey a full interest in the securities so credited, i.e., all the rights under Article 9. It implies that, subject to non-Convention law, the interest conferred by a credit is determined by the transaction between the transferor and the transferee.

As the Commentary observes, the question then arises as to whether the debit and credit entries in one transaction are to be regarded as effecting a single transfer of property from A to B, or whether the debit must be analysed as extinguishing an interest of A, and the credit as creating an interest of B.[28]

Coming back to the question of the nature of the interest created by a credit of securities to a securities account. What is the Convention's response to this important issue of link between debit and credit? Nothing, and this is regrettable. Consistent with what it calls a *functional* approach, the Convention does not take any view on this issue, but leaves non-Convention law to decide. It may link the debit and credit involved in a transfer of securities so as to make sure that none is reversed without all others being reversed as well (in line with the principle), but it may also consider the credit and the debit as dealing with different interests.

It is clear that UNIDROIT is not taking a stance on the appropriateness of the 'no credit without debit' rule. We note that several examples of validity conditions were discussed by UNIDROIT's Committee of Governmental Experts (CGE) and the Diplomatic Conference. It was clearly understood that non-Convention law may, as in many countries, link debits and credits that form part of the same transfer of intermediated securities and that consequently a credit will be invalid or unable to be reversed if it cannot be linked with the corresponding debit.

8.3.2.3 Position of the Legal Certainty Group

As we have seen, Recommendation 9 of the LCG deals with the integrity of the issue.[29]

27 Art. 11(2). 28 Kanda et al., *Official Commentary*, s. 11–4.

29 See Recommendation 9.a: 'EU legislation should provide that an account provider has to maintain a number of book-entry securities that corresponds to the aggregate number of book-entry securities credited to the accounts of its account holders or held for its own account.'

The Group has taken the same concept of integrity as French law.[30] To enforce this integrity, the LCG states that a 'mechanism should be in place designed to avoid imbalances at the level of account providers'. To do that, it logically identifies two methods: obligation to hold sufficient securities and the no credit without debit rule (an acquisition is only valid if there is a corresponding sale). The LCG commented: 'This principle is applied in a number of Member States.' But it also adds the following nuance which has serious consequences: 'However, as it is closely linked to the underlying legal concept of securities holding and settlement, it would not work in other jurisdictions.'[31]

In addition, the Group even criticises the name of the principle for being potentially misleading.[32] And it also calls into question its practicality for cases where it could be difficult to identify the purchaser and seller.[33] The LCG notes: 'Under the "no credit without debit" principle, a direct transfer of "ownership" (i.e. seller transfers ownership to the buyer) might be seen as the most stringent form to protect the integrity of the issue. Conceptually, there are never more securities validly credited than issued (unless the fungible pool of securities at the level of the central securities depository is reduced).' And it notes that one of the characteristics of this system is the technique of conditional credits: 'One characteristic of such system is the technique of conditional credits' whereby 'a legal system avoids that credits which are not immediately covered by debits lead to a situation where more securities are validly credited than issued'.[34]

30 'As the issuer has issued a certain number of securities, the chain of account providers must ensure that that the total number of securities belonging to a specific issue does not exceed the number of securities originally issued.'

31 Second Advice of the Legal Certainty Group, Solutions to Legal Barriers related to Post-Trading within the EU, August 2008, 69.

32 *Ibid.*, 69: 'The name of this principle is somewhat misleading. It appears to be a mere accounting tool but it is also used to describe a conceptual approach to the acquisition and disposition of securities, where 'ownership' is transferred from a properly identified alienator to the properly identified acquirer.'

33 *Ibid.*, 69: 'While it might be technically simpler to apply this principle in a situation where both seller and buyer have their accounts with the same account provider, in countries where this principle is applicable it does not stop there but applies to all types of securities acquisition and disposition, even if it might be (technically) difficult to identify seller and buyer. Logically, this principle could also be applied in cases where the interest is passed onward in the chain of holding, requiring the account provider to maintain at all times sufficient cover with the upper-tier account provider (in such systems, this requirement goes beyond a mere accounting requirement) and giving substantive effect to any breach of that requirement, i.e. where the account provider violates this requirement, the next-in-line person does not receive any interest.'

34 *Ibid.*, 70: 'This practice is mindful to the fact that in commercial practice bookings are effected before all requirements for the acquisition of the asset (or interest therein) have

All this is positive. However, the conclusion comes as no surprise: like UNIDROIT, the LCG does not take a view, again in the interests of a functional approach: 'However, to elevate this principle to a binding common rule would touch upon the Member States' fundamental legal concepts, including the determination of the nature of the investor's interest which should be avoided under the functional approach taken by the present Advice.'

The draft Securities Law Directive, Article 5 ('Methods for acquisition and disposition') provides that acquisition is evidenced by a credit and disposition by a debit and then sets out the conditions under which the credit may take place. There are no corresponding conditions for the debit. Article 6 (Legal effectiveness of acquisitions and dispositions) states that no further steps than those set out in Principle 4 paragraphs 1 and 5 should be required to render an acquisition or disposition effective between the account holder and the account provider and against third parties. This is tantamount to condemning the 'no credit without debit rule'.

8.4 Conclusion

No single holding system is 'better' than another. Each system has its own history, is part of a cultural environment and meets specific needs and purposes. It would be a caricature to contrast 'dynamic' systems with 'static' ones, or 'indirect' ones with 'direct' ones. Similarly, all systems attempt to provide the greatest possible protection for investors whilst facilitating liquidity for collateral or other purposes. There are no 'good' or 'bad' systems, but some models are more influenced than others by their legal and cultural environment.

The American system is based on a coherent and even brilliant intellectual construction, the merits of which cannot be ignored. However, it was designed and developed to meet the practical difficulties inherent in the securities holding system in the USA in the mid-1980s, at a time when the industry was at risk of being stifled due to the cumbersome and archaic nature of the model at the time. It was a solution to the problems of US intermediaries. Since the 2008 financial crisis, with the disaster it brought in its wake for a whole swathe of investors, this model should be treated with circumspection as its underlying rationale meets a vision of

been fulfilled, in particular that the interest of the seller is validly extinguished or that the account provider has received sufficient coverage.'

regulation that today seems outmoded. Promoting liquidity and collateralisation of securities for the benefit of intermediaries was a pre-crisis concern. It is no longer the case today. Moreover, it has become apparent that promoting liquidity cannot only create a systemic legal risk if there is a failure along the securities holding chain, but can even accelerate the conditions for a new crisis by allowing the not totally secure 'collateral' bubble to 'inflate'.

Modern financiers have something in common with the alchemist of old: both are seeking the philosopher's stone that will turn lead into gold; or in today's world, credit (collateral) into money. Both believe in it implicitly and are not discouraged by experience to the contrary.

Legal uncertainty (which implies that a security entitlement has the same legal value and certainty as the security itself) creates financial uncertainty.

PART II

Impact on securities laws of selected European jurisdictions

9

Intermediated securities under Belgian law: assessing the impact of the Geneva Securities Convention on the regulatory environment

MICHEL TISON AND LIENTJE VAN DEN STEEN

9.1 Introduction

The purpose of this chapter is to highlight the potential impact of the 2009 UNIDROIT Convention on Substantive Rules for Intermediated Securities (hereinafter 'the Convention') on the Belgian legal regimes for intermediated securities. After a brief description of the current regimes for intermediated securities under Belgian law, we will outline the main features of these regimes, regarding the nature of the right incorporated into book-entry securities, the rules pertaining to the lower-tier and upper-tier level of intermediated securities, and the protection in case of insolvency of the intermediary. For each sub-theme, we will examine to what extent the Belgian rules are likely or are required to undergo modifications in view of the Convention.

9.2 The legal framework for intermediated securities in Belgian law

9.2.1 Fragmented regimes but harmonised in substance

In Belgian company law, securities[1] can be distinguished according to their form, into bearer securities, registered securities[2] or dematerialised securities.[3]

1 For a description of securities ('effecten'/'valeurs mobilières'), see Van Ryn and Heenen, *Principes de droit commercial*, No. 95.

2 Fredericq, *Traité de droit commercial belge*, IV, No. 332–3.

3 Explanatory Memorandum, *Parl. Documents.* Chamber of Representatives (51), 1974/001, 11.

Bearer securities are securities issued as a physical document which incorporates the rights attached to the security. The person holding the document is presumed to be the legal owner of the rights 'materialised' into this document. Bearer securities used to be the most widespread form of securities used in Belgium, as they combined both easy transferability in face-to-face transactions and anonymity for the owner. The latter inferred obvious advantages, either in tax matters (possible tax avoidance on liberalities or inheritance tax) or in other instances of concealment of property (e.g. to deceive creditors seeking an attachment).

Ownership of registered securities appears from a register, held by the issuing company (or a professional registrar).

Dematerialised securities were conceived under Belgian law as a separate form of securities that lack a 'physical' existence, but exist merely through registration into a securities account held by a settlement institution or financial intermediary.[4] The person in whose name the securities account is opened with the financial intermediary is considered to be the legal owner of the securities credited on that account. End-investors holding the dematerialised securities can never 'exit' the account-based system of securities holdings unless it is possible to convert the securities into another form.

The introduction of 'dematerialised' securities did not follow a single route. An initial legal regime for dematerialised securities was created in 1991 in the area of public debt securities,[5] followed shortly thereafter by the possibility for private issuers to issue dematerialised short-term debt securities under the form of treasury certificates.[6] In both instances, the function of CSD was entrusted to the National Bank of Belgium. In 1995, the Companies Code introduced an additional layer of dematerialised securities rules, by enabling public limited liability companies to issue securities in dematerialised form. However, the regime only became effective after the creation of the settlement system by Royal Decree, which took place not earlier than in 2006. The delay was due mainly to political disagreement on the designation of the CSD for the system of

4 The settlement institutions referred to are Euroclear Belgium or the National Bank of Belgium (NBB). The categories of financial intermediaries (mainly credit institutions) allowed to open securities accounts with these clearing houses or to operate dematerialised securities accounts solo, are specifically enumerated in the Royal Decree of 16 January 2006 on dematerialised company securities.

5 Law of 2 January 1991 on the public debt securities, *Official Gazette*, 25 January 1991.

6 Law of 22 July 1991 on commercial paper and certificates of deposit, *Official Gazette*, 21 September 1991.

dematerialised company securities. Eventually, a compromise was found in splitting the CSD functions according to the nature of the dematerialised company securities: while the National Bank of Belgium was designated as CSD for dematerialised company bonds only, Euroclear Belgium was recognised as settlement organisation for all dematerialised company securities, including bonds.

Moreover, the law of 14 December 2005 (see below) created yet a new form of book entry dematerialised securities that functions as a residual category for those issuers that were not yet allowed to issue dematerialised securities.[7]

In reality, bearer securities were the dominant form for securities for a long time. This was not perceived as problematic for the smooth operation of financial markets. The difficulties for effecting physical paper transfers when settling securities transactions in bearer securities were solved by creating a regime of 'immobilised securities', laid down in the well-known Royal Decree No. 62 of 10 November 1967.[8] This regime aimed at facilitating the transfer of listed (bearer) securities in a cost-effective way, by creating a system of 'fungible deposit' of securities. The securities were deposited with a financial intermediary (lower tier), and ultimately deposited with an upper-tier central securities depository (CIK, presently Euroclear Belgium[9]) or an affiliated depository. The ownership of the deposited securities was reflected in a system of securities accounts, thus enabling the securities to be transferred rapidly and safely, while keeping the physical documents safely under deposit with the CSD.

From the perspective of the owner of the securities, the system of 'immobilisation' created by Royal Decree No. 62 was not only optional, but also reversible:[10] at any given time, the owner of the securities account in which the securities were registered could recollect the bearer

7 E.g. certificates issued by foundations or structured notes issued by financial institutions or SPVs, that do not qualify as 'bonds' within the meaning of the Companies Code.

8 Royal Decree No. 62 of 10 November 1967, *Official Gazette*, 14 November 1967. The initial text, as modified, was coordinated by Royal Decree of 27 January 2004, *Official Gazette*, 23 February 2004.

9 The Royal Decree originally set up the CIK (*Caisse Interprofessionnelle de Dépôt et de Virement de Titres – Interprofessionele Effectendeposito- en Girokas*) as the Central Securities Depository (CSD) of the system of immobilised securities. The CIK was funded by the financial institutions, and was the predecessor to Euroclear Belgium.

10 This is less true for financial intermediaries, when executing orders in listed securities: for securities listed on a Belgian regulated market, credit institutions and investment firms are obliged to settle the transaction through an account-based securities settlement system (Art. 28bis Law of 2 August 2002 on financial supervision).

securities from the (central) depository, restoring their physical nature.[11] Unlike the dematerialised, bearer or registered securities, the 'fungible securities' under Royal Decree No. 62 do not constitute a separate 'form' of securities: the immobilisation of securities does not alter the legal nature of the securities entered into the system (the securities remain 'bearer' securities), but merely transform the individualised ownership right on specified securities into a co-ownership right on a pool of securities of the same nature held by the depository.

The situation described above underwent important changes following the Law of 14 December 2005,[12] which provided for the abolition of bearer securities, albeit through a phasing-out regime rather than a 'big bang'. As part of this phasing-out process, all listed bearer securities held on securities accounts under the regime of Royal Decree No. 62 were automatically transformed into dematerialised securities as from 1 January 2008. Furthermore, as from the same date, it became impossible to issue new bearer securities under Belgian law. Holders of bearer securities that were not automatically transformed into dematerialised securities must opt for their transformation into either registered or dematerialised securities before the end of 2013. The overall effect of the abolition of bearer securities under Belgian law will be a shift from 'immobilisation' towards 'dematerialisation' of securities, notably for listed securities. At the end of the phasing-out process in 2014, only registered and dematerialised securities will subsist as valid forms of securities under Belgian law. However, the 'immobilisation' regime of Royal Decree No. 62 will remain important for the safekeeping of foreign securities on a securities account, usually held with Euroclear Bank as ICSD.

11 It should be noted, however, that even before the abolition of bearer securities under Belgian law, the costs charged by issuers and financial intermediaries for the physical delivery of bearer securities, either at the moment of initial issuance or subsequently, created strong disincentives for investors to exit the regime of immobilised securities. In fact, many (listed) bearer securities were never printed in bearer form when issued, but introduced directly into the account-based system through the issuance of a single global certificate under the form of a bearer security, that was deposited with the CSD, with allocation of the securities to the end-investors directly through the system of securities accounts. This system not only proves to be cost-efficient for the issuer, but it also allocates the cost of creation of physical securities to the investor asking for their delivery. As of 2008 it is no longer possible to 'reverse' the process: the securities credited to an account, even if immobilised, must remain on the account and be converted into either dematerialised or registered securities.

12 *Official Gazette* 23 December 2005.

In conclusion, Belgian law does not have, at present, a 'one size fits all' legal regime for intermediated securities. Various legal regimes continue to coexist, depending on both the issuer and the form of securities, and their fragmented subsistence is mainly due to path-dependent and political factors. Each of the distinct legal regimes for intermediated securities regulates in more or less detail the rights attached to the securities, their transfer and vesting of security interests, the protection of account holders in the case of insolvency of the intermediary, upper-tier attachment of securities, bona fide third party protection etc. However, those fragmented regimes have been mostly aligned with each other.

In view of their relative importance, we will focus below on the regimes for dematerialised corporate securities on the one hand, and on the immobilised securities of Royal Decree No. 62 on the other. Both qualify as 'intermediated securities' under Article 1 of the Convention.

9.2.2 The nature of investors' rights on securities held in an account with an intermediary

Belgian law expressly stipulates that the dematerialised and immobilised securities represent a right *in rem* (an ownership right), albeit of an intangible nature.[13] However, the right *in rem* cannot be individualised, to the extent that a multiplicity of securities owners hold account positions in similar securities with the same intermediary. It is therefore specified that the account position represents an undivided right *in rem* (i.e. a *joint* property right) on the pool of similar securities held by the intermediary or the CSD, as the case may be, which is to be exercised against the intermediary who keeps the account.[14] The situation under Belgian law is similar to the approach in numerous other jurisdictions (e.g. Luxembourg, the Netherlands) that opted for a characterisation as a right *in rem* rather than a right *in personam* (a claim).

As a rule, the actual exercise of the property rights on the securities (or other rights *in rem* such as a pledge) is only possible against the intermediary with whom the account is held.[15] Consequently, no rights can be

13 See, for dematerialised securities: Art. 468, para. 5 Companies Code; for immobilised securities: Art. 2, para. 3, Royal Decree No. 62 of 10 November 1967.

14 With regard to dematerialised company securities, the undivided property right relates to the universality of similar securities registered in the name of the settlement institution with the issuer of the securities (Art. 468, para. 5 Companies Code).

15 See, for dematerialised securities: Art. 471 Companies Code; for immobilised securities: Art. 13, Royal Decree No. 62 of 10 November 1967.

exercised on the aggregate 'omnibus' account held by the intermediary with the CSD, nor directly against the issuer of the securities. However, there are exceptions to this rule in the situation of insolvency or other situations of default (*concursus creditorum*) affecting one of the actors in the system (see below).

9.2.3 Lower-tier level: transactions with dematerialised or immobilised securities

9.2.3.1 Transfer of securities

The dematerialisation and immobilisation regimes under Belgian law expressly contain a provision according to which the transfer of securities is realised by crediting the account of the beneficiary of a transfer.[16] However, unlike in French law, the moment of transfer of ownership has not been fixed. It was widely accepted that this provision does not modify the principle of transfer *solo consensu* as between the transferor and the transferee.[17] However, the latter rule does not fit with the settlement cycle which occurs when securities are being transferred from one account to another. An alternative view takes into account the 'fungible' nature of the securities, and therefore holds that the transfer *inter partes* will occur whenever the securities that are the object of the transfer are specified. By their very nature, such securities cannot be specified through an individual number or other individual characteristics, but only when they are isolated from other securities on the transferor's account or the pool of securities held by the transferor's or transferee's financial intermediary. Hence, the specification that triggers the transfer of ownership from the transferor to the transferee will occur only when the transferee's account has been credited.[18] This coincides with the perfection of the transfer *erga omnes*.

9.2.3.2 Incidents in the transaction chain

Specific rules have been introduced to ensure that the transfer is not disrupted by a revocation of the transfer order, the insolvency or other

16 See, for dematerialised securities: Art. 468, para. 2 Companies Code; for immobilised securities: Art. 6, RD No. 62 of 10 November 1967, which is, however, less explicit in this regard.

17 Tison, 'De uitgifte van gedematerialiseerde vennootschapseffecten', at 239 et seq.; Sunt, 'Dematerialisatie van vennootschapseffecten', at 455 et seq.

18 Van den Steen, *De effectenrekening*, at 534.

events of default during the clearing and settlement process. These rules stem from the European Settlement Finality Directive, implemented into Belgian law by the Law of 28 April 1999. Finality is realised mainly through two principles. First, in order to ensure the smooth operation of the settlement systems, the introduction of a transfer order in the system will as a rule be irrevocable from a certain point on, to be determined in the operating regulations of the system.[19] Second, the insolvency or any other event of default affecting the transferor or any of the intermediaries in the settlement system in the course of the transfer will not affect the completion of the transfer.

Other incidents in the transaction chain can stem from the occurrence of a transfer of securities by a non-owner, or a transfer effected without instruction by the owner. In this regard, the question arises to what extent bona fide acquirers of securities are protected against possible claims by the *verus dominus*. The protection of bona fide third parties who have acquired dematerialised securities, either directly or indirectly, from a person who was not entitled to dispose of these securities, could avoid possible disruptions of the smooth functioning of the accounts system, as it would avoid the unwinding of transactions following successful property disputes.

As a rule, dematerialised securities, as immaterial goods,[20] would not benefit from the protection that is granted by Article 2279 Belgian Civil Code to the bona fide possessor of tangible movable property. Belgian law did not tackle this issue in a consistent way before 2005: most regimes did not contain specific third-party protection provisions. Consequently, the interests of the rightful owner took priority over those of the bona fide third party in situations of erroneous or fraudulent transfers.[21] The Law of 14 November 2005 remedied what was perceived as a possible threat for the orderly functioning of the account-based securities transfer systems, by declaring Article 2279 of the Civil Code applicable to all regimes

19 Compare Art. 3, para. 5, Law of 28 April 1999 (implementing the Settlement Finality Directive), which gives effect to the irrevocable character of the transfer order when provided for in the contractual arrangements of the system.

20 In fact, the rights deriving from a credit position on a securities account in dematerialised or immobilised securities are explicitly characterised by law as 'immaterial': See for dematerialised securities: Art. 468, para. 5 Companies Code; for immobilised securities: Art. 2, para. 3 Royal Decree No. 62 of 10 November 1967.

21 Only for public debt securities did the Law of 2 January 1991 offer protection to the bona fide acquirer in situations where an intermediary had disposed of clients' securities for its own account.

of intermediated securities.[22] This implies that the mere possession of securities (i.e. the credit on a securities account) will provide a valid title for the right *in rem* to the benefit of the bona fide acquirer of intermediated securities, which can be opposed to the 'dispossessed' previous owner.[23]

In theory the dematerialisation system is 'closed-ended': the aggregate sum of all account positions should at all times equal the number of securities issued in dematerialised form or immobilised through 'fungible' deposit. Hence, no transfers may be initiated which would result in a debit position on a securities account, and there must be reconciliation on a regular basis.[24]

9.2.4 Upper-tier level: protection of client securities

9.2.4.1 Segregation of accounts and prohibition of upper-tier attachment

A critical element in investor protection with regard to dematerialised and immobilised securities, concerns the elimination of third-party claims on the investors' securities as aggregated in the upper-tier account held with the CSD or an affiliated intermediary. Particularly, account holders run the risk that creditors of the intermediary with whom the securities are held, or creditors of other account holders could make claims on the securities held by that intermediary on their behalf at a higher level with the CSD or an affiliated party. Therefore, upper-tier attachment on the omnibus account held with the CSD or an affiliated party is prohibited by law.[25] In view of its general wording, the prohibition applies to the creditors of both the intermediary itself and the account holders.

Following the MiFID directive, the previously existing strict regulatory requirements under Belgian law imposing a clear-cut segregation between the pooled 'customer' account ('omnibus account') and the

22 See, for dematerialised securities: Art. 475bis Companies Code; for immobilised securities: Art. 19 Royal Decree No. 62 of 10 November 1967.

23 Van den Steen, *De effectenrekening*, at 577.

24 See also Court of Appeal Antwerp, 21 November 2002, *Droit bancaire et financier*, 2003/V, at 313.

25 See, for dematerialised securities: Art. 472 Companies Code; for immobilised securities: Art. 11, Royal Decree No. 62 of 10 November 1967. The protection thus offered to investors through a specific statutory provision is not affected by the controversial judgment of the Cour de Cassation of 27 January 2011 in the 'Carpa' case, that allowed the attachment by the personal creditors of a barrister of the client account held by the barrister in his personal name with the bank. See Cour de Cassation 27 January 2011, *Droit bancaire & financier* 2012/I, 59.

securities owned (both economically and legally) by the intermediary, have been replaced by a more functional obligation: the securities held by the financial intermediary at the upper level must clearly distinguish, in the books of the upper level intermediary, the clients' securities from the intermediary's own securities.[26] This will usually be realised by maintaining segregated accounts for own securities and clients' securities with the CSD or its affiliated intermediary, thus insulating the client (omnibus) account from third-party claims. However, it is not excluded to use other means to 'separate' the securities, provided they offer an equivalent protection to the clients, although it remains unclear which other techniques could effectively offer such a similar 'insulation effect' to the benefit of the lower-tier account holders.[27]

9.2.4.2 Client protection against insolvency of the financial intermediary or the CSD

9.2.4.2.1 Insolvency of the financial intermediary The insolvency of an intermediary with whom securities accounts are held is likely to affect the rights of the investors pertaining to the securities credited on their accounts. The protection of those rights is mainly realised through techniques of 'bankruptcy-remoteness' of the omnibus account by keeping the pool of securities owned by the investors outside the realm of the intermediary's bankruptcy.

In summarising the relevant legal protection offered under Belgian law to the owners of dematerialised or immobilised securities against the insolvency of the financial intermediary, three levels can be distinguished.

First, the financial intermediary with whom the investor holds the securities account may become insolvent or enter into default. In this case, the rights of the different securities owners of a same security will be executed collectively on the aggregate 'customer' account ('omnibus account') held by the intermediary with the CSD (or an affiliate member). The account held with the CSD is protected against competing claims from other creditors of the insolvent intermediary. In view of the legal obligation for the intermediaries to separate the clients' securities from their own positions, the credit position on the 'omnibus' account held

26 See Art. 66 Royal Decree of 3 June 2007, *Official Gazette*, 18 June 2007, which implements Arts. 16 et seq. of Directive 2006/73/EC.

27 See also Deguée, 'La protection', at 10, who rightly points out that a reporting system whereby the intermediary would regularly notify what proportion of the global account is represented by the intermediaries' own securities, would not appear to offer such equivalent protection.

with the CSD should normally correspond to the sum of the individual clients' account positions held with the intermediary, and consequently offer full compensation to the investors.

There may be situations where the number of securities credited on the omnibus account is inferior to the sum of individual account positions. In this situation, a further distinction should be made according to whether or not clients have agreed to the reuse of securities. If the shortfall occurred without clients' consent to reuse the securities, the ensuing losses will be collectivised to all securities holders, as the available securities will be attributed to them in proportion to their holdings. If the insolvent intermediary personally holds securities of the same nature, the securities holders may, however, exercise the remainder of their claims on these securities, held by the intermediary with the CSD or an affiliated intermediary; this stems from the presumption that the intermediary has used clients' securities for its own account. This right will prioritise all competing claims from other creditors and the property right of the intermediary itself.[28] If, on the contrary, the client has given his consent to the reuse of his securities by the intermediary, a recent change in the Belgian legislation, inspired by the financial crisis, would substantially affect the client's protection in the event of insolvency or other default of the financial intermediary: the client's claim would, to the extent that the consent to reuse was given, be subordinated to those of the clients who did not grant permission to reuse, and therefore will only be admitted to claim his securities on the omnibus account after all other clients have been compensated.[29] It should be noted that the conditions under which the client should obtain the permission from the client to use the client's securities have been aligned with the MiFID regime in 2007: the client should give his express and prior consent to the use of securities by the financial intermediary who holds them.[30] However, this requirement is generally regarded as a weak protection for the investor, as permission should, according to the wording of the MiFID 'level 2' directive 2006/73/EC or the Belgian implementing legislation, not be

28 See, for dematerialised securities, Art. 471, paras. 2, 3 and 5 Companies Code; for immobilised securities: Art. 13, paras. 2, 3 and 5 Royal Decree No. 62 of 10 November 1967.

29 This subordination regime was inserted by law of 2 June 2010 into Art. 471, para. 3 Companies Code (dematerialised securities) and Art. 13, para. 4 Royal Decree No. 62 of 10 November 1967 (immobilised securities). The entry into force of either of both provisions still has to be determined by way of Royal Decree.

30 See Art. 77bis, Law of 6 April 1995, implementing Art. 13(7) of 'level 2' directive 2006/73/EC.

specific.[31] Hence, the consent to reuse the securities could be included in the general contract terms to which the client has adhered when opening a securities account.[32] This could open the door for widespread use of clients' securities as collateral by the financial intermediary, with potentially devastating effects for investors if the financial intermediary entered into default. Recent events indicate that this is not a purely hypothetical issue.[33]

9.2.4.2.2 Insolvency of the CSD Second – a hypothesis that in pre-financial crisis times was deemed not to be very likely, a situation of insolvency or default could affect the CSD directly. In this situation, the securities owners may execute their rights collectively on the financial instruments held by the CSD in custody or given by the latter into sub-custody. The protection is similar to the event of insolvency of an intermediary: the financial instruments held by the CSD are protected against claims from other creditors, and the CSD's own securities of the same nature will be attributed to the securities owners if the latter have not managed to fully recover their securities.[34]

Furthermore, such a CSD would be placed under a strict prudential supervision by the National Bank of Belgium, the Belgian supervisory

31 A further indication that the drafters of MiFID do not consider an 'express' consent to be a synonym for a 'specific' consent under the form of a separate agreement, can be found in the 'best execution' regime of Art. 21(3) MiFID: the directive requires that the inclusion in the execution policiy of the possibility to execute orders in financial instruments outside a regulated market or MTF, is subject to the obligation for the investment firm to obtain the 'prior express consent' from its clients. The provision then clarifies that this consent may be obtained in the form of a general agreement.

32 See, however, Deguée, 'Nouvelle législation', at 240: The author contends, without supporting his point of view, that the consent to reuse the securities cannot be given through the acceptance of the general contract terms. It is, moreover, debatable whether Belgian law could 'gold-plate' the requirement contained in the MiFID 'level 2' directive 2006/73/EC, by requiring a specific consent to reuse the securities, in view of the 'maximum harmonisation' clause of Art. 4 of the same directive (see also Deguée, 'La protection', at 14). Previously, the requirement under Belgian law to obtain a written consent was deducted from the criminal sanction of the use, by the intermediary, of client securities for its own account without written permission. (*Ibid.*).

33 See, notably, the circumstances surrounding the failure of MF Global.

34 Art. 12, para. 2 Royal Decree No. 62 of 10 November 1967. For dematerialised securities, a similar regime is applicable: see Art. 471, para. 1, first indent, Companies Code, that cross-refers to the relevant provision of Royal Decree No. 62. In view of the immaterial nature of dematerialised securities, the owners will execute their rights on the account balance held by the CSD in the books of the issuer.

authority.[35] In case this CSD does not properly function or does not comply with the law, is at risk of becoming insolvent or could disrupt the Belgian or international markets, the government can (by way of Royal Decree) impose several measures, among which disposal (i.e. transfer or sale) of assets and liabilities, including the transfer of the client assets consisting of financial instruments. The Royal Decree will determine the price that will be paid to the owners of the assets that are being transferred.

Finally, the bankruptcy or similar event of default of the issuer of the securities enables the securities account owner to exercise his (financial) claims directly against the issuer (e.g. claim for reimbursement of the capital of a bond).

Attention must also be drawn to the provision that enables the Belgian government to take ad hoc measures in case of a sudden crisis on the financial markets, or in case of a severe threat of systemic crisis. By way of Royal Decree, additional rules or regulations derogating from the legal framework on dematerialised or immobilised securities can be issued. Such 'crisis' regulations are only valid for a year and thus lose binding powers after twelve months unless they are ratified by law. [36]

9.2.5 Investors' rights vis-à-vis the issuer

As for the relationship between the issuer and the owner of dematerialised securities, the dematerialisation of the securities does not alter the full exercise by the owner of the rights attached to the securities, whether pecuniary (dividends, interests, redemption of capital, etc.) or associative (voting right, preferential subscription right etc.). However, specific arrangements are required in order to organise the exercise of these rights, in the absence of a direct connection between the issuer and the investor.

The account holder or the CSD must deliver a certificate which states the number of securities credited on the securities account of the investor. To be able to participate in the general meeting of shareholders, the certificate delivered to the investor must also state that these securities cannot be disposed of until after the general meeting. This must ensure that no person exercises voting rights with shares that have been transferred between the moment of issue of the certificate and the moment of the

35 Art. 36/26 of the Law of 22 February 1998 on the organic statute of the National Bank of Belgium. The market supervision on these institutions is exercised by the Financial Services and Markets Authority (FSMA).

36 Art. 36/24, para. 1, 1° of the Law of 22 February 1998 on the organic statute of the National Bank of Belgium.

meeting itself. In case a registration date is used (for listed companies), the certificate will refer to the number of shares held on this registration date, being the fourteenth day preceding the shareholder meeting; after this date the shares can be disposed of again.[37]

The chain of operators in the account-based system (CSD and account holders) is used to effect the discharge of pecuniary obligations by the issuer towards the investor. With a view to increasing legal certainty, the payment by the issuer to the CSD will discharge the former of its obligations towards the investor. The same principle applies to all further payments down the system, from the CSD to the subsequent account holders, and, ultimately, to the investor.

9.3 The impact of the Geneva Securities Convention on Belgian law

In general, the Belgian legal framework for dematerialised and immobilised securities has gained a strong reputation in providing a robust system with a high degree of legal certainty for all actors involved. It has been quoted as one of the most 'advanced' systems in the world.[38] It is therefore noteworthy to analyse to what extent Belgian law will need adaptations to implement the Geneva Securities Convention. We will further clarify this in the following paragraphs, using the same structure as for the above description of the existing system.

9.3.1 Scope of the UNIDROIT intermediated securities regime

The Convention defines 'intermediated securities' as 'securities credited to a securities account or rights or interests in securities resulting from the credit of securities to a securities account'.[39] The notion of 'securities' is defined in a functional way, referring generally to all financial instruments or financial assets which are capable of being credited to a securities account.[40] The form of the underlying asset of the account position is irrelevant: in view of this functional approach, the Convention regime will cover both the immobilised securities and the dematerialised securities regime in Belgian law. Also, the Convention does not contain any restriction regarding the type of issuer. Consequently, the separate

37 See Art. 536, para. 2 Companies Code.

38 Guynn, *Modernising Securities Ownership, Transfer and Pledging Laws*, p. 77.

39 Convention, Art. 1(b). 40 Convention, Art. 1(a).

regime for dematerialised public debt securities is covered by the Convention as well.

9.3.2 The nature of the investors' rights on securities held in an account with an intermediary

It is well known that the Convention adopts a functional approach to the characterisation of the right resulting from the securities account position: instead of characterising the securities position into existing legal categories, the Convention describes the desired outcome to be achieved, leaving it to each legislator to translate the concepts into national law. Article 9 describes the rights of the account holders with regard to the securities credited to their account: this includes, in a nutshell, the right to receive and exercise any rights attached to the securities, the right to effect a disposition or grant an interest; the right, by instructions to the relevant intermediary, to cause the securities to be held otherwise than through a securities account, to the extent permitted by the applicable law, the terms of the securities and, to the extent permitted by the non-Convention law, the account agreement or the uniform rules of a securities settlement system, and any other rights provided by the local law. Such rights are effective against third parties. This is further reinforced by Article 10 of the Convention, which states, *inter alia*, that the intermediary must allocate securities or intermediated securities to the rights of its account holders so as to be unavailable to its creditors.

Under this functional approach, the Convention does not impair the characterisation, under Belgian law, of the right of the securities account holder as an undivided co-ownership right (*in rem*). As the 'owner' of the securities, the account holder may exercise all rights, both pecuniary and associative, attached to the securities, under the conditions specified in express legal provisions. The account holder can dispose of the securities by transferring, selling, donating etc. and can – to the extent permitted by the relevant rules – require the securities to be converted into another form (i.e. be transposed into registered form). It must be noted that due to the above-mentioned legislation on the gradual abolishment of bearer shares, it is no longer possible to exit the immobilised securities system by reclaiming similar bearer securities in paper form.

Article 10 of the Convention further specifies the obligations incumbent on the intermediary in order to enable its account holders to receive and exercise their rights under the Convention. This includes the obligation to allocate securities to its account holders so as to be unavailable to its creditors, the prohibition to dispose of clients' securities without their authorisation, as further specified in Article 15 of the Convention, and the obligation regularly to pass on information to account holders relating to intermediated securities. While the protection of clients' securities against claims from creditors of the intermediary is expressly provided for in the specific regimes for dematerialised and immobilised securities, other aspects are dealt with more generally in the supervisory regime applicable to financial intermediaries authorised to act as securities custodians. This is the case of the requirement that the intermediary obtains the express and prior consent from the account holder to use its securities for its own account.[41] Similarly, the MiFID conduct of business regime provides for a general obligation regularly to inform the client on the account position.[42]

9.3.3 *Transfer of intermediated securities*

Article 11 of the Convention on Substantive Rules for Intermediated Securities lays down the rule that acquisition or disposition of intermediated securities takes place through the credit or debit of the securities account of the account holder. Moreover, the credit of the securities account is sufficient to render the acquisition effective against third parties.

As discussed above, the immobilised and dematerialised securities regimes under Belgian law do not clarify to what extent the account position is exclusive in determining the property rights regarding the account-based securities. However, in view of the requirement to specify the object of a disposal or acquisition of securities, it may be submitted that even *inter partes* a transfer will only be perfected upon the credit of the securities account of the beneficiary. Moreover, the Convention leaves some room for the application of non-Convention law regarding the conditions under which a credit or debit can be invalidated or reversed,

41 See Art. 77bis, Law of 6 April 1995 on the supervision of investment firms. Where the intermediary is acting as a sub-custodian, the prior consent requirement has been laid down in the MiFID 'level 2' directive 2006/73/EU, as implemented in Belgian law by Art. 69 of the Royal Decree of 3 June 2007, *Official Gazette* 18 June 2007.

42 See, notably, Art. 21(8) of Directive 2004/39/EU, that obliges investment firms and credit institutions to give adequate report on the service provided to their clients. The regime equally applies to 'ancillary' services, including the custody of securities by those institutions. See also Art. 43 of Directive 2006/73/EC, that further specifies this obligation as regards the custody of securities: the intermediary must provide the client at least once a year an account statement. Belgian law implemented these requirements in Art. 26(8) Law of 2 August 2002 on financial supervision c.q. Art. 76 Royal Decree of 3 June 2007.

thereby allowing Contracting States to hold that the account positions do not necessarily reflect the actual property situation between parties to a transaction.

Article 12 of the Convention contains other methods for granting interests (including security interests, such as pledges) in intermediated securities notably through control agreements and earmarking – by way of an opt-in into the national legislation. The difficulty under Belgian law is that, specifically with regard to pledges of securities, Belgian law traditionally required 'dispossession' as a condition for the validity and effectiveness against third parties of the security interest. The dispossession requires that the pledgor no longer has the possibility to dispose of the securities. It is therefore not sufficient to grant some form of publicity to the pledge, by ensuring that third parties are aware of the fact that an agreement to vest a security interest has been concluded between parties. The principle of earmarking has been accepted in the Belgian banking practice but has not been expressly recognised by law. It has been asserted that an earmarked account can be recognised as such and is blocked for the pledgor, and can thus be considered to be fulfilling the requirement of dispossession. The recognition of control agreements is much more controversial as it would need to be established that the control agreement satisfies the 'dispossession' requirement. From a legal certainty perspective, there is a need for further clarification of this aspect under Belgian law. Recently, the Belgian Parliament adopted a law[43] seeking to amend the general law of pledges on movable goods and rights. The law will enable a pledge to be established by agreement without mandatory dispossession, whereby publicity will be ensured through a system of public registration. Hence, Belgian law will recognise control agreements as a valid technique for pledging movable assets, including intermediated securities. The new regime will enter into force no later than 1 December 2014.

Belgian law does not expressly deal with the invalidity and reversal of securities account entries – this is a matter governed by the general principles of the Civil Code; only the protection of a bona fide acquisition by a third party has been recognised, by declaring the protection offered by Article 2279 Belgian Civil Code ('*possession vaut titre*') applicable to the holding of account-based securities. The Convention rules on the 'innocent' acquisition (Article 18) are much more detailed, and may require modifications to the Belgian law regime in two respects. First, in identifying the 'innocent' acquirer, the UNIDROIT Convention excludes

43 See for the text: Parliamentary Documents, Chamber of Representatives (53) 2463/007 (10 Jan. 2013).

from the protection regime not only persons who have actual knowledge of competing interests in securities, but also persons who 'ought to know'. Under Belgian law, by contrast, bona fide is presumed, and the rebuttal of the presumption would require demonstration of actual knowledge by the acquirer of the violation of a competing interest. Hence, the current Belgian regime can be seen as more acquirer-protective that the system envisaged by the Convention. Second, a minor difference stems from the non-application of the 'innocent acquirer' regime to acquisitions by way of gift or otherwise gratuitously (Article 18(3) of the Convention). In protecting the bona fide possessor of securities in a general way, Belgian law does not further distinguish according to the causes of the bona fide acquisition. Hence, the Belgian regime should be further refined to comply with the Convention.

9.3.4 Treatment of upper-tier attachment

The upper-tier attachment of intermediated securities of an account holder is expressly prohibited by Article 22 of the Convention. This is in line with the Belgian legislation which expressly states that the securities account held with the settlement institution (such as Euroclear) may not be attached by e.g. the account holder's creditors. The prohibition laid down in Article 22 of the Convention appears to be broader, to the extent that the attachment may not affect a securities account of any person other than the account holder, while the relevant provisions under Belgian law focus on attachment of the upper-tier account. However, the characterisation of the securities account position under Belgian law as an undivided right *in rem* ensures a similar effect: prohibiting the upper-tier attachment on the omnibus account held by the intermediary protects the undivided ownership rights of other account holders.

9.3.5 Protection against insolvency of the financial intermediary

The functional approach underpinning the Convention implies that no reference is made to any characterisation of the rights of the account holders. In the same sense, Article 26 of the Convention describes the mechanism that should operate in case of insolvency of the intermediary. If the aggregate number or amount of intermediated securities allocated to the account holders is inferior to the aggregate number or amount of securities of that description credited to the securities accounts of these account holders, this shortfall shall be borne by all the account holders to whom the relevant securities have been allocated, in proportion to the respective number or amount of securities of that description credited to their securities accounts.

The Belgian legislation is in line with the shortfall regime provided for in the Convention: based on the characterisation of the account position as an undivided ownership right, a shortfall in the event of insolvency of the intermediary will be borne, proportionally, by all account holders of similar securities. Belgian law even offers more protection to the account holders than provided for in Article 26 of the Convention: if the intermediary itself holds securities of the same type for its own account, these will be allocated, by priority over the rights of the other insolvency creditors, to fulfil the claims of the account holders. This rule can be considered to be part of 'non-Convention law' under Articles 20(1) and 28(3) of the Convention, and should therefore not be abolished when implementing the Convention. More delicate is the recently introduced 'subordination' of the restitution claim by an account holder who has authorised the intermediary to reuse his securities, when a shortfall occurs after the latter's insolvency. As the shortfall regime does not seem to provide for any exception to proportional loss sharing, one could conclude that such subordination does not comply with the Convention. However, the specificity of the relationship between the account holder and the intermediary following the authorisation to reuse should be taken into account: the authorisation granted by the account holder to the intermediary to reuse the securities credited on the account could be characterised, under Belgian law, as a securities loan to the intermediary, generating a transfer of property of the securities that the intermediary uses for its own account. As a consequence, these securities can no longer be considered to be 'allocated' to the account holders within the meaning of Article 25 of the Convention, but are allocated to the intermediary itself. This implies that the account holder will no longer benefit from the loss-sharing regime in case of shortfall, as provided for in Article 26 of the Convention. From this point of view, the subordination regime under Belgian law does not conflict with the shortfall provision of the Convention.

A further complicating factor could stem from the nature of the shortfall provision in private international law. Indeed, the shortfall provision under Belgian law can be characterised as a provision of insolvency law, regulating the priority right of account holders over other creditors in the event of an insolvency of the intermediary. This implies that, in the more exceptional situation where a foreign financial intermediary is connected to a securities settlement system governed by Belgian law, the rights of account holders will be governed by the *lex concursus* – that will most probably coincide with the law of the registered office of the foreign financial intermediary. Consequently, account holders run the risk of not being able to invoke the shortfall regime, including the possible priority right over the securities owned by the intermediary, against the foreign bankruptcy trustee.

9.3.6 Investors' rights vis-à-vis the issuer

As already mentioned, the Belgian co-ownership model confers to the account holder the right to receive dividends which will be passed on from the issuer via the accounts system to the account holder. The account holder will be able to exercise his voting rights by using a certificate delivered by the intermediary, stating the amount of securities held on a certain date by the account holder. This is consistent with Article 9 of the Convention, which states that the right to receive and exercise any rights attached to the securities may be exercised against the relevant intermediary or the issuer of the securities, or both, in accordance with this Convention, the terms of the securities and the applicable law.

The right to effect a disposition or to cause the securities to be held otherwise than through a securities account, to the extent permitted can, according to Article 9, only be exercised against the relevant intermediary. Under Belgian law, it makes sense that any transfer will only be executed by the intermediary. However, the right to cause the securities to be held otherwise than through a securities account could also refer to the conversion into registered shares. Whereas it is clear that this must be done with the assistance of the intermediary, the right to request the conversion into registered form for corporate securities (Article 462 Companies Code) must be exercised against the issuer in the first place.

9.4 Private international law rules in Belgium

The 2004 Code of Private International Law contains a single conflict rule for the rights pertaining to account-based securities. These will be governed by the law of the state where the registration on individual securities accounts is made. It is furthermore presumed that the registration is located in the main establishment of the person keeping the register (i.e. the bank or settlement institution) (Article 91 *juncto* Article 94 Code of PIL). Thus, the account-based securities can be located at the place where the settlement system, holding the securities account, is established.[44] It applies both to 'immobilised' securities, falling under the Royal Decree No. 62, and to dematerialised securities.

The scope of the conflict rule is broad: it encompasses all aspects relating to the existence, the nature, the substance and size of rights *in rem* (such as pledges or title transfer) vested on a financial instrument, This approach was confirmed by Article 9(2) of the European 'Settlement Finality' Directive 1998/26/EEC,[45] which states that when securities held in a settlement system are provided as collateral, the determination of the rights of such entities as holders of collateral security in relation to those securities shall be governed by the law of the Member State where the deposit system is located, or where the institution holding the account is located. Although technically the directive only applies in the case of collateral delivered to central banks or participants in a settlement system and in the context of that system, it confirms that the perfection of collateral in Euroclear generally should also be governed by Belgian law. Moreover, Article 17 of the Financial Collateral Law of 15 December 2004, transposing Article 9, paragraph 2 of the Financial Collateral Directive, states that the legal nature and proprietary consequences, enforceability, realisation and the matter of bona fide third-party acquisition, are governed by the law of the state where the relevant account is held. This is the account on which the pledged or transferred securities are credited.

In other words, the Belgian PRIMA approach is in line with the approach consecrated in the Belgian Code on International Private Law, and does not follow the rules laid down in the 2006 Hague Convention on the law applicable to certain rights in respect of securities held with an intermediary. As Belgium (as all other European Union Member States) has not signed this Convention, there is no need to modify the current private international law regime.

44 A similar approach was already mentioned in Art. 4 of the Royal Decree No. 62, according to which Euroclear (as indeed any other institution operating under Royal Decree No. 62) may redeposit the securities it holds with any sub-custodian in Belgium or abroad, and that the rules set out by Royal Decree No. 62 with regard to the perfection of pledges remain applicable in that case. This implies that Belgian law will govern the perfection and enforcement of a pledge over securities kept in Euroclear, irrespective of a possible re-deposit of the securities by Euroclear with a foreign sub-custodian.

45 Directive of 19 May 1998 on settlement finality in payment and securities settlement systems, OJ L166/45, 11 June 1998. The directive has been implemented in Belgium by the law of 28 April 1999; see in particular Art. 8 para. 2 Law of 28 April 1999, which implements Art. 9(2) of the Directive.

9.5 Conclusion

The presence of the Euroclear system in Belgium has been critical in drawing the attention of lawmakers to continuously improving the legal framework of intermediated securities, in order to maximise the protection of investors and the sound functioning of the securities settlement systems. This brief overview illustrates that a fairly complex legal framework is needed to maximise legal certainty of issuers, investors and operators in settlement systems for immobilised and dematerialised securities.

However, this is not to say that the current legal framework has achieved a status of perfection. Several issues, such as the moment of transfer of ownership, should be further clarified. Others, such as the application by law of Article 2279 Civil Code, by its nature not applicable to intangible goods such as dematerialised securities, need further refinement.

Due to its upscale level of protection, the Convention does not introduce significant improvements to the Belgian legislation nor does it require major amendments. In essence, it appears that the impact of the Convention on the existing system can be regarded to a large extent as a non-issue. The combination of both the neutrality regarding the characterisation of the rights in an account-based system, and the room left for 'non-convention law' in the Convention, enables most elements of the existing regulatory system to remain unchanged.

The most important changes would be the clarifications with regard to third-party beneficiary protection, and the extension of the transfer possibilities to transfer methods other than the mere credit/debit of securities accounts. However, due to the voluntary nature of such transfer methods, it remains to be seen whether the Belgian legislator would be keen on implementing them, especially in light of the strategic importance of Euroclear, and the comparative advantage of the existing legal framework offering a high degree of legal certainty and stability. Even when said rules of the Convention would not be expressly introduced into the Belgian legislation, the Convention would certainly be a useful tool for interpretation and further reference.

Bibliography

Beaupain, L., 'Compte courant de valeurs mobilières' [1968] *Revue de la Banque*, 273–89.

Benjamin, J., 'Immobilised Securities: Perfection of Security Interests' [1999] *J.I.F.M.*, 68–71.

Bernasconi, C., 'Indirectly Held Securities: a New Venture for the Hague Convention on Private International Law' [2001] *Yearbook of Private International Law*, 63–100.

Cerfontaine, C., 'Effectenbewaarneming door financiële instellingen' in Tilleman, B. and Du Laing, B. (eds.), *Bankcontracten* (Bruges: Die keure, 2004), 477–519.

CESR/ECB, 'Standards for Securities Clearing and Settlement in the European Union', September 2004, ESR/04–561, www.cesr-eu.org/.

Dabin, L., 'La dématerialisation et la circulation scripturale des valeurs mobilières dan le cadre des marchés financiers' [1997] *Revue internationale de droit économique*, 291–317.

Deguée, J.-P., 'La protection des avoirs de clients après MiFID' [2008] *Droit bancaire et financier*, 3–22.

'Nouvelle législation sur le renforcement des mesures de redressement en cas de crise' [2011] *Revue de droit commercial belge*, 238–40.

Del Marmol, A., 'Aspects juridiques du fonctionnement d'un système de comptes-titres – rapport de la loi du 6 août 1993' [1994] *Revue de la Banque*, 152–61.

Fredericq, L., *Traité de droit commercial belge*, vol. IV (Ghent: Rombaut, 1946).

Goode, R., 'The Nature and Transfer of Rights in Dematerialised and Immobilised Securities', in Oditah, F. (ed.), *Future of the Global Securities Market* (Oxford: Clarendon Press, 1996), 107–30.

Group of Thirty, *Clearance and Settlement Systems in the World's Securities Markets* (London: 1987).

Guynn, R. D., *Modernizing Securities Ownership, Transfer and Pledging Laws* (London: Capital Markets Forum, 1996).

IOSCO/BIS, 'Recommendations for Securities Settlement Systems', November 2001, available on BIS website.

Lambrecht, Ph., 'La société et son capital' in Centre Jean Renauld (ed.), *Droit des sociétés: les lois des 7 et 13 avril 1995* (Brussels: Bruylant/Academia, 1995), 45–104.

Meunier, V., 'Les systèmes belges de clearing d'opérations sur valeurs mobilières' [1994] *Revue de la Banque*, 144–51.

Schrans, G. and Steennot, R., *Algemeen deel van het financieel recht* (Antwerp: Intersentia, 2003).

Schwarcz, S. L., 'Intermediary Risk in the Indirect Holding System for Securities' [2002] 12 *Duke Journal of Comparative and International Law*, 309–34.

Servaes, B., 'Het immobiliseren van effecten: het Belgisch juridisch kader', in Jan Ronse Instituut (ed.)., *Nieuw vennootschaps- en financieel recht 1999* (Kalmthout: Biblo, 2000), 513–27.

Sunt, C., 'Dematerialisatie van vennootschapseffecten', in Byttebier, K., Feltkamp, R. and Francois, A. (eds.), *De gewijzigde Vennootschapswet 1995* (Antwerp: Kluwer, 1996).

Tison, M., 'De uitgifte van gedematerialiseerde vennootschapseffecten: bemerkingen bij de wet van 7 april 1995', in Braeckmans, H. and Wymeersch, E. (eds.), *Het gewijzigde vennootschapsrecht 1995* (Antwerp: Maklu, 1996), 227–61.

'Competing for Legal Certainty: The Regime of Dematerialised Securities in Belgian Law', in de Vauplane, H. (ed.), *20 ans de dématérialisation des titres en France* (Paris: Banque Editeur, 2005), 254–75.

Tyteca, J., 'De dematerialisatie van aandelen en obligaties', in Jan Ronse Instituut (ed.), *De nieuwe vennootschapswetten van 7 en 13 april 1995* (Kalmthout: Biblo, 1995) 61–91.

UNIDROIT Study Group on Harmonised Substantive Rules Regarding securities Held with an intermediary, Position Paper of the UNIDROIT Study Group on Harmonised Substantive Rules Regarding Indirectly Held Securities, August 2003, www.UNIDROIT.org/.

Van den Steen, L., *De effectenrekening* (Antwerp: Intersentia, 2009).

Van der Haegen, M., 'Le système Euroclear' [1994] *Revue de la Banque*, 138–43.

'La loi du 7 avril 1995 sur les titres dématérialisés: régime des actions et obligations dématérialisées émises par les sociétés anonymes de droit belge' [1996] *Revue Pratique des Sociétés*, 5.

Van der Haegen, M. and Fontaine, A., 'Les dispositions de la loi du 2 août en matière de compensation et de liquidation d'opération sur instruments financiers' [2003] *Droit bancaire et financier*, 69–84.

van Houtte, H. (ed.), *The Law of Cross-Border Securities Transactions* (London: Sweet & Maxwell, 1999).

van Ryn, J. and Heenen, J., *Principes de droit commercial*, vol. III (Brussels: Bruylant, 1981).

10

The Geneva Securities Convention, the future European legislation, and their impact on French securities laws

PHILIPPE LANGLET

10.1 Introduction

We should start by pointing out that, on the whole, the general principles articulated in both the Geneva Securities Convention (the 'Convention') and the EU Documents are largely compatible with French law.[1] Instead of running a strict text analysis, the purpose of this chapter is to highlight practical examples of discrepancies between the Convention and the future EU legislation, against the backdrop of the French securities laws.

It should be remembered that all the work leading up to the EU Legal Certainty Project and the Convention originated from the well-known Giovannini report issued in 2003. At that time, the speed, cost and safety of cross-border securities transactions were considered too burdensome and unsatisfactory by actors in the securities sector. It therefore appeared necessary to tackle those issues which are the main drivers of all the work achieved in securities law relating to the EU Legal Certainty Project and the Convention.

It followed that several experts within the Legal Certainty Group produced a huge work surveying competing legal systems.[2] Specifically, each

1 EU Commission, Legislation on Legal Certainty of Securities Holding and Dispositions, Consultation Document of the Services of the Directorate-General Internal Market and Services, November 2010, DG Markt G2 MET/OT/acg D(2010) 768690; Legislation on Legal Certainty of Securities Holding and Dispositions, Member States Working Group, Updated Compilation of 17 September 2010 of the rules and explanatory notes discussed so far.

2 Second Advice of the Legal Certainty Group, Solutions to Legal Barriers related to Post-trading within the EU, August 2008; Legal Certainty Group, Horizontal answers to the Questionnaire, 24 April 2006.

existing legal system of securities holding was identified and analysed, and several approaches were considered to reconcile them all. It was then that the functional approach appeared to offer the best solution.

However, in 2007 and 2008, when the financial crisis occurred, the whole financial and banking system appeared to be about to collapse. The crisis revealed that an account provider (a 'too-big-to-fail' financial institution) in the holding chain could be in default and become bankrupt. Such a scenario raises two questions: first, who is liable to return the securities to the rightful owner in case of an account provider's bankruptcy? Secondly, who is the actual owner of the securities?

A careful reading of both the EU documents and the Convention from an operational risk perspective seems to suggest that the lessons learnt from the financial crisis aimed at restoring confidence in the banking system have not been sufficiently reflected in either draft.

The answers to the two questions above offer an illustration: first, the Convention and the EU documents do not provide strict securities registration obligations at the upper level, and expose investors to the risk of loss in case of bankruptcy of the account provider (section 10.2). Secondly, the Convention and the EU documents fail clearly to define who is the owner of securities, and therefore expose banks acting as account providers to a significant risk of loss (section 10.3).

10.2 Pro rata sharing of securities loss in case of bankruptcy of the account provider

10.2.1 Under the future EU legislation and the Convention

The duty imposed on the account provider to register its own securities at the upper level of the chain does not exist in the EU documents[3] and is left to non-Convention law in the Convention.[4]

3 Art. 5(2) of the Updated Compilation only refers to 'Account of its Account Holders'.

4 Art. 24 of the Convention ('Holding or availability of sufficient securities'):

> (1) An intermediary must, for each description of securities, hold or have available securities and intermediated securities of an aggregate number or amount equal to the aggregate number or amount of securities of that description credited to:
>
> (a) securities accounts that it maintains for its account holders other than itself; and
> (b) if applicable, securities accounts that it maintains for itself. . . .
>
> (4) This Article does not affect any provision of the non-Convention law . . . , relating to the method of complying with the requirements of this Article or the allocation of the cost of ensuring compliance with those requirements or otherwise relating to the consequences of failure to comply with those requirements.

Recommendation 9a of the Second Advice of the Legal Certainty Group provides that an account provider has to maintain securities in a quantity corresponding to the aggregate of all securities credited to the account of its account holders or held for its own account. This pertinent recommendation was skipped in the last text proposal.

In Article 24 of the Convention, the obligation imposed on the account provider to maintain securities in a quantity corresponding to the aggregate of all securities held for its own account is left to non-convention law and disappears from Article 5(2) of the Updated Compilation of September 2010.

Therefore, in case of bankruptcy of the account provider, the account holders cannot take advantage of the pro rata sharing rule (Article 11(2) of the Updated Compilation[5] and Article 26 of the Convention[6]) in respect to the securities held by the defaulting account provider for its own account.

Consequently, in the event of a securities shortfall, an individual or a bank acting as account holder will not recover its securities, because there are more securities credited at the bankrupt account provider level than securities registered in its name at the upper level.

To avoid such an imbalance, the account provider should have the duty to hold at the upper level of the holding chain sufficient securities

5 Art. 11 ('Protection of account holders in case of insolvency of account provider'). Art. 11(2) provides that 'Member States shall ensure that the law applicable in the insolvency of an account provider provides for a mechanism governing the distribution of the shortage in the event of an insufficient number of securities or account-held securities in the sense of Art. 5 paragraph 2 being held by an insolvent account provider.'

6 Art. 26 ('Loss sharing in case of insolvency of the intermediary'):

> (1) This Article applies in any insolvency proceeding in relation to an intermediary unless otherwise provided by any conflicting rule applicable in that proceeding.
>
> (2) If the aggregate number or amount of securities and intermediated securities of any description allocated under Art. 25(1) to an account holder, a group of account holders or the intermediary's account holders generally (as the case may be) is less than the aggregate number or amount of securities of that description credited to the securities accounts of that account holder, that group of account holders or the intermediary's account holders generally, the shortfall shall be borne:
>
> (a) if securities and intermediated securities have been allocated to a single account holder, by that account holder; and
> (b) in any other case, by the account holders to whom the relevant securities have been allocated, in proportion to the respective number or amount of securities of that description credited to their securities accounts.
>
> (3) To the extent permitted by the non-Convention law, if the intermediary is the operator of a securities settlement system and the uniform rules of the system make provision in case of a shortfall, the shortfall shall be borne in the manner so provided.

equivalent to the number of securities credited to its client's account as well as the number of securities credited to its own account.

It makes economic sense that it is up to the account provider to guarantee any securities shortfall because, in the vast majority of cases, such securities shortfall results directly from the bankrupt account holder's own negligence. It is therefore fair to compel the account holder to indemnify its client(s).

Nevertheless, in practice, we acknowledge that, on the settlement side of the transactions, and for technical reasons, the imbalance mentioned above exists in some jurisdictions in the context of a set of transactions (securities lending and borrowing, short selling, failure to deliver to receive, administrative debit, fraud, etc.).

10.2.2 Under French law

Under French law, registration of the account holder's own securities at the upper level of the chain is compulsory. Nevertheless, section 1300 of the French Civil Code[7] could lead to the extinction of the account provider's obligation, in the event of the failure to register the securities pertaining to the account provider at an upper level. (Indeed, how could a bank be entitled to recover its own securities from itself?) In addition, in the event of the account provider's bankruptcy, section L 211–10 of the French Monetary and Financial Code requires that the securities held by the account provider for its own account be extended to the account holder to cover any securities shortfall.[8] Similar pro rata sharing schemes already exist under the systems of Luxembourg and Belgium.

We should underline that given the absence of a comparable scheme under the English system, there is no hope that the account holders (investors) would be able to recover the securities they had deposited with

7 Art. 1300 French Civil Code: where the capacities of creditor and debtor are united in the same person, a merger is made as of right which extinguishes both claims.

8 Art. L 211–10 Code Monétaire et Financier:

> In case of bankruptcy procedure of an intermediary listed in art. 213–3, 'l'administrateur judiciaire ou le liquidateur', with the 'administrateur provisoire ou le liquidateur' named, in such a case, by the 'Autorité de contrôle prudentiel', checks security by security that the aggregate amount of all the securities registered in an account opened within another intermediary or within the central securities depository in the name of the defaulting intermediary, notwithstanding the nature of such account, is sufficient to permit the intermediary to fulfil its obligations towards the account holders. In the event that there is an insufficient number of securities, each security is allocated to the relevant account holder on a pro rata basis; the latter may wire transfer to a securities account held by another intermediary or by the issuer from which they obtain the securities.

Lehman Brother International Europe in UK to cover the shortfall they have endured. More than two years after Lehman Brother International Europe's bankruptcy, to the best of our knowledge, no one has been able to recover their securities!

10.3 How could the uncertain definition of the owner of securities lead to an unfair result at the banks' expense?

10.3.1 Madoff clawback procedure

The Madoff clawback procedure is a reflection of the risk to which banks are exposed when they act as intermediaries because the underlying legislation does not clearly spell out who the real owner of the securities is. A clawback claim is generally asserted by a bankruptcy trustee to recover money paid out to investors in a Ponzi scheme before the discovery of the scheme.

In the *Bernard Madoff* case, a US court initiated liquidation proceedings against the company Bernard L Madoff Investment Securities LLC ('BLMIS') and all those whose assets were held or managed by, or invested in BLMIS (for example all the Fairfield family British Virgin Islands funds).

BLMIS is in this example the defaulting account provider in the holding chain.

By cascade, the Fairfields' funds, which were sued by BLMIS's receiver, in turn brought a civil action against banks that acted as intermediaries on behalf of the actual owners of the relevant funds' shares (beneficial owners) to recover USD 4.644 billion in redemptions before, respectively, the New York Supreme Court, US Federal Bankruptcy Court and the High Court of Justice of the British Virgin Islands.

This chain of lawsuits revealed a rather odd and unfair situation where banks (registered within the books of the transfer agent of the Fairfields' funds) were sued based on the allegation, inter alia, that the banks were unjustly enriched to the detriment of both the Fairfields' funds and the current holders of Fairfield shares!

In other words, Fairfields' funds sought to recover all redemption payments made before the six-year statute of limitations ran out.

We should emphasise at this stage that the banks were just receiving and transmitting subscription or redemption orders given by the final beneficial owners based on their own risk analysis. In the vast majority of cases, banks never promoted or sold in their volition the shares pertaining to the Fairfields' funds. To provide more detail, the transfer agent of the relevant funds is a company registered under Luxembourg laws. Further, pursuant to applicable Luxembourg laws and circulars,[9] the banks, even though they only acted as nominees, vis-à-vis third parties were treated as the actual owners of the shares pertaining to the Fairfields' funds. As such, they were entitled or subject to, as the case may be, all attached rights and obligations.

Such an unfair and contested recovery device directed against the banks is no more than 'fishing in deep pockets'. This is a tremendously practical reason to avoid both the Convention and the future EU legislation, which allow uncertainty as to who the actual owner of the relevant securities is. The indirect holding pattern is one of the means that allow the first financial intermediary in the chain to be sued for reimbursement even if such account provider is not entitled to receive ownership rights and obligations of the actual owner.

By comparison, because the French regime is a direct holding system, there is a direct relationship between the issuer and the final investor, and thus there is no doubt in the end as to who the beneficial owner is. On the contrary, the Convention – and, to a certain extent, the future EU legislation – by permitting the existence of rights or assets derived from the initially issued securities at each level of the holding chain, promote confusion regarding who the actual owner of the securities is, which in the end opens the door to unfair procedures against the banks acting as intermediaries, on the grounds that they appear to be vested with the rights derived from the securities. The multi-tier holding system legitimates the account holder's claims against the account provider because the latter seems to be vested with actual property rights and obligations.

10.3.2 The bundle of rights concept in the Convention and the future EU legislation is not compatible with French law

The Convention and the future EU legislation are inspired by Article 8 of the United States Uniform Commercial Code. Multiple book entries embedded in the multi-tier holding system which are promoted by the future EU legislation and the Convention create new or 'derivative rights' at each level of the chain (with negative effects – e.g. over-voting at shareholders' meetings and securities inflation). The subsequent securities

9 IML 91/75 CSSF 02/77.

become distinct from the initial issued securities.[10] Finally the securities sold or given as collateral are different from the initial securities; they are a mere entitlement against the account provider.

Under French law, and for the vast majority of the authors, the security book entry materialises the security. Through the securities registration in a book entry, the account provider acknowledges the existence of the ownership rights (*usus, fructus and abusus*) created by the issuer in favour of the account holder. There is no additional right created in favour of the account holder. Therefore, due to the direct holding pattern, only one securities owner exists. The owner of the securities alone enjoys ownership rights and obligations in respect to the relevant security. He is the only actual owner. Only he can be sued in a clawback claim.[11]

Under French law the book entry is the security. Such security is evidenced in the securities account held in the security owner's account. The investor has full ownership rights on his security and has a direct claim on the issuer which permits him to escape from the account providers' creditors. Despite dematerialisation, the cornerstone of the French legal system is that the securities owner enjoys full ownership rights on his security whether or not the security is in paper form. In fact in order to fully protect the investor, the ultimate consequences of the dematerialisation process have not been incorporated into the French legal regime.[12]

For the reasons stated above, the multi-tier holding system promoted by EU documents and the Geneva Convention contradicts the French system where the actual owner is the only actor who enjoys all ownership rights in respect to a security.

10.4 Conclusion

Because the bankruptcy of an intermediary in the chain is no longer hypothetical (following the Lehman collapse), it is no longer necessary to foster the rapidity, volume and collateralisation of transactions through the creation of securities entitlements at each level of the holding chain/reuse. The focus should be on the protection of investors and the

10 Gourio, A. and Thebault, L., 'Le droit européen des titres financiers: l'heure du choix', [2010] *European Banking and Financial Law Review (Euredia)*, 325–35; Mojuye, B. 'Les droits intermediés en common law américain', [2010] *Revue de Droit Bancaire et Financier*, 6–15.

11 See above section 10.3.1.

12 de Vauplane, H. and Nizard, Frédéric, 'Les titres inscrits en compte en droit international privé', in *Mélanges AEDBF III*, July 1, 2001, 401–23.

soundness/safety of the financial/banking system. The Convention and the future EU legislation are not in line with French law principles. The pillars of reform should include stronger regulation of account providers, the integrity of securities issues and a better tracking of securities owners. It seems too late for the Convention, but it is still time for the future EU legislation to draw from the lessons learned during the crisis and to build a legal system that better protects investors against the bankruptcy of intermediaries (account providers).

11

The Geneva Securities Convention, the future European legislation, and their impact on German law

ULRICH SEGNA

11.1 Introduction

Unlike the United States, Japan and Switzerland – taking three prominent examples – Germany has not so far modernised its legal framework for intermediated securities. The main statutory basis for the holding and transfer of securities by way of book entries on securities accounts, the Securities Deposit Act (*Depotgesetz*), dates back to 1937 and has not been substantially changed since then. Certainly, there have been several more or less important amendments, such as *Depotgesetz* section 9a, which was enacted in 1972 to clarify that global certificates are capable to serve as a basis for book entries, *Depotgesetz* section 5(4), which was adopted in 1985 in order to allow a German CSD (*Wertpapiersammelbank*) to establish a mutual account relationship (*gegenseitige Kontoverbindung*) for purposes of cross-border securities settlements with a foreign CSD, or the special conflict-of-laws rule in *Depotgesetz* section 17a, by which Article 9(2) of the Settlement Finality Directive of 1998 (the 'PRIMA' rule) was implemented into German law.[1] Nevertheless, the basic principles and concepts for the holding and disposition of intermediated securities have remained the same over the past decades. This holds especially true with regard to the concept of co-ownership, which is laid down in *Depotgesetz* sections 6 and 24(2). This concept applies to all fungible securities held in

1 Directive 98/26/EC of the European Parliament and of the Council of 19 May 1998 on settlement finality in payment and securities settlement systems, OJ L166/45, as amended by Directive 2009/44/EC of the European Parliament and of the Council of 6 May 2009 amending Directive 98/26/EC on settlement finality in payment and securities settlement systems and Directive 2002/47/EC on financial collateral arrangements as regards linked systems and credit claims, OJ L146/37.

collective safe custody (*Sammelverwahrung*) with the only German CSD, Clearstream Banking AG in Frankfurt am Main. It follows the general rules of the German Civil Code (*Bürgerliches Gesetzbuch*, hereafter BGB) for the transfer of movables (sections 929 et seq.) to such a large extent that it appears not misleading to say that Germany maintains a strong civil law tradition in this respect.[2]

Although the existing legal framework for intermediated securities has not caused serious practical problems so far,[3] it is widely believed that the traditional concepts have not kept pace with the development of modern financial markets, and that for this reason they can no longer be regarded as a sound legal basis for the holding and disposition of securities.[4] The adoption of the Geneva Securities Convention and the discussion of the harmonisation of securities law at EU level have made it even more evident that there is an urgent necessity to think about a thorough modernisation of German deposit law. This is all the more true, given that some academics take the view that the implementation of the Geneva Securities Convention would require a fundamental conceptual change, arguing that a co-ownership concept like the 'good old' German one is not compatible with this instrument.[5]

However, it should be noted that there has been no consensus up to now as to which alternative approach the German law should choose instead. Dorothee Einsele, a law professor from Kiel and member of the UNIDROIT Study Group preparing the draft Convention, has recommended the implementation of a trust concept ('*Treuhand*') in which the ultimate account holder would no longer be regarded as the legal owner of the securities, but only as the beneficial owner, as is the case under the *Gutschrift in Wertpapierrechnung* system, which applies to securities purchased and deposited abroad.[6] Other experts support a full

2 Kanda, 'Legal Rules on Intermediated Securities: The Japanese Situation', at 230.

3 See Scherer and Gallei, 'UNIDROIT draft Convention and German securities law', at 474 et seq., stating that the existing legal framework 'works extremely smooth and well in practice, and has never led to any significant legal disputes'.

4 See Einsele, *Wertpapierrecht als Schuldrecht;* Lehmann, *Finanzinstrumente.*

5 Kronke, 'Das Genfer UNIDROIT-Übereinkommen über materiellrechtliche Normen für intermediär-verwahrte Wertpapiere und die Reform des deutschen Depotrechts'; Mülbert, 'Vom Ende allen sachenrechtlichen Denkens im Depotrecht durch UNIDROIT und die EU'; Mülbert, 'Vom Ende allen sachenrechtlichen Denkens im österreichischen und deutschen Depotrecht durch UNIDROIT und die EU'; see also Voß, 'Die Securities Law Directive und das deutsche Depotrecht'.

6 Einsele, *Wertpapierrecht als Schuldrecht*, 561–96; see also Einsele, 'Das Treuhandmodell als Alternative zum geltenden Recht', at 14–28.

dematerialisation of all shares and bonds issued under German law, being convinced that the main legal risk stems from the fact that the German securities settlement system is widely based on the use of certificates.[7] Furthermore, in May 2008 the Federal Ministry of Justice published a position paper on the reform of German securities deposit law in which it brought up for discussion the question of whether the co-ownership concept should be replaced by a new *sui generis* approach in accordance with the Swiss Federal Intermediated Securities Act (FISA).[8] Since the German and the Swiss legal frameworks for the holding and transfer of securities by book entry were largely based on the same principles before the FISA entered into force (1 January 2010), it is not surprising that the FISA is widely considered to be the most important international benchmark for the modernisation of German deposit law.[9]

The present contribution has neither the ambitious aim to provide a deepened and comprehensive analysis of the current German legal framework for intermediated securities, nor that of presenting a sophisticated proposal for its modernisation. Instead, it focuses primarily on the crucial question of whether it is true that the two harmonisation initiatives on the international and the European level, the Geneva Securities Convention and the EU project of what is commonly referred to as the 'Securities Law Directive' (SLD), have brought about the necessity for a conceptual change. Since the traditional co-ownership model is indeed the most problematic one in this context, this seems to be a good reason to concentrate exclusively on this model and to leave aside the concept of *Gutschrift in Wertpapierrechnung*.[10] Consequently, section 11.2 takes a closer look at the main characteristics and problems of the co-ownership concept in order to provide a background for the analysis which follows. Section 11.3 deals with the impact of the Geneva Securities Convention,

7 See (with remarkable differences in detail) Lehmann, *Finanzinstrumente*, 250–523; Peters, *Wertpapierfreies Effektensystem*, 125–53; Habersack/Mayer, 'Globalverbriefte Aktien', 1678–84; see also Zahn and Kock, 'Die Emission von unverbrieften Schuldtiteln durch die Europäische Zentralbank', 1955–67.

8 Bundesministerium der Justiz, Eckpunktepapier zur Reform des Depotrechts of 29 May 2008.

9 Saager, 'Depotrecht im Umbruch', at 25.

10 The concept of 'Gutschrift in Wertpapierrechnung' applies to securities which are purchased and deposited abroad at a foreign custodian selected by the domestic (first-tier) custodian or Clearstream Banking AG, as the case may be; for a short description see Einsele, 'Modernising German Law', at 256–7; Than, 'The Legal Framework for Safe Custody, Administration and Transfer of Securities in Germany', at 242–3.

and section 11.4 with the impact of the EU harmonisation initiative. Finally, section 11.5 draws some conclusions.

11.2 The co-ownership concept and its main problems

11.2.1 Main characteristics

As already mentioned, the concept of co-ownership applies in the case where certificated securities such as shares or private bonds are held in collective safe custody with Clearstream Banking AG.[11] This so-called *Girosammelverwahrung* is by far the most common form of holding securities in safe custody in Germany, and is mandatory for all domestic issues traded on the German stock exchanges. The main characteristics of the co-ownership concept, applied since 1925 and codified more than ten years later by the Securities Deposit Act of 1937,[12] are the following:

- The ultimate account holders (investors) are co-owners of the respective fungible pool of securities stored in the vault of Clearstream Banking AG. The size of their co-ownership interest is determined by the size of their participation in the pool (section 6(1) *Depotgesetz*). Such a pro rata co-ownership is a right *in rem* (*Recht am Wertpapier*) with all its consequences: it is neither Clearstream, nor the relevant intermediary, but the ultimate account holder who holds legal title to the securities and who is therefore recognised as the shareholder or creditor.[13] Consequently, all rights attached to the securities (*Rechte aus dem Wertpapier*), such as voting rights or the right to receive dividends, are attributed to the ultimate account holder. The intermediaries in the holding chain are, of course, obliged to render administration services to their customers (the collection of dividends and interests etc.), but they do not

11 Additionally, this concept also applies to federal and state bonds, which are completely dematerialised, i.e. there is no certificate at all. Instead, federal and state bonds are issued by registering claims in the name of Clearstream Banking AG in a special public register, the so-called 'Schuldbuch'. According to s. 6(2) of the Federal Act regulating the Management of Federal Debts of July 12, 2006 (*Gesetz zur Regelung des Schuldenwesens des Bundes* [*Bundesschuldenwesengesetz* – BSchuWG]), all claims registered in the name of Clearstream Banking AG (*Sammelschuldbuchforderungen*) shall be treated as fungible pools of certificated securities held in collective safe custody.

12 For a short historical overview, see Heinsius and Horn and Than, *Depotgesetz*, s. 5 para. 1–9.

13 Than, 'The Legal Framework for Safe Custody, Administration and Transfer of Securities in Germany', at 238.

have any property rights in the securities. There is no division into legal and beneficial ownership as under the *Gutschrift in Wertpapierrechnung* regime.

The fact that the investor holds a pro rata property interest in the fungible pool of securities reflects one of the general ideas behind this concept: the commingling of securities of the same issue modifies the form of ownership, but it interrupts neither the investor's direct legal title to the securities nor his relationship with the issuer, thus ensuring that the investor's legal position is as safe as if the securities were held in separate safe custody. Since co-ownership rights in securities are effective against all persons as any other rights *in rem*, there is consequently no need to say that the investors are protected against an intermediary´s insolvency by the general rules of the Insolvency Act (*Insolvenzordnung*). According to section 47 of the Insolvency Act they are entitled to separate their securities (*Aussonderungsrecht*).

Looking at this characteristic feature of the German co-ownership model, it should be clear why the term 'indirect holding system', which was often used especially in connection with the Hague Securities Convention and also in the very beginning of the UNIDROIT project, is completely misleading. The co-ownership model is indirect only in the sense that several intermediaries are standing between the issuer and the investor. It is, however, a 'direct ownership' concept in the sense that, as in the physical world of paper securities, the investor – as the last account holder in the chain – has a direct interest in the underlying securities and a direct legal relationship with the issuer, regardless of the number of intermediaries involved in the holding of the securities.

– A second main feature may be seen in the fact that not only Clearstream but also the various account holders in the holding chain, i.e. the intermediaries further up the chain and the final investors, are considered to be possessors of the whole bulk of securities. While Clearstream can obviously be classified as the direct possessor of the certificates since it holds them physically (*unmittelbarer Besitzer*), the lower-tier intermediaries and the ultimate account holders are regarded as indirect co-possessors of the first or of the second degree (*mittelbare Mitbesitzer ersten bzw. zweiten Grades*). Based on the account agreement, Clearstream mediates co-possession of the underlying documents in favour of its own customer, the first-tier intermediary, who in turn mediates co-possession in favour of the ultimate account holder. According to the traditional legal doctrine, this indirect co-possession manifests itself in the book entry on the securities account maintained with Clearstream in respect to the first-tier intermediary.[14]

- These two premises form the conceptual ground for the common opinion in Germany that (co-ownership rights in) securities can be acquired and transferred in accordance with the general rules applicable to the transfer of movables (BGB section 929 et seq.). Pursuant to BGB section 929, the transfer of ownership in movable property requires (1) an agreement between the transferor and the transferee that the ownership passes to the transferee and (2) the delivery of possession. In a simple two-party transaction it is usually not difficult to ascertain whether these two requirements are fulfilled or not. If a typical stock exchange transaction is settled through Clearstream Banking AG, the application of this provision proves to be more complex, since it is not clear at first sight between which parties the transfer of ownership takes place and which role the intermediaries play in the settlement process. For a number of reasons which do not need further explanation here, it is a general consensus that the title to the securities should pass directly from the selling investor to the buying investor and that, consequently, there should be no interim acquisition on behalf of the various intermediaries involved in the settlement process, even for a short moment.

As the agreement required by BGB section 929 has to be concluded between the transferor and the transferee, it is therefore inevitable to build up 'a complex structure of legal declarations starting from the seller mandating his custodian bank to sell and transfer ownership of his securities via such custodian bank, the Central Securities Depository holding physical possession of securities, the bank executing the corresponding purchase order on to the purchaser'.[15] As regards the second requirement of BGB section 929, the delivery of possession no longer consists of certificates being handed out physically to the buyer. Instead, the buyer acquires indirect co-possession of the certificates by receiving a credit on his securities account immediately after the execution of the purchase order by his intermediary ('T+0').

Nevertheless, it should be noted that this credit becomes legally effective only under the implied condition that the buyer's intermediary in

14 For the details see Micheler, *Property in Securities*, 208–9.

15 Than, 'The Legal Framework for Safe Custody, Administration and Transfer of Securities in Germany', at 247. For the details see Dechamps, *Wertrechte im Effektengiroverkehr*, 49–60.

turn receives a corresponding credit on his account with Clearstream Banking AG.[16] Pursuant to the conditions on transactions at the German stock exchanges, such transactions must be performed on the second performance day following the day the transaction is entered into ('T+2').[17] In consequence, the transfer of co-ownership takes place the moment the seller's intermediary fulfils its obligation to 'deliver' the securities, i.e. when the securities are credited to the securities account of the buyer's intermediary. Thus, the credit on the buyer's securities account on T+0 is made on the condition that the respective trade is duly settled on T+2. The conditions on transactions on the German stock exchanges also provide that the purchaser is required to pay the price for the relevant securities upon delivery, but no earlier than on the second day of performance after entering into the transaction.[18] Therefore, stock exchange transactions are settled by Clearstream on a DVP basis. Clearstream shall ensure that title to securities passes concurrently with payment, thus eliminating the principal risk inherent in the given transaction.

11.2.2 Main problems

In its First Advice of 2006, the Legal Certainty Group argued that 'Germany has a specific and clear legal basis for holding securities in book entry form and for transferring ownership of such securities'.[19] For a lawyer who is familiar with the state of discussion in Germany, this assessment was somewhat surprising, since there is a widely held view among experts that the traditional co-ownership concept shows some serious uncertainties. This may be illustrated by two examples:

- First, it is said that it is not only artificial, but even impossible to consider the final investor as indirect co-possessor of the securities deposited with Clearstream. The reason is that indirect possession requires that the investor has a right against his intermediary to request delivery of individual certificates equivalent to the book entries in his favour. According to *Depotgesetz* section 7(1), this right undoubtedly exists

16 Than, 'The Preliminary Draft UNIDROIT Convention and Capital Market Practice in Germany', at 269.

17 See for example § 4(1) of the Conditions for Transactions on the Frankfurter Wertpapierbörse (2 July 2012).

18 See for example § 4(2) of the Conditions for Transactions on the Frankfurter Wertpapierbörse (2 July 2012).

19 Legal Certainty Group, *Practical Examples of Legal Barriers, Annex to the Advice of the Group*, July 2006, 2.

when the fungible pool of securities consists of individual certificates. However, since more than 95 per cent of all securities are issued in the form of global certificates which are stored permanently at Clearstream, the investors consequently have no right to obtain any separate certificates (*Depotgesetz* section 9a(3)). Therefore, it is concluded that the prerequisites for indirect possession are not fulfilled in this case with the result that the application of the general rules for the transfer of movables is impossible. This, in turn, means that there is no legal basis for the possibility of bona fide acquisition.[20]

One might well doubt whether this objection is justified. It holds true that in such cases when a permanent global certificate forms the basis of the book entries, the individual investor does not have the right to request delivery of individual certificates. However, that does not necessarily mean that he cannot be considered as indirect co-possessor. While analysing the applicability of BGB sections 929 et seq, one must consider that the account holder, based on the account agreement, has the power to instruct his intermediary to transfer the securities to another account. By concluding the account agreement, the intermediary has agreed to comply with the account holder's orders to effect a disposition. One can understand this contractual power of the account holder as a functional equivalent to the right to obtain certificates (*Herausgabeanspruch*), although it must be admitted that from a methodological point of view this idea reaches the limit of what appears to be feasible. Nevertheless, in a judgment given in 2004 the German Federal High Court (*Bundesgerichtshof*) took a very similar position, stating that in the world of intermediated securities the transfer of possession by way of handing over certificates physically has been replaced by making book entries on securities accounts. Especially in the case when a permanent global note has been deposited, performing such book entries would be the only possible way for an intermediary to fulfil the account holder's right to request the delivery of certificates.[21]

- Secondly, one of the most controversial questions in the current discussion is whether good faith acquisition is possible under the co-ownership concept. It is a common opinion that, for reasons of efficiency and financial stability, provisions on the protection of a bona

20 See in detail Einsele, *Wertpapierrecht als Schuldrecht*, 65–88; Habersack and Mayer, 'Globalverbriefte Aktien', at 1680–1.

21 *Amtliche Sammlung der Entscheidungen des Bundesgerichtshofs in Zivilsachen* (BGHZ), vol. 161, 189 at 191–2; see also Berger, 'Verpfändung und Verwertung von Aktien', at 582.

> fide acquirer form an indispensable element of the legal framework for intermediated securities. However, it is widely believed in Germany that the intended result – bona fide acquisition – cannot be achieved by the application of the general rules of property law. The rationale underlying these rules – in particular BGB section 932 – is that the ability of the seller to bring an asset into the physical possession of the buyer entitles him to assume that the seller also had the authority to dispose this asset.[22] This underlying explanation leads some German scholars to believe that the buyer of a co-ownership interest is not protected by the rules on good faith acquisition. Their main argument is that when the buyer acquires co-possession, no aspect of the transfer process indicates which fraction of the ownership right to the bulk belonged to the buyer. Considering that it is only the book entries that evidence the amount or number of rights that the account holder owns, the prevailing legal opinion in Germany is that book entries may be regarded as the legal basis for the possibility of bona fide acquisition.[23] However, Dorothee Einsele has raised some fundamental concerns against this approach. In her opinion, 'book entries lack the quality of a legal basis for the possibility of bona fide acquisition since the acquirer has no inside view of the operation of the system and bank secrecy laws do not allow for it to verify whether the transferor in turn acquired the right'.[24]

In the author's opinion, all these considerations and reservations have made matters much more complicated than they should be. It has been demonstrated above that the problem of co-possession could be solved by regarding the account holder's contractual power to instruct his intermediary to transfer the securities to another account as a functional equivalent to a *Herausgabeanspruch*. Consequently, the ability of the transferor to cause the intermediary to effect such a transfer should be considered a sufficient basis for a bona fide acquisition.[25] Nevertheless, it should be admitted that this is no more than a compromise solution that cannot hide the fact that there is a considerable lack of transparency and clarity in German law.

22 Micheler, *Property in Securities*, 212.

23 Heinsius and Horn and Than, *Depotgesetz*, 1975, s. 6 para. 91; Dechamps, *Wertrechte im Effektengiroverkehr*, 115–56; Mahler, *Rechtsgeschäftliche Verfügungen*, 132–6; Horn, 'Die Erfüllung von Wertpapiergeschäften', 14–15.

24 Einsele, 'Modernising German Law', at 252–3.

25 Kunz, *Ausgewählte Rechtsprobleme des Zentralen Kontrahenten*, 439–40.

11.3 The impact of the Geneva Securities Convention

Another question is whether the Geneva Securities Convention makes it necessary to replace the co-ownership concept.

11.3.1 Functional approach

The answer to this question is predetermined by the functional approach taken by the Convention. It would go far beyond the scope of this chapter to provide a detailed description and analysis of this approach.[26] However, it should be remembered that it is based on the assessment of the Study Group that the most promising way to establish a common legal framework for intermediated securities would be to concentrate on a very few key questions that call for global uniform rules, given that it would be extremely difficult, if not impossible for political reasons to achieve full harmonisation within a reasonable time frame. Taking into account that there is a wide diversity in the legal and doctrinal characterisation of the position of account holders around the world, the Study Group recognised that 'a harmonised rule should be regarded as appropriate if, but only if, it is clearly required for the reduction of legal or systemic risk or for the promotion of market efficiency'.[27] Consequently, the Convention focuses on a carefully selected list of key issues (rights of the account holder, transfer of intermediated securities etc.), using a language which is as neutral as possible, formulating rules only by reference to their results, and leaving a fair number of related matters to 'non-Convention law', as defined in Article 1(m). In particular, the Convention does not attempt to override the whole of the underlying domestic legal doctrine that is the vehicle for producing the results that arise in securities transactions and settings within its scope.[28] Its rules have been designed to be strictly independent from the legal characterisation of the rights created or evidenced by book entries in securities accounts so they can be implemented by a Contracting State without requiring it to change that characterisation.[29]

From a German point of view, there is no reason to criticise the key terms 'intermediary' and 'intermediated securities' as being not

26 See Thévenoz, 'The Geneva Securities Convention: objectives, history, and guiding principles', Ch. 1 of this book.
27 UNIDROIT Study group, position paper August 2003, 14.
28 Mooney and Kanda, 'Core Issues', at 75.
29 Thévenoz, 'Intermediated Securities', at 414.

sufficiently neutral.[30] Although it is true that these terms have been completely unknown in German law to date – the Securities Deposit Act uses only the terms *Verwahrer* (custodian) and *Wertpapiere* – and may be more familiar to lawyers with an Anglo-American background, there is no doubt that the definitions contained in Article 1 are wide and flexible enough to cover all types of 'national' account providers and all types of rights which can arise from the credit of securities to a securities account. When carefully read, these definitions should not provoke the misunderstanding that an 'intermediary' is in every case part of a holding arrangement where the legal relationship between the issuer and the final investor is interrupted, as it is for example the case within the security entitlement concept of Article 8 UCC. A different question is whether the relevant provisions of the Convention, both taken for their own and as a whole, meet the requirement of being sufficiently neutral. To answer this question, we shall now examine two of the cornerstones of the Convention: Article 9 dealing with the rights of the account holder, and Article 11 dealing with the disposition and acquisition of intermediated securities by debit and credit.

11.3.2 Rights of the account holder (Article 9)

Article 9 is one of the most representative examples for the functional approach taken by the Convention. Fully consistent with this approach, it does not attempt to characterise the legal nature of the rights and interests arising from the credit of securities to a securities account.[31] Instead, it specifies the core attributes of intermediated securities by describing both in economic and legal terms 'what it is that is conferred to the account holder by the credit of securities to a securities account'.[32] 'Consequently, in a cross-border holding chain, where different laws may apply to "the same" securities credited to the relevant securities accounts, Article 9(1) makes sure that the basic content of the rights remains identical and that account holders always know that they receive at least . . . these rights.'[33] Article 9(1)(a) provides that the account holder receives 'the right to receive and exercise any rights attached to the securities, including dividends, other distributions and voting rights'. But an account holder that is an intermediary receives these economic benefits only if it 'is acting for its own account' – and can therefore be considered as 'ultimate account holder' – or 'if so provided by the non-Convention law'. The account

30 For a different view from the Austrian perspective see Pöch, 'UNIDROIT – Entwurf einer Wertpapier-Konvention', at 307.

31 Kanda et al., *Official Commentary*, s. 9–2.

32 Mooney and Kanda, 'Core Issues', at 83.

33 Kanda et al., *Official Commentary*, s. 9–1.

holder also receives the right to effect a disposition under Article 11, or to grant an interest under Article 12,[34] and the right to instruct the intermediary to cause the securities to be held otherwise than through a securities account, though this right is subject to numerous limitations.[35] Finally, Article 9(1)(d) provides that a credit to a securities account confers 'such other rights, including rights and interests in securities, as may be conferred by the non-Convention law'. Its wording corresponds perfectly to the definition of 'intermediated securities' in Article 1(b), which are defined as 'securities credited to a securities account or rights or interests in securities resulting from the credit of securities to a securities account'.

Given that Article 9 should be understood as offering a compromise between the different concepts for the characterisation of the account holder's legal position,[36] it is at least misleading, if not incorrect, to say that the Convention makes it necessary to distinguish between a beneficial owner who acquires merely a limited position as described in Article 9(1)(a) and a legal owner who acquires the 'full' position of a shareholder or bondholder as provided by the non-Convention law according to Article 9(1)(d).[37] It is true that Article 9(1)(a) does not grant the 'full' position of a legal owner to the ultimate account holder, but only in the sense that it specifies the minimum content of that account holder's legal position. A credit on a securities account must at least confer the rights attached to the securities to the account holder at the lowest tier of the holding chain, since these rights form the economic substance of the securities.[38] Nevertheless, the non-Convention law shall be free to fill the bundle of rights resulting from a credit of securities to a securities account with additional components. In particular, in jurisdictions where the notion of *Mitgliedschaft* is not limited to the rights described in Article 9(1)(a), the Convention fully recognises that the additional rights conferred by the non-Convention law are also an integral part of the rights comprised in intermediated securities and enjoy the same treatment as all other Article 9(1) rights. Accordingly, the non-Convention law may also provide that the ultimate account holder obtains a property interest in the securities held by the top-tier intermediary. Therefore, it can be concluded that Article 9 does not exclude a co-ownership concept such as the German one.

34 Art. 9(1)(b). 35 Art. 9(1)(c). 36 Mooney and Kanda, 'Core Issues' at 85.

37 Mülbert, 'Vom Ende allen sachenrechtlichen Denkens im Depotrecht durch UNIDROIT und die EU', at 451.

38 Kanda et al., *Official Commentary*, para 9–15; Thévenoz, 'Intermediated Securities', at 424.

11.3.3 *Transfer of intermediated securities (Article 11)*

Nevertheless, it is argued that it is rather Article 11 than Article 9 that has brought along the necessity of a conceptual change. It is believed that under this Article, debits and credits have to be treated as two operational steps strictly separated from each other, and that this so-called 'separation principle' does not permit the non-Convention law to provide for a derivative acquisition of intermediated securities, i.e. for a model in which the (property) interest acquired by the buyer is nothing else than the seller's interest transferred. Consequently, it is concluded that Article 11 does not leave any room for a concept in which the relevant debits and credits on the various tiers of the holding system are linked together in a manner that a specific property right passes directly from the seller to the buyer when a securities transaction is settled. This restrictive interpretation of Article 11 is based on the assumption that debits and credits *each* have a constitutive effect and that it is therefore impossible to regard them as effecting a *single* transfer of property from investor A to investor B.[39]

It is doubtful whether this is the only possible way to understand Article 11. It is true that this provision distinguishes sharply between debits and credits: subject to Article 16, intermediated securities are acquired by an account holder by the credit of securities to that account holder's securities account[40]; and subject to Articles 15 and 16, intermediated securities are disposed of by an account holder by the debit of securities to that account holder's securities account.[41] However, there are at least two reasons which may justify the assumption that a derivative acquisition is compatible with the Convention. First, it should be borne in mind that Article 11 deals with debits and credits as universally recognised *methods* for the acquisition and disposition of intermediated securities. Consistent with the functional approach, it does not take any view as to the *legal nature* of the rights created or represented by book entries in securities accounts. As credits and debits are tightly connected with legal characterisation issues, it can be assumed that it is also up to the non-Convention law to decide whether the several book entries on the various tiers of the holding system are to be considered as dealing with one and the same interest or with different interests.[42]

39 Mülbert, 'Vom Ende allen sachenrechtlichen Denkens im Depotrecht durch UNIDROIT und die EU', at 451; Voß, 'Die Securities Law Directive', at 210.

40 Art. 11(1). 41 Art. 11(3).

42 Kanda et al., *Official Commentary*, s. 11–4; Thévenoz, 'Intermediated Securities', at 434 et seq.

Secondly, it must be taken into account that it is for the non-Convention law to determine the validity of a credit and that both debits and credits may be subject to a condition. Article 16 implies 'that nothing in the Convention affects the application of rules of the non-Convention law that render a credit invalid or liable to be reversed if and when it cannot be traced back to a matching debit or when the matching debit is invalid or liable to be reversed, as is the case on various jurisdictions'.[43] This, in turn, indicates that the non-Convention law is *not* obliged to treat debits and credits as two operational steps strictly separated from each other. When properly read, Article 11 does not contain a 'separation principle' in the sense that under all circumstances a debit on a securities account must be analysed as extinguishing an interest and a credit on a securities account as creating a *new* interest. Rather, Article 16 allows Contracting States 'to thoroughly interconnect debits and credits so that they become the two sides of the very same coins'.[44] Consequently, the non-Convention law is by all means permitted to adopt or maintain a 'no credit without debit rule' which is based on the idea that a discrete ownership interest in a fungible pool of securities is transferred directly from investor A to investor B.[45]

11.4 European legislation on legal certainty of securities holding and dispositions

As far as the future European legislation is concerned, it is not possible to give a final assessment of its impact on the German substantive law at the present time, as no formal proposal has been adopted by the Commission and transferred to the European legislator so far. In September 2010, when the Luxembourg conference on Intermediated Securities was held, all the indications were that a directive would be the instrument of choice. Consequently, the discussions at this conference focused on the future 'Securities Law Directive' (SLD). During recent months, however, it has become apparent that it is probably safer to speak more neutrally about the future 'European legislation on legal certainty of securities

43 Kanda et al., *Official Commentary*, s. 11–12.

44 Thévenoz, 'Transfer of intermediated securities', Ch. 6 of this book (under section 6.2.1).

45 Than, 'Der funktionale Ansatz in der UNIDROIT Geneva Securities Convention', at 245–6. Contra: Scherer and Gallei, 'UNIDROIT draft Convention and German securities law', at 475, arguing that 'even if such causal dependency between debit and credit entry could be construed under the Draft Convention, its provisions on acquisitions in *bona fide* would counteract this result'.

holding and dispositions', since it is no longer clear whether the future EU instrument will be a Directive, a Regulation or something else.[46] However, the Second Advice of the Legal Certainty Group of August 2008,[47] the Updated Compilation of the rules and explanatory notes discussed so far by the Member States Working Group of 17 September 2010[48] and the Consultation Document of December 2010,[49] allow a first cautious forecast of the scope, the methodological approach and the main building blocks of the future EU instrument, although they do not purport to represent or to pre-judge the formal proposal of the Commission.

11.4.1 Functional approach

These documents strongly indicate that the future EU instrument will be based on a functional approach as well, acknowledging that a full harmonisation of the Member States' legal framework for intermediated securities is neither possible nor necessary to achieve a sufficient level of legal certainty in securities markets. One could even predict that the EU instrument will be more functional than the rules of the Convention. For instance, the terms 'intermediary' and 'intermediated securities' cannot be found in the Updated Compilation of 17 September 2010. Instead, this document uses an alternative set of key terms which may be considered as offering a higher degree of neutrality, such as 'account provider' as defined in Article 2(c),[50] 'account holder' as defined in Article 2(d),[51]

46 See Paech, Ch. 2 of this book, at pp. 26–7.

47 *Solutions to Legal Barriers related to Post-Trading within the EU, Second Advice of the Legal Certainty Group*, August 2008.

48 EU Commission, Legislation on Legal Certainty of Securities Holding and Dispositions, Member States Working Group, Updated Compilation of the rules and explanatory notes discussed so far of 17 September 2010, G2/PhP D(2010).

49 EU Commission, Legislation on Legal Certainty of Securities Holding and Dispositions, Consultation document of the Services of the Directorate-General Internal Market and Services of December 2010, DG Markt G2 MET/OT/acg D(2010) 768690.

50 '"Account provider" means a person who: maintains securities accounts for account holders and is authorised in accordance with Art. 5 of Directive 2004/39/EC to provide services listed in Annex I Section A indent (9) of Directive 2004/39/EC or is a Central Securities Depository as defined in . . . and, in either case, is acting in that capacity; in relation to Arts. 4 to 14, if not subject to the law of a Member State, in the course of a business or other regular activity maintains securities accounts for others or both for others and for its own account and is acting in that capacity'.

51 '"Account holder" means a person for whom an account provider maintains a securities account, whether that person is acting for its own account or for others, including in the capacity of account provider.'

'securities' as defined in Article 2(a)[52] and 'account-held securities' as specified in Article 4.[53] Apart from that, however, there is no significant difference between the Convention and the EU documents with regard to the extent of harmonisation and the technique by which harmonisation is to be achieved. In particular, the EU documents also concentrate on some important main issues of securities holding and dispositions and do not aim at any reconstruction or fundamental change to national legal concepts.[54]

11.4.2 Rights of the account holder

This may be demonstrated by having a short look at Article 4 of the Updated Compilation, which deals with the rights of the account holder.[55] Like Article 9 of the Convention, this provision circumscribes the minimum content of the account holder's legal position, without determining the general conceptual nature of this position. Article 4(1) specifies that the credit of securities to a securities account shall at least confer the following rights to the account holder:

(a) the right to exercise and receive the rights attached to the securities if the account holder is the ultimate account holder as defined in Article 2(e)[56] or if, in any other case, the applicable law confers the right to that account holder;
(b) the right to effect a disposition under Article 5;
(c) the right to instruct the account provider to arrange for holding the securities with another account provider or otherwise than with an account provider, as far as permitted under the applicable law, the terms of the securities and, to the extent permitted by the law of the Member State, the account agreement and the rules of a securities settlement system.

52 '"Securities" means financial instruments or financial assets, other than cash, as listed in Annex I Section C of Directive 2004/39/EC, which are capable of being credited to a securities account.'
53 See also Principles 1 and 3 of the EU Consultation Document.
54 *Second Advice of the Legal Certainty Group*, 41; EU Consultation Document, Background comment to Principle 3.
55 See also Principle 3 of the EU Consultation Document.
56 '"Ultimate account holder" means an account holder which is not acting in the capacity of account provider for another person.'

It follows from Article 4(1)(a) that the national law will continue to determine whether or not a credit to a securities account confers upon an account holder the position of a beneficiary of all rights attached to the securities and what the exact content of the legal position of other account holders in the holding chain would be.[57] Furthermore, Article 4(4) expressly provides that the 'Member States may characterise the legal nature of account held securities as any form of property, equitable interest or other right as far as the characteristics flowing from the legal nature do not contravene paragraphs 1 to 3 or any provision of this Directive.' There can therefore be no doubt that the national law may attribute additional features to the legal position described in Article 4(1), e.g. a co-ownership right in a fungible pool of securities, which implies that the ultimate account holder has to be regarded as the direct legal owner of the securities. This is also made clear in the comment to Principle 3 of the EU Consultation Document, which states 'the applicable (national) law remains decisive for the legal nature of the right aquired by an account holder upon crediting of an account. For example, where the applicable law qualifies the right of an account holder as a classical property right, the legal position (a) can be called "property", (b) must cover the minimum content described above, and, (c) can additionally have legal attributes that property in this jurisdiction normally has.'

11.4.3 Methods for acquisition and disposition

However, the crucial point is once again whether the rules dealing with the acquisition and disposition of intermediated securities will call for a conceptual change in German law. When drafting these rules, the EU Commission was facing the difficulty that under the law of the EU Member States there is a wide variety of book entry and non-book entry methods for effecting all types of acquisition and disposition of intermediated securities, in particular for the creation of security interests. It does not seem that the future EU instrument will undertake the attempt to restrict these different methods or to attribute specific methods to specific forms of acquisition or disposition.[58] Instead, Article 5(1) of the Updated Compilation provides that all Members are required to recognise credits and debits as one – and probably the most important – method for

57 *Second Advice of the Legal Certainty Group*, 41.
58 *Second Advice of the Legal Certainty Group*, 43–9.

acquisition and disposition of account-held securities and limited interests therein.[59] Additionally, Article 5(5) makes available a catalogue of several other methods used throughout the EU, like 'earmarking' as defined in Article 2(p), and concluding a control agreement as defined in Article 2(q). Moreover, Article 6(1) clarifies that it is up to the Member States 'to characterise the legal nature of dispositions over account-held securities effected under one of the methods listed in Article 5 as far as the legal nature does not contravene the provisions of this directive'.[60] According to the Second Advice of the Legal Certainty Group, assignment, transfer, pledge, mortgage, floating charge and all other traditional legal concepts underlying the settlement of securities transactions or the creation of limited security interests could still be used in each jurisdiction. Harmonisation would only happen on the level of the factual requirements of each and every legal concept.[61]

Against this background, it is far from obvious that Article 5(1) must be understood as laying down a 'separation principle' in the strict sense that a Member State is not permitted to connect debits and credits in a manner that a discrete ownership right passes directly from the seller to the buyer when a particular securities transaction is settled.[62] It is true that, at first glance, this provision draws a sharp line between debits and credits as mandatory methods for effecting dispositions or acquisitions respectively, as Article 11 of the Convention is supposed to do on the international level. Nevertheless, one may ask whether Article 6(1), which must be interpreted in the light of the neutrality principle underlying the Directive, would make any sense if a derivate acquisition would be excluded. This is the more true as pursuant to Article 6(6), Member States may stipulate that the effectiveness of a debit or credit can be made subject to a condition. There is not much fantasy needed to assume that this provision has been added to the Compilation considering the fact that there are legal concepts such as the German co-ownership model where debits and credits are co-dependent as a matter of law, providing that no buyer can acquire a co-ownership right in a fungible pool of securities without the former co-owner relinquishing it.

59 See also Principle 4 of the EU Consultation Document.

60 See also Principle 5 of the EU Consultation Document.

61 *Second Advice of the Legal Certainty Group*, 45.

62 Mülbert, 'Vom Ende allen sachenrechtlichen Denkens im Depotrecht durch UNIDROIT und die EU', at 456; Voß, 'Die Securities Law Directive', at 210.

11.5 Conclusion

It has been demonstrated that neither the Convention nor the future EU instrument make it necessary to change the German legal framework for intermediated securities fundamentally. Thanks to their functional approach, the traditional co-ownership concept can be maintained. However, since this concept shows a considerable lack of clarity and certainty, especially with regard to the question of whether the final investor can be regarded as indirect co-possessor of the securities deposited with Clearstream, and whether there is a sufficient legal basis for bona fide acquisition, there is at least the necessity for a 'small' modernisation of the German Securities Deposit Act. Apart from this, the harmonisation process on both the European and the international levels offers the excellent opportunity to put the co-ownership concept to the test as a whole and to discuss whether it should be replaced by a more modern approach, such as the Swiss Federal Intermediated Securities Act (FISA). This opportunity should not be missed.

Bibliography

Berger, C., 'Verpfändung und Verwertung von Aktien' [2009] *Zeitschrift für Wirtschafts- und Bankrecht (WM)*, 577–85.

Dechamps, C., *Wertrechte im Effektengiroverkehr* (Cologne: Carl Heymanns, 1989).

Einsele, D., *Wertpapierrecht als Schuldrecht. Funktionsverlust von Effektenurkunden im internationalen Rechtsverkehr* (Tübingen: Mohr Siebeck, 1995).

'Wertpapiere im elektronischen Bankgeschäft' [2001] *Zeitschrift für Wirtschafts- und Bankrecht (WM)*, 7–16.

'Modernising German Law: Can the UNIDROIT Project on Intermediated Securities Provide Guidance?' [2005] *Uniform Law Review*, 251–61.

'Das Treuhandmodell als Alternative zum geltenden Recht', in T. Baums and A. Cahn (eds.), *Die Zukunft des Clearing und Settlement* (Berlin: de Gruyter, 2006), 3–28.

Habersack, M. and Mayer, C., 'Globalverbriefte Aktien als Gegenstand sachenrechtlicher Verfügungen? – Ein (weiteres) Plädoyer für die Ablösung der Globalurkunde durch Wertrechte –' [2000] *Zeitschrift für Wirtschafts- und Bankrecht (WM)*, 1678–84.

Heinsius, T., Horn, A. and Than, J., *Depotgesetz. Kommentar zum Gesetz über die Verwahrung und Anschaffung von Wertpapieren vom 4. Februar 1937* (Berlin/New York: de Gruyter, 1975).

Horn, N., 'Die Erfüllung von Wertpapiergeschäften unter Einbeziehung eines Zentralen Kontrahenten an der Börse – Sachenrechtliche Aspekte –', *Zeitschrift für Wirtschafts- und Bankrecht (WM)*, Sonderbeilage 2/2002.

Kanda, H., 'Legal Rules on Intermediated Securities: The Japanese Situation', in H. de Vauplane (ed.), *20 ans de dématérialisation des titres en France. Bilan et perspectives nationales et internationales* (Paris: La Revue Banque, 2005), 223.

Kanda, H., Mooney, C., Thévenoz, L. and Béraud, S., with the assistance of T. Keijser, *Official Commentary on the UNIDROIT Convention on Substantive Rules for Intermediated Securities* (Oxford University Press, 2012).

Kronke, H., 'Das Genfer UNIDROIT-Übereinkommen über materiellrechtliche Normen für intermediär-verwahrte Wertpapiere und die Reform des deutschen Depotrechts' [2010] *Zeitschrift für Wirtschafts- und Bankrecht (WM)*, 1625–35.

Kunz, J. H., *Ausgewählte Rechtsprobleme des Zentralen Kontrahenten* (Frankfurt am Main: Peter Lang, 2009).

Lehmann, M., *Finanzinstrumente. Vom Wertpapier- und Sachenrecht zum Recht der unkörperlichen Vermögensgegenstände* (Tübingen: Mohr Siebeck, 2009).

Mahler, F., *Rechtsgeschäftliche Verfügungen über sonder- und sammelverwahrte Wertpapiere des Kapitalmarktes* (Frankfurt am Main: Peter Lang, 2006).

Micheler, E., *Property in Securities. A Comparative Study* (Cambridge University Press, 2007).

Mooney, C. W. and Kanda, H., 'Core Issues under the UNIDROIT (Geneva) Securities Convention on Intermediated Securities: Views from the United States and Japan', in L. Gullifer and J. Payne (eds.), *Intermediated Securities. Legal Problems and Practical Issues* (Oxford: Hart Publishing, 2010), 69–130.

Mülbert, P. O., 'Vom Ende allen sachenrechtlichen Denkens im Depotrecht durch UNIDROIT und die EU' [2010] *Zeitschrift für Bankrecht und Bankwirtschaft (ZBB)*, 445–58.

'Vom Ende allen sachenrechtlichen Denkens im österreichischen und deutschen Depotrecht durch UNIDROIT und die EU', in P. Apathy et al. (eds.), *Festschrift für Helmut Koziol* (Vienna: Jan Sramek Verlag, 2010), 1055–76.

Peters, K., *Wertpapierfreies Effektensystem. Eine Untersuchung der faktischen und rechtlichen Möglichkeiten einer Weiterentwicklung des herrschenden Effektenwesens* (Baden-Baden: Nomos, 1978).

Saager, S., 'Depotrecht im Umbruch' [2005] *Die Bank*, 22–5.

Scherer, P. and Gallei, R., 'UNIDROIT draft Convention and German securities law: friend or foe?' [2009] *Journal of International Banking Law and Regulation (JIBLR)*, 470–6.

Than, J., 'The Legal Framework for Safe Custody, Administration and Transfer of Securities in Germany', in H. de Vauplane (ed.), *20 ans de dématérialisation des titres en France. Bilan et perspectives nationales et internationales* (Paris: La Revue Banque, 2005), 233–49.

'The Preliminary Draft UNIDROIT Convention and Capital Market Practice in Germany' [2005] *Uniform Law Review*, 263–70.

'Der funktionale Ansatz in der UNIDROIT Geneva Securities Convention vom 9. Oktober 2009', in S. Grundmann et al. (eds.), *Festschrift für Klaus Hopt* (Berlin/New York: de Gruyter, 2010), 231–46.

Thévenoz, L., 'Intermediated Securities, Legal Risk, and the International Harmonization of Commercial Law' [2008] 13 *Stanford Journal of Law, Business & Finance*, 384–452.

Voß, T., 'Die Securities Law Directive und das deutsche Depotrecht' [2010] *Europäisches Wirtschafts- und Steuerrecht (EWS)*, 209–11.

Wust, B., *Die grenzüberschreitende Verbuchung von Wertpapieren. Möglichkeiten und Grenzen moderner Kollisionsnormen im Hinblick auf unterschiedliche materiellrechtliche Berechtigungen an Wertpapieren* (Berlin: Duncker & Humblot, 2011).

Zahn, A. and Kock, S., 'Die Emission von unverbrieften Schuldtiteln durch die Europäische Zentralbank – Abkehr vom Verbriefungserfordernis für Effekten: Perspektiven für private Emittenten?' [2009] *Zeitschrift für Wirtschafts- und Bankrecht (WM)*, 1955–67.

12

The Geneva Securities Convention: a Spanish perspective

FRANCISCO GARCIMARTÍN*

12.1 Introduction

The Spanish legislator has established a sound legal framework for book-entry securities. This legal framework contains rules dealing with (i) the creation of book-entry securities, (ii) the acquisition and disposition of the rights *pertaining to* book-entry securities, including the creation of security interests, and (iii) the exercise of the rights *arising from* the securities (Articles 7–9 *Ley del Mercado de Valores*, LMV, and *Real Decreto* 116/1992, RD 116/92). According to this legal framework, the rights of the investors and collateral takers over book-entry securities are characterised as proprietary-law rights and, therefore, are adequately protected in case of insolvency of the intermediary or of the collateral provider.

Nevertheless, such a legal regime only applies to book-entry securities held with the Spanish Central Securities Depository (CSD), or with a direct participant in the Spanish CSD. There are no special rules dealing with indirect holding situations, whether of (i) investors holding Spanish securities through low-tier intermediaries (i.e. not directly with a participant in the Spanish CSD); or (ii) Spanish investors holding foreign securities through a Spanish intermediary.[1] There are, so to speak, two different worlds: the 'regulated world' (securities in the Spanish CSD) and the 'non-regulated world' (foreign securities and down-tier investors in Spanish securities). The UNIDROIT Convention on Substantive Rules

* This chapter has been elaborated in the context of research project DER2009–11876, financed by the Spanish Ministry of Science and Technology.

1 Actually, the only rule dealing with this second type of situation is Art. 70*ter*(f) LMV (Ley del Mercado de Valores), which, in case of insolvency of a Spanish custodian that maintains the assets of its clients in an omnibus account with a sub-custodian, recognises the Spanish CNMV (Comisión Nacional del Mercado de Valores) the right to withdraw those assets from the insolvency estate in favour of the clients of the custodian.

for Intermediated Securities (the Convention) and the future EU legislation will offer a useful legal instrument to fill this *lacuna*. Nevertheless, its application may at the same time provoke certain difficulties as regards their compatibility with the 'regulated world'.

This chapter is organised as follows. First, I will outline the main features of the Spanish rules applicable to book-entry securities. Secondly, I will try to imagine how a Spanish lawyer would approach the Convention, or, in other words, how the Convention would fit within the conceptual framework of a Spanish lawyer. And finally, I will analyse certain problems or difficulties that the ratification of the Convention by Spain may raise. The intention of this chapter is to demonstrate that even if the interaction between the Convention and Spanish Law may provoke certain problems, the functional approach adopted by the former allows us to overcome them with relative ease.

12.2 Outline of the Spanish system

12.2.1 Spanish securities held directly in the Spanish CSD or in a participant in the Spanish CSD

12.2.1.1 Point of departure

Under Spanish law, securities can be represented in two ways: by means of a physical document (certificate), and by means of an electronic book entry. In the first case, the security, i.e. the contractual claim vis-à-vis the issuer, is incorporated into a piece of paper and transferable by physical delivery (or by endorsement and physical delivery, in the case of registered securities).[2] In the second case, the security is represented by an entry recorded in an electronic registry. In principle, the issuer may choose the means of representation. Nevertheless, when securities are going to be listed in a regulated market, they must be represented by book entries. With regard to these type of securities, Spain, like other countries, has opted for a fully dematerialised system (rather than for an immobilisation system).[3] In quantitative terms, the vast majority of Spanish securities (listed companies, sovereign bonds, etc.) are evidenced *only* by electronic means.

2 Under Spanish law, registered securities are transferable by endorsement. The inscription in the registry of the issuer is not a condition for the transfer of the proprietary rights over the security; it only entitles the person to exercise corporate rights vis-à-vis the issuer.

3 See Art. 5–12 LMV.

In order to avoid any misunderstanding, it is important to underline what we mean by the word 'representation'. That is, what do we mean when we say that something (a piece of paper or a book entry) 'represents' the security? A look at this concept will allow us to understand many of the traits of the Spanish system.

When a security is represented in the form of a physical document, it means that all the rights and obligations vis-à-vis the issuer are now attached to the document, i.e. 'incorporated' into a document. The incorporation of an intangible (a contractual right) into a tangible asset (a paper) is obviously a fiction. But a legal fiction (something between a *fictio iuris* and a *fictio juristae*) and, therefore, it has a fundamental consequence: according to the law, (i) the creation, (ii) the transfer and (iii), the exercise of the rights can take place as a consequence of the creation, the delivery and the presentation of the document. Furthermore, the incorporation of an intangible into a piece of paper permits the application of the rules of circulation laid down for tangible assets, in particular, the publicity linked to the physical possession of an asset. For instance, the good faith acquirer is protected to the extent that he has relied on the appearance offered by the possession of the transferor.

When the legal system recognises that a security can also be represented by means of an electronic record (a book entry), this is another fiction. One fiction, i.e. *the paper represents the rights*, is replaced by another fiction, i.e. *the electronic entry represents the rights*. But it is also a legal fiction with normative consequences. The legal systems can presume that in the case of book-entry securities, the rights arising from the security are now attached to inscriptions in the electronic registry. Therefore, the creation, the transfer, and the exercise of the rights take place as a consequence of entries in an electronic registry.

Spanish law has followed such an approach. Thus:

1. Book-entry securities are *created* by the registration in the corresponding electronic registry (Article 8 LMV).
2. The *transfer* of the securities is carried out by electronic book-entries and, therefore, a debit and a credit in the accounts have equivalent effects to the delivery of the document in the case of bearer securities (Article 9 LMV). The same applies for the creation of a security interest pertaining to the securities: registration of the pledge, i.e. earmarking or similar visibility in the account, is equivalent to the transfer of possession of the certificate (Article 10 I LMV). Furthermore, the Law makes it expressly clear that the security interest is effective against third parties from the time when the corresponding entry (earmarking) has been made (Article 10 II LMV).

3. Thirdly, the exercise of the rights arising from the securities is conditioned upon the inscription of the acquisition in the corresponding electronic registry. That is, the entitlement to exercise the rights is linked to the inscription in the registry: the person who is shown as legitimated in the registry is deemed to be the owner of the securities and is, consequently, entitled to exercise the rights attached to the securities vis-à-vis the issuer (Article 11 I LMV). This issuer, in turn, is in principle only liable vis-à-vis the person who is shown in the corresponding registry.

The ideas summarised above were the starting point of the Spanish legislator in the late 1980s when it decided to set forth a model of dematerialisation of securities. The Spanish law is construed on the assumption that the new means of representation (book entry) does not call for a radical change in the legal and conceptual framework traditionally applied to securities.[4] Naturally, some modifications were necessary to adapt the legal regime to the technical and operational particularities of book-entry securities. But not radical changes. The legislator considered that the Spanish legal system offered enough tools to adapt the basic principle of the traditional law to the new way of representation without reducing the protection of investors. Basically, the technical adaptations required were to replace the physical possession of the certificate, as instrument of protection, with entries in a centralised electronic registry. Such electronic registry could fulfil a function equivalent to the possession of the physical document. For instance, the obligation of custody of the documents in the case of materialised securities is replaced by the obligation of keeping the book-entry registry; the principle of good faith acquisition based on the appearance of physical possession is replaced by the acquisition based on the appearance of the entries in the electronic registry; the transmission by delivery of the document is replaced by the modification in the registry (by means of credits and debits), and so on.

As we will see in the next paragraph, to meet those objectives it was deemed necessary to borrow certain principles from the real-estate registry regime (see Article 16 of the RD 116/92), such as the principle of 'central registry', i.e. the book-entries that represent the security are only those carried out in the Spanish central registry either at the level of the

4 It is recommended to read the article produced by one of the 'fathers' of the new regulation, Paz-Ares, 'La desincorporación de los títulos-valor', at 90–9. See also Recalde, 'Los valores negociables', at 301. But this is not 'typical Spanish': see Khimji, 'Intermediary Credit Risk', 287 et seq., *passim* (arguing that under English, US and Canadian law, a perfectly adequate solution to intermediary risk is available under the traditional law of property); see also with regard to English law, Macfarlane and Stevens, 'Interests in Securities', at 34–54.

Central Securities Depositary (CSD) or at the level of its participants, priority, i.e. the act which first accesses the register will have priority over those which access subsequently, and the chain of entitlements, i.e. in order to register the transfer of securities, the prior registration in favour of the transferor will be necessary.

12.2.1.2 Architecture: CSD and its participants as central registry

The Spanish system is based on the idea of a central registry where entries take place (i.e. central record-keeping based on accounting entries). The structure of such a book-entry registry depends on whether the securities are listed in a regulated market or not. Here, we are only dealing with the former.

For securities listed in Spanish regulated markets, the book-entry registry is structured in a two-tier system (Articles 29 et seq. of RD 116/92). In such a system the registry is entrusted jointly to the Central Securities Depository (Iberclear) and to its participant entities (the 'participants'). The registry is structured in two levels. First, a central registry, managed by Iberclear, containing the aggregate balances of securities issued in two types of accounts opened by Iberclear for each participant: (i) an account in which the securities owned by each participant are held; and (ii) another account, different and entirely segregated from the latter, that reflects the total amount of securities held by each participant on behalf of its clients. Second, a so-called detailed registry, managed by the participants, in which each of them maintains the accounts opened by each investor (individual accounts), and in which the detail of securities credited in the name of each client is recorded. Hence, the name of each individual investor is only shown in the detail registry held by the participants in the CSD.

In spite of the above, the law considers both levels as parts of the same registry (see recitals of RD 119/92, 'a system of two tiers which is not contrary to the idea of a unique electronic registry even though it is articulated through a central registry and detailed registries'). The system guarantees the connection between those two levels via a code: the so-called register references (*referencias de registro* or RR).[5] This allows the

5 Note that the system is being reconsidered by the Spanish legislator. A document on a 'Proposal for amendment of the Spanish system of registration, clearing and settlement' was published by the Spanish securities regulator, the CNMV on 14 January 2011 and was open to public consultation until 28 February 2011. That document envisages certain significant

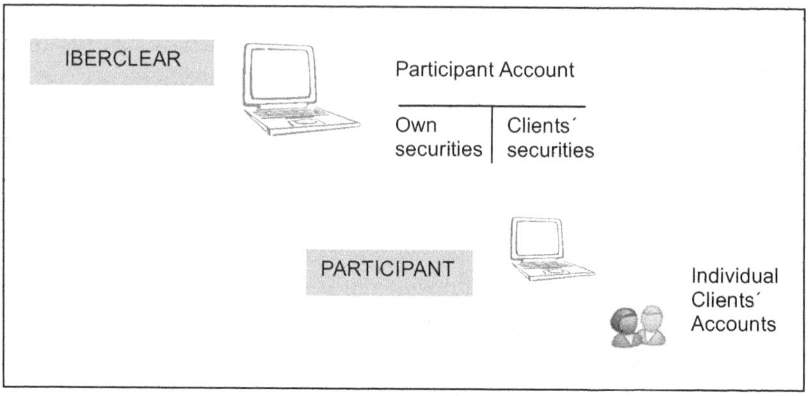

Figure 12.1 Spanish book-entry registry system

system to keep a historical register of all operations and account entries. All operations are numbered, and Iberclear or the Stock Exchange – depending on the type of transaction – communicates this number to the participants who, in turn, file it away in order to facilitate later enquiries about a given operation or to resolve incidents. Hence, individual accounts are maintained by the participants, and therefore the name of the investor is only shown at the down-tier level, whereas the RRs corresponding to the acquisition of securities by each investor are granted by a centralised system and are recorded at both levels: the CSD and the corresponding participant.

The RR number is electronically linked to a certain and traceable amount of fungible securities. To the extent that there is a central registry with a historical record of all transactions on securities, we can consider that investors are owners of a discrete amount of fungible securities, i.e. direct holders of a certain amount of securities vis-à-vis the issuer and also vis-à-vis third parties.

12.2.1.3 Consequences

Here is a highlight of some of the consequences of the regime described above, in particular: (i) investors whose names appear in the

changes in the Spanish system of registration, clearing and settlement of securities. Among such changes, one of the most important refers to the substitution of the register references system as a way to track the ownership of equity securities by a system of control of securities balances in both the central and detailed registry (as happens already with debt securities). This proposal entailed the amendment of the LMV and the RD 116/92. The amendment to the LMV was adopted in October 2011 and the new implementing measures were expected to have been adopted during the second half of 2012.

corresponding registry have a direct proprietary right pertaining to the securities; (ii) these rights are conditioned upon the existence of a valid and effective credit; and (iii) since the CSD and its participants play a key role as managers of the registry, they are subject to a regime of strict liability.

12.2.1.4 A system of direct proprietary rights

Under Spanish law, the model of a centralised record system based on formal accounting entries makes it possible to maintain the conceptual framework of direct holding. The name of the owners of the securities (i.e. investors) must appear in the detailed registries of the participants in Iberclear, and those owners have (i) direct ownership rights pertaining to the securities and (ii) are entitled vis-à-vis the issuer to receive and enjoy the rights arising from the securities. Accordingly, as owners, the account holders can dispose of the securities, encumber them or transfer them to another participant in Iberclear. Since the account holder is entitled to exercise the rights attached to the securities, if the issuer does not fulfil its obligations, the account holder is the only person authorised to sue the issuer – he must act as plaintiff in his own capacity. In order to exercise the rights arising out of the securities, the investor may need the assistance of the intermediary, but in doing so, the intermediary exercises rights of the investor in the capacity of an attorney or of an agent.

Following such an approach, the Spanish legislator has not considered it necessary to create a 'new type of property' to cope with the book-entry securities world. In some jurisdictions, the legislator has opted for the creation of a new entitlement defined as the package of rights that a person has against the person's own intermediary with respect to the positions carried in the person's securities account. Settlement of securities trade will involve termination of one person's security entitlement and acquisition of a new security entitlement by another person. That transaction is not, however, a transfer of the *same entitlement* from one person to another.[6] The model is based on the idea of extinction and creation of rights. Spanish law, on the contrary, has maintained the traditional approach. There is no division of entitlements 'in tiers', nor any sort of split ownership between investors and intermediaries. Neither is there a difference between legal and beneficial owner. Nor is there room for any kind of legal entitlement different from the underlying security, not even for any kind of co-ownership of a pool of securities. It is important to emphasise this point: under Spanish law (corporate or property law), neither

6 See para. 5 of the Official Comment to Art. 8–501 UCC.

the CSD nor its participants have any proprietary right to the securities of its investors. *Intermediaries are mere record-keeping institutions.*

Furthermore, if the property rights fall upon the securities, the transfer of these property rights entails the transfer of the original securities and the rights arising therefrom. That is why, in these systems, it is conceptually easy to understand the idea of 'no credits without corresponding debits'. One can only acquire a thing if there is somebody elsewhere who has lost it. The introduction of the fungibility element does not necessarily call for a reconsideration of this principle to the extent that the system is able to allocate portions of fungible securities. This is precisely what happens under Spanish law. As we have already seen, all transferors and transferees are directly or indirectly connected with a central programme. The system assigns portions of securities to account holders. Each portion corresponds to a number, which is also reflected in the central registry. When a transfer takes place, one register reference (RR) is cancelled (the one corresponding to the debit) and a new one is issued (the one corresponding to the credit).[7] From a legal standpoint, this guarantees the exactness in the matching of credits and debits, and therefore explains why the basic principle of the Spanish law is that there cannot be credits without corresponding debits (see Articles 16 and 32.2 of the RD 116/92: 'No credit or debit can be practised if the corresponding reference registry number has not been cancelled and issued').

12.2.1.5 Credits and debits

Although legal scholars have different views, according to the general understanding among practitioners and the Spanish securities regulator, the CNMV, an entry at the lower level (i.e. at the detailed registry of each participant) can only be made when the corresponding register reference number has been assigned at the upper level (Iberclear). This also entails that only those credits supported at the upper level by RR numbers are valid and effective. And, therefore, only those credits supported by a valid RR at the upper level are deemed to attribute proprietary rights pertaining to the securities. Furthermore, in case of insolvency of a participant in Iberclear, the securities are moved by the Spanish Stock Exchange Commission ex officio and at no cost to another participant (and if no firm is willing to accept them, to the CSD directly), and shall be allocated according to the RR mechanism as first criterion, i.e. if there is a deficit,

7 But see n. 5 above. The new Act expressly envisages the pro-rata rule as the solution directly applicable in cases of deficits (Art. 12*bis*4).

the securities should firstly be allocated to those investors whose credits are supported by a valid RR. A pro-rata criterion would only be applied in the remote hypothesis that the RR mechanism could not work (for example, due to operational mistakes or disorders in the books of the participant).[8]

Excursus. Under Spanish law, credits and debits imply more than a legal relationship. They require a record in the registry, and in a particular way: through the Iberclear scheme (for listed securities). So, unlike in other countries where a credit may take place by a mere confirmation to the account holder or by any other means that identifies the security as belonging to the purchaser,[9] under Spanish law an investor only acquires a proprietary right when the inscription in the 'two-tier central registry' takes place. The investor may have paid and may have received a confirmation by his intermediary, but if a formal credit under the rules of the central system has not taken place, the investor does not have a proprietary right pertaining to the securities (naturally, he may have a contractual claim against his intermediary or may get the benefits of public or private insurance). This may be good or bad policy, but it is a corollary of a model of book-entry securities based on a two-tier centralised registry.

In his well-known article in the *UCLA Law Review*, Professor Rogers put forth the following example:

> Suppose that at time 1, Broker acquires 10,000 shares of XYZ Co. common stock for its own property account at a time when none of Broker's customers are holding XYZ Co common stock through it. Thereafter Customer places a purchase order for 10,000 shares of XYZ Co. common stock through broker, to be credited to Customer's securities account with Broker. Broker takes Customer's money and falsely reports to Customer that it has purchased 10,000 shares for Customer's account, but in fact, Broker does not do so. If Broker fails... Under revised Article 8, the answer is clear: Customer wins.[10]

This paragraph is very useful to illustrate the different approach to the concept of 'credit' and 'debit'. Under a fully regulated and centralised

8 This may seem unfair, but it is coherent under the traditional principles of proprietary law. Since it is possible to identify by the RR mechanism whose securities are missing, according to those principles, the corresponding party should bear the loss, see www.cnmv.es/Portal/GPage.aspx?id=RefSCLV&lang=es .

9 See Mooney and Kanda, 'Core Issues', 69 at 86.

10 Rogers, 'Policy Perspective on Revised U.C.C. Art. 8', 1431 at 1515.

book-entry system, the fact that Broker reports to the Customer the acquisition of the securities does not imply the acquisition of the ownership of the securities, so Customer would not have any proprietary right pertaining to the securities. Nothing has been credited. For the same reasons, ideas like 'the creation of a security entitlement is not dependent upon whether an intermediary actually holds or acquires a financial asset'[11] are conceptually very difficult to accept.

12.2.1.6 Liability

The relationships between the investor and its intermediary are framed within a contract of custody and administration of securities. The content of this contract has been typified by practice and enshrined in a model contract. According to the provision of the contract, the two main obligations of the intermediary are (i) to hold in custody the securities, which basically means to hold the corresponding amount of securities at the level of the CSD; (ii) to facilitate to the account holders the exercise of the corporate rights arising from the securities. Since the intermediaries fulfil a registry function, which has legal proprietary consequences, Spanish law has laid down a principle of strict liability. Any failure to make the corresponding entries, inaccuracies and delays therein and infringement in general of the rules laid down for maintaining registers will give rise to liability of the entity in breach or, as the case may be, of the CSD, in relation to those who have suffered loss, in the absence of exclusive fault of the latter.

A final clarification is worthy of note. As has been said, Spanish law does not envisage special rules for the hypothesis where there is more than one intermediary and, therefore, the person whose name appears in the detail registry of a participant in Iberclear is a mere custodian acting on behalf of third parties (the investors). In principle, these investors are not deemed to be the owners of the securities and are not entitled vis-à-vis the issuer. From a civil law perspective, it could be argued that these investors only have contractual rights vis-à-vis the intermediary; it could also be argued that, under the general rules of the Civil Code, they have a proprietary right to the extent that they could offer full evidence that the registered person was a mere fiduciary owner. This latter understanding seems more sensible, but this result is not explicitly contemplated by the

11 Spink and Pare, 'The Uniform Security Transfer Act', 321 at 363; Mooney and Kanda, 'Core Issues', 69 at 86.

Securities Law and could only be achieved by resorting to the general principles of civil law.

12.3 The Convention: conceptual framework

The Convention is drafted following the so-called functional approach. The concepts employed are neutral and adaptable to different legal regimes. However, once the Convention is incorporated into a legal system, the instrument has to be read under the conceptual categories of the corresponding legal system. In this section, we are trying to imagine how a Spanish lawyer would read the Geneva Convention or, in other words, how the Geneva Convention would fit within the conceptual framework of a Spanish lawyer.

The two main aspects that a Spanish lawyer would first underline are related to the nature of the rules of the Convention.

1. The provisions of the Convention are of a private-law nature, rather than a public-law nature. The Convention deals with the rights and obligations between investors, intermediaries, issuers and third parties, including the insolvency administrator. In principle, it does not deal with regulatory obligations of participants in this market.
2. Within this private-law scope, the Conventions seeks to define the legal position of account holders, and does it by adding up three set of rules: (i) rules dealing with the contractual aspects, i.e. rights vis-à-vis the intermediary based on the account agreement; (ii) rules dealing with the proprietary aspects, i.e. rights pertaining to the securities valid and effective against third parties, including the insolvency administrator; and (iii) (very limited) rules dealing with the corporate aspects.

12.3.1 Contractual rights

First, the set of contractual rights includes the rights vis-à-vis the intermediary based on the account agreement, and its correlative obligations. The contractual obligations are mainly laid down in Articles 9, 10, 23, 24 and 28 of the Convention. The content of these contractual obligations can be divided in two groups of rules: one related to the custody obligations and another related to the administration obligations.

1. The intermediary is obliged to hold the securities credited to its clients' accounts. This idea is enshrined in Articles 9, 10, 15, 16 or 24: the intermediary must hold the credited securities, which means holding sufficient securities, and must transfer or encumber them under the instructions of its clients.

2. The intermediary is obliged to administer the securities in the interest of its account holder. This idea is enshrined in Articles 9, 10 and 23: the intermediary must facilitate the exercise of the rights pertaining to the securities and arising from the securities in the interest of its account holders.

With regard to these core contractual rights, there is no difference from Spanish law, which, furthermore, offers an adequate regulated legal framework to specify those rights and the corresponding obligations and liabilities.

12.3.2 Proprietary rights

Secondly, the set of proprietary rights refer to the rights of the account holder(s) pertaining to the securities and opposable vis-à-vis third parties, in particular creditors of the intermediary in an insolvency scenario. These rights are defined by three groups of rules: rules recognising the 'proprietary rights' pertaining to the securities (static situation), rules dealing with the transfer of the securities or the creation of security rights (dynamic situation), and rules dealing with an insolvency scenario.

1. Static aspects: the rule recognising the proprietary rights pertaining to the securities is established in Article 9 (and indirectly Article 22: that forbids upper-tier attachments).
2. Dynamic aspects: the rules dealing with the transfer of the securities and the creation of limited proprietary interest in them are contained in Articles 11 (credits and debits), 12 (other methods), 13 (non-Convention law), 15–16 (non-authorised dispositions, invalidity and reversals), 18 (good-faith acquirer) and 19–20 (priorities).
3. Insolvency: the regime of the rights pertaining to the securities in an insolvency scenario are contained in Articles 14 (2) and 25–7.

Also the basic content of those rights coincides with the corresponding provisions of Spanish law.

12.3.3 Corporate rights

Finally, the Convention does not cover the area of corporate law, in particular the relationships between account holders and the issuers of the securities (Article 8). However, it contains a couple of rules which require Contracting States to recognise indirect holding structures and certain consequences such as the splitting of voting. This is not a problem from a Spanish law perspective, since the provisions of the Convention are equivalent to the rules of Directive 2007/36/EC.

12.4 The Convention: selected issues

12.4.1 General comment

As has been pointed out, the principles underlying the Convention are perfectly compatible with the solutions adopted by the Spanish legislator. In both cases, the approach is similar. On the one hand, from a proprietary rights standpoint, the account holders have rights pertaining to the book-entry securities credited to their accounts which are effective vis-à-vis third parties and, accordingly, sufficiently protected in case of insolvency of the intermediary. On the other hand, from a contractual rights standpoint, intermediaries have contractual obligations to hold the securities belonging to their account holders and to administrate the rights attached to those securities in the interest of their account holders. Furthermore, the Convention would have an important added value for Spain. Since the Spanish legislator has not laid down special rules for the rights of Spanish investors in foreign securities held with an intermediary, the Convention would address this *lacuna*.

Nevertheless, there are certain aspects of the Convention that have given rise to certain concern among Spanish lawyers. The following paragraphs describe these aspects and analyse whether that concern is justified or not.

12.4.2 Acquisition of securities: credits

The concept of *credit* plays a pivotal function in the Convention. The entire text revolves around the idea that a credit of securities to a securities account confers on the account holder a set of rights which are enforceable vis-à-vis third parties, including the insolvency administrator of the intermediary (Articles 9 and 11). That is, account holders acquire intermediated securities by way of a credit. In order to ensure the real effectiveness of this idea, the Convention imposes an obligation upon the intermediary to hold sufficient securities to cover the securities credited to its account holders (Article 24). And, finally, the Convention includes an allocation rule (Article 25) and a loss-sharing rule (Article 26): securities held by the intermediary are first allocated to the rights of the account holder, and in case of insolvency of the intermediary, if there is a shortfall (i.e. the intermediary does not hold sufficient securities to match the securities actually credited to its account holders), the loss is shared by all the account holders on a pro-rata basis. The beneficiaries of this loss-sharing rule are determined by the 'credits' in the registries of the intermediary.

Example 1. Int-1 has three account holders: A, B and C. All of them have invested in the shares issued by Company X, A 100, B 50 and C 50, and these shares have been credited respectively to their accounts in Int-1. Int-1, in turn, has a securities account with an upper-level intermediary, Int-2, where those 200 X shares are credited. According to the Convention, A, B, and C have rights pertaining to those securities which are effective against third parties, including the insolvency administrator. Hence, if Int-1 goes bankrupt, the X shares securities are allocated to A, B and C, and not to the general creditors of Int-1.

Example 2. In that case, if Int-1 by fraud or mistake only has 150 X-shares at the upper-level, these 150 X-shares are distributed on a pro-rata basis among A, B and C.

Example 3. In that case, if Int-1 has a segregated account at the upper-level, and in its own account there are 25 X-securities, and in the account of their clients, 150 X-shares, the 25 X-shares will be allocated to A, B, and C, and not to the general creditors of Int-1 (Article 25). Hence, the 175 X-shares will be distributed on a pro-rata basis among A, B, and C.

Under Spanish law, and with regard to securities deposited in the Spanish CSD, the solution would be slightly different. As explained, and according to the dominant view among practitioners, in principle a mere credit in the account is not sufficient to acquire rights pertaining to the securities. Only those credits supported by a valid registered reference would confer those rights. A participant in Iberclear cannot make a valid and effective credit to one of its client's accounts until it has received the corresponding RR number from the CSD. As a corollary of this, in the event of the insolvency of a participant in the Spanish CSD, if there is a shortfall, the distribution will not be on a pro-rata basis, but will be based on the RR mechanism: since by looking at the system it will be possible to assign specific amounts of securities to specific account holders, the shortfall will be first allocated to those investors whose credits are not supported by a valid

RR.[12] Additionally, since the accounts of each participant are segregated in the CSD (and Spain is one of those jurisdictions that draws proprietary law consequences from the segregation mechanism), the securities credited in its own account will not be allocated to its account holders. Hence, the results in the former examples would be different.

Example 1. Let us imagine that Int-1 is a participant in the Spanish CSD, and X is a Spanish listed company. A, B, and C are clients of Int-1. A has bought 100 X shares and these shares have been credited to his account with the corresponding RR which coincide with an RR that Int-1 has in the client's account at the CSD level. B has also bought 50 X-shares in the same condition as A, and C also. However, by fraud or mistake, the 50 X-shares credited to C's securities account are not supported by a corresponding RR at the CSD level. In this case, if Int-1 goes bankrupt, A and B will be allocated their X-shares, but C will be considered an unsecured creditor. Since the RR mechanism makes it possible to identify whose shares are missed, the pro-rata rule does not apply. Furthermore, C will not have any priority pertaining to the X-shares that Int-1 may have in its own account at the CSD level.

The Convention, nevertheless, allows Spain to maintain such an approach. On the one hand, the Convention allows contracting states to make a declaration according to which if the intermediary maintains segregated accounts at the upper level, the securities credited for its own account will not be allocated to its account holders (Article 25(5)). And, on the other hand, the application of the pro-rata rule is conditioned upon two circumstances: (i) that the securities have not been allocated to a particular account holder (Article 26(2)(a)) and the RR's numbers can be deemed as a form of allocating the shortfall to particular account holders), and (ii) that there is no (domestic) conflicting rule applicable in the insolvency proceeding (Article 26(1)).

12.4.3 *Transfers of securities: debit, credit and title*

According to Spanish law, the transfer of proprietary rights pertaining to any assets requires three elements: (i) the title of the transferor to the securities (i.e. the transferor has the right to dispose of the securities),

12 But see n. 5 above. The new amendments expressly opt for a pro-rata rule. Therefore, once it has been implemented, the Spanish systems will be parallel to the approach of the Convention.

(ii) a valid contract, and (iii) the delivery of the securities. These three conditions are called for in order to pass property.

The Spanish legislator has followed the same approach in the case of book-entry securities registered in the Spanish CSD.

With regard to the first element, the Spanish legal system is based upon the principle of derivative acquisition (or *nemo dat quod non habet* principle): a person only acquires ownership rights pertaining to the securities credited to his account if the transferor was entitled to dispose of those ownership rights. An exception aimed at the protection of bona fide purchasers is, however, included (Article 12.2 RD 116/92). If the bona fide principle applies, the original owner loses his rights pertaining to the securities and will only be entitled to a personal claims vis-à-vis the responsible person.

With regard to the second element, the Spanish legal system is not based upon the principle of abstraction: a mere delivery is not enough to transfer ownership and, therefore, the mere credit of securities to a securities account does not create a valid proprietary right in favour of the account holder. It requires a valid contract – a valid contract which is a sufficient title to produce the effect of a transfer of ownership. According to Spanish law, the protection of the bona fide purchaser does not include the protection with regard to a defective contract.

And, finally, the delivery of assets is also necessary. In the context of book-entry securities, the Spanish legislator has expressly clarified that the delivery takes place by means of book entries, i.e. debit and the corresponding credit (Article 9 LMV and Article 12.2 RD 116/92). It has substituted physical delivery of the document by book-entries in the corresponding registry.

The same legal framework applies, mutatis mutandis, to the creation of limited proprietary rights pertaining to book-entry securities, such as a pledge. Instead of credits and debits, in these cases, the transfer of possession may take place by a designating entry, but not by other methods. Spanish law practitioners are reluctant to accept a control agreement (without 'visibility' in the account) as a method to create a security interest over book-entry securities; hence, Spain will presumably opt for excluding the application of Article 12(3)(c) of the Convention.

The Convention follows a different approach. The regime applicable to the transfer of book-entry securities is articulated in three steps.

First, the text of the Convention takes as a starting point the idea that the acquisition occurs by the mere credit of securities to the account (Article 11(1)), and that no further step is necessary or will be required by the non-Conventional Law (Article 11(2)). Thus, the Convention, unlike the Spanish law, does not require any agreement or contract to transfer and to acquire the rights pertaining to the securities.

Second, the Convention leaves certain room for the non-Convention law in Article 16. According to this provision, the non-Convention law determines whether and in what circumstances a debit, a credit or a designating entry is invalid and/or liable to be reverse, and the consequences thereof. With regard to the Spanish law, the reference to the non-Convention law in Article 16 may safeguard the application of two conditions: a credit is not valid (i) without a corresponding underlying title, typically a contract, to transfer property or (ii) if the transferor is not the owner of the securities. And even more, the condition that the credit must be linked to a corresponding debit under the rules described above. If any of these conditions fails, from a property law perspective, the transferee never acquired ownership rights pertaining to the securities, even though they were credited to his securities account. In this sense, the rules of the Convention, including the reference to non-Convention law in Article 16, can fit within Spanish law.

Thirdly, Article 16 of the Convention is subject to Article 18. Hence, if the acquirer qualifies as an innocent person under this provision, he will acquire property rights pertaining to the securities credited to his account, regardless of whether the credit was not effective according to the Spanish law; for example, due to a defect in the underlying contract or the lack of ownership of the transferor.

Two comments are noteworthy with regard to Article 18.

1. This provision protects vis-à-vis any interference of the non-Convention law under Article 16. As the Official Commentary states, 'it is important to note that all requirements for the validity of a credit set out by the non-Convention law do not displace the protection of an innocent acquirer under Article 18' (§ 11–13). Therefore, the bona fide acquirer is protected regardless of whether the credit was not effective according to the non-Convention law; for example, due to a defect in the underlying contract or the lack of ownership of the transferor. This is not the case under the Spanish law, since the bona fide principle in our legal system only protects the acquirer vis-à-vis a defect on the power of disposition of the transferor, and not against a defect in the title. However, in practical terms, the consequences will not be very relevant, since in these jurisdictions the acquirer is usually protected under other doctrines.[13]

13 See, UNIDROIT 2008 – CONF. 11 – Doc. 8, 10–11

2. Article 18 only envisages the protection of the innocent acquirer, but the consequences of this protection with regard to the original owner of the securities are referred to the non-Convention law. This can be explained if we recall that the Convention is formally based on a principle of separation (though it does not impose it[14]). The wording of the Convention separates the debit and the credit sides of the transaction. Article 18 only deals with the 'credit side' and establishes a harmonised rule of protection of the innocent acquirer in this regard; however, it does not deal with the debit side. This aspect is left to the non-Convention law.[15]

This reference to the non-Convention law allows the Spanish law to maintain its characterisation of the transfer of securities as a sole transaction. If the acquirer qualifies as innocent, according to the Spanish rules, the original owner will lose his rights pertaining to the securities. Only if it were not possible to identify the transferor (i.e., the legitimate owner), for example, because the securities were not debited to a particular account, would the losses be shared among the account holders of the intermediary.

Bibliography

Khimji, Mo. F., 'Intermediary Credit Risk: A Comparative Law Analysis of Proprietary Rights in Indirectly Held Securities' [2005] *Journal of Business Law* 287–325.

14 The idea is clearly explained in Kanda et al., *Official Commentary*, s. 11–4. There are two possible general approaches to a transfer of intermediated securities: (i) either to consider the debit and credit entries as part of one transaction which entails a single transfer of property from the transferor to the transferee, or (ii) to consider them as different transactions, the debit entails the extinction of an interest of the transferor vis-à-vis his intermediary and the credit the creation of an interest of the transferee vis-à-vis its own intermediary. One group of jurisdictions follows the former approach and another group the latter. The Convention is neutral on this point and, in principle, is compatible with both (though in cross-border cases the result may be unclear).

15 See, with different examples, UNIDROIT 2008 – CONF. 11- Doc. 8, section 7.2. The idea can be summarised as follows. With regard to the 'debit side' of the transaction, the non-Convention law may typically establish: (a) either that the original owner has lost his rights over the intermediated securities and only has a contractual claim vis-à-vis the intermediary or any other liable person (this is probably the solution under those legal systems based on the principle that if someone acquires an asset under the bona fide principle, someone must lose it), or (b) that the original owner has not lost his rights over the securities. In this case, the original owner still qualifies as an account holder, and the allocation of securities will be governed by Arts. 25 and 26 of the Convention (loss-sharing rule). As has been said, Art. 18 is a rule on the qualification of a person as account holder, but not a rule on the allocation of securities (*ibid.*).

Macfarlane, B. and Stevens, R., 'Interests in Securities: Practical Problems and Conceptual Solutions', in L. Gullifer and J. Payne (eds.), *Intermediated Securities. Legal Problems and Practical Issues* (Oxford: Hart Publishing, 2010), 33–59.

Mooney, C. W. and Kanda, H., 'Core Issues under the UNIDROIT (Geneva) Convention on Intermediated Securities: Views from the United States and Japan', in L. Gullifer and J. Payne (eds.), *Intermediated Securities. Legal Problems and Practical Issues* (Oxford: Hart Publishing, 2010), 69–130.

Paz-Ares, C., 'La desincorporación de los títulos-valor', in *El nuevo mercado de valores* (Madrid, Colegios Notariales de España, 1995), 81–106.

Recalde, A., 'Los valores negociables', in A. Ureba, and J. Martinez-Simancas (eds.), *Derecho del mercado financiero* (Madrid: Cívitas, 1994) vol. I-2, 265–310.

Rogers, J. S., 'Policy Perspective on Revised U.C.C. Article 8' [1996] 43 *UCLA L. Rev.*, 1431–.57.

Spink, E. T. and Pare M. A., 'The Uniform Security Transfer Act: Globalized Commercial Law for Canada' [2004] 19 *Bank. & Fin L. Rev.*, 321–91.

13

The Geneva Securities Convention and the Swiss intermediated securities law reform

HANS KUHN

13.1 Introduction

In Switzerland, a sweeping reform of the legal framework underpinning the holding of securities by financial intermediaries and their transfer became effective on 1 January 2010. The Federal Intermediated Securities Act (FISA),[1] a statute governing the rights and duties of investors and intermediaries in intermediated holding systems and regulating the methods for the disposition of intermediated securities, was at the heart of this reform. At the same time, Switzerland adopted the Hague Securities Convention (HSC),[2] putting the conflict of laws rules applicable to intermediated securities on new and firmer ground.

The reform of intermediated securities legislation in Switzerland has been much influenced by the work undertaken since 2001 by UNIDROIT in this field, resulting in the adoption of the Geneva Securities Convention (the 'Convention') by a diplomatic conference in 2009. The FISA is almost completely in line with the Convention and can be understood as a possible model for the implementation of the Convention into domestic law. More importantly, the Convention, from a Swiss perspective, may be seen as a necessary part of a safe and sound legal framework for the holding of securities across borders. It is clear that the possibilities of a national legislator wishing to ensure cross-border compatibility

1 Bundesgesetz vom 3. Oktober 2008 über Bucheffekten (*Bucheffektengesetz*, BEG)/Loi fédérale du 3 octobre 2008 sur les titres intermédiés (LTI)/Legge federale del 3 ottobre 2008 sui titoli contabili (Legge sui titoli contabili, LTCo) AS 2009, 3577. All versions available at www.admin.ch/ch/i/rs/c957_1.html. An unofficial English translation of the Act is available from the author.

2 Convention of 5 July 2006 on the Law Applicable to Certain Rights in Respect of Securities held with an Intermediary. The text can be found at www.hcch.net/index'en.php?act=conventions.text&cid=72 .

of legal systems are limited. Harmonisation across borders was therefore a necessary complement to modernisation of the domestic legal framework.

This chapter explains in more detail the interaction between the domestic reform of intermediated securities legislation in Switzerland and the international harmonisation effort undertaken by UNIDROIT. It is organised in five sections. Section 13.2 provides a brief overview of the history and the policy objectives of the Swiss reform exercise. Section 13.3 outlines the core element of the Swiss act and compares those with the Geneva Securities Convention. Section 13.4 then discusses the options a national legislator has to tackle cross-border issues. Section 13.5 concludes by making the point that the FISA is a real-life example for a modern legislation implementing the Convention.

13.2 History and policy objective of Switzerland's securities law reform

13.2.1 Key legal concepts under previous law

Intermediation of securities-holding dates back in Switzerland to the early 1970s, when the Schweizerische Effektengiro AG ('Sega') was set up as a national central securities depository.[3] The immobilisation of securities was initially based on the concept of collective custody. Over the years, Switzerland's financial services industry achieved an almost complete immobilisation and a far-reaching dematerialisation of securities. Amazingly, these fundamental changes in operational arrangements were tackled without the legal framework being amended in any major way.[4] In fact, until the FISA became effective, intermediation and dematerialisation were based entirely on traditional concepts of securities law and generally applicable provisions of contract, property, and insolvency law.

According to the concept of collective custody, fungible certificated securities of the same kind, belonging to a number of different depositors, are kept in a so-called global depot.[5] The depositors (i.e. the ultimate investors) are pro-rata co-owners of the pool of fungible securities held

3 Sega later merged with the ICSD Intersettle to form SegaInterSettle (SIS). Today it is SIX SIS AG, part of the SIX Group AG, the Swiss financial infrastructure group.

4 See Message, BBl 2006, pp. 9321 et seq.; Expert Group Report, 8–9. See also Kuhn, 'Modernisierung', 127 et seq.; Kuhn, 'Bucheffektenmodell', 31 et seq.

5 See von der Crone and Bilek, 'Aktienrechtliche Querbezüge', at 202/203.

by the central securities depository.[6] The intermediaries in the chain of custody are not owner of the securities, but they have (indirect or, in the case of the CSD, direct) possession of the certificate.[7] Since (certificated) securities qualify as chattels (*Sache, chose*) under Swiss law and therefore are to be segregated from the bankruptcy estate (Article 242 Federal Act on Debt Collection and Bankruptcy – DEBA), client securities were protected in the event of the insolvency of the intermediary.[8] Securities held in collective custody were transferred by way of transfer of possession (Article 967(1) Code of Obligations – CO): the transferor would instruct his custodian to holding possession on behalf of the transferee (*Besitzanweisung, transfert de possession*). The foundation in traditional property law concepts also permitted the good-faith acquisition of securities from a transferor who lacked the necessary power to dispose. The system of collective custody was further developed in the 1980s when the concept of global certificates was introduced. Global certificates are certificated securities representing several securities, or the whole, of a particular issue of securities. The legal foundation of the system of global certificates was basically the same as the concept of collective custody.[9]

In practice, both the concept of collective custody and that of global certificates could apply only to fungible securities, i.e. bearer securities or securities in order form made fungible by way of a blank endorsement. It did not work for nominal shares, which were not fungible. In the late 1990s, the Swiss financial services industry therefore introduced a fully dematerialised model for nominal shares.[10] This model rested on the concept of uncertificated securities (*Wertrecht, droit-valeur*). The concept was legally recognised in 1995 when the Stock Exchange Act (SESTA) was enacted. Article 2(a) SESTA defined uncertificated securities as 'non-certificated rights functionally equivalent [to certificated securities]'. The provision had no material content and it was left to scholars and practitioners to flesh out the underlying concept. According to the prevailing view in the Swiss academic literature, uncertificated securities were pure

6 See Message, BBl 2006, 9327.

7 Message, BBl 2006, 9327.

8 Hess and Friedrich, 'Bucheffektengesetz', at 100 with references; Message, BBl 2006, 9329.

9 FISA-Kuhn, Prel. Cmts. FISA, N 5.

10 The so-called nominal share model with deferred printing of title (*Namenaktienmodell mit aufgeschobenem Titeldruck modèle actions nominatives avec impression différée*) left the investor the right to request the production of a physical title. In the nominal share model with abolished printing of title (*Namenaktienmodell mit aufgehobenem Titeldruck modèle actions nominatives avec impression supprimée*) this right was fully abolished. See Message, BBl 2006, 9324.

contractual rights.[11] It followed that such securities could be disposed of pursuant to the provisions on the assignment and pledge of claims (respectively Article 164 seq. CO and Article 900(1) Civil Code – CC). Both a transfer and a pledge required a written agreement signed by the assignor/pledgor.[12] Since uncertificated securities do not qualify as chattels under Swiss law, they did not fall under the scope of Article 242 DEBA and therefore were not subject to segregation in the insolvency of an intermediary. This lacuna was closed by a 1994 amendment to the Banking Act (Articles 16 and 37b BA)[13] providing for the segregation of certain types of non-corporeal assets deposited with a bank in the event of the bank's insolvency. The qualification as mere contractual rights also excluded the possibility of a bona fide acquisition.[14]

13.2.2 History and policy objectives of FISA

This legal framework, developed by commercial lawyers on the basis of generally applicable rules of contract, property, and insolvency law, worked satisfactorily for well over three decades and without challenge in a court of law.[15] Nevertheless, Swiss legal scholars had for some time been calling for a comprehensive reform of the legal foundations of the custody business.[16] With respect to uncertificated securities (*Wertrechte, droits-valeurs*), in the late 1990s a broad consensus emerged that the legislative

11 See Message, BBl 2006, 9328; von der Crone and Bilek, 'Aktienrechtliche Querbezüge', at 201; Forstmoser and Lörtscher, 'Namenaktien', at 51 et seq.; Zobl and Lambert, 'Entmaterialisierung', at 129; Meier-Hayoz and von der Crone, *Wertpapierrecht*, § 25 para. 28.

12 See Zobl and Lambert, 'Entmaterialisierung', at 129; Hess and Friedrich, 'Bucheffektengesetz', at 102; ATF/BGE 115 II 468.

13 Version in Annex 17 of the BA dated 16 December 1994 (AS 1995, 1227).

14 Message, BBl 2006, 9332.

15 No judicial decision has yet been published in Switzerland relating to the issues now covered by FISA. The Federal Tribunal was once called to decide on a similar arrangement, but the case did not involve financial intermediaries: see ATF/BGE 112 II 406 = JdT (1987), I 487. After publication of the Expert Group Report, the Swiss Takeover Board published a recommendation including a detailed discussion of the shortcomings of the former legal framework, see Swiss Takeover Board, 27 June 2005, *Recommendation re: Victory/Unaxis.*

16 See Zobl and Lambert, 'Entmaterialisierung', at 129; Druey, 'Entmaterialisierung', at 69 et seq.; Meier-Hayoz, 'Abschied vom Wertpapier', at 398; Meier-Hayoz and von der Crone, *Wertpapierrecht*, § 25 para. 39; Forstmoser and Lörtscher, 'Namenaktien', at 64; contra: Kleiner, 'Abschied vom Wertpapier', at 295; see also Hess and Friedrich, 'Bucheffektengesetz', at 102 with references.

framework was totally inadequate.[17] The initiative for legal reform was finally taken by the industry, which in 2001 set up a Working Group of financial market lawyers to discuss the need and potential for reform. The final trigger was the increasing difficulty of providing institutional clients and foreign regulators with a satisfactory explanation of the legal framework for the Swiss custody business.[18] At the same time, it was clearly understood that a reliable and transparent legal framework would constitute an important competitive edge in the custody business, an industry of the greatest importance to Switzerland.[19]

The Working Group quickly concluded that reform was indeed needed. It rejected proposals for a piecemeal approach through amendments to the relevant provisions of the Civil Code, the Code of Obligations and the Bankruptcy Act. It commissioned Prof. Hans Caspar von der Crone, of Zurich University, to prepare a draft Act codifying and supporting the operational framework for the holding and transferring of securities held with an intermediary. The draft for a Securities Custody Act[20] (*Wertpapierverwahrungsgesetz*, WVG) published in early 2003 basically codified the existing concepts, i.e. securities in collective custody, global certificates, and uncertificated securities (*Wertrechte, droits-valeurs)*. The draft took up the traditional concept that investors have a 'modified and labile co-ownership' interest in the pool of securities deposited with a central securities depository (see Articles 7 (securities in collective custody) and 11 (global certificates) WVG). This concept was then applied analogously to uncertificated securities (Article 18 WVG). The draft also recognised the constitutive effect of credits to a securities account for the transfer of, or the creation of interests in, securities held in collective custody, a concept equally applicable to any form of intermediation (see Articles 21–6 WVG). The draft included provisions aimed at protecting the integrity of the system, in particular a duty to ensure reconciliation (Article 16 WVG). While the draft relied on traditional concepts of property law, it

17 See Message, BBl 2006, 9331 et seq. Scholars were somewhat reluctant to express a strong opinion, but in the course of the legislative process there were few if any attempts to defend the existing framework for uncertificated securities as being sufficient or satisfactory.

18 See Kuhn, 'Bucheffektenmodell', at 37; Thévenoz, 'New Legal Concepts', at 304.

19 See Thévenoz, 'New Legal Concepts', at 304.

20 See 'Entwurf zu einem Bundesgesetz über die Verwahrung und Verwaltung von Wertpapieren und Bucheffekten' dated 6 January 2003, accessible at www.vondercrone.ch. For a discussion of the draft, see von der Crone and Kessler and Gersbach, 'Entwurf zu einem schweizerischen Wertpapierverwahrungsgesetz'.

identified and tried to address most of the issues that must be resolved by any modern legislation on intermediated securities.

In 2003 the Federal Department of Finance (DoF) commissioned a second Working Group with representatives from several federal offices and the financial services industry to review the draft Act and to prepare the ratification of the Hague Securities Convention. The Working Group started with the draft Securities Custody Act, but soon realised that there was no point in trying to build a modern legal framework for the holding of securities through financial intermediaries on the basis of concepts designed in the nineteenth century. The Working Group therefore developed the concept of intermediated securities (*Bucheffekten, titres intermédiés*) as a new kind of property sui generis. The group went on to revise the rules aimed at protecting the integrity of the system, adopting a bottom-up approach. The Working Group concluded its work in May 2004 and delivered the preliminary draft FISA and the report to the Departments of Finance and Justice on 15 June 2004.[21] In 2006 the Federal Council submitted its draft and message to the parliament.[22] After extensive discussions in the Law Committees of the State Council and the National Council the FISA was adopted by both chambers of parliament on 3 October 2008 without any opposition.

13.3 Key concepts of FISA compared with the Convention

13.3.1 Form, terminology and structure

The FISA has 36 Articles, divided into eight chapters. The first Chapter (Articles 1–5) defines the purpose and scope of the act and provides definitions of certain key terms. Of crucial importance in this Chapter are Article 3, which contains a statutory definition of the key concept of intermediated securities, and Article 4, with a list of financial intermediaries which qualify as custodians under the Act. This list of domestic custodians is limited to regulated entities (Article 4(1)), whereas in

21 See Bericht der vom Eidg. Finanzdepartement eingesetzten technischen Arbeitsgruppe zum Entwurf eines Bundesgesetzes über die Verwahrung und Übertragung von Bucheffekten (Bucheffektengesetz) und zur Ratifikation des Haager Übereinkommens über die auf bestimmte Rechte an Intermediär-verwahrten Wertpapieren anzuwendende Rechtsordnung (Haager Wertpapierübereinkommen), Bern, 15. Juni 2004.

22 See 'Botschaft zum Bucheffektengesetz sowie zum Haager Wertpapierübereinkommen vom 15. November 2006', BBl 2006, 9315–9454.

the international context the FISA does not impose such a requirement (Article 4(2)) because not all jurisdictions require all custodians to be regulated and supervised.[23]

Chapter 2 (Articles 6–8) regulates how intermediated securities are created and extinguished. Chapter 3 (Articles 9–12) deals with the extension of the custody relationship into the vertical dimension by including one or more sub-custodians (Articles 9–10) and imposes a duty on custodians to maintain enough intermediated securities to safeguard the integrity of the intermediated holding system (Article 11 FISA).

Chapter 4, one of two principal chapters, begins by determining the rights of the account holder vis-à-vis his or her custodian (section 1, Articles 13–16). Section 2 (Articles 17–20) provides for the protection of the property of account holders in the insolvency of a custodian, and section 3 (Articles 21–3) deals with rights and interests of a custodian in the intermediated securities it maintains on behalf of its account holders.

The second principal chapter, Chapter 5 (Articles 24–32), sets up the legal framework for disposal of intermediated securities. Section 1 (Articles 24–5) defines three possible ways to dispose of intermediated securities, including creating security interests in them, by way of a credit to a securities account (Article 24), or by entering into a control agreement (Article 25), or by entering into a security agreement in favour of the custodian (Article 26). Section 2 (Articles 27–8) deals with reversals of erroneous debits and credits, and Section 3 (Articles 29–30) with good-faith acquisition and priority issues.

Chapter 6 (Articles 31–2) provides a legal framework for the realisation of security interests Chapter 7 (Article 33) contains liability provisions and Chapter 8 (Articles 34–6) contains interim and final clauses.

13.3.2 Intermediated securities

One of the striking features of FISA is the introduction of a new legal category of assets,[24] called intermediated securities. This reliance on a new concept was a critical step in overcoming the limits set by traditional property or contract law, which were both inadequate to capture the realities of the intermediated holding systems.[25] The choice of a new legal

23 FISA-Graham-Siegenthaler, Art. 4 FISA, N 8, 26.

24 Message, BBl 2006, 9339, 9345 ('ein neues Vermögensobjekt *sui generis*'). See also Expert Group Report, 42.

25 FISA-Thévenoz, Art. 3 FISA, N 1.

concept required new terms in all three official languages (*Bucheffekten, titres intermédiés, titoli contabili*). It thus reflects a fundamental policy choice, a 'paradigm shift'.[26]

Article 3(1) defines intermediated securities as (i) personal or corporate rights of a fungible nature against an issuer which are (ii) credited to a securities account and may be (iii) disposed of in accordance with the provisions of the Act. Article 3(2) complements this definition by making it clear that intermediated securities are effective against the intermediary and any third party, i.e. *erga omnes*. This point is further emphasised by stating explicitly that intermediated securities are 'beyond the reach of other creditors of the [intermediary]'.

Through this definition, FISA recognises a direct relationship between the issuer and the investor, a conceptual feature that distinguishes intermediated securities as defined by the Act clearly from an Article 8 UCC securities entitlement. This makes it necessary to make a distinction between the account holder, defined as the person in whose name a securities account is maintained (Article 5(b)), and the investor who is defined as an account holder who is not an [intermediary], or an [intermediary] who holds intermediated securities for its own account (Article 5(c)). Thus, each investor is an account holder, but not all account holders are investors. Finally, according to Article 13(1) '[t]he creation of intermediated securities does not affect the rights of investors against the issuer'.

Intermediated securities are created in a two-step-process: first by the immobilisation of certificated securities or the registration of uncertificated securities in a single main registry maintained usually by the CSD, and second by crediting the securities to a securities account (Article 6). This process can be reversed, i.e. intermediated securities are extinguished by debiting a securities account and delivering certificated securities to the investor (Article 8).

While both FISA and the Geneva Securities Convention use the same term to describe the object of their regulation,[27] the content of the definition is not exactly the same. According to Article 1(b) of the Convention, intermediated securities are 'securities credited to a securities account or

26 *Ibid.*, Art. 3 FISA, N 1; Thévenoz, 'Du dépôt collectif', passim.

27 This is no coincidence. When the UNIDROIT Committee of Governmental Experts looked for a shorter defined term for the phrase used by the Hague Securities Convention ('securities held with an intermediary'), it opted for 'titres intermédiés' and 'intermediated securities' at the suggestion of the Canadian delegation, which explicitly referred to the Swiss draft Act. See FISA-Thévenoz, Art. 3 FISA, N 6.

rights or interests in securities resulting from the credit of securities to a securities account'. Article 1(a) of the Convention defines securities as 'any shares, bonds or other financial instruments or financial assets (other than cash) which are capable of being credited to a securities account and of being acquired and disposed of in accordance with the provisions of the Convention'. Article 3 FISA is more restrictive than the definitions in the Convention.[28] However, the difference is a matter of legal approach rather than of substance, and intermediated securities within the meaning of the FISA also qualify as intermediated securities within the meaning of the Convention.[29]

13.3.3 Protection of the integrity of intermediated holding system

Intermediated holding systems have a number of advantages over direct holding systems, including the reduction of risks inherent to traditional securities systems like theft, loss, or forgery.[30] On the other hand, intermediated holding systems exhibit specific risks arising from the participation of a majority of intermediaries in a particular chain of custodians or in a transfer of intermediated securities.[31] The main risk is that the positions of investors, credited to the investor's securities account maintained by its intermediary, are not fully covered at all times by holding at an upper-tier level ('shortfall').

The Convention deals with these risks – arising in all intermediated systems[32] – in its Chapter IV, headed 'Integrity of the Intermediated Holding System'. The chapter includes ten articles, dealing with a broad range of issues relating to the account holder's position in the relevant intermediary's insolvency (Article 21), the prohibition of 'upper-tier attachments' (Article 22), instructions to the intermediary (Article 23), the prevention of shortfalls (Articles 24 and 25) and the allocation of losses in case of an insolvency of the intermediary (Articles 26 and 27). Other rules are dealing with the intermediary's obligations and liability (Article 28), the position of issuers (Article 29) and set-off (Article 30).

FISA tackles these issues in a number of provisions scattered over Chapters 3 and 4. The legal framework aimed at safeguarding the integrity of the intermediated holding systems is quite different from Chapter IV of the Convention both in terms of structure and language. However, in terms of policy and results, FISA is understood to be fully in line with the Geneva Securities Convention.

28 See FISA-Thévenoz, Art. 3 FISA, N 52 et seq. for further details.
29 *Ibid.*, Art. 3 FISA, N 52, 55. 30 See Message, BBl 2006, 9323, 9340.
31 *Ibid.*, 9340. 32 Official Commentary, Cmt. IV-1, 117.

A first core provision aimed at preserving the system's integrity is Article 11, which imposes an obligation on each custodian to hold intermediated securities 'at least equal to the total of intermediated securities credited to the securities accounts of its account holders' (Article 11(1)). If the total number of available securities is less than the total number of credited securities, the custodian has to acquire intermediated securities to the extent of the shortfall 'without delay' (Article 11(2)). While at first glance this language appears quite strict, the provision actually works in a rather flexible way because it deems as available securities 'readily available rights to delivery of intermediated securities from other custodians' (Article 11(3)(c)). This broad definition permits the contractual settlement of transactions, where the credit to the account holder's securities account occurs at the trade date (T+0), i.e. before the custodian has received delivery (usually at T+3).[33]

A second core element for ensuring the system's integrity is the framework to protect client positions in an insolvency of the custodian. Article 17 provides for the segregation of client positions from the intermediary's insolvency estate. The segregation extends to intermediated securities credited to a securities account that the custodian holds with an upper-tier custodian (a so-called sub-custodian Article 17(1)(a)) and includes also 'readily available claims of the custodian to receive delivery of intermediated securities' (Article 17(1)(c)). The segregation extends furthermore to the intermediary's proprietary positions if those are commingled with client positions (Article 17(2)). If after segregation of client positions and commingled proprietary positions a shortfall subsists, the shortfall shall be covered by allocation of non-commingled proprietary positions (Article 19(1)). Finally, Article 19(2) provides for a pro-rata loss-sharing rule, i.e. the available intermediated securities are allocated in proportion to the intermediated securities credited to the account holders' securities accounts.

13.3.4 Disposition of intermediated securities

13.3.4.1 General

Chapter 5 dealing with the disposition of intermediated securities is another core element of FISA. Disposition (*Verfügung, disposition*) is

33 See FISA-Witmer, Art. 11 FISA, N 10 et seq. The preservation of the contractual settlement is in line with the Act's policy objective to respect, to the extent possible, 'the operational reality of existing systems'. See FISA-Kuhn, Prel. Cmts. FISA, N. 25 Expert Group Report, p. 32.

what is called a 'transfer' under the Convention. It comprises both the transfer of ownership in intermediated securities from one person (the transferor) to another person (the transferee), as well as the creation of a security interest in intermediated securities (see Articles 25 and 26). Furthermore, the creation of a ususfruct also qualifies as a disposition (Articles 25(3)).[34]

Chapter 5 of FISA is firmly rooted in a concept of derivative acquisition of intermediated securities, i.e. of transferring particular legal positions from one person to another person. This is not easy to reconcile with the realities of the intermediated holding system.[35] A transfer of intermediated securities from the seller to the purchaser usually involves a whole series of debits and credits to several securities accounts maintained by a number of custodians. Credits and debits are sometimes not made in sequential order and normally cannot be traced end-to-end, e.g. when a central counterparty (CCP) is involved in a transaction. From a conceptual point of view, it is clear that the concept of securities entitlement, codified by Article 8 of the Uniform Commercial Code (UCC), is much better suited to deal with these realities. However, in Switzerland this approach was rejected in the course of the securities law reform as being a departure too drastic from fundamental legal concepts deeply ingrained in the DNA of civil lawyers.

Under general principles of Swiss property law, a disposition requires (i) an underlying contract, (ii) an act of disposition and (iii) either the transferor's power to dispose, or the transferee's good faith with respect to such power. The FISA deals only with some but not with all of these requirements, in particular with the methods of disposition. Nonetheless, it fits in well into the general dogmatic framework of Swiss property law.

13.3.4.2 Valid underlying contract?

Under general Swiss property law principles, the validity of the transfer of movable or immovable property depends upon the validity of the underlying contract (causality principle).[36] The situation is unclear for the assignment of claims, the majority view being in favour of the abstraction principle, i.e. claims or receivables are validly assigned even if the

34 FISA-Eigenmann, Art. 25 FISA, N 39 et seq.

35 *Ibid.*, Prel. Cmts. Arts. 24–6 FISA, N 9.

36 See Kuhn, *Kreditsicherungsrecht*, 114. For the transfer of immovable property this so-called causality principle is codified in Art. 974(2) CC. For the transfer of movable property it has been recognised by the Federal Tribunal in ATF/BGE 55 II 302.

underlying contract is void or has been revoked.[37] For intermediated securities FISA does not expressly tackle this issue.[38] However, FISA regulates a number of points which usually depend on the abstract or causal nature of the disposition. In particular, Article 15(2) provides that the 'custodian shall not be obliged or entitled to verify the legal grounds for the instruction'.[39] An instruction given by the account holder has to be executed by the custodian irrespective of whether it is based on a valid underlying contract. Also, the lack of a valid underlying contract does not result in the reversal of a debit or a credit (Article 27).[40] A seller may reclaim intermediated securities if they were transferred without a valid underlying contract, but he can do so only based on the rules on unjust enrichment (Article 62 seq. CO).[41] As a result the legal situation under FISA corresponds to a situation where the abstraction principles applies.[42]

13.3.4.3 Methods for the disposition of intermediated securities

FISA provides for three methods of disposition:

- by way of a credit to the securities account of the transferee (Article 24(1) – see Article 11 of the Convention);
- by way of the transferor entering into a control agreement with the custodian (Article 25 – see Article 12(3)(c) of the Convention); or
- by way of the transferor entering into a security agreement with its custodian (Article 26 FISA – Article 12(3)(a) of the Convention).

Unlike the Convention in Article 12(3)(b), FISA does not recognise the designating entry as a method for the disposition of intermediated securities. The Working Group considered this method, but dismissed it for several reasons. First, a designating entry is nothing more than an electronic record relating to a certain securities account. Normally this record

37 Kuhn, *Kreditsicherungsrecht*, 402–3.

38 The legislator expressly refused to take a view on this primarily dogmatic issue, see Foëx, 'Les actes de disposition', 83 at 89.

39 Vgl. Foëx, 'Les actes de disposition', at 88; Eigenmann, 'Projet de loi', at 111.

40 FISA-Kuhn, Art. 27 FISA, N 55 et seq.; see also Legal Certainty Group, Second Advice, 54.

41 Botschaft, BBl 2006, 9378; FISA-Eigenmann, Prel. Cmts Arts. 24–6 FISA, N 18.

42 See Foëx, 'Les actes de disposition', at 89; FISA-Eigenmann, Prel. Cmts Arts. 24–6 FISA, Rz. 18; Dalla Torre et al., 'Sicherheiten', 17 fn. 7; for a different view see Eigenmann, 'Projet de loi', at 111; Zbinden, *Das Pfandrecht an Aktien*, 25 et seq., Hess and Stöckli, 'Das Bucheffektengesetz', at 118; Eigenmann, SZW 2006, at 111.

can be read only by the custodian maintaining the securities account, not by third parties. A designating entry therefore does not provide any reasonable kind of publicity. Second, a designating entry can legally be effective in any event only if it is made with the consent, or upon the instruction, of the account holder. A designating entry made without such consent has no legal relevance whatsoever. If this is the case, it seems reasonable to focus on the account holder's agreement, which led quite naturally to the concept of control agreement. Lastly, the Working Group found that if the concept of designating entry was to be adopted, detailed secondary legislation would have been required in order to clarify what does and what does not constitute a designating entry. The rejection of the concept of designating entry therefore was based on purely pragmatic considerations and is not an expression of a particular dogmatic view.

13.3.4.3.1 Credit to a securities account The disposition by way of credit (Article 24 FISA) requires (i) a valid instruction (Article 24(1)(a)) and (ii) a credit to a securities account (Article 24(1)(b)). The disposition is completed when the credit has been made (Article 24(2)). Unlike the Convention – and this is one of few discrepancies –FISA does not require a corresponding debit being made. The rationale for this approach is avoiding a period in which the securities would be without an owner.[43]

An effective disposition requires an instruction given by the transferor. FISA does not define the term instruction, but legislative history shows that this is understood as a unilateral contractual expression of will by the account holder, directed at, and subject to reception by, the intermediary (*einseitige, rechtsgeschäftliche und empfangsbedürftige Willenserklärung*).[44] FISA seems to be the first intermediated securities statute expressly dealing with this concept.[45] The Convention deals with the instruction in a more comprehensive way, covering both the account holder's power to issue instructions (positive aspect, see Article 9 of the Convention) and the prevention of third-party interference in the account holder's rights (negative aspect, see Article 23 of the Convention). While FISA does not clearly distinguish the positive and the negative side of instruction, both aspects are at least implicit in the concept underlying Article 24(1)(a), and FISA should be interpreted accordingly.[46]

43 FISA-Eigenmann, Art. 24 FISA, N 22; Foëx, 'Les actes de disposition', at 89.
44 Message, BBl. 2006, 9359 see also FISA-Kuhn, Art. 15 FISA, N 9.
45 FISA-Kuhn, Art. 15 FISA, N 8. 46 *Ibid.*, Art. 15 FISA, N 2, 13 et seq., 20.

While FISA vests the credit to a securities account with legal effect, it also recognises that credits can be materially defective, e.g. when a debit is made without a valid and proper instruction from the account holder, or when an instruction is not executed properly, or when a credit does not correspond to an underlying instruction. FISA, in its Articles 27 and 28, deals with methods for the unilateral correction of incorrect book entries by way of a reversal of debits or credits. Article 27 grants the account holder whose accounts has been debited incorrectly a right to have the debit reversed if (i) it was made without valid and proper instruction (Article 27(1)(a)), (ii) the instruction was seriously defective (Article 27(1)(b)), or (iii) the corresponding credit was not executed correctly or within the customary term (Article 27(1)(c)). Article 28 grants the custodian the right to reverse a credit without the account holder's consent or cooperation if (i) the corresponding debit has been reversed (Article 28(1)(a)), or (ii) the credit did not correspond to the underlying instruction (Article 28(1)(b)). The rules on the reversal of debits and credits are amongst the most innovative provisions introduced by FISA.[47] The Geneva Securities Convention refers issues arising from the reversal of credits and debits to non-Convention law and, to the extent permitted by non-Convention law, to the account agreement or the uniform rules of a securities settlement system (Article 15 of the Convention).

13.3.4.3.2 Control agreement Article 25 FISA provides for the creation and perfection of a security interest (or another limited interest like the usufruct, see Article 25(3)) in intermediated securities by way of entering into a control agreement. The control agreement is an agreement between the account holder and the custodian whereby the custodian 'agrees irrevocably that the custodian must carry out instructions from the secured party without further consent or cooperation from the part of the account holder' (Article 25(1)). Of course, the control agreement is also one of the alternative methods provided for by the Geneva Securities Convention (Article 12(3)(a) of the Convention).

A security interest created by way of a control agreements is perfected (i.e. becomes effective *erga omnes*) once the agreement is concluded (Article 25(1)). No further act of perfection is required. While it will normally be in the custodian's own interest to block the relevant securities account, or earmark the pledged securities, in order to be able to comply with the

47 *Ibid.*, Prel. Cmts. Arts. 17–28 FISA, N 20 et seq.

obligations under the control agreement, under Swiss law the earmarking has no legal relevance and is no perfection requirement.[48]

The control agreement is the act of disposition for the creation of security interests in intermediated securities without a transfer to the secured party's securities account. It has clearly to be distinguished from the underlying contract (pledge agreement, *pactum fiduciae*).[49] FISA defines the control agreement as a bilateral agreement between the account holder (collateral provider) and the custodian, while the secured party needs not to be a party to the control agreement.[50] In such a case the control agreement is to be qualified as a contract in favour of a third party (Article 112 CO), and the secured party has the right directly to seek its performance (Article 112(2) CO).[51] Nothing prevents the parties from entering into a tripartite agreement.[52] It should be pointed out, however, that an agreement between the collateral provider and the secured party of which the custodian is merely notified does not qualify as a control agreement under FISA. This is in fact a major divergence between FISA and the Geneva Securities Convention.[53]

FISA defines control as the secured party's right to dispose of intermediated securities 'without any further consent or cooperation on the part of the account holder' (i.e., *positive control* Article 25(1)). The Act does not require the collateral provider to be fully excluded from dispositions relating to intermediated securities credited to its securities account (*negative control*).[54] However, the parties are free to enter into this kind of agreement, or to combine aspects of positive and negative control.[55]

13.3.4.3.3 Security interest in favour of custodian Security interests in favour of the relevant custodian in intermediated securities held with such custodian may be created and perfected by simply entering into a security agreement. Since the secured party – the custodian – already has control over the collateral the act of disposition is limited to entering into

48 See Foëx, 'Les actes de disposition', at 95.
49 Dalla Torre et al., 'Sicherheiten', 20.
50 See FISA-Eigenmann, Art. 25 FISA, N 16.
51 *Ibid.*, Art. 25 FISA, N 17.
52 *Ibid.*, Art. 25 FISA, N 16.
53 *Ibid.*, Art. 25 FISA, N 16.
54 See Dalla Torre et al., 'Sicherheiten', 21; Foëx, 'Les sûretés sur les titres', at 135; Bensahel and Micotti and Villa, 'L'objet et le rang des sûretés', at 332 et seq.; Lanz, 'Aktientransfers', at 209.
55 See Dalla Torre et al., 'Sicherheiten', 21.

the security agreement.[56] No further act is required in order to perfect the security interest.[57] In particular, no earmarking is required.[58]

The security agreement is not subject to any formal requirements. It may be part of general contract terms if those have become part of the contractual agreement between collateral provider and secured party. In the legislative process, this was a point of contention. The Federal Council had proposed that the security agreement must be in written form and signed by the collateral provider in order to make it perfectly clear to account holders that the custodian has a security interest in the intermediated securities credited to their securities account. The parliament, however, rejected this proposal.[59]

The custodian's security interest is extinguished when intermediated securities are transferred to another securities account (Article 26(2) FISA). Intermediated securities cannot be transferred from one account to another account without the custodian's cooperation. The execution of a transfer instruction issued by the account holder therefore has to be understood as the custodian waiving its security interests in the intermediated securities.

13.3.4.4 Transferor's power to dispose or transferee's good faith

13.3.4.4.1 Power to dispose Also under general Swiss property law principles, an effective disposition requires the disposing party to have the power or authority to dispose.[60] This is also a requirement under FISA. Only an instruction issued by the competent account holder is legally effective (Article 24(1)(a)). If an account is debited based on an instruction issued by a person who is not the account holder, the account holder has a legally enforceable claim against the intermediary to have the debit reversed (Article 27(1)(b)(2)). Power or authority to dispose is also a prerequisite for an effective disposition if the disposition is made by way of entering into a control agreement (Article 25) or a security agreement (Article 26).[61]

56 Foëx, 'Les actes de disposition', at 97; Eigenmann, 'Projet de loi', at 112.

57 Dalla Torre et al., 'Sicherheiten', at 23.

58 Foëx, 'Les actes de disposition', at 97.

59 See Message, BBl 2006, 9372.

60 FISA-Eigenmann, Prel. Cmts Arts. 24–6 FISA, N 14 ff. Foëx, 'Les actes de disposition', at 85.

61 Foëx, 'Les actes de disposition', at 96 et seq.

The power to dispose is vested in the person for whom the custodian maintains the account, i.e. the account holder (Article 5(b)).[62] The account holder may or may not be the beneficiary, e.g. if he acts as a trustee or a nominee. The power to dispose can be granted by way of agreement, e.g. by entering into a control agreement (Article 25), or a right of use (Article 22).

If a (regular) pledge was granted by way of a credit to a securities account (Article 24), the account holder/pledgee has power to dispose only if authorised by the pledgor. Since the intermediated securities are not earmarked as being subject to a pledge, the pledgee has the (factual) power to dispose without such authorisation. However, in such a case the third-party purchaser acquires as a good-faith acquirer (Article 29(1)(a)).

13.3.4.4.2 Good faith If the transferor had no power to dispose, Article 29 FISA protects the transferee if he acquires intermediated securities or rights in intermediated securities (i) for value and (ii) in good faith. Article 29 has been modelled after the property law provisions on good-faith acquisition (Articles 933, 973 CC),[63] but differs in a number of practical and dogmatic points. First, the good faith acquisition of property rights in movables and immovables is based on the protection of the transferee relying on an appearance attributable to the transferor.[64] In the corporeal world, this appearance is created by the transferor having possession of the movable or being registered in the land register as the owner of an immovable. There is no similar basis of appearance in the world of intermediated securities, because the disposition is based on actions (credits and debits to securities accounts) which are not really accessible to third parties and which are therefore not public.

The dogmatic basis for the good-faith acquisition of intermediated securities therefore is the credit to a securities account (positive element) and the absence of information regarding defects in the disposition (negative element).[65] In other words, the transferee is protected if (i) intermediated securities have been credited to his securities account, and (ii) he did not have any information regarding the transferor lacking the requisite authority to dispose. This concept is clearly expressed by the Convention in Article 18(1) and (2), whereas it remained somewhat blurred in FISA's legislative history. However, nothing prevents Article 29 being construed in line with the Geneva Securities Convention.

62 FISA-Eigenmann, Prel. Cmts. Arts. 24–6 FISA, N 14.

63 Foëx, 'Les actes de disposition', at 85. 64 *Ibid.*, at 86. 65 *Ibid.*, at 86.

The good-faith protection provided for by Article 29 applies only if the acquisition is made for value (Article 29(1)). With respect to this requirement, FISA is fully in line with the Geneva Securities Convention (Article 18(3) of the Convention). It should be noted that the 'for value' requirement is new to Swiss law. The Federal Council's message justified it on the grounds that gratitious acquisitions do not involve interests of third parties participating in commercial transactions worthy of protection.[66] Any acquisition that is not made 'by way of gift or otherwise gratitously' is for value payment, in other words is not necessary for an acquisition to be deemed to be for value.[67] It goes without saying that the perfection of a security interest is a 'for value' disposition.[68]

FISA does not define a particular good-faith standard. The expert commission discussed this approach but finally rejected it. Whether a transferee is in good faith therefore has to be determined based on general principles. The famous Article 3 CC provides for a general assumption that a person is acting in good faith, but prohibits a person from invoking the presumption of good faith if he or she has failed to exercise 'the diligence required by the circumstances' (Article 3(2) CC). Relevant circumstances to be considered include terms and usages observed in a particular business.[69] With respect to securities transactions, the large trading volumes, the speed of the transactions and the fact that the organisation of the clearing and settlement usually excludes dispositions by unauthorised persons.

13.3.5 Priorities

The Federal Intermediated Securities Act deals with priority issues in Article 30. Article 30(1) starts from the proposition that the first disposition has priority over subsequent dispositions, following the Roman law adage *prior tempore, potior iure.*[70] Paragraphs (2) and (3) derogate from the 'first in time is first in right' ground rule in two specific cases:

1. when a priority conflict arises between an interest created by control agreement (Article 25(1)) and an interest in favour of the custodian (Article 26) the interest in favour of the custodian is then subordinated to the interest of the secured party (Article 30(2)); and

66 Message, BBl 2006, 9377.

67 FISA-Foëx, Art. 29 FISA, N 25 see also Lanz, 'Aktientransfers', at 222; von der Crone and Bilek, 'Aktienrechtliche Querbezüge', at 206.

68 See Art. 18(3) of the Convention.

69 Message, BBl 2006, 9377.

70 Codex 8, 17, 3 and 2. See FISA-Kuhn, Art. 30 FISA, N 1 et seq.

2. when a priority conflict arises between an interest created under FISA and an assignment of intermediated securities. In this case, the assignee's rights are always subordinated to the rights acquired by a disposition under the act, regardless of the time of the assignment (Article 30(3)).

The scope of the priority rules was one of the most controversial issues in the course of the preparation of the Geneva Securities Convention.[71] The final text of Article 19 of the Convention now makes it clear that it covers only interests that become effective against third parties under Article 12 (control agreement, agreement with the custodian designating entry), or Article 13 (non-Convention law method). It does not apply to interests acquired by credit pursuant to Article 11 of the Convention. The scope of the priority provisions was not subject to the same intensive discussions when the Swiss act was prepared, and both legislative history and the text of Article 30 FISA remain silent in this respect. However, nothing prevents learning from the UNIDROIT experience, and construing Article 30 FISA in line with Article 19 of the Convention.[72]

13.3.6 *Security interests in intermediated securities*

The Federal Intermediated Securities Act does not distinguish between pledges and full title security interests, but rather uses the term 'security interests' (see Article 25, 26, 31, 32). The term is not defined by the Act, but legislative history makes it clear that it includes both limited rights (i.e. pledges) as well as full title security interests. Put differently, the Act did not intend to replace the dichotomy of limited and full title security interests by a uniform security interest. Parties therefore are free to define a security interest as a (regular or irregular) pledge, a fiduciary title transfer for security purposes and, or a non-fiduciary full-title security interest.[73] Moreover, the Act does regulate the right of retention (Article 21) as a statutory security interest.

The distinction between partial and full title security interests is in particular relevant for the ownership in intermediated securities which remains with the pledgor in the case of a (regular) pledge and which passes to the secured party in case of an irregular pledge or a full-title security interest.[74] The attribution of ownership is relevant in particular

71 See Kanda et al., *Official Commentary*, s. 19–2 et seq. for a history of the debates.

72 See FISA-Kuhn, Art. 30 FISA, N 9 et seq.

73 Kuhn, *Kreditsicherungsrecht*, 476. 74 *Ibid.*, 476.

for the right of use and the treatment of collateral in the secured party's insolvency.[75]

13.4 FISA's cross-border dimension

Cross-border compatibility was a key concern in the law reform process from the outset, and was defined by the Working Group as the single most important policy objective.[76] Since the possibilities of a national legislator ensuring cross-border compatibility are limited, Switzerland decided to follow closely and support to the extent possible the multilateral harmonisation of intermediated securities law undertaken since 1999 by the Hague Conference for Private International Law and since 2003 by the International Institute for the Unification of Private Law (UNIDROIT).

Of particular importance was the influence of the work undertaken by UNIDROIT. Prof. Luc Thévenoz, a member of the Swiss Working Group, also served as a member in the Restricted Study Group and the various drafting groups preparing the Geneva Securities Convention. The author first served as chairman of the Swiss Working Group commissioned to prepare the draft FISA, and later for UNIDROIT as chairman of the Committee of Governmental Experts and of the Committee of the Whole of the Diplomatic Conference. It can hardly be overstated how important the insights gained in the course of the international negotiations were in developing a deep understanding of the issues and the possible solutions for the national legislation.

However, it should also be pointed out that the reform exercise in Switzerland was well advanced when the Restricted Study Group delivered the preliminary draft convention on 23 December 2004. The Swiss Working Group had concluded its work in the spring of that year and its report was published on 15 June 2004. Since the Working Groups proposals were adopted more or less in toto by the Federal Council, later discussions at the international level had only very limited impact on the black-letter text of FISA. Hence, it would be an overstatement to say that FISA has been modelled upon the Convention. It is the more remarkable that on many points, very similar solutions have been found in the course of the domestic law reform exercise and in the international negotiations. Moreover, interpretation of the text of the Swiss Act can and should take into account the insights gained in the course of the preparation of the Geneva Securities Convention.

75 *Ibid.*, 503 et seq. 76 Expert Group Report, 32 et seq.

Another measure to ensure maximum cross-border compatibility was the decision to implement in Switzerland, as part of the legal reform, the EU Finality and Financial Collateral Directives,[77] even though Switzerland, which is not a Member State of the European Union, of course was under no obligation to do so.

Another pillar of the Swiss securities law reform was a complete overhaul of the private international law rules regarding intermediated securities. Prior to 2010, the conflict of laws provisions relevant for determining the law applicable to the holding and the transfer of intermediated securities were confusing, inconsistent, and at times virtually impossible to apply.[78] Hence, a reform was urgent. Switzerland therefore supported the work undertaken by the Hague Conference on Private International law and became, together with the United States, the first signatory of the Hague Securities Convention. When it became clear that the Convention would encounter resistance in the European Union, the Federal Council reviewed all available options, including waiting for an EU solution and drafting domestic conflict of laws rules. It finally concluded that a ratification of the Hague Securities Convention would be the best solution.[79] Since it was (and still is) unclear when the Convention will enter into force as a matter of public international law, the Federal Council decided to have it applied as Swiss domestic law until such time as it enters into force on an international level. This was technically achieved by introducing a new Article 108c in the Private International Law Act (PILA), which refers all issues regarding the law applicable to intermediated securities to the Hague Securities Convention. This reference is constitutive for the time being and will become purely declarative once the HSC enters into force as an international instrument.[80]

13.5 Conclusions

There is hardly any business which is more international than the securities business. The holding of securities across borders therefore is today the rule, rather than the exception. This is particularly true for an international financial centre such as Switzerland. The cross-border dimension

77 Directive 2002/47/EC of the European Parliament and of the Council of 6 June 2002 on financial collateral arrangements, OJ L168/43–50.

78 See Zobl, 'Internationale Übertragung', at 105 et seq.; Girsberger and Guillaume, 'Aspects', 15 et seq.; see also Message, BBl 2006, 9400.

79 For a discussion of the available policies see Message, BBl 2006, 9398 et seq.

80 Message, BBl 2006, 9410.

was therefore a key concern throughout the securities law reform exercise undertaken in Switzerland since 2001. Since the possibilities for a national legislator to ensure cross-border compatibility of legal systems are limited, harmonisation of the legal framework on a global level was an integral part of Switzerland's strategy to implement a modern and resilient legal framework for the holding of securities through intermediaries. Switzerland therefore has actively supported the work undertaken by UNIDROIT.

The Federal Intermediated Securities Act, which was adopted by the parliament in 2008 and became effective in 2010, is not a copy of the Geneva Securities Convention. Nonetheless, the Act is understood to be to a very large degree compatible with the Convention. This is due, on the one hand, to the fact that the work undertaken by UNIDROIT has strongly influenced the drafting of the Swiss Act. On the other hand this is also evidence that certain solutions to a particular problem are unavoidable. Even where the Act's provisions differ from the text of the Convention, FISA can and should be interpreted in a way which is consistent with the Convention.

FISA can also be seen as a possible model for the implementation of the Convention in a civil law jurisdiction. FISA is firmly rooted in, and fits into, the dogmatic framework of Swiss property law. At the same time, the Act was not, as it were, built on a greenfield site, but rather aimed at supporting operational systems which worked perfectly well. Remodelling such systems is usually an extremely expensive exercise. It was therefore a cornerstone of the Swiss securities law reform that FISA should respect existing systems and practices, and impose changes only if there was a cogent reason for doing so.

Bibliography

Abegglen, S., 'Zulässigkeit der Bestellung eines Pfandrechts an Bucheffekten mittels Umbuchung nach Art. 24 BEG – eine dogmatische Einordnung' [2011] *Recht*, 112–17.

Ammann, H.-P., 'Bucheffektengesetz und Haager Wertpapierübereinkommen, Vorlage für Finanzplatz Schweiz von strategischer Bedeutung' [2006] *Der Schweizer Treuhänder (ST)*, 524–6.

Bahar, R., 'Foreign Securities and the Act on Book-Entry Securities' [2009] *CapLaw*, Nr. 74

Bärtschi, H., 'Die rechtliche Umsetzung des Bucheffektengesetzes' [2009] *Aktuelle Juristische Praxis (AJP)*, 1071–87.

Baumgartner, F., 'Reguläre Pfandrechte und pfandrechtsähnliche Sicherheiten an Bucheffekten' [2011] *Aktuelle Juristische Praxis (AJP)*, 1355–68.

Bensahel, F., Micotti, S. and Villa, M., 'L'objet et le rang des sûretés selon la loi sur les titres intermédiés (LTI), Questions choisies' [2009] *SemJud* II, 321–69.

Bericht der vom Eidgenössischen Finanzdepartement eingesetzten technischen Arbeitsgruppe zum Entwurf eines Bundesgesetzes über die Verwahrung und Übertragung von Bucheffekten (Bucheffektengesetz) und zur Ratifikation des Haager Übereinkommens über die auf bestimmte Rechte an Intermediärverwahrten Wertpapieren anzuwendende Rechtsordnung (Haager Wertpapierübereinkommen), Bern, 15 June 2004 (cit. Expert Group Report).

Blum, O., 'Rechtsmängel bei der Übertragung von Aktien' [2007] *Aktuelle Juristische Praxis (AJP)*, 694–8.

Brunner, C., *Wertrechte – nicht verurkundete Rechte mit gleicher Funktion wie Wertpapiere, Ein Beitrag zur rechtlichen Erfassung des Effektengiroverkehrs* (Bern: Stämpfli, Berner Bankrechtliche Abhandlungen Band 1, 1996).

Costantini, R., 'Kollisionsrechtliche Aspekte des Bucheffektengesetzes. Zur Praktikabilität stufenweiser Anknüpfung unter dem Haager Wertpapierübereinkommen' [2010] *Schweizerische Juristen-Zeitung (SJZ)*, 366–70.

'The New Act on Book-Entry Securities' [2009] *CapLaw*, Nr. 55.

Die drei Anknüpfungsgegenstände des internationalen Effektenrechts, Eine Strukturtheorie der Effektenverwahrung im Hinblick auf die Bestimmung des relevanten Intermediärs im Sinne des Haager Wertpapierübereinkommens (Zürich/Basel/Genf: Schulthess, 2008).

Dalla Torre, L. and Germann, M., '12 Antworten zum neuen Bucheffektengesetz' [2009] *Gesellschafts- und Kapitalmarktrecht (GesKR)*, 573–82.

Dalla Torre, L. et al., 'Sicherheiten nach Bucheffektengesetz – Theoretische und praktische Aspekte' [2010] *Recht* 10–29.

Dallèves, L., 'La dématérialisation des papiers-valeurs: un décalage croissant entre droit et réalité' [1987] *Die Schweizerische Aktiengesellschaft (SAG)*, 43–9.

'Le sequestre des titres déposés à la SEGA' [1978] *Schweizerische Juristen-Zeitung (SJZ)*, 85–8.

Defferrard, F. [1999] *Le transfert des actions nominatives liées non cotées* (Fribourg: Travaux de la Faculté de Droit de l'Université de Fribourg, vol. 188, 1999).

Dietschi, N. and Messer, R., 'Collaterals in connection with the Act on Book-Entry Securities' [2009] *CapLaw*, Nr. 72.

Druey, J. N., 'Die Entmaterialisierung des Wertpapiers. Einige rechtsvergleichende Hinweise' [1987] *Die Schweizerische Aktiengesellschaft (SAG)*, 65–70.

Eggen, M., 'Sicherheiten an Wertrechten – eine Untersuchung der Rechtslage ab Inkrafttreten des Bucheffektengesetzes' [2009] *Schweizerische Zeitschrift für Wirtschafts- und Finanzmarktrecht (SZW)*, 116–27.

'Bemerkungen zur Verpfändung von Wertpapieren' [2009] *Gesellschafts- und Kapitalmarktrecht (GesKR)*, 540–7.

Egger, W., 'Rechtsprobleme im Zusammenhang mit der Sammelverwahrung', in P. Forstmoser (ed.), *Rechtsprobleme der Bankpraxis* (Bern/Stuttgart: Bankwirtschaftliche Forschungen Band 36, 1976), 109–28.

Eigenmann, A., 'La réalisation des sûretés sur les titres intermédiés', in J.-T. Michel (ed.), *Placements collectifs et titres intermédiés: Le renouveau de la place financière suisse, Travaux de la journée d'étude organisée à l'Université de Lausanne le 7 novembre 2007* (Lausanne: CEDIDAC, 2007), 127–44.

'Projet de loi sur le dépôt et le transfert des titres intermédiés, aspects choisis' [2006] *Schweizerische Zeitschrift für Wirtschafts- und Finanzmarktrecht (SZW)*, 104–18.

Etter, E., 'Ubi rem meam invenio – ibi eam vindico, Gedanken zur Sammelverwahrung von Wertschriften' [1978] *Schweizerische Juristen-Zeitung (SJZ)*, 101–6.

Favre, O., *Die Berechtigung von Depotkunden an auslandsverwahrten Effekten. Verwahrungskonzepte und ihre Bedeutung im internationalen Privatrecht aus schweizerischer Sicht* (Zürich/Basel/Genf: Schulthess, Schweizer Schriften zum Bankrecht Band 72, 2003).

Foëx, B., 'Gages sur les droits-valeurs: développements récents', in F. Bianchi (ed.), *Mélanges publiés par l'Association des Notaires Vaudois à l'occasion de son centenaire* (Zürich: Schulthess 2005) 235–254.

'Les actes de disposition sur les titres intermédiés', in J.-T. Michel (ed.), *Placements collectifs et titres intermédiés: Le renouveau de la place financière suisse, Travaux de la journée d'étude organisée à l'Université de Lausanne le 7 novembre 2007* (Lausanne: CEDIDAC, 2007), 83–106.

'Les sûretés sur les titres détenus auprès d'une banque en Suisse selon la loi sur les titres intermédiés', in L. Thévenoz and C. Bovet (eds.), *Journée 2008 de droit bancaire et financier* (Zürich: Schulthess, 2009), 123–46.

'Sûretés mobilières: proposition pour une réforme' [2007] *Zeitschrift für Schweizerisches Recht (ZSR)* II, 291–337.

'Transfert et engagement des valeurs mobilières 'intermédiées' en droit suisse', in L. Thévenoz/C. Bovet (eds.), *Journée 2003 de droit bancaire et financier* (Zürich: Schulthess, 2004), 55–76.

Forstmoser, P. and Lörtscher, T., 'Namenaktien mit aufgeschobenem Titeldruck: ein Konzept zur Rationalisierung der Verwaltung und des Handels von Schweizer Namenaktien' [1987] *Die Schweizerische Aktiengesellschaft (SAG)*, 50–64.

Gautschi, G., 'Im Ausland hinterlegte Wertpapiere im Konkurs, bei Arrestlegung oder Pfändung gegenüber Depotkunden einer Schweizer Bank' [1969] *Schweizerische Juristen-Zeitung (SJZ)*, 249–52.

Girsberger, D. and Guillaume, F., 'Aspects de droit international privé du transfer et du nantissement des papiers-valeurs et des droit-valeurs détenues dans un système de dépôt collectif', in L. Thévenoz and C. Bovet (eds.), *Journée 2003 de droit bancaire et financier* (Zürich: Schulthess, 2004), 15–55.

Girsberger, D. and Hess, M., 'Das Haager Wertpapierübereinkommen' [2006] *Aktuelle Juristische Praxis (AJP)*, 992–1008.

Gomez-Richa, L. and Veuve, J., 'Les titres intermédiés et leurs instruments financiers sous-jacents' [2010] *Gesellschafts- und Kapitalmarktrecht (GesKR)*, 6–34.

Graham-Siegenthaler, B., 'Übertragung und Verwahrung von Wertpapieren im nationalen und internationalen Recht' [2005] *recht*, 185–94.

Guillaume, F., 'L'electio juris comme règle de rattachement des titres intermédiés, ses effets sur les droits des tiers et ses conséquences dans une procédure d'insolvabilité', in A. Bonomi, E. C. Ritaine and B. Volders (eds.), *La loi applicable aux titres intermédiés: La Convention de La Haye du 5 juillet 2006 – Une opportunité pour la place financière suisse?* (Zürich: Schulthess, 2006), 67–83.

'Les titres détenus auprès d'un intermédiaire (titres intermédiés) en droit suisse – Aspects de droit materiel et de droit international privé' [2005] *Euredia*, 247–70.

'Les titres intermédiés en droit international privé', in J.-T. Michel (ed.), *Placements collectifs et titres intermédiés – Le renouveau de la place financière suisse, Travaux de la journée d'étude organisée à l'Université de Lausanne le 7 novembre 2007* (Lausanne: 2008), 145–73.

Handschin, L., 'Papierlose Wertpapiere', dissertation, Basel 1987 (Basel/Frankfurt A.M.: Helbing & Lichtenhahn 1987).

Hess, M. and Friedrich, A., 'Das neue Bucheffektengesetz (BEG) – Hinweise auf Grundlagen und praktische Auswirkungen' [2008] *Gesellschafts- und Kapitalmarktrecht (GesKR)*, 98–118.

Hess, M. and Stöckli, K., 'Bestellung von Sicherheiten an Bucheffekten' [2010] *Schweizerische Juristen-Zeitung (SJZ)*, 153–62.

'Das Bucheffektengesetz aus der Optik des Kapitalmarktrechts', in T. U. Reuter and T. Werlen (eds.), *Kapitalmarkttransaktionen V* (Zürich: Schulthess, 2010), 1–57.

'Das Bucheffektengesetz: Grundzüge und Missverständnisse' [2010] *Anwaltsrevue*, 115–20.

Hess, M. and Zbinden, A., 'Das reguläre Pfandrecht an Bucheffekten, Ein Beitrag zur Frage der Errichtung des Pfandrechts an Bucheffekten nach Art. 24 Bucheffektengesetz (BEG)' [2011] *Gesellschafts- und Kapitalmarktrecht (GesKR)*, 346–58.

Hofstetter, B., 'Regelung der Verwahrung und Übertragung von Bucheffekten' [2004] *Jusletter* 20 Dezember 2004.

Huber, H. G., 'Verarrestierbarkeit von Wertpapieren, welche durch inländische Banken im Ausland verwahrt werden' [1969] *Schweizerische Juristen-Zeitung (SJZ)*, 149–54.

Kleiner, B., 'Bankdepot – auswärtsliegende Titel und deren Pfändung bzw. Verarrestierung' [1968] *Schweizerische Juristen-Zeitung (SJZ)*, 211.

'Zäher Abschied vom Wertpapier im Effektenbereich' [1995] *Schweizerische Zeitschrift für Wirtschafts- und Finanzmarktrecht (SZW)* 290–5.

Kocher, R. F., *Namenaktien mit aufgeschobenem Titeldruck im Vollstreckungsrecht* (Zürich: Juris Druck + Verlag, 1990).

Kroll, M. J., 'Arrest von Wertrechten in Sammelverwahrung' [1994] *Schweizerische Zeitschrift für Wirtschafts- und Finanzmarktrecht (SZW)*, 244–50.

Krummenacher R., *Die Verpfändung von Namenaktien mit aufgeschobenem Titeldruck, Unter besonderer Berücksichtigung der statutarischen Behandlung von Namenaktien mit aufgeschobenem Titeldruck sowie der in der Praxis verwendeten Pfandverträge und Allgemeinen Geschäftsbedingungen* (Basel: Helbing & Lichtenhahn 1999).

Kuhn, H., *Schweizerisches Kreditsicherungsrecht* (Bern: Stämpfli, 2011).

'Das neue Bucheffektenmodell des schweizerischen Rechts', in T. Baums and A. Cahn (eds.), *Die Zukunft des Clearing und Settlement* (Berlin: de Gruyter, 2006), 29–61.

'Die Modernisierung des Rechts der mediatisierten Wertpapierverwahrung in der Schweiz', in P. Nobel (ed.), *Aktuelle Rechtsprobleme des Finanz- und Börsenplatzes Schweiz,* Heft 13 (Bern: Stämpfli, 2006), 125–44.

Kuhn, H., Graham-Siegenthaler, B. and Thévenoz, L. (eds.), *The Federal Intermediated Securities Act (FISA) and the Hague Securities Convention (HSC)* (Bern: Stämpfli, 2010) (cit. FISA-Author).

Kunz, P., 'Legislative Aktivitäten im Finanzmarktrecht – zum Entwurf für ein neues Bundesgesetz über Bucheffekten (Bucheffektengesetz, BEG)', in S. Emmenegger (ed.), *Anlagerecht, Schweizerische Bankrechtstagung 2007* (Basel: Helbing Lichtenhahn, 2007), 25–57.

Lanz, M., 'Aktientransfers unter dem neuen Bucheffektengesetz', in T. U. Reutter and T. Werlen (eds.), *Kapitalmarkttransaktionen IV* (Zürich/Basel/Genf: Schulthess, 2009), 189–223.

Lanz, M. and Favre, O., 'Inhaberaktien in der Form von Wertrechten. Neue Möglichkeiten unter Art. 973c OR', *Gesellschafts- und Kapitalmarktrecht (GesKR)*, 548–53.

Lehmann, M., *Finanzinstrumente, Vom Wertpapier- und Sachenrecht zum Recht der unkörperlichen Vermögensgegenstände* (Tübingen: Mohr Siebeck, 2009)

Meier-Hayoz, A., 'Abschied vom Wertpapier?' [1986] 122 *Zeitschrift des Bernischen Juristenvereins (ZBJV)*, 385–401.

Meier-Hayoz, A. and von der Crone, H. C., *Wertpapierrecht,* 2nd edn (Bern: Stämpfli, 2000).

Olgiati, L., 'Schweizerische Nominees im Aktienregister amerikanischer Publikumsgesellschaften, Eine Analyse der Rechtsstellung des Anlegers unter besonderer Berücksichtigung seines Interessenwahrungsanspruchs gegenüber der schweizerischen Depotbank', dissertation, Zürich 1995.

Piotet, D., 'Titres intermédiés: rupture avec les principes généraux de la codification', in *Placements collectifs et titres intermédiés: Le renouveau de la place financière suisse, Travaux de la journée d'étude organisée à l'Université de Lausanne le 7 novembre 2007* (Lausanne: CEDIDAC, 2007), 107–25.

Rickenbacher, R., *Globalurkunden und Bucheffekten im schweizerischen Recht, Ein Beitrag zur Rationalisierung des Wertpapiergeschäfts* (Zürich: Schulthess, Schweizer Schriften zum Bankrecht Band 58, 1981).

Roth, G. H., 'Zur Zukunft des Wertpapierrechts' [2011] *Basler Juristische Mitteilungen*, 169–97.

Schlegel, A., *Die schweizerische Effekten-Giro AG und ihre Beziehung zum Bankkunden in der Verwahrung von Wertpapieren* (Bern: Haupt 1983).

Steinauer, P.-H., 'Les droits réels face à la dématérialisation des papiers-valeurs', in Association Franco-Suisse de Paris II, *Le centenaire du Code civil suisse. Colloque du 5 avril 2007* (Paris: Société de législation comparée, 2008), 145–67.

Steiner, C. and Büchi, R., 'Vom Wertrecht zur Bucheffekte – Kristallisation aus dem Nichts?' [2007] *Gesellschafts- und Kapitalmarktrecht (GesKR)*, 73–8.

Thévenoz, L., 'Du dépôt collectif des valeurs mobilières aux titres intermédiés: un saut épistémologique', in R. Waldburger et al. (eds.), *Wirtschaftsrecht zu Beginn des 21. Jahrhunderts, Festschrift für Peter Nobel zum 60. Geburtstag* (Bern: Stämpfli, 2005), 681–711.

'Intermediated Securities, Legal Risk, and the International Harmonization of Commercial Law' [2007] 13 *Stanford Journal of Law, Business & Finance*, 384–452.

'Switzerland – New Legal Concepts regarding the Holding of Investment Securities for a Civil Law Jurisdiction: The Swiss Draft Act', *Uniform Law Review* 2005, 301–37.

'Titres intermédiés: l'état de fait', in L. Thévenoz and C. Bovet (eds.), *Journée 2003 de droit bancaire et financier* (Zürich: Schulthess, 2004), 1–14.

Trigo Trindade, R., 'Loi sur les titres intermédiés: adaptation de statuts antérieurs à la loi?', in T. Trindade and H. P. C. Bovet (eds.), *Economie, Environnement, Ethique, Liber Amicorum Anne Petitpierre-Sauvain* (Zürich: 2009), 379–89.

von Ballmoos T., *Der wertpapierrechtliche Verkehrsschutz unter spezieller Berücksichtigung des stückelosen Effektenverkehrs* (Bern/Stuttgart/Vienna: Haupt, 1993).

von der Crone, H. C. and Bilek, E., 'Aktienrechtliche Querbezüge zum geplanten Bucheffektengesetz (BEG)' [2008] *Schweizerische Zeitschrift für Wirtschafts- und Finanzmarktrecht (SZW)*, 193–207.

von der Crone, H. C., Kessler, F. J. and Gersbach, A., 'Der Entwurf zu einem schweizerischen Wertpapierverwahrungsgesetz (WVG)', in P. Nobel (ed.), *Aktuelle Rechtsprobleme des Finanz- und Börsenplatzes Schweiz*, Heft 11 (Bern: Stämpfli, 2004), 135–54.

Weber, R. H., 'Elektronische Abwicklung von Effektentransaktionen', in W. Wiegand (ed.), *E-Banking – Die einzelnen Rechtsgeschäfte, Berner Bankrechtstag Band 9* (Bern: Stämpfli, 2003), 45–74.

Wechsler, R., *Die Abwicklung von Effektenhandelsgeschäften* (Bern/Stuttgart/Vienna: Haupt, 1996).

Wiegand, W., 'Die Bucheffekte – Ein neues Vermögensrecht?', in P. Apathy et al. (eds.), *Festschrift für Helmut Koziol* (Vienna: Jan Sramek Verlag, 2010), 1125–37.

Zbinden, A., *Das Pfandrecht an Aktien. Ausgewählte dogmatische und praktische Aspekte des Pfandrechts an Aktien in Form von Wertpapieren, Wertrechten und Bucheffekten* (Bern: Stämpfli, Abhandlungen zum schweizerischen Recht Heft 773, 2010).

Zbinden, A. and Hess, M., 'Das reguläre Pfandrecht an Bucheffekten, Ein Beitrag zur Frage der Errichtung des Pfandrechts an Bucheffekten nach Art. 24 Bucheffektengesetz (BEG)' [2011] *Gesellschafts- und Kapitalmarktrecht (GesKR)*, 346–58.

Zobl, D., 'Internationale Übertragung und Verwahrung von Wertpapieren (aus schweizerischer Sicht)' [2001] *Schweizerische Zeitschrift für Wirtschafts- und Finanzmarktrecht (SZW)*, 105–21.

Zobl, D. and Lambert, C., 'Zur Entmaterialisierung der Wertpapiere' [1991] *Schweizerische Zeitschrift für Wirtschafts- und Finanzmarktrecht (SZW)*, 117–39.

Appendix

UNIDROIT Convention on Substantive Rules for Intermediated Securities

EU Consultation Document 'Legislation on Legal Certainty of Securities Holding and Dispositions'

UNIDROIT Convention on Substantive Rules for Intermediated Securities

Geneva, 9 October 2009

The states signatory to this convention

CONSCIOUS of the growth and development of global capital markets and recognising the benefits of holding securities, or interests in securities, through intermediaries in increasing the liquidity of modern securities markets,

RECOGNISING the need to protect persons that acquire or otherwise hold intermediated securities,

AWARE of the importance of reducing legal risk, systemic risk and associated costs in relation to domestic and cross-border transactions involving intermediated securities so as to facilitate the flow of capital and access to capital markets,

MINDFUL of the need to enhance the international compatibility of legal systems as well as the soundness of domestic and international rules relating to intermediated securities,

DESIRING to establish a common legal framework for the holding and disposition of intermediated securities,

BELIEVING that a functional approach in the formulation of rules to accommodate the various legal traditions involved would best serve the purposes of this Convention,

HAVING due regard for non-Convention law in matters not determined by this Convention,

EMPHASISING the importance of the integrity of a securities issue in a global environment for intermediated holding in order to ensure the exercise of investors' rights and enhance their protection,

EMPHASISING that this Convention is not intended to harmonise or otherwise affect insolvency law except to the extent necessary to provide for the effectiveness of rights and interests governed by this Convention,

RECOGNISING that this Convention does not limit or otherwise affect the powers of Contracting States to regulate, supervise or oversee the holding and disposition of intermediated securities or any other matters expressly covered by the Convention, except in so far as such regulation, supervision or oversight would contravene the provisions of this Convention,

MINDFUL of the importance of the role of intermediaries in the application of this Convention and the need of Contracting States to regulate, supervise or oversee their activities,

HAVE AGREED upon the following provisions:

Chapter I – Definitions, sphere of application and interpretation

Article 1
Definitions

In this Convention:

(a) 'securities' means any shares, bonds or other financial instruments or financial assets (other than cash) which are capable of being credited to a securities account and of being acquired and disposed of in accordance with the provisions of this Convention;
(b) 'intermediated securities' means securities credited to a securities account or rights or interests in securities resulting from the credit of securities to a securities account;
(c) 'securities account' means an account maintained by an intermediary to which securities may be credited or debited;
(d) 'intermediary' means a person (including a central securities depository) who in the course of a business or other regular activity maintains securities accounts for others or both for others and for its own account and is acting in that capacity;
(e) 'account holder' means a person in whose name an intermediary maintains a securities account, whether that person is acting for its own account or for others (including in the capacity of intermediary);

(f) 'account agreement' means, in relation to a securities account, the agreement between the account holder and the relevant intermediary governing the securities account;

(g) 'relevant intermediary' means, in relation to a securities account, the intermediary that maintains that securities account for the account holder;

(h) 'insolvency proceeding' means a collective judicial or administrative proceeding, including an interim proceeding, in which the assets and affairs of the debtor are subject to control or supervision by a court or other competent authority for the purpose of reorganisation or liquidation;

(i) 'insolvency administrator' means a person (including a debtor in possession if applicable) authorised to administer an insolvency proceeding, including one authorised on an interim basis;

(j) securities are 'of the same description' as other securities if they are issued by the same issuer and:

  (I) they are of the same class of shares or stock; or

  (II) in the case of securities other than shares or stock, they are of the same currency and denomination and are treated as forming part of the same issue;

(k) 'control agreement' means an agreement in relation to intermediated securities between an account holder, the relevant intermediary and another person or, if so provided by the non-Convention law, between an account holder and the relevant intermediary or between an account holder and another person of which the relevant intermediary receives notice, which includes either or both of the following provisions:

  (i) that the relevant intermediary is not permitted to comply with any instructions given by the account holder in relation to the intermediated securities to which the agreement relates without the consent of that other person;

  (ii) that the relevant intermediary is obliged to comply with any instructions given by that other person in relation to the intermediated securities to which the agreement relates in such circumstances and as to such matters as may be provided by the agreement, without any further consent of the account holder;

(l) 'designating entry' means an entry in a securities account made in favour of a person (including the relevant intermediary) other than the account holder in relation to intermediated securities, which, under the account agreement, a control agreement, the uniform rules of a securities settlement system or the non-Convention law, has either or both of the following effects:

(i) that the relevant intermediary is not permitted to comply with any instructions given by the account holder in relation to the intermediated securities as to which the entry is made without the consent of that person;

(ii) that the relevant intermediary is obliged to comply with any instructions given by that person in relation to the intermediated securities as to which the entry is made in such circumstances and as to such matters as may be provided by the account agreement, a control agreement or the uniform rules of a securities settlement system, without any further consent of the account holder;

(m) 'non-Convention law' means the law in force in the Contracting State referred to in Article 2, other than the provisions of this Convention;

(n) 'securities settlement system' means a system that:

(i) settles, or clears and settles, securities transactions;

(ii) is operated by a central bank or central banks or is subject to regulation, supervision or oversight by a governmental or public authority in relation to its rules; and

(iii) has been identified as a securities settlement system in a declaration made by the Contracting State the law of which governs the system on the ground of the reduction of risk to the stability of the financial system;

(o) 'securities clearing system' means a system that:

(i) clears, but does not settle, securities transactions through a central counterparty or otherwise;

(ii) is operated by a central bank or central banks or is subject to regulation, supervision or oversight by a governmental or public authority in relation to its rules; and

(iii) has been identified as a securities clearing system in a declaration made by the Contracting State the law of which governs the system on the ground of the reduction of risk to the stability of the financial system;

(p) 'uniform rules' means, in relation to a securities settlement system or securities clearing system, rules of that system (including system rules constituted by the non-Convention law) which are common to the participants or to a class of participants and are publicly accessible.

Article 2
Sphere of application

This Convention applies whenever:

(a) the applicable conflict of laws rules designate the law in force in a Contracting State as the applicable law; or
(b) the circumstances do not lead to the application of any law other than the law in force in a Contracting State.

Article 3
Applicability of declarations

If the law of the forum State is not the applicable law, the forum State shall apply the Convention and the declarations, if any, made by the Contracting State the law of which applies, and without regard to the declarations, if any, made by the forum State.

Article 4
Principles of interpretation

In the implementation, interpretation and application of this Convention, regard is to be had to its purposes, the general principles on which it is based, its international character and the need to promote uniformity and predictability in its application.

Article 5
Central bank and regulated intermediaries

A Contracting State may declare that this Convention shall apply only to securities accounts maintained by:

(a) intermediaries falling within such categories as may be described in the declaration, which are subject to authorisation, regulation, supervision or oversight by a government or public authority in relation to the activity of maintaining securities accounts; or
(b) a central bank.

Article 6
Excluded functions

This Convention does not apply to the functions of creation, recording or reconciliation of securities, vis-à-vis the issuer of those securities, by a person such as a central securities depository, central bank, transfer agent or registrar.

Article 7
Performance of functions of intermediaries by other persons

1. A Contracting State may declare that under its non-Convention law a person other than the relevant intermediary is responsible for the performance of a function or functions (but not all functions) of the relevant intermediary under this Convention, either generally or in relation to intermediated securities, or securities accounts, of any category or description.
2. A declaration under this Article shall:
   (a) specify, if applicable, the relevant category or description of intermediated securities or securities accounts;
   (b) identify, by name or description:
      (i) the relevant intermediary;
      (ii) the parties to the account agreement; and
      (iii) the person or persons other than the relevant intermediary who is or are responsible as described in paragraph 1; and
   (c) specify, in relation to each such person:
      (i) the functions for which such person is so responsible;
      (ii) the provisions of this Convention that apply to such person, including whether Article 9, Article 10, Article 15 or Article 23 applies to such person; and
      (iii) if applicable, the relevant category or description of intermediated securities or securities accounts.
3. Unless otherwise provided in this Convention, if a declaration under this Article applies, references in any provision in this Convention to an intermediary or the relevant intermediary are to the person or persons responsible for performing the function to which that provision applies.

Article 8
Relationship with issuers

1. Subject to Article 29(2), this Convention does not affect any right of the account holder against the issuer of the securities.
2. This Convention does not determine whom the issuer is required to recognise as the shareholder, bondholder or other person entitled to receive and exercise the rights attached to the securities or to recognise for any other purpose.

Chapter II – Rights of the account holder

Article 9
Intermediated securities

1. The credit of securities to a securities account confers on the account holder:
   (a) the right to receive and exercise any rights attached to the securities, including dividends, other distributions and voting rights:
      (i) if the account holder is not an intermediary or is an intermediary acting for its own account; and
      (ii) in any other case, if so provided by the non-Convention law;
   (b) the right to effect a disposition under Article 11 or grant an interest under Article 12;
   (c) the right, by instructions to the relevant intermediary, to cause the securities to be held otherwise than through a securities account, to the extent permitted by the applicable law, the terms of the securities and, to the extent permitted by the non-Convention law, the account agreement or the uniform rules of a securities settlement system;
   (d) unless otherwise provided in this Convention, such other rights, including rights and interests in securities, as may be conferred by the non-Convention law.
2. Unless otherwise provided in this Convention:
   (a) the rights referred to in paragraph 1 are effective against third parties;
   (b) the rights referred to in paragraph 1(a) may be exercised against the relevant intermediary or the issuer of the securities, or both,

in accordance with this Conven-tion, the terms of the securities and the applicable law;

(c) the rights referred to in paragraph 1(b) and 1(c) may be exercised only against the relevant intermediary.

3. If an account holder has acquired a security interest, or a limited interest other than a security interest, by credit of securities to its securities account under Article 11(4), the non-Convention law determines any limits on the rights described in paragraph 1 of this Article.

Article 10
Measures to enable the exercise of rights

1. An intermediary must take appropriate measures to enable its account holders to receive and exercise the rights specified in Article 9(1).
2. An intermediary must, at least:
   (a) protect securities credited to a securities account, as provided in Article 24;
   (b) allocate securities or intermediated securities to the rights of its account holders so as to be unavailable to its creditors, as provided in Article 25;
   (c) give effect to any instructions given by the account holder or other authorised person, as provided by the non-Convention law, the account agreement or the uniform rules of a securities settlement system;
   (d) not dispose of securities credited to a securities account without authorisation, as provided in Article 15;
   (e) regularly pass on to account holders information relating to intermediated securities, including information necessary for account holders to exercise rights, if provided by the non-Convention law, the account agreement or the uniform rules of a securities settlement system; and
   (f) regularly pass on to account holders dividends and other distributions received in relation to intermediated securities, if provided by the non-Convention law, the account agreement or the uniform rules of a securities settlement system.
3. This Convention does not require the relevant intermediary to establish a securities account with another intermediary or to take any action that is not within its power.

Chapter III – Transfer of intermediated securities

Article 11
Acquisition and disposition by debit and credit

1. Subject to Article 16, intermediated securities are acquired by an account holder by the credit of securities to that account holder's securities account.
2. No further step is necessary, or may be required by the non-Convention law or any other rule of law applicable in an insolvency proceeding, to render the acquisition of intermediated securities effective against third parties.
3. Subject to Articles 15 and 16, intermediated securities are disposed of by an account holder by the debit of securities to that account holder's securities account.
4. A security interest, or a limited interest other than a security interest, in intermediated securities may be acquired and disposed of by debit and credit of securities to securities accounts under this Article.
5. Nothing in this Convention limits the effectiveness of debits and credits to securities accounts which are effected on a net basis in relation to securities of the same description.

Article 12
Acquisition and disposition by other methods

1. Subject to Article 16, an account holder grants an interest in intermediated securities, including a security interest or a limited interest other than a security interest, to another person if:
   (a) the account holder enters into an agreement with or in favour of that person; and
   (b) one of the conditions specified in paragraph 3 applies and the relevant Contracting State has made a declaration in relation to that condition under paragraph 5.
2. No further step is necessary, or may be required by the non-Convention law or any other rule of law applicable in an insolvency proceeding, to render the interest effective against third parties.
3. The conditions referred to in paragraph 1(b) are as follows:
   (a) the person to whom the interest is granted is the relevant intermediary;
   (b) a designating entry in favour of that person has been made;
   (c) a control agreement in favour of that person applies.

4. An interest in intermediated securities may be granted under this Article so as to be effective against third parties:
   (a) in relation to a securities account (and such an interest extends to all intermediated securities from time to time standing to the credit of the relevant securities account);
   (b) in relation to a specified category, quantity, proportion or value of the intermediated securities from time to time standing to the credit of a securities account.
5. A Contracting State may declare that under its law:
   (a) the condition specified in any one or more of the sub-paragraphs of paragraph 3 is sufficient to render an interest effective against third parties;
   (b) this Article shall not apply in relation to interests in intermediated securities granted by or to parties falling within such categories as may be specified in the declaration;
   (c) paragraph 4, or either sub-paragraph of paragraph 4, does not apply;
   (d) paragraph 4(b) applies with such modifications as may be specified in the declaration.
6. A declaration in relation to paragraph 3(b) shall specify whether a designating entry has the effect described in Article 1(l)(i) or Article 1(l)(ii) or both.
7. A declaration in relation to paragraph 3(c) shall specify whether a control agreement must include the provision described in Article 1(k)(i) or Article 1(k)(ii) or both.
8. The applicable law determines in what circumstances a non-consensual security interest in intermediated securities may arise and become effective against third parties.

Article 13
Acquisition and disposition under non-Convention law

This Convention does not preclude any method provided by the non-Convention law for:

(a) the acquisition or disposition of intermediated securities or of an interest in intermediated securities; or
(b) the creation of an interest in intermediated securities and for making such an interest effective against third parties,

other than the methods provided by Articles 11 and 12.

Article 14
Effectiveness in insolvency

1. Rights and interests that have become effective against third parties under Article 11 or Article 12 are effective against the insolvency administrator and creditors in any insolvency proceeding.
2. Paragraph 1 does not affect the application of any substantive or procedural rule of law applicable by virtue of an insolvency proceeding, such as any rule relating to:
   (a) the ranking of categories of claims;
   (b) the avoidance of a transaction as a preference or a transfer in fraud of creditors; or
   (c) the enforcement of rights to property that is under the control or supervision of the insolvency administrator.
3. Paragraph 1 does not apply to the rights and interests to which Article 21(1) applies.
4. Nothing in this Convention impairs the effectiveness of an interest in intermediated securities against the insolvency administrator and creditors in any insolvency proceeding if that interest has become effective by any method referred to in Article 13.

Article 15
Unauthorised dispositions

1. An intermediary may make a debit of securities to a securities account, make or remove a designating entry or otherwise dispose of intermediated securities only if it is authorised to do so:
   (a) in relation to a debit, by the account holder and, if applicable, the person to whom an interest in the relevant intermediated securities has been granted under Article 12;
   (b) in relation to a designating entry, by the account holder;
   (c) in relation to the removal of a designating entry, by the person in whose favour the designating entry has been made;
   (d) in relation to any other disposition, by the account holder and, if applicable, the person to whom an interest in the relevant intermediated securities has been granted under Article 12; or
   (e) by the non-Convention law.
2. The non-Convention law and, to the extent permitted by the non-Convention law, the account agreement or the uniform rules of a

securities settlement system determine the consequences of: an unauthorised debit; an unauthorised removal of a designating entry; subject to Article 18(2), an unauthorised designating entry; or any other unauthorised disposition.

Article 16
Invalidity, reversal and conditions

Subject to Article 18, the non-Convention law and, to the extent permitted by the non-Convention law, the account agreement or the uniform rules of a securities settlement system determine whether and in what circumstances a debit, credit, designating entry or removal of a designating entry is invalid, is liable to be reversed or may be subject to a condition, and the consequences thereof.

Article 17
Terms used in Chapter III

In this Chapter:

(a) 'acquirer' means:
  (i) an account holder to whose securities account securities are credited; or
  (ii) a person to whom an interest in intermediated securities is granted under Article 12;
(b) in determining whether a person ought to know of an interest or fact:
  (i) the determination must take into account the characteristics and requirements of securities markets, including the intermediated holding system; and
  (ii) the person is under no general duty of inquiry or investigation;
(c) an organisation actually knows or ought to know of an interest or fact from the time when the interest or fact is or ought reasonably to have been brought to the attention of the individual responsible for the matter to which the interest or fact is relevant;
(d) 'defective entry' means a credit of securities or designating entry that is invalid or liable to be reversed, including a conditional credit or designating entry that becomes invalid or liable to be reversed by reason of the operation or non-fulfilment of the condition;
(e) 'relevant time' means the time that a credit is made or the time referred to in Article 19(3).

Article 18
Acquisition by an innocent person

1. Unless an acquirer actually knows or ought to know, at the relevant time, that another person has an interest in securities or intermediated securities and that the credit to the securities account of the acquirer, designating entry or interest granted to the acquirer violates the rights of that other person in relation to its interest:
   (a) the right or interest of the acquirer is not subject to the interest of that other person;
   (b) the acquirer is not liable to that other person; and
   (c) the credit, designating entry or interest granted is not rendered invalid, ineffective against third parties or liable to be reversed on the ground that the credit, designating entry or interest granted violates the rights of that other person.
2. Unless an acquirer actually knows or ought to know, at the relevant time, of an earlier defective entry:
   (a) the credit, designating entry or interest is not rendered invalid, ineffective against third parties or liable to be reversed as a result of that defective entry; and
   (b) the acquirer is not liable to anyone who would benefit from the invalidity or reversal of that defective entry.
3. Paragraphs 1 and 2 do not apply to an acquisition of intermediated securities, other than the grant of a security interest, made by way of gift or otherwise gratuitously.
4. If an acquirer is not protected by paragraph 1 or paragraph 2, the applicable law determines the rights and liabilities, if any, of the acquirer.
5. To the extent permitted by the non-Convention law, paragraph 2 is subject to any provision of the uniform rules of a securities settlement system or of the account agreement.
6. This Article does not modify the priorities determined by Article 19 or Article 20(2).

Article 19
Priority among competing interests

1. This Article determines priority between interests in the same intermediated securities which become effective against third parties under Article 12 or Article 13.

2. Subject to paragraph 5 and Article 20, interests that become effective against third parties under Article 12 have priority over any interest that becomes effective against third parties by any other method provided by the non-Convention law.
3. Interests that become effective against third parties under Article 12 rank among themselves according to the time of occurrence of the following events:
   (a) if the relevant intermediary is itself the holder of the interest and the interest is effective against third parties under Article 12(3)(a), when the agreement granting the interest is entered into;
   (b) when a designating entry is made;
   (c) when a control agreement is entered into or, if the relevant intermediary is not a party to the control agreement, when the relevant intermediary receives notice of it.
4. If an intermediary has an interest that has become effective against third parties under Article 12 and makes a designating entry or enters into a control agreement with the consequence that an interest of another person becomes effective against third parties, the interest of that other person has priority over the interest of the intermediary unless that other person and the intermediary expressly agree otherwise.
5. A non-consensual security interest in intermediated securities arising under the applicable law has such priority as is afforded to it by that law.
6. As between persons entitled to any interests referred to in paragraphs 2, 3 and 4 and, to the extent permitted by the applicable law, paragraph 5, the priorities provided by this Article may be varied by agreement between those persons, but any such agreement does not affect third parties.
7. A Contracting State may declare that under its non-Convention law, subject to paragraph 4, an interest granted by a designating entry has priority over any interest granted by any other method provided by Article 12.

Article 20
Priority of interests granted by an intermediary

1. Except as provided by paragraph 2, this Convention does not determine the priority or the relative rights and interests between the rights of account holders of an intermediary and interests granted by that

intermediary so as to be effective against third parties under Article 12 or Article 13.

2. An interest in intermediated securities granted by an intermediary so as to become effective against third parties under Article 12 has priority over the rights of account holders of that intermediary unless, at the relevant time, the person to whom the interest is granted actually knows or ought to know that the interest granted violates the rights of one or more account holders.

Chapter IV – Integrity Of The Intermediated Holding System

Article 21
Effectiveness in the insolvency of the relevant intermediary

1. Rights and interests of account holders of a relevant intermediary that have become effective against third parties under Article 11 and interests granted by such account holders that have become effective under Article 12 are effective against the insolvency administrator and credi-tors in any insolvency proceeding in relation to the relevant intermediary or in relation to any other person responsible for the performance of a function of the relevant intermediary under Article 7.
2. Paragraph 1 does not affect:
   (a) any rule of law applicable in the insolvency proceeding relating to the avoidance of a transaction as a preference or a transfer in fraud of creditors; or
   (b) any rule of procedure relating to the enforcement of rights to property that is under the control or supervision of the insolvency administrator.
3. Nothing in this Article impairs the effectiveness of an interest in intermediated securities against the insolvency administrator and creditors in any insolvency proceeding referred to in paragraph 1, if that interest has become effective by any method referred to in Article 13.

Article 22
Prohibition of upper-tier attachment

1. Subject to paragraph 3, no attachment of intermediated securities of an account holder shall be made against, or so as to affect:
   (a) a securities account of any person other than that account holder;

(b) the issuer of any securities credited to a securities account of that account holder; or
(c) a person other than the account holder and the relevant intermediary.

2. In this Article 'attachment of intermediated securities of an account holder' means any judicial, administrative or other act or process to freeze, restrict or impound intermediated securities of that account holder in order to enforce or satisfy a judgment, award or other judicial, arbitral, administrative or other decision or in order to ensure the availability of such intermediated securities to enforce or satisfy any future judgment, award or decision.
3. A Contracting State may declare that under its non-Convention law an attachment of intermediated securities of an account holder made against or so as to affect a person other than the relevant intermediary has effect also against the relevant intermediary. Any such declaration shall identify that other person by name or description and shall specify the time at which such an attachment becomes effective against the relevant intermediary.

Article 23
Instructions to the intermediary

1. An intermediary is neither bound nor entitled to give effect to any instructions in relation to intermediated securities of an account holder given by any person other than that account holder.
2. Paragraph 1 is subject to:
   (a) the provisions of the account agreement, any other agreement between the intermediary and the account holder or any other agreement entered into by the intermediary with the consent of the account holder;
   (b) the rights of any person (including the intermediary) who holds an interest that has become effective against third parties under Article 12;
   (c) subject to Article 22, any judgment, award, order or decision of a court, tribunal or other judicial or administrative authority of competent jurisdiction;
   (d) any applicable provision of the non-Convention law; and
   (e) if the intermediary is the operator of a securities settlement system, the uniform rules of that system.

Article 24
Holding or availability of sufficient securities

1. An intermediary must, for each description of securities, hold or have available securities and intermediated securities of an aggregate number or amount equal to the aggregate number or amount of securities of that description credited to:
   (a) securities accounts that it maintains for its account holders other than itself; and
   (b) if applicable, securities accounts that it maintains for itself.
2. An intermediary may comply with paragraph 1 by:
   (a) procuring that securities are held on the register of the issuer in the name, or for the account, of its account holders;
   (b) holding securities as the registered holder on the register of the issuer;
   (c) possession of certificates or other documents of title;
   (d) holding intermediated securities with another intermediary; or
   (e) any other appropriate method.
3. If at any time the requirements of paragraph 1 are not complied with, the intermediary must within the time permitted by the non-Convention law take such action as is necessary to ensure compliance with those requirements.
4. This Article does not affect any provision of the non-Convention law, or, to the extent permitted by the non-Convention law, any provision of the uniform rules of a securities settlement system or of the account agreement, relating to the method of complying with the requirements of this Article or the allocation of the cost of ensuring compliance with those requirements or otherwise relating to the consequences of failure to comply with those requirements.

Article 25
Allocation of securities to account holders' rights

1. Securities and intermediated securities of each description held by an intermediary as described in Article 24(2) shall be allocated to the rights of the account holders of that intermediary, other than itself, to the extent necessary to ensure compliance with Article 24(1)(a).
2. Subject to Article 20, securities and intermediated securities allocated under paragraph 1 shall not form part of the property of the

intermediary available for distribution among or realisation for the benefit of creditors of the intermediary.

3. The allocation required by paragraph 1 shall be effected by the non-Convention law and, to the extent required or permitted by the non-Convention law, by arrangements made by the relevant intermediary.
4. The arrangements referred to in paragraph 3 may include arrangements under which an intermediary holds securities and intermediated securities in segregated form for the benefit of:
   (a) its account holders generally; or
   (b) particular account holders or groups of account holders, in such manner as to ensure that such securities and intermediated securities are allocated in accordance with paragraph 1.
5. A Contracting State may declare that, if all securities and intermediated securities held by an intermediary for its account holders, other than itself, are in segregated form under arrangements such as are referred to in paragraph 4, under its non-Convention law the allocation required by paragraph 1 applies only to those securities and intermediated securities and does not apply to securities and intermediated securities held by an intermediary for its own account.
6. This Article applies notwithstanding the commencement or continuation of an insolvency proceeding in relation to the intermediary.

Article 26
Loss sharing in case of insolvency of the intermediary

1. This Article applies in any insolvency proceeding in relation to an intermediary unless otherwise provided by any conflicting rule applicable in that proceeding.
2. If the aggregate number or amount of securities and intermediated securities of any description allocated under Article 25(1) to an account holder, a group of account holders or the intermediary's account holders generally (as the case may be) is less than the aggregate number or amount of securities of that description credited to the securities accounts of that account holder, that group of account holders or the intermediary's account holders generally, the shortfall shall be borne:
   (a) if securities and intermediated securities have been allocated to a single account holder, by that account holder; and
   (b) in any other case, by the account holders to whom the relevant securities have been allocated, in proportion to the respective number

or amount of securities of that description credited to their securities accounts.

3. To the extent permitted by the non-Convention law, if the intermediary is the operator of a securities settlement system and the uniform rules of the system make provision in case of a shortfall, the shortfall shall be borne in the manner so provided.

Article 27
Insolvency of system operator or participant

To the extent permitted by the law governing a system, the following provisions shall have effect notwithstanding the commencement of an insolvency proceeding in relation to the operator of that system or any participant in that system and notwithstanding any invalidation, reversal or revocation that would otherwise occur under any rule applicable in an insolvency proceeding:

(a) any provision of the uniform rules of a securities settlement system or of a securities clearing system in so far as that provision precludes the revocation of any instruction given by a participant in the system for making a disposition of intermediated securities, or for making a payment relating to an acquisition or disposition of intermediated securities, after the time at which that instruction is treated under the rules of the system as having been entered irrevocably into the system;
(b) any provision of the uniform rules of a securities settlement system in so far as that provision precludes the invalidation or reversal of a debit or credit of securities to, or a designating entry or removal of a designating entry in, a securities account that forms part of the system after the time at which that debit, credit, designating entry or removal of a designating entry is treated under the rules of the system as not liable to be reversed.

Article 28
Obligations and liability of intermediaries

1. The obligations of an intermediary under this Convention, including the manner in which an intermediary complies with its obligations,

may be specified by the non-Convention law and, to the extent permitted by the non-Convention law, the account agreement or the uniform rules of a securities settlement system.

2. If the substance of any such obligation is specified by the non-Convention law or, to the extent permitted by the non-Convention law, the account agreement or the uniform rules of a securities settlement system, compliance with it satisfies that obligation.
3. The liability of an intermediary in relation to its obligations is governed by the non-Convention law and, to the extent permitted by the non-Convention law, the account agreement or the uniform rules of a securities settlement system.
4. An intermediary may not exclude liability for its gross negligence or wilful misconduct.

Article 29
Position of issuers of securities

1. The law of a Contracting State shall permit the holding through one or more intermediaries of securities that are permitted to be traded on an exchange or regulated market, and the effective exercise in accordance with Article 9 of the rights attached to such securities that are so held, but need not require that all such securities be issued on terms that permit them to be held through intermediaries.
2. In particular, the law of a Contracting State shall recognise the holding of such securities by a person acting in its own name on behalf of another person or other persons and shall permit such a person to exercise voting or other rights in different ways in relation to different parts of a holding of securities of the same description; but this Convention does not determine the conditions under which such a person is authorised to exercise such rights.

Article 30
Set-off

As between an account holder that holds intermediated securities for its own account and the issuer of those securities, the fact that the account holder holds the securities through an intermediary or intermediaries shall not of itself, in any insolvency proceeding in relation to the issuer, preclude the existence or prevent the exercise of any rights of set-off which would have existed and been exercisable if the account holder had held the securities otherwise than through an intermediary.

Chapter V – Special Provisions In Relation To Collateral Transactions

Article 31
Scope of application and definitions in Chapter V

1. This Chapter applies to collateral agreements under which a collateral provider grants an interest in intermediated securities to a collateral taker in order to secure the performance of any existing, future or contingent obligations of the collateral provider or another person.
2. Nothing in this Chapter impairs any provision of the non-Convention law which provides for additional rights or powers of a collateral taker or additional obligations of a collateral provider.
3. In this Chapter:
   (a) 'collateral agreement' means a security collateral agreement or a title transfer collateral agreement;
   (b) 'security collateral agreement' means an agreement between a collateral provider and a collateral taker providing (in whatever terms) for the grant of an interest other than full ownership in intermediated securities for the purpose of securing the performance of relevant obligations;
   (c) 'title transfer collateral agreement' means an agreement, including an agreement providing for the sale and repurchase of securities, between a collateral provider and a collateral taker providing (in whatever terms) for the transfer of full ownership of intermediated securities by the collateral provider to the collateral taker for the purpose of securing or otherwise covering the performance of relevant obligations;
   (d) 'relevant obligations' means any existing, future or contingent obligations of a collateral provider or another person;
   (e) 'collateral securities' means intermediated securities delivered under a collateral agreement;
   (f) 'collateral taker' means a person to whom an interest in intermediated securities is granted under a collateral agreement;
   (g) 'collateral provider' means an account holder by whom an interest in intermediated securities is granted under a collateral agreement;

(h) 'enforcement event' means, in relation to a collateral agreement, an event of default or other event on the occurrence of which, under the terms of that collateral agreement or by the operation of law, the collateral taker is entitled to realise the collateral securities or a close-out netting provision may be operated;

(i) 'equivalent collateral' means securities of the same description as collateral securities;

(j) 'close-out netting provision' means a provision of a collateral agreement, or of a set of connected agreements of which a collateral agreement forms part, under which, on the occurrence of an enforcement event, either or both of the following shall occur, or may at the election of the collateral taker occur, whether through the operation of netting or set-off or otherwise:

(k) the respective obligations of the parties are accelerated so as to be immediately due and expressed as an obligation to pay an amount representing their estimated current value or are terminated and replaced by an obligation to pay such an amount;

(l) an account is taken of what is due from each party to the other in relation to such obligations, and a net sum equal to the balance of the account is payable by the party from whom the larger amount is due to the other party.

Article 32
Recognition of title transfer collateral agreements

The law of a Contracting State shall permit a title transfer collateral agreement to take effect in accordance with its terms.

Article 33
Enforcement

1. On the occurrence of an enforcement event:

   (a) the collateral taker may realise the collateral securities delivered under a security collateral agreement by:

      (i) selling them and applying the net proceeds of sale in or towards the discharge of the relevant obligations; or

      (ii) appropriating the collateral securities as the collateral taker's own property and setting off their value against, or applying their value in or towards the discharge of, the relevant obligations, provided that the collateral agreement provides for realisation in this manner and specifies the basis on which collateral securities are to be valued for this purpose; or

(b) a close-out netting provision may be operated.

2. If an enforcement event occurs while any obligation of the collateral taker to deliver equivalent collateral under a collateral agreement remains outstanding, that obligation and the relevant obligations may be the subject of a close-out netting provision.

3. Collateral securities may be realised, and a close-out netting provision may be operated, under this Article:

(a) subject to any contrary provision of the collateral agreement, without any requirement that:

(i) prior notice of the intention to realise or operate the close-out netting provision shall have been given;

(ii) the terms of the realisation or the operation of the close-out netting provision be approved by any court, public officer or other person; or

(iii) the realisation be conducted by public auction or in any other prescribed manner or the close-out netting provision be operated in any prescribed manner; and

(b) notwithstanding the commencement or continuation of an insolvency proceeding in relation to the collateral provider or the collateral taker.

Article 34
Right to use collateral securities

1. If and to the extent that the terms of a security collateral agreement so provide, the collateral taker shall have the right to use and dispose of the collateral securities as if it were the owner of them (a 'right of use').

2. If a collateral taker exercises a right of use, it thereby incurs an obligation to replace the collateral securities so used or disposed of (the 'original collateral securities') by delivering to the collateral provider, not later than the discharge of the relevant obligations, equivalent collateral or, if the security collateral agreement provides for the delivery of other assets following the occurrence of any event relating to or affecting any securities delivered as collateral, those other assets ('replacement collateral').

3. Replacement collateral acquired or identified by the collateral taker before the relevant obligations have been fully discharged shall:

(a) in the same manner as the original collateral securities, be subject to an interest under the relevant security collateral agreement, which shall be treated as having been created at the same time as the interest in relation to the original collateral securities was created; and

(b) in all other respects be subject to the terms of the relevant security collateral agreement.

4. The exercise of a right of use shall not render invalid or unenforceable any right of the collateral taker under the relevant security collateral agreement or the non-Convention law.

Article 35

Requirements of non-Convention law relating to enforcement

Articles 33 and 34 do not affect any requirement of the non-Convention law to the effect that the realisation or valuation of collateral securities or the calculation of any obligations must be conducted in a commercially reasonable manner.

Article 36

Top-up or substitution of collateral

1. If a collateral agreement includes:
   (a) an obligation to deliver additional collateral securities:
      (i) in order to take account of changes in the value of the collateral delivered under the collateral agreement or in the amount of the relevant obligations;
      (ii) in order to take account of any circumstances giving rise to an increase in the credit risk incurred by the collateral taker as determined by reference to objective criteria relating to the creditworthiness, financial performance or financial condition of the collateral provider or other person by whom the relevant obligations are owed; or
      (iii) to the extent permitted by the non-Convention law, in any other circumstances specified in the collateral agreement; or
   (b) a right to withdraw collateral securities or other assets on delivering collateral securities or other assets of substantially the same value, the delivery of securities or other assets as described in sub-paragraphs (a) and (b) shall not be treated as invalid, reversed or declared void solely on the basis that they are delivered during

a prescribed period before, or on the day of but before, the commencement of an insolvency proceeding in relation to the collateral provider, or after the relevant obligations have been incurred.

2. A Contracting State may declare that paragraph 1(a)(ii) shall not apply.

Article 37
Certain insolvency provisions disapplied

If Article 36 does not apply, a collateral agreement or the delivery of collateral securities under such agreement shall not be treated as invalid, reversed or declared void solely on the basis that the agreement is entered into or the collateral securities are delivered during a prescribed period before, or on the day of but before, the commencement of an insolvency proceeding in relation to the collateral provider.

Article 38
Declarations in relation to Chapter V

1. A Contracting State may declare that this Chapter shall not apply.
2. A Contracting State may declare that this Chapter shall not apply:
   (a) in relation to collateral agreements entered into by natural persons or other persons falling within such categories as may be specified in the declaration;
   (b) in relation to intermediated securities that are not permitted to be traded on an exchange or regulated market;
   (c) in relation to collateral agreements that relate to relevant obligations falling within such categories as may be specified in the declaration.

Chapter VI – Transitional Provision

Article 39
Priority

1. This Convention does not affect the priority of interests granted under the law in force in a Contracting State before the date on which this Convention has entered into force in relation to that Contracting State.
2. A Contracting State may declare that a pre-existing interest shall retain the priority it enjoyed before the relevant date only if, at any time before that date, the interest has become effective against third parties

by satisfying a condition specified in the declaration made by that Contracting State in accordance with Article 12(5)(a).

3. In this Article:
   (a) 'pre-existing interest' means any interest, other than a non-consensual security interest, that has been granted under the law in force in a Contracting State before the date this Convention has entered into force in relation to that Contracting State, other than by a credit to a securities account;
   (b) 'the relevant date' means the date stated by a Contracting State in the declaration made under this Article and that date shall not be later than two years after the effective date of that declaration.
4. Article 45(5) does not apply to the declaration provided for in this Article.

Chapter VII – Final Provisions

Article 40
Signature, ratification, acceptance, approval or accession

1. This Convention shall be open for signature in Geneva on 9 October 2009 by States participating in the diplomatic Conference to adopt a Convention on Substantive Rules regarding Intermediated Securities held at Geneva from 1 September 2008 to 12 September 2008 and from 5 October 2009 to 9 October 2009 (the Geneva Conference). After 9 October 2009 this Convention shall be open to all States for signature at the Headquarters of the International Institute for the Unification of Private Law (UNIDROIT) in Rome, and at such other places as the Depositary may determine, until it enters into force in accordance with Article 42.
2. This Convention shall be subject to ratification, acceptance or approval by States that have signed it.
3. Any State that does not sign this Convention may accede to it at any time.
4. Ratification, acceptance, approval or accession is effected by the deposit of a formal instrument to that effect with the Depositary.

Article 41
Regional Economic Integration Organisations

1. A Regional Economic Integration Organisation that is constituted by sovereign States and has competence over certain matters governed by

this Convention may similarly sign, accept, approve or accede to this Convention. The Regional Economic Integration Organisation shall in that case have the rights and obligations of a Contracting State, to the extent that the Organisation has competence over matters governed by this Convention. If the number of Contracting States is relevant in this Convention, the Regional Economic Integration Organisation shall not count as a Contracting State in addition to its Member States that are Contracting States.

2. The Regional Economic Integration Organisation shall, at the time of signature, acceptance, approval or accession, make a declaration to the Depositary specifying the matters governed by this Convention in relation to which competence has been transferred to that Organisation by its Member States. The Regional Economic Integration Organisation shall promptly and formally notify the Depositary in writing of any changes to the distribution of competence, including new transfers of competence, specified in the declaration under this paragraph.
3. Any reference to 'Contracting State', 'Contracting States' or 'State Party' in this Convention applies equally to a Regional Economic Integration Organisation if the context so requires.

Article 42
Entry into force

1. This Convention enters into force on the first day of the month following the expiration of six months after the date of the deposit of the third instrument of ratification, acceptance, approval or accession between the States that have deposited such instruments.
2. For each State that ratifies, accepts, approves or accedes to this Convention after the deposit of the third instrument of ratification, acceptance, approval or accession, this Convention enters into force in relation to that State on the first day of the month following the expiration of six months after the date of the deposit of its instrument of ratification, acceptance, approval or accession.

Article 43
Territorial units

1. If a Contracting State has two or more territorial units in which different systems of law are applicable in relation to the matters dealt with in this Convention, it may, at the time of signature, ratification,

acceptance, approval or accession, make an initial declaration that this Convention is to extend to all its territorial units or only to one or more of them, and may modify its declaration by submitting another declaration at any time.

2. Any such initial declaration is to be made in writing and formally notified to the Depositary and shall state expressly the territorial units to which this Convention applies.
3. If a Contracting State has not made any declaration under paragraph 1, this Convention shall apply to all territorial units of that State.
4. If a Contracting State extends this Convention to one or more of its territorial units, declarations permitted under this Convention may be made in relation to each such territorial unit, and the declarations made in relation to one territorial unit may be different from those made in relation to another territorial unit.
5. In relation to a Contracting State with two or more territorial units in which different systems of law are applicable in relation to the matters dealt with in this Convention, any reference to the law in force in a Contracting State or to the law of a Contracting State shall be construed as referring to the law in force in the relevant territorial unit.

Article 44
Reservations

No reservations may be made to this Convention.

Article 45
Declarations

1. Declarations authorised by the provisions of the Convention, other than the declaration provided for in Article 41(2) and the initial declaration provided for in Article 43(1), may be made at any time.
2. Declarations, and confirmations of declarations, are to be made in writing and formally notified to the Depositary.
3. A declaration made by a Contracting State prior to the entry into force of the Convention for that State shall take effect simultaneously with the entry into force of the Convention for the State concerned. A declaration of which the Depositary receives formal notification after such entry into force shall take effect on the first day of the month following the expiration of six months after the date of the receipt of

the notification by the Depositary. Declarations made at the time of signature are subject to confirmation upon ratification, acceptance or approval.

4. A Contracting State that makes a declaration under this Convention may modify or withdraw it at any time by a formal notification in writing to the Depositary. The modification or withdrawal shall take effect on the first day of the month following the expiration of six months after the date of the receipt of the notification by the Depositary.
5. Notwithstanding the previous paragraphs, this Convention shall continue to apply, as if no declaration, modification or withdrawal of a declaration had been made, in relation to all rights and interests arising prior to the effective date of such declaration, modification or withdrawal.

Article 46
Denunciations

1. Any State Party may denounce this Convention by formal notification in writing to the Depositary.
2. Any such denunciation shall take effect on the first day of the month following the expiration of six months after the date of receipt of the notification by the Depositary. If a longer period for that denunciation to take effect is specified in the notification, it shall take effect upon the expiration of such period after receipt of the notification by the Depositary.
3. Notwithstanding the previous paragraphs, this Convention shall continue to apply, as if no such denunciation had been made, in relation to all rights, interests and obligations arising prior to the effective date of any such denunciation.

Article 47
Evaluation meetings, revision Conferences and related matters

1. Not later than 24 months after the entry into force of the Convention, and in principle every 24 months thereafter as the circumstances warrant, the Depositary shall convene an Evaluation Meeting, to which will be invited the Contracting States, the States and Observers participating in the Geneva Conference, the member States of UNIDROIT as well as other invited Observers.

2. The Agenda of the Evaluation Meeting may include the following matters:
   (a) the implementation and operation of the Convention;
   (b) whether any modification to this Convention or to the Official Commentary is desirable.
3. The Depositary will take due account of the results of the Evaluation Meeting and, if appropriate, may convene a diplomatic Conference.
4. The amendments adopted by the diplomatic Conference referred to in paragraph 3 will enter into force on such a date as will be determined by the Conference in relation to Contracting States that ratify, accept or approve these amendments.
5. After the entry into force of the amendments referred to in paragraph 4, the States that will ratify, accept, approve or accede to this Convention will be bound by the Convention as amended.

Article 48
Depositary and its functions

1. Instruments of ratification, acceptance, approval or accession shall be deposited with UNIDROIT, which is hereby designated the Depositary.
2. The Depositary shall:
   (a) inform all Contracting States of:
      (i) each new signature or deposit of an instrument of ratification, acceptance, approval or accession, together with the date thereof;
      (ii) the date of entry into force of this Convention;
      (iii) each declaration made in accordance with this Convention, together with the date thereof;
      (iv) the withdrawal or amendment of any declaration, together with the date thereof; and
      (v) the notification of any denunciation of this Convention together with the date thereof and the date on which it takes effect;
   (b) transmit certified true copies of this Convention to all Contracting States; and
   (c) perform such other functions customary for depositaries.

IN WITNESS WHEREOF the undersigned Plenipotentiaries, having been duly authorised, have signed this Convention.

DONE at Geneva, this ninth day of October, two thousand and nine, in a single original in the English and French languages, both texts being equally authentic, such authenticity to take effect upon verification by the Secretariat of the Conference under the authority of the President of the Conference within one hundred and twenty days hereof as to the consistency of the texts with one another.

EU Consultation Document 'Legislation on Legal Certainty of Securities Holding and Dispositions'

EUROPEAN COMMISSION
Internal Market and Services DG
FINANCIAL SERVICES POLICY AND FINANCIAL MARKETS
Financial markets infrastructure

Brussels,
DG Markt G2 MET/OT/acg D(2010) **768690**

LEGISLATION ON LEGAL CERTAINTY OF SECURITIES HOLDING AND DISPOSITIONS

Important comment: this document is a working document of the Internal Market and Services Directorate General of the European Commission for discussion and consultation purposes. It does not purport to represent or pre-judge the formal proposal of the Commission.

CONSULTATION DOCUMENT OF THE SERVICES OF THE DIRECTORATE-GENERAL INTERNAL MARKET AND SERVICES

1. This public consultation has been prepared by the services of the Internal Market Directorate General of the European Commission. It seeks feedback from Member States, market participants and other stakeholders, including investors, on improving the legal framework for holding and disposing securities and the exercise of rights attached to securities in the context of the Internal Market. Although the issue and any possible solutions are legal in nature, the underlying problems have a significant economic impact. The present lack of legal clarity and certainty in the field covered by this consultation has a concrete impact on cross-border investment in Europe. Any future legislation in this field will need to complement and will be without prejudice to the existing EU legal framework concerning, for instance, markets and trading in financial

instruments (cf. Directive 2004/39/EC – MiFID – and its implementation measures).

Preliminary remarks

2. In 2004, the Commission set out a roadmap for future action with a view to enhancing the safety and efficiency of post-trading arrangements across Europe[1]. It advocated, amongst other proposals, pursuing work in the field of legal barriers to a safe and efficient post-trading landscape. It mandated a group of legal experts, the Legal Certainty Group, to advise the Commission Services on whether legislation in the field of securities holding and dispositions should be improved, and if so, how it should be carried out. The Group presented its Advice to the Commission in August 2008[2] and was also the subject of a public conference held on 23 October 2008 in Brussels.

3. A *first* public consultation on this issue was held between 16 April and 11 June 2009. The Services prepared a first set of draft provisions which were discussed with Member States' experts between February and June 2010. In view of the progress of discussions and further reflection on legal details, the Commission services would like to submit the outcome of this process to a *further* public consultation.

4. This consultation paper contains 22 sections which cover the full scope of the possible legislative approach. Note, however, that some issues that were raised in the first consultation paper, notably the issue of free access to CSDs by issuers, will be dealt by a separate strand of work.

5. *Importantly, the approaches and suggestions contained in this paper remain work in progress and are exclusively published for discussion and consultation purposes. It does not purport to represent or pre-judge any possible formal proposal of the Commission.*

6. This consultation will open on 05/11/2010 and close on 01/01/2011. Answers, to one or several of the questions below, can be submitted to markt-consultationsld@ec.europa.eu.

7. Contributions, together with the identity of the contributor, will be published on the website of the Directorate-General for Internal Market and Services, unless the contributor objects to their publication.

1 'Clearing and Settlement in the European Union – the way forward', Communication from the Commission to the Council and the European Parliament, COM (2004) 312 final, 28.04.2004.

2 'Second Advice of the Legal Certainty Group on Solutions to Legal Barriers related to Post-Trading within the EU', August 2008, http://ec.europa.eu/internal_market/financial-markets/clearing/certainty_en.htm.

Information about the respondent

In order to correctly assess responses received, respondents are requested to provide the following information.

- Name and address of the respondent
- Field of activity of the respondent
  - Does the respondent (or in the case of an association, its members) conduct domestic or cross-border securities operations in the EU/EEA area?
  - If yes, in which form does your entity conduct these operations?
- If the respondent is a securities account provider, please indicate whether the activity relating to holding and dispositions of account-held securities is
  - made in the context of a European regulated activity (e.g. banking and/or investment services);
  - made in the context of national regulations (e.g. for the service of safekeeping of securities; or as a CCP, SSS or CSD authorised or supervised by a public authority).
- If the respondent is an association of stakeholders, how many members do you represent and what is your membership structure?

Questionnaire

This paper presents specific and articulated principles which are followed by an explanation for those principles. As the Commission's first public consultation of 2009 already presented the general issues at stake and sought feedback at a high-level of generality on the possible approaches, this paper, of necessity enters into greater detail and granularity. This avoids duplication of the issues discussed during the first public consultation. A glossary of terms is included at the end of this Paper to assist stakeholder in understanding the precise meaning of the terms adopted.

1 Objectives

1.1 Principles

1. EU law should regulate the legal framework governing the holding and disposition of securities held through securities accounts and the processing of rights flowing from securities held through securities accounts.

2. The legislation should not harmonise the legal framework governing the question of whom an issuer has to recognise as the legal holder of its securities.

1.2 Background

The last forty years have been characterised by the sharp development of book-entry securities to the detriment of paper based securities. Today, throughout Europe, depending on the Member States and on the type of securities (listed or not listed) the percentage of securities entered into a book-entry form varies from 100% to 85%[3]. Usually, the more recent the financial market, the more it is dematerialised. This phenomenon is addressed through different terms ('dematerialisation', 'immobilisation', 'registered form', 'electronic book-entries'), which address different approaches and legal issues but which all converge on a situation where securities are no longer transferred in paper form but through securities accounts kept by account providers acting on behalf of account holders. Whereas, in the past, securities were transferred from 'hand to hand', today, securities are mostly transferred by 'book-entries', requiring the recourse to a 'securities account' and the intervention of a third party, the 'account provider', which is an intermediary (often a bank or an investment firm). The same phenomenon exists outside the EU, especially in Switzerland, the US, Canada, Japan, China, Brazil and other developed and emerging markets.

In some national holding arrangement, only one single account provider intervenes in the holding of securities. In other Member States it might be a multitude of 'account providers', one holding for the other ('holding chain'). This market reality is usually addressed by the national law. It is important to note that from a *domestic* point of view, most Member States' legislation concerning book-entry securities works perfectly well for *purely domestic* situations. However, the legal frameworks differ considerably. Where a holding chain crosses borders, different laws are applicable to the same underlying securities. Yet, the relevant laws of Member States are usually incompatible and legal uncertainty arises, for example because different laws identify different 'owners' of the same underlying security. This is current legal reality and uncontested amongst legal experts.

As a result, in the EU the cross-border holding and disposition (outright sale, pledge, etc) of securities held through securities accounts across borders:

3 'Summary of the First Public consultation on the harmonisation of securities law', April-June 2009, http://ec.europa.eu/internal_market/financial-markets/docs/securitieslaw/first_consultation_summary_en.pdf.

a. suffers from legal uncertainty and it is often not clear what an investor owns,
b. is ineffective, and
c. does not allow investors to exercise the rights attached to those securities (receipt of dividends or interests, voting, agreeing to corporate measures like stock splits, etc) without major obstacles.

It is therefore necessary to make the holding and disposition safer and easier from a legal point of view by ensuring that the core mechanisms of Member States' legal frameworks are compatible. Some of the difficulties are legal in nature, others are operational. The following three actions are required for consideration:

1) *all* account providers must be regulated at EU-level and should be subject to a detailed authorisation and supervision framework notably the one provided by MIFID;

2) conflict-of-laws arrangements (answering the question of which law is applicable) must be clarified and brought in line with existing EU measures (Settlement Finality and the Financial Collateral Directives);

3) substantive law arrangements (answering the question of what the applicable laws say in substance) need to be made compatible;

4) the full exercise of investor rights must be guaranteed.

Of central importance is that measures at EU level should not seek to harmonise the legal framework governing the question of whom an issuer has to recognise as the legal holder of its securities. It is not only extremely difficult to harmonise the national laws of legal ownership of shares between Member States, but it is also unnecessary. A functional approach should suffice. Equally, EU law should not cover the functions of creation, recording or reconciliation of securities, against the issuer of those securities, by a person such as a central securities depository, central bank, transfer agent or registrar.

1.3 Question

Q1: Do you agree that the envisaged legislation should cover the objectives described above? If not, please explain why. Are any aspects missing (please consider also the following pages for a detailed description of the content of the proposal)?

2 Shared Functions

2.1 Principles

1. It should be possible for Member States to provide that a person other than the account provider is responsible for the performance of certain, but not all, functions of an account provider. In such a case, references made in EU law to an account provider aim at the person responsible for performing the function to which the relevant provision applies.

2. The Commission would need to be notified accordingly and could specify the exact content of the notification. The Commission should publish on its website a list of Member States allowing for the sharing of account-provider functions, including all relevant specifications.

2.2 Background

In some jurisdictions account providers actually share the task of maintaining a securities account with one or even more, other service providers which are not considered as account providers. It is important that EU legislation smoothly applies to such holding patterns. This is in particular the case in 'transparent systems' (Sweden, Finland, Greece and others), where by virtue of the national law, the Central Security Depository (CSD) that has entered the securities into a book entry form is considered as the sole securities account provider. All other intermediaries are considered as purely transparent 'account operators' which intervene in the managing of the account on a contractual basis, being neither account holder nor account provider.

In these situations there is a need for clarification as to how and to whom the provisions of the envisaged legislation apply. Therefore, there is a need for a mechanism for the identification of

(i) the person who is the account provider of the account holder;

(ii) the functions which are performed by the *other person* (the one which is not the account provider but takes over some functions);

(iii) the provisions of the Convention which apply to that *other person* instead of applying to the account provider.

A main purpose of a specific provision would be to clarify that such holding patterns are actually covered. The principle should contain the following elements (i) it should generally recognise the existence of holding patterns involving shared functions, (ii) it should specify which quality of involvement the other person must have; (iii) it should state that the rules of the envisaged legislation are applicable to that *other* person performing account provider functions; (iii) it should contain an element of publicity, e.g. by notifying the pattern to the Commission.

However, a general identification of such persons on the basis of the terms 'outsourcing' or 'legal representation' would be insufficient in the view of the Commission Services. Therefore, the provision should use the criterion of 'responsibility' for delimitation. The *other person* should be 'responsible' for the performance of a function or functions covered by the envisaged legislation. In that respect, 'Responsible' would mean legally responsible vis-à-vis the account holder, i.e. the person must have an own, independent role regarding the fulfilment of the function, including an element of legal accountability towards the account holder.

The envisaged functions of an account provider could probably include: (i) receive and execute instructions; (ii) be the operational addressee for the exercise of corporate rights, (cf. sections 16 to 21).

As the arrangement of shared functions and the application of the envisaged legislation and Member States' law to this situation have a legal effect on third parties, in the view of the Commission's services the sharing of functions should not be left to private contractual arrangements alone. Therefore, sharing functions should be allowed or provided for under the relevant Member State's law.

For the same reasons, arrangements regarding the sharing of functions would need to be made public. A notification to the Commission with subsequent publication in a web-site based list could suffice. The exact content of that notification could contain (a) the class of assets concerned, and, (b) the entities concerned (i.e. who is account provider and who is *the other person*) and their respective share in the functions.

2.3 Questions

Q2: Would a Principle along the lines set out above adequately accommodate the functioning of so-called transparent holding systems?

Q3: If not: can you explain which aspect is not correctly addressed and what could be improved? Which are, if applicable, the repercussions on your business model?

Q4: Do you know any specific difficulties of connecting transparent holding systems to non-transparent holding systems?

3 *Account-held securities*

3.1 Principles

1) The national law should clarify that securities standing to the credit of a securities account confer upon the account holder at least the following rights:

(a) the right to exercise and receive the rights attached to the securities if the account holder is the ultimate account holder or if, in any other case, the applicable law confers the right to that account holder;
(b) the right to effect a disposition under one of the harmonised methods (cf. below);
(c) the right to instruct the account provider to arrange for holding the securities with another account provider or otherwise than with an account provider, as far as permitted under the applicable law, the terms of the securities and, to the extent permitted by the national law, the account agreement and the rules of a securities settlement system.

2) The national law should make sure that account holders which act in the capacity of account provider for a third person exercise the rights (b) and (c), above, in accordance with the instructions of that person (see below).

3) In case of acquisition of a security interest or other limited interest in account-held securities the national law of should be able to restrict the rights (a)-(c), above.

4) The national law should be allowed to characterise the legal nature of account-held securities as any form of property, equitable interest or other right as far as the characteristics flowing from the legal nature is in accordance with the rights (a)-(c), above, and the remainder of any legislation.

3.2 Background

The most relevant aspect of any legislative action in the field of securities held through account providers would certainly relate to the requirements which need to be fulfilled in order to render the acquisition of securities or of a security interest in securities, legally effective (see sections 4 *et seq.*, below). However, the certainty that an account holder acquires such position must be accompanied by the knowledge of what he has exactly acquired. This is because account holders need to be sure to what extent the acquired position can be used: to participate in a corporation, to receive dividends or similar payments, to sell the securities or realise their value in case a security provider does not fulfil his obligations, etc.

The legal design of the acquired position must provide clarity regarding these elements. To this extent, and as confirmed by stakeholders in the first public consultation, there is a clear need for harmonisation. Consequently, a common legal framework could provide for a legal position of the acquiring account holder which comprises a set of legal attributes in the sense of a minimum content, without determining the exact legal characterisation of that position. In other words: the common legal framework would not harmonise the property laws of Member States but limit itself to setting out what the attributes of that law would be. This is referred to as a functional approach which should achieve the following substantive elements:

First, the legal nature of the right credited to accounts might change in a holding chain which crosses jurisdictional borders (i.e. with different laws applicable to the various parts of the chain). Account holders might have, in respect of the same underlying securities, conceptually differing rights (full property, shared property, right sui generis, equitable interest) depending on their position in the holding chain and the national law applicable to their accounts. This is the reason for which this second consultation paper continues to refer to the formal envelop of the rights credited to accounts, rather to its actual legal content. However the terms have been changed. While, the first consultation paper of April 2009 referred to the term 'book-entry securities', it became clear that 'book-entry securities' can be misunderstood. Confusion may arise as to whether Member States were to be required to introduce a new category of securities – book-entry securities – in their legal system. This would not be the case. The concept has therefore been refined and renamed as 'account-held securities'.

Second, account holders need to be sure *what* they receive. This is because they may expect to be able to use the asset in one or more ways (participate in a corporation, receive dividends or similar payments, sell the securities, use them as collateral or realise their value in case a security provider does not fulfil his obligations, etc.) Consequently, legal framework must provide for a legal position that is harmonised in the sense that the account holder receives these essential elements of minimum content. As the applicable law would remain national law, a legal approach must focus solely on achieving this result without determining the exact legal characterisation of the acquired position. The most important elements are the following:

- the ultimate account holder can exercise the rights flowing from the securities (dividends, voting rights); 'non-ultimate' account holders can exercise the rights only if so determined by the national law (e.g. because they are identified by the national law as 'shareholder'), which is actually often the case under the current legal arrangements. EU law addressing the exercise of rights would be in a position to guarantee that the ultimate account holder at least controls the exercise of the rights, cf. below, sections 15–20;

- any account holder can 'dispose' of the securities, i.e. relinquish them or use them to provide a security interest, however, if he is not the ultimate account holder, he can do so only on instruction (see paragraph 2);
- an account holder must be able to change the holding situation (which does not represent a 'disposition' in the sense of the second indent) either by moving the securities to another account provider or by retrieving certificates (to the extent that this is possible under the applicable law and other relevant rules).

Third, Where a crediting occurs with a view to creating a security interest (pledge *et.al.*, or other limited interest, like usufruct), it is necessary that the applicable law can restrict the right to exercise the corporate rights or dispose of the security, (depending on the nature of the interest, e.g. pledge as opposed to repo).

Fourth, There is agreement that it would be too complicated (and unnecessary) to conceptually harmonise Member States' laws on the above issues.

Therefore, the applicable (national) law remains decisive for the legal nature of the right acquired by an account holder upon crediting of the account. For example, where the applicable law qualifies the right of an account holder as a classical property right, the legal position (a) can be called 'property', (b) must cover the minimum content described above, and, (c) can additionally have legal attributes that property in this jurisdiction normally has. However, (a)-(c) are subject to the requirement that neither the legal qualification nor the attributes coming with it can contradict the remainder of the common legal framework. This principle applies regardless of the qualification of the right under national law as 'property', 'property sui generis', 'equitable interest' or other, (see paragraph 4 of the draft Principle).

This principle refines the understanding of who is potentially identified as the person called upon to exercise the rights flowing from the securities by the applicable company law. In some situations, company law attributes the exercise of the rights to an account holder which is not the ultimate account holder of the securities in question but one of the account providers involved in the holding chain (in particular if the company register determines the shareholder), see paragraph 1(a). This needs to be taken into account. As a consequence the case of the 'non-ultimate' account holder entitled to exercise the rights needs to be included explicitly, in order to respect national company law analysis.

In all cases, the envisaged principles on the exercise of corporate rights, (see below principles 15 to 20) guarantee that the ultimate account holder either exercises itself or is at least in control of the exercise by the legal holder.

3.3 Questions

Q5: Would a principle along the lines described above provide Member States with a framework allowing them to adequately define the legal position of account holders?

Q6: If not, which legal aspects that belong, in your opinion, to an adequate legal position of each account holder could not be realised by the national law under an EU framework as described above? What are the practical problems that might occur in your opinion, if Member States were bound by a framework as described above? Which are, if applicable, the repercussions on your business model?

Q7: The Geneva Securities Convention (www.unidroit.org/english/conventions/2009intermediatedsecurities/main.htm) provides for a global harmonised instrument regarding the substantive law (= content of the law) of holding and disposition of securities, covering the same scope as those parts of the present outline dealing this subject. Most EU Member States and the EU itself have participated in the negotiations of this Convention. Both the present approach and the Convention are compatible with each other.

- If applicable, does your business model comprise securities holdings or transactions involving non-EU account holders or account providers?
- Is it, in your opinion, important to achieve global compatibility regarding the substantive law of securities dispositions, or would EU-wide compatibility suffice?

4 Methods for acquisition and disposition

4.1 Principles

1. The national law should provide for acquisitions and dispositions of account-held securities and limited interests therein to be effected by crediting an account and debiting an account respectively.

2. The national law should provide that an account provider may credit the accounts of its account holders, for each description of securities, only

if it holds a corresponding number of securities of the same description by

(a) having available account-held securities in a securities account maintained for the account provider by another account provider;
(b) arranging for securities to be held on the register of the issuer in the name, or for the account, of its account holders;
(c) holding securities as the registered holder on the register of the issuer;
(d) possessing relevant securities certificates or other documents of title; or
(e) creating the initial electronic record of securities for the issuer in accordance with the applicable law.

and that an account provider continuously holds that corresponding number.

3. If the applicable law allows crediting and debiting to be made conditional it should also define the extent to which such conditional crediting or debiting is taken into account in determining the number of securities referred to in the preceding paragraphs. Credits to a securities account the effectiveness of which is subject to a condition must be identifiable as such in the account.

4. If a corresponding number (paragraph 2) is not held, the account provider should promptly apply either or both of the following mechanisms in order to re-establish compliance:

(a) reverse erroneous credits;
(b) provide additional securities of the relevant description, to be held by one of the methods provided for in paragraph 2.

The sharing of any cost entailed by the provision of additional securities pursuant to subparagraph can be subject to a contractual agreement between the account provider and those account holders holding securities of the relevant description at the time of the occurrence of the loss in non-segregated accounts only in cases where the account provider held securities of the relevant description with another account provider pursuant to Article 17(3) subparagraphs (a) and (b) of the MiFID.

5. The applicable national law may in addition allow for acquisitions and dispositions being effected under one or more of the following methods:

(a) earmarking account-held securities in an account, or earmarking a securities account, and the removing of such earmarking;
(b) concluding a control agreement; or
(c) concluding an agreement with and in favour of an account provider.

4.2 Background

There is general agreement that a separation in two distinct principles is logical. A first principle should deal with the operational side of acquiring and disposing through accounts, comprising the methods for acquisition and dispositions and the corresponding duties of the account provider. A second principle should set out the requirements for the legal effectiveness of acquisitions and dispositions, under regular circumstances as well as in situations in which the account provider is not compliant with the operational duties. Methods are addressed in the present section, legal effectiveness in the following sections.

Different methods are used throughout Member States to realise one or the other type of acquisition and disposition.

- Book-entry methods
  - crediting of an account;
  - debiting of an account;
  - earmarking of securities in an account or of a securities account;
  - removing of an earmarking.
- Non-book-entry methods
  - conclusion of a control agreement;
  - conclusion of an agreement with and in favour of the account provider.

There is a general agreement that among these six book entry methods, crediting and debiting form the minimum common denominator that should be generally provided for under any law (see paragraph 1). The four other methods should be recognised in a crossborder context but not necessarily imposed or allowed to local account holder – account provider relationships (see paragraph 5).

In particular crediting and debiting determine the actual number of securities in the holding chain and must be used consistently and in such a way that the number of securities maintained by the account provider for the account of its account holder always equates the number of securities held by the former through one of the five methods distinguished under paragraph 2. As a matter of fact, instead of providing for a rough ex ante 'no-credit-without-debit-rule', that is difficult to address in legal terms (civil law cannot forbid neither 'error' nor 'fraud'), the Commission Services suggests having recourse to an ex post rule as provided under paragraph 2 seeking the final *result* rather than detailing the initial *methods*. Furthermore, this ex-post solution allows the identification of two corrective methods in case of shortfall, as provided under paragraph 4.

Only in limited circumstances involving crossborder holdings with third countries (notably cases regulated under Article 17 (3) of the MiFID Implementing Directive), it might be worth considering the sharing of costs between the account holder and the account provider. This is the purpose of the last indent of paragraph 4 of the draft Principle.

As concerns paragraph 3 concerning 'conditional credits', it must be read in conjunction with Principal 5 paragraph 6 (see below)

4.3 Questions

Q8: Would a principle along the lines described above allow for a framework which effectively avoids that more securities are credited to account holders than had been originally issued by the issuer?

Q9: If not, how could a harmonised EU-framework better guarantee that account providers do not create excess securities by over-crediting client accounts (keeping in mind that all account providers are either banks or MiFID regulated entities)? Please distinguish between regulating the account providers' behaviour and issues relating to the effectiveness of excess credits made.

Q10: Is the principle relating to the passing on of costs of a buy-in appropriate? If not, in which way should it be changed and why? What would be the repercussions on your business model?

5 Legal effectiveness of acquisitions and dispositions

5.1 Principles

1. The legal nature of dispositions over account-held securities effected under one of the methods listed in Principle 4 would be determined by the national law, as far as the legal nature does not contravene the principles.

2. No further steps than those set out in Principle 4 paragraphs 1 and 5 should be required to render an acquisition or disposition effective between the account holder and the account provider and against third parties.

3. To the extent that the requirements of Principle 4 paragraph 2 are not met, and until measures under Principle 4 paragraph 4 are successfully applied, the national law, or the rules of a settlement system in accordance with the applicable law, should determine, subject to Principle 8 below, whether and in what circumstances a credit is legally ineffective, liable to be reversed or subject to a condition, and the consequences thereof.

4. Acquisitions and dispositions arising by mandatory operation of the national law are effective and have the legal attributes, in particular rank, attributed by that law.

5. Effectiveness in the above sense does not determine whom an issuer has to recognise as legal holder of its securities.

6. The effectiveness can be made subject to a condition in accordance with national law.

7. The national law prescribes whether the credit is legally ineffective, liable to be reversed or subject to a condition, and the consequences thereof if the terms of issue of the relevant securities, in accordance with the national law under which the securities are constituted, require the agreement of the issuer for an acquisition to be legally effective.

8. The national law may provide for reasons which trigger ineffectiveness of acquisitions and dispositions effected under a control agreement or an agreement with and in favour of the account provider and regulate the consequences of such ineffectiveness.

5.2 Background

As regards the side of legal effectiveness of acquisition and disposition, certainty requires the assurance that, from a specific point in time, acquisitions and dispositions can no longer be 'undone' and are 'good against' third parties. Acquisitions and dispositions should be effective once they are established under one of the six methods set out above, establishing at the same time the effectiveness between account holder and account provider, the effectiveness against the insolvency administrator and the creditors in any insolvency proceeding and the effectiveness *vis-à-vis* third persons. This is the purpose of Paragraphs 1 to 2.

In this respect, there is agreement regarding the principle that if an innocent account holder is protected against reversal of earlier credits a solution is required as regards the avoidance of the creation of 'legally effective excess securities'. This question can however be left to the applicable (national) law. However, every national rule must effectively avoid legally effective excess securities.

Paragraph 6 deals (together with paragraph 3 of Principle 4) deals with Conditional Credit. Conditional credits are used in particular in the context of contractual settlement, i.e. an agreement between account provider and account holder under which the account holder immediately receives the acquired securities, even if the account provider has not yet received them (in particular because the settlement cycle is T+2 or T+3). Typically, Member States' law determines that the credit is not legally effective until the account provider receives the securities through the settlement system. In more general terms, conditional credits establish a linkage between effectiveness of a book entry and factors external to the account. Therefore, 'Conditional credits' should be possible under the applicable law. But since, conditional credit is an exception to the principle of effectiveness; it has to be identified marked accordingly in the book-entry system. This is the reason for which Paragraph 3 of Principle 4 provides that 'credits to a securities account the effectiveness of which is subject to a condition must be identifiable as such in the account.'

A recognition of conditional credits leads to a situation where two different types of credit can be made to an account: the 'regular' credit having immediate effect, and the conditional credit which is not immediately effective. For this reason, conditions should be made transparent from the account (which would create additional administrative burden for the account provider) or at the least limited in time, (cf. Section 5 Paragraph 3 of the principle). A non transparent condition in itself may not be an issue as long as the effects are confined within one system or intermediary, for instance by blocking conditional credits until the condition is fulfilled. However, if such non-transparent conditional credits could be passed down a chain of intermediated holdings into a jurisdiction where credits are always legally effective in the moment they occur, creation of uncovered excess-securities might be the result.

Some Member States allow for 'restricted registered shares'. Under this regime, the terms of the issue can provide that any legally effective acquisition of securities is subject to prior consent of the issuer. Until the consent is given, the securities are not acquired. These regimes should be recognised as part of national corporate law and remain unchanged.

5.3 Questions

Q11: Would a principle along the lines described above provide Member States with a framework allowing them to determine legal effectiveness and ineffectiveness to an extent sufficient to safeguard basic domestic legal concepts, like e.g. the transfer of property?

Q12: If not, please specify how and to what extent national legal concepts would be incompatible. Please specify the practical problems linked to these Background, and, if applicable, the repercussions on your business model.

6 *Effectiveness in insolvency*

6.1 Principles

1. Acquisitions and dispositions that have become effective under the methods described in Principles 4 and 5 should be equally effective against the insolvency administrator and creditors in any insolvency proceeding.

2. The principle contained in Paragraph 1 does not affect the application of any substantive or procedural rule of law applicable by virtue of an insolvency proceeding, such as any rule relating to:

(a) the ranking of categories of claims [in the case of violation of the methods described in Principles 4 and 5];
(b) the avoidance of a transaction as a preference or a transfer in fraud of creditors; or
(c) the enforcement of rights to property that is under the control or supervision of the insolvency administrator.

6.2 Background

The most important aspect here is the protection of account holders' securities in the event of the insolvency of the account provider. Any EU-initiative must make it crystal clear that the insolvency administrator of the insolvent account providers does not have access to the securities or interests therein established by one of the harmonised methods. This protection is probably already implicitly granted by the preceding envisaged Principles. However, because of the overarching importance of this aspect, and in order to remove doubts regarding the question whether the insolvency administrator is a 'third party', the insolvency situation should be addressed in an additional, separate rule from the principle presented under question 5 above.

National insolvency law often contains rules targeted at the protection of the creditors of the insolvent entity. In particular, there are rules for the recapture of assets transferred by the debtor to the detriment of his creditors in a suspect period prior to the commencement of the insolvency proceedings, especially in cases of alleged or actual fraud. It should be avoided by any EU-initiative to harmonise or to affect these rules. In addition, there should be no interference with rules on ranking of claims [in the case of violation of the methods described above] and methods of enforcement in insolvency. As there is a wide range of such rules, there needs to be a rather general statement of this principle, ideally accompanied by rule examples such as the ones provided under paragraph 2 of the principle above.

6.3 Questions

Q13: Would a principle along the lines described above provide for a framework allowing effective protection of client securities in case of insolvency of an account provider?

Q14: If not, which measures needed for effective protection could not be taken by Member States under the proposed framework?

7 Reversal

7.1 Principle

1. The national law should ensure that Book entries can only be reversed under the following circumstances:

(a) in the case of crediting provided that the account holder consents to the reversal;
(b) in the case of erroneous crediting which was not authorised by the account holder, subject to Article 9;
(c) in the case of debiting which was not authorised by the account holder, or a third person who has acquired an interest in the relevant account-held securities;
(d) in case of earmarking which was not authorised by the account holder, subject to Article 9;
(e) in case of removal of an earmarking which was not authorised by the person in whose favour it was made.

2. Paragraph 1 should be, to the extent permitted by the applicable law, subject to any rule of a securities settlement system.

3. The national law should specify the extent to which consent in the sense of paragraph 1(a) can be given in a general manner and any formal requirements for giving such consent.

7.2 Background

In parallel to the principle of effectiveness, once an effective book-entry position is effectively established, there needs to be clarity on the conditions under which it can be subsequently 'undone' and what the legal consequences in such a case would be.

There is general agreement that totally comprehensive effectiveness of acquisition and disposition of account-held securities is unpractical. Therefore, once an effective account-held position is established, there needs to be clarity on the conditions under which it can be subsequently 'undone' and what the legal consequences in such a case would be. The future harmonised legislation should therefore provide for reasons allowing for 'reversal'.

The set of reasons allowing for reversal should be very restricted, in order to guarantee maximum certainty regarding the validity of an acquisition. There are a number of cases of possible reversal which are all borrowed from general principles of law and which should be maintained for the area of account-held securities.

First, the obvious exception is that the account holder agrees that a crediting is reversed. Second, it must be possible to reverse a crediting which the account holder did not want to obtain, either because it objected explicitly or because it did not give general or special authorisation to credit securities to its account. Third, where an unauthorised debit violates the rights of the account holder or a third person which had a security interest in the account-held securities, reversal of the debiting (= re-crediting) must be possible. Fourth, where an earmarking of account-held securities in favour of a third party was not authorised by the account holder, it must be possible to reverse the earmarking (= delete it). Fifth, where a valid earmarking is removed without the consent of its beneficiary (in particular: secured party), the removal can be reversed (= re-earmark).

7.3 Questions

Q14: Is the list of cases allowing for reversal complete? Are cases listed which appear to be inappropriate? Are cases missing? What are, if applicable, the repercussions on your business model?

Q15: Should national law define the extent to which general consent to reversal can be given in standard account documentation? What are, if applicable, the repercussions on your business model in case your jurisdiction would take a restrictive approach to this question and limit the possibility of general consent to reversal?

8 Protection of acquirers against reversal

8.1 Principle

The national law should ensure that

(a) an account holder is protected against reversal of a crediting;
(b) a person in whose favour an earmarking has been made is protected against reversal of this earmarking

unless it knew or ought to have known that the crediting or earmarking should not have been made.

8.2 Background

A comprehensive legal system on acquisition and disposition of securities requires a rule of 'good faith acquisition'. In the account-held environment, under the assumption that reversal must be allowed in certain cases, the absence of such a good faith acquisition rule may have very serious systemic consequences. An attempt to unwind a sequence of acquisitions because one of these acquisitions had been invalid could cause serious strain to participants and, possibly, to systems. In most jurisdictions, there are rules in place protecting the parties involved in such a situation against the risk of unwinding a sequence of acquisitions. These rules resemble each other as regards their general result, while differing considerably as regards their exact legal construction, some of them focusing on the contractual liability of the account provider towards the account holder whereas other focus more on the inalterability of the ownership right of the good faith acquirer.

An account holder's ability to rely on a credit in his account (with limited exceptions) is the linchpin for a regime of enhanced cross-border legal certainty in the present context. Therefore, a harmonised protection rule is of utmost importance and only a high degree of uniformity can significantly eliminate the threat of unexpected reversal of book entries. For this reason, a common framework would need to be based on a purely functional provision without allusions to traditional legal concepts and employ neutral terminology in order to avoid misinterpretation.

8.3 Questions

Q16: Do you agree with the 'test of innocence' as proposed ('knew or ought to have known') ? Do you know of any practical obstacle that could flow from its application in your jurisdiction? What would be the negative consequences in that case?

9 Priority

9.1 Principle

1. The national law should provide that Priority rules prescribe that

(a) interests in the same account-held securities which are acquired by earmarking rank amongst themselves in chronological order;
(b) interests in the same account-held securities which are acquired by control agreement or an agreement with and in favour of the account provider rank amongst themselves in chronological order;

(c) interests in account-held securities which are acquired by earmarking have priority over interests acquired in the same account-held securities by means of a control agreement or an agreement with and in favour of the account provider.

2. An acquisition of securities, account-held securities or interests therein effected under Articles 5 should prevail over any other method permitted by the national law.

3. Parties should be able to deviate from the above rules by agreement. Such agreement cannot affect the rights of third parties.

4. Security interests or other limited interests created by mandatory operation of the applicable law should have the priority attributed by that law.

9.2 Background

As a further issue, harmonisation at EU-level of rules on priority of interests appears to be necessary. 'Interests' is a generic term to designate the legal position conferred by a book entry, whether it is a right of ownership as defined under the applicable law or whether it is a security interest such as the one provided through a collateral arrangement.

Priority conflicts between several market participants with respect to the same accountheld securities can, and do in practice, arise. The national laws this question in different manners. Future harmonised legislation would need to provide appropriate rules, striking a balance between the various methods for acquiring securities and interests therein on the basis of the following criteria: first, the chronological order in which competing rights or interests are established, second, the different nature of the methods used, third, an agreement by the parties to alter the order of priority, and, fourth, policy decisions that give absolute protection of certain claims.

The chronological order is a classical means of determining an order of priority with respect to rights and interests created in the same assets. Generally, rights and interests created earlier in time prevail over others created subsequently.

A more difficult issue is whether interests created by means of specific methods should have a 'better' priority although they have been established later in time as compared to other interests created with respect to the same securities but by different methods. There is large support for the view that book-entries to an account should have constitutive effect as regards acquisition and disposition of securities and that the use of book-entries generally increases transparency. Against this background, interests created by bookentries should be attributed a priority rank that is more favourable than the priority rank granted to interests created under non-account-held methods. This idea, however, can logically only apply to earmarking, as crediting and debiting are not within the scope of the priority provisions.

The principle of contractual freedom of the parties allows for the order of priority to be changed by them. However, such agreement may not affect the rights of third parties. On the basis of policy decisions, national law often attributes a certain rank to certain claims (for example the tax or social security authorities might have a super-priority over the assets of a debtor). The envisaged Principle is not intended to change priority or rank which is attributed to a non-consensual interest.

9.3 Questions

Q17: Will a principle along the lines set out above, under which the applicable law would need to afford an inferior priority to interests created under a control agreement, be appropriate and justified against the background that control agreements are not 'visible' in the relevant securities account? If not, please explain why.

Q18: Have you encountered difficulties regarding the priority/rank of an interest created under a mechanism comparable to a control agreement in the context of a priority contest, or, more generally, in an insolvency proceeding? If yes, please specify.

Q19: Would there be negative practical consequences for your business model flowing from a Principle along the lines set out above? If yes, please specify.

10 Protection of account holders in case of insolvency of account provider

10.1 Principle

1. The national law should ensure that In the event of insolvency of the account provider securities and account-held securities held by the account provider for its account holders should be unavailable for distribution among or realisation for the benefit of creditors of the account provider.

2. The national law applicable in the insolvency of an account provider should provide for a mechanism governing the distribution of the shortage in the event of an insufficient number of securities or account-held securities in the sense of Principle 4 paragraph 2 being held by an insolvent account provider.

10.2 Background

It is impossible to exclude operational failure hundred per cent. An account provider might, intentionally or accidentally, credit more securities to its clients' accounts than it holds itself, and fail to apply the remedies of reversal and buy-in properly and timely. This risk is particularly high in pre-insolvency situation. Therefore, there needs to be a rule stating the consequences of a shortage of securities in the event of insolvency of the account provider (*cf.* Section 4 above) is the insolvency of the account provider. The national law should provide for a mandatory mechanism that eliminates the imbalance between the aggregate number of securities credited to accounts and the number of securities issued, in order to protect issuers and prevent systemic instability by clearly and immediately answering the question who owns what.

Some commentators proposed that in case the account provider holds securities for its own account, these securities should be attributed to its account holders. However, such a principle would result in granting an unjustified super-priority to securities account holders, over any other types of creditors of an insolvent account provider, including other clients.

Similarly, any funds still available in the insolvent estate cannot be used, in analogy to the Principle contained under Section (paragraph 2.a), to buy in missing securities. Consequently, as there is no possibility left to *increase* the number of securities held by the insolvent account provider for its account holders, the only possible solution is to *diminish* the number of securities credited to the accounts of the account provider's clients. For reasons of account holder protection and stability of the system, any arbitrary allocation of the loss to one or the other account holder should be avoided. Originally, there seemed to be support for a harmonised rule on how a potential shortfall should be shared, which provided for a *pro rata* sharing of the holdings ('mandatory mutualisation of the loss'). The background for this proposal was first, that it would be very difficult to argue for the loss to be born by individual account holders. Even in the event where it is possible to identify one or more account providers that are 'closer' to the facts that actually caused the loss (for example: those account holders that received credits on their accounts at the time the loss occurred) they would become victim of the account provider's mistake or misbehaviour in a rather arbitrary manner. Second, individualisation of losses would generally bear the risk of producing further failures, notably of those affected by the individualised loss, with the potential of a chain reaction of insolvencies.

Nevertheless, a harmonised loss sharing rule at EU-level would impinge on rules of national insolvency law addressing the issue and potentially distort prioritisation of account holders' and security providers' interests. Therefore, the envisaged principle only proposes that the national law should contain a clear and predictable solution, leaving the details and mechanisms of such solution should to national policy.

10.3 Questions

Q20: Would a Principle along the lines described above pave the way for the national legal frameworks to effectively protect client securities in case of the insolvency of an account provider?

Q21: If not: Which mechanisms should be available which could not be implemented under a framework designed along the lines described above. Please specify.

Q22: Should the sharing of a loss in securities holdings (occurring, for example, as a consequence of fraud by the account provider) be left to national law ? Would you prefer a harmonised rule, following the *pro rata* principle or any other mechanism?

11 Instructions

11.1 Principle

1. An intermediary should neither be bound nor entitled to give effect to any instruction in relation to account-held securities of an account holder given by any person other than that account holder.

2. Paragraph 1 is subject to:

(a) any agreement between account holder and account provider;
(b) the rights of any person, including the intermediary, who has acquired an interest in the relevant account-held securities;
(c) any judgement, award, order or decision of a court or other judicial or administrative authority of competent jurisdiction;
(d) any rule of the applicable law;
(e) if the account provider is the operator of a securities settlement system, the rules of that system, to the extent permitted by the law governing the system.

11.2 Background

As crediting, debiting and earmarking are capable of immediately affecting market participants' legal positions towards account-held securities, the envisaged legislation must make sure that the account provider follows only the instruction of the account holder.

However, there are various well reasoned exceptions: in particular, the account provider and the account holder could contractually agree on another person being authorised to give instructions, for example in case of a family member being mandated to make any disposition; or, the national law might provide for the power to instruct the account provider in the context of tutelage or similar. Additionally, the right to instruct might also depend on whether a security interest over the relevant account-held securities had been established, and similar cases.

11.3 Questions

Q23: Would a Principle along the lines described above provide for a framework allowing the national law to effectively apply restrictions on whose instructions to follow for purposes of investor protection, notably in connection with the envisaged Principle contained under section 4 (Paragraph 2)? If not, please explain why.

12 Attachment by creditors of the account holder

12.1 Principle

The national law should provide that Creditors of an account holder may attach accountheld securities only at the level of the account provider of that account holder.

12.2 Background

There are two scenarios which need special attention when it comes to attaching accountheld securities, as opposed to attaching other interest or chattel: on one hand the prohibition of 'upper-tier attachment' (present section 12), and, on the other hand, the attachment of segregated client accounts (see below section 13). Whilst both mechanisms relate to 'attachments' they deal in fact with two different issues.

The term 'Prohibition of upper-tier attachment' is commonly used to refer to the risk that a securities account with an account provider at a higher tier in the holding pattern may be subject to a legal claim (typically through court proceedings) to freeze or attach the account in order to enforce a claim against a person alleged to hold an interest through an account provider at a lower tier. This phenomenon occurs in the following forms:

- In holding arrangements where legal relationships exist only between the account holder and its own direct account provider the account holder has no rights against any higher-tier account provider. Hence, there is nothing to attach at the higher-tier account provider level. The taking up of an 'upper-tier prohibition rule' in such a legal context is thus merely stating the obvious and serves as a clarification.

- In holding arrangements where the investor is considered to be the direct owner of the securities all the way down the holding chain, upper-tier attachment is conceivable. Two scenarios must be distinguished:
  - First, the investor, as legal owner of the securities, can only be identified as such by his own direct account provider, the higher-tier account provider being unable to do so; in this case higher-tier identification is not possible. Consequently, the upper-tier prohibition rule is important and adds actual legal value.
  - Second, the investor, as legal owner of the securities is identified or identifiable at the direct *and* at the higher-tier account provider level; in this case, higher-tier identification is possible and a legal and a policy issue arise. The following key elements are of importance: (i) where the investor has a direct account relationship with the higher-tier account provider, its direct account provider acting merely as an 'account operator', there is no issue of upper-tier attachment because there is only one securities account (maintained by the upper-tier entity and administered by the account operator; (ii) where the direct account provider of the account holder holds itself an account with a highertier account provider which is subdivided in as many sub accounts as there are direct investors and the identity of the investors is disclosed to the higher-tier account provider one may conceive an 'upper-tier attachment'. This depends, however, in particular on, first, the identification of the decisive record (direct account provider/higher-tier account provider) of the investor's rights, and, second, a solid information transfer system between the direct and the higher-tier account provider to ensure that they receive the same information in real time.

12.3 Questions

Q24: Would a Principle along the lines described above provide Member States with a framework allowing them, in combination with the envisaged Principle on shared functions, to effectively reflect operational practice regarding attachments in your jurisdiction? If not, please explain why.

Q25: Have you ever encountered, in your business practice, attempts to attach securities at a tier of the holding chain which did not maintain the decisive record? If yes, please specify.

13 Attachment by creditors of the account provider

13.1 Principle

The national law should prohibit that creditors of an account provider attach securities credited to accounts opened in the name of that account provider with a second account provider, as far as these accounts are identified as containing securities belonging to the first account provider's customers. Where the law provides for a presumption that accounts opened by an account provider with a second account provider contain securities belonging to customers, the presumption should apply.

13.2 Background

The goal of a rule on prohibition of the attachment of segregated client accounts by creditors of the account provider is to enhance investor protection and to allow for an efficient functioning of holding through securities accounts in structures using multiple tiers and omnibus accounts.

Articles 13(7) and 13(8) of MiFID and Article 16(1)(d) of the MiFID Implementing Directive already require that credit institutions and investment firms 'must take the necessary steps to ensure that any client financial instruments deposited with a third party (. . .) are identifiable separately from the financial instruments belonging to the investment firm and from financial instruments belonging to that third party, by means of differently titled accounts on the books of the third party or other equivalent measures that achieve the same level of protection'. This segregation rule is designed to safeguard client securities in case of insolvency of the account provider and to prevent the use by the account provider of client securities for own account.

In the context of this initiative aimed at harmonising the framework for securities holding and dispositions, it is appropriate to regulate specifically the situation and rights of account providers' creditors. Therefore, the idea is to provide that those creditors may not attach accounts which are identified as 'client accounts' with a higher-tier account provider.

It is worth noting that in some countries there is a rebuttable presumption that an account that an account provider has with an upper-tier account provider *always* contains clients' assets, which is probably the strongest protection possible. Such national rule should be maintained and respected.

13.3 Questions

Q26: Would the proposed framework for protecting client accounts be sufficient? Should the presumption that accounts opened by an account provider with another intermediary generally contain client securities become a general rule? If not, please explain why.

14 Determination of the applicable law

14.1 Principle

1. The national law should provide that any question with respect to any of the matters specified in paragraph 3 arising in relation to account-held securities should be governed by the national law of the country where the relevant securities account is maintained by the account provider. Where an account provider has branches located in jurisdictions different from the head offices' jurisdiction, the account is maintained by the branch which handles the relationship with the account holder in relation to the securities account, otherwise by the head office.

2. An account provider is responsible for communicating in writing to the account holder whether the head office or a branch and, if applicable, which branch, handles the relationship with the account holder. The communication itself does not alter the determination of the applicable law under paragraph 1. The communication should be standardised.

3. The matters referred to in paragraph 1 are:

(a) the legal nature of account-held securities;
(b) the legal nature and the requirements of an acquisition or disposition of account-held securities as well as its effects between the parties and against third parties;
(c) whether a disposition of account-held securities extends to entitlements to dividends or other distributions, or redemption, sale or other proceeds;
(d) the effectiveness of an acquisition or disposition and whether it can be invalidated, reversed or otherwise be undone;
(e) whether a person's interest in account-held securities extinguishes or has priority over another person's interest;
(f) the duties, if any, of an account provider to a person other than the account holder who asserts in competition with the account holder or another person an interest in account-held securities;
(g) the requirements, if any, for the realisation of an interest in account-held securities.

4. Paragraph 1 determines the applicable law regardless of the legal nature of the rights conferred upon the account holder upon crediting of account-held securities to his securities account.

14.2 Background

Many dispositions in securities involve a cross-border element. Therefore, more than one jurisdiction may be relevant to these dispositions. As already mentioned, not only the legal concepts applying to securities held through account providers vary considerably, but similarly the conflict-of-laws rules do not conform to each other. Three directives address the issue, amongst other questions, notably Article 9(1) of the Financial Collateral Directive, Article 9(2) of the Settlement Finality Directive, and Article 24 of the Winding-Up Directive.

The status quo raises three questions: First, the conflict-of-laws rules as contained in the three directives are based on slightly different criteria. The envisaged legislation should bring the three rules in line with each other so as to ensure consistency and predictability.

Second, these rules exclusively apply to the relatively limited scope of the directives, notably to those organisations covered by their personal scope. The envisaged legislation should apply to all account holders and account providers. Consequently, a uniform conflict-of-laws rule for all market participants would be useful.

Third, taking Article 9(1) of the Financial Collateral Directive, which is the most recent one, as a conceptual starting point, it becomes clear that that in some (admittedly rare) cases the interpretation of where securities accounts are 'located' could diverge. That means, before settling on a uniform conflict-of-laws rule for the entire environment, the rule itself needed to be clarified as regards the so called 'connecting factor.

The connecting factor of the conflict-of-laws rule should be based on the factual criterion similar to the criterion used in the three directives, i.e. where a securities account is 'maintained'. However, more guidance is needed for proper interpretation of this criterion, in particular as regards multi-branch entities. In this respect, regard has to be given to the reasonable perspective of the account holder, which expects that the national law of the country is applicable where the branch is located which handles the relationship with the account holder in relation to the securities account. In deciding which branch is servicing the client, the question of through which branch the account was opened, which branch handles the commercial relationship with the account holder, and which branch administers payments or corporate actions relating to the securities credited to the securities account, and similar aspects, will have to be taken into account, whereas the place of the location of supporting technology or of call or mailing centres should be disregarded. However, these additional guidelines as to which branch handles the relationship should not figure as cumulative elements of the connecting factor but rather as clarifying elements of interpretation figuring in the recitals of the instrument (*cf.* paragraph 1 of the envisaged Principle).

In addition to clarifying the connecting factor itself improvement of *ex-ante* legal certainty is necessary. As the connecting factor is fact-based and subject to legal interpretation, ultimately confined to the judge, it is basically a criterion delivering an *ex post* view. However, increased legal certainty requires active reliable *ex ante* knowledge of the applicable law. Paragraph 2 of the envisaged Principle cuts the Gordian knot by prescribing a practical solution, allowing for a fact based connecting factor while at the same time increasing *ex ante* predictability: account provider should always be in a position to tell where an account is maintained, i.e. which branch handles the client relationship. This certainty should be transferred to the account holder by communicating the relevant location. The account provider should be responsible for the correct fulfilment of this duty and the competent authority should be in a position to intervene where the communication does not reflect the location where the account is actually serviced. However, there needs to be a clarification that the approach remains entirely fact based and that the communication must not be able to alter the underlying analysis of where the account is actually maintained. A judge will have to look at the facts, not at the communication, in order to determine the applicable law. In case the factual analysis and the communication differ, the factual analysis prevails and the account provider will be responsible for any incorrect communication in this regard (*cf.* Paragraph 2 of the envisaged Principle).

There is agreement that a conflict-of-laws rule should roughly cover what is dealt with in the substantive law part regarding holding and disposition of account-held securities. However, there are additional elements which need to be covered by the conflict of laws rule, notably those that are closely connected to the matter but are, in the substantive law part, left to autonomous national legislation. For instance, the characterisation of the legal nature of the rights arising from crediting securities accounts would need to be included. Furthermore, there are aspects addressed in the substantive part which should not be governed by the conflict-of-laws rule, for instance the loss sharing mechanism in case of insolvency. Consequently, a detailed list of issues setting out the scope of the conflict-of-laws rule needs to be included in a separate paragraph, (*cf.* paragraph 4 of the envisaged Principle).

There needs to be a clarification that all securities credited to a securities account are covered by the conflict-of-laws rule, regardless the legal nature that national law attributes to them. This aspect is particularly important where national law characterises certain account-held securities in a cross-border context as being of contractual or similar nature (*cf.* paragraph 5 of the envisaged Principle).

There might be additional benefit in harmonising the way by which the location is communicated to the account holder, for example in a separate document, on the account statement, or even as part of the account number. This rather technical issue would benefit from some degree of standardisation.

14.3 Questions

Q27: Would a Principle along the lines described above allow for a consistent conflict-of-laws regime? If not: Which part of the proposal causes practical difficulties that could be addressed better?

Q28: Would the mechanism of communicating to the client, whether the head offices or a branch (and if a branch, which one) is handling the relationship with the client, add to *ex ante* clarity? Is it reasonable to hold the account provider responsible for the correctness of this information? If applicable, would any negative repercussions on your business model occur?

Q29: The Hague Securities Convention (www.hcch.net/index_en.php?act=conventions.text&cid=72) provides for a global harmonised instrument regarding the conflict-of-law rule of holding and disposition of securities, covering the same scope as the proposal outlined above and the three EU Directives. Most EU Member States and the EU itself have participated in the negotiations of this Convention. The proposed principle 14 differ from the Convention as regards the basic legal mechanism for the identification of the applicable law. However, the scope of principle 14 is the same than the scope of the Convention: property law, collateral, effectiveness, priority. Do you agree that this will facilitate the resolution of conflicts with third country jurisdictions ? If not, please explain why.

15 Cross-border recognition of rights attached to securities

15.1 Principle

1. the national law governing a securities issue as well as the national law governing the holding of securities should not discriminate against the exercise of rights attached to securities held in another jurisdiction on the sole grounds that the relevant securities are held in a specific manner, in particular

- through one or more account providers,
- through an account provider acting in its own name but for the account of its account holders,
- through accounts in which securities of two or more account holders are held in an indistinguishable manner.

2. The national law should remain free to prescribe which holding methods account providers should offer to their account holders.

15.2 Background

The national law is often tailored to match domestic holding patterns and might in certain cases not correctly mirror securities holdings in other jurisdictions thus making the exercise of rights attached to the relevant securities cumbersome or impossible. It is therefore appropriate to require national law not to discriminate the exercise of rights attached to securities on the sole grounds that they are held under a holding pattern which differs from the holding pattern in the issuer's jurisdiction, as for instance the holding through more than one account providers in general, or through so called nominee or omnibus accounts which might exist in a number of jurisdictions.

Articles 13(4), (5) and 10(1), (3) of the Shareholders' Rights Directive address this issue regarding voting rights and general meetings in respect of publicly traded shares, but not in relation to *other* types of securities (in particular bonds) or other types of rights attached to securities, as for instance the acceptance of a takeover-bid or the exercise of a subscription or exchange right. Therefore, the envisaged Principle would generalise the mutual recognition of holding patterns to all types of securities.

15.3 Questions

Q30: Would a general non-discrimination rule along the lines set out above be useful? Have you encountered problems regarding the cross-border exercise of rights attached to securities?

Q31: If applicable, would a Principle along these lines have (positive or negative) repercussions on your business model? Please specify.

16 Passing on information

16.1 Principle

1. The national law should require that Information with respect to securities received by an account holder, which is not the ultimate account holder, from its account provider or from the issuer should be passed on

to its account holder or, if possible, to the ultimate account holder without undue delay as far as information

(a) is necessary in order to exercise a right attached to the securities which exists against the issuer; and
(b) is directed to all legal holders of securities of that description.

2. The account provider of the ultimate account holder must pass on information with respect to the exercise of rights attached to securities received from the ultimate account holder to the issuer of the securities or, if applicable, the following account provider without undue delay, as far as information is provided by the ultimate account holder in the course of the exercise of a right attached to the securities.

16.2 Background

Account providers, as the central element of modern securities holding and settlement, have to ensure a harmonised level of basic assistance to investors as regards the exercise of rights enshrined in securities. The first level of basic assistance, which concerns all account providers of a holding chain concerns obligation to pass on information relating to the exercise of rights attached to the securities.

Information and messages regarding the exercise of corporate rights released by the issuer need to reach the ultimate account provider in order to enable it to determine the exercise of and receive the rights attached to securities. Equally, information and messages directed by the ultimate account holder towards the issuer need to reach the latter in order to achieve that objective. All financial intermediaries acting as account providers in a holding chain should be obliged to pass on to the following link in that holding chain the information which they receive in that capacity.

Since the flow of information and messages potentially available upstream and downstream might be considerable, and considering that financial intermediaries in their role as account provider incur cost for processing it, it is appropriate to limit the flow of information and messages to the necessary.

As the information available on the side of the issuer might be vast in terms of content and possible sources, the necessary should consist of information and messages stemming from the issuer itself, as opposed to those stemming from third parties, which are being processed through the holding chain and which are necessary for the exercise of rights while at the same time being directed to all legal holders of the relevant class of securities, as opposed of being directed to individual ones. The term 'necessary' refers to information and messages which are *conditio sine qua non* for the exercise of rights attached to securities. For the obligation to process it is irrelevant whether information is also publicly available. The right and corresponding duty is without any prejudice to obligations of the issuer flowing from company law (transparency, etc.).

Information and messages stemming from the ultimate account provider should be processed only if they relate to the exercise of or the receipt of a right attached to the relevant securities.

Since the cost incurred by financial intermediaries for processing information and messages upstream and downstream will vary considerably depending on the number of financial intermediaries involved, the type of information or message, the degree of standardisation and the complexity of holding arrangements and since a regulation of the repartition of this burden amongst issuers, financial intermediaries and ultimate account holders would probably carve in stone current market complexity it is appropriate to leave the sharing of the financial burden to the market itself and control of the cost to open competition.

The duty to pass on information and messages as such should not be subject to a contractual opt-out as information should be processed to the extent to which ultimate account holders are entitled to determine the exercise of the rights. In other words, the extent of information to be processed is directly accessory to the range of rights the exercise of which can be determined by the ultimate account holder. Consequently, to the extent ultimate account holder opt out from the right to determine the exercise of and receive certain rights attached to securities (*cf. infra*), information and messages relating to relevant rights would not need to be processed. A separate opt-out provision in respect of the duty to process information and messages is therefore not appropriate.

Standardisation plays a primordial role for the development of cross-border investment. Given that the consistent and timely processing of information heavily depends on the standardisation of operational procedures and key dates used by issuers and financial intermediaries, the Commission strongly encourages market led standardisation in this field. In order to streamline existing standardisation practices, future legislation may foresee a mechanism that would facilitate and monitor market-led standardisation and install a regulatory option should market-led standardisation fail.

16.3 Questions

Q32: Is the duty to pass on information adequately kept to the necessary minimum? Is it sufficient?: If applicable, would there be any (positive or negative) repercussion of such a Principle on your business model? Please specify.

Q33: How do you see the role of market-led standardisation regarding the passing on of information? What are your views on a regulatory mechanism for streamlining standardisation procedures?

17 Facilitation of the ultimate account holder's position

17.1 Principle

1. The national law should require that the account provider of the ultimate account holder should be bound to facilitate the determination of the exercise of rights attached to securities by the ultimate account holder against the issuer or a third party as requested by the ultimate account holder.

2. Such facilitation must at least consist in the account provider of the ultimate account holder

(a) arranging for the ultimate account holder or a third person nominated by the ultimate account holder being the representative of the legal holder with respect to the exercise of the relevant rights, if the account provider or a third person is the legal holder of securities, in which case Article 11 of the Shareholders' Rights Directive applies correspondingly; or,

(b) exercising the rights attached to the securities upon authorisation and instruction and for the benefit of the ultimate account holder, if the account provider or a third person is the legal holder of the securities; or,

(c) providing the ultimate account holder, regardless of whether it is the legal holder of the securities or not, with evidence confirming its holdings and it being enabled to exercise the rights attached to the securities against the issuer or a third party, under a general framework guaranteeing the integrity of the number of available rights and the position of the legal holder of the securities in respect of lit. (c) of paragraph 2. The content and form of the evidence to be provided should be specified and standard forms should be developed, in particular to define under which conditions issuers should recognise such evidence for purposes of exercising rights attached to securities.

3. The extent to which the obligations following paragraphs 1 and 2 can be made subject to a contractual agreement between the ultimate account holder and its account provider as well as the formal requirements to be met by such agreement should be subject to restrictions for purposes of client protection.

17.2 Background

Any mechanism actually enabling the ultimate account holder to determine the exercise of and receive the rights attached to securities needs to recognise the position of the legal holder of the relevant securities (shareholder, bondholder) as determined by the national law governing the securities issue. Thus, the position of an ultimate account holder which is not the legal holder in the context of exercising and receiving rights attached to securities can only be a position derived from the legal holder's position.

The first classical means of enabling the ultimate account holder to determine the exercise of or receive the rights attached to securities is making it the legal representative of the legal holder for the purpose of exercising and receiving the rights. The envisaged legislation should take into account that the ultimate account holder might wish to have a third person determining the exercise of the rights, in particular where the securities are credited to the ultimate account holders securities account under a security interest while the security arrangement, in accordance with the applicable law, provides for the rights still to be attributed to the grantor of the security interest (*cf.* also Section 3, paragraph 3 of the envisaged Principle).

The second classical means is for the ultimate account holder to direct and authorise the exercise and receipt of rights attached to securities by the legal holder by being entitled to give instructions to it.

It is therefore appropriate to require the availability and recognition of these two methods under all Member States' law and confer on ultimate account holders which are not legal holders themselves a right to be made representative, or to be able to direct and authorise the exercise respectively.

The two described methods build on the correct identification of the legal holder of securities, as the position of the ultimate account holder is to be derived from the legal position of the former. However, in a cross-border context, the identification might be difficult and cumbersome, in particular in the scenario of multi-level holding chains crossing three or more jurisdictions and there might be uncertainty whether the ultimate account holder itself is legal holder or whether it is not. The ultimate account holder's right to become representative or to give instructions under the methods described above can only materialise if the link to the legal holder can be traced timely and reliably. It appears therefore appropriate to include a third method which evidences the position of the ultimate account holder *vis-à-vis* the issuer. In order to respect the rights of legal holders and to avoid uncertainty regarding a potential simultaneous exercise of the relevant rights by both the legal holder and the ultimate account holder at the same time it is necessary that such method is built as a closed system with the issuer providing the root for the evidence to be distributed amongst ultimate account holders. No such system exists on a universal basis and technical standards as for instance regarding bar-codes as evidence entitling to voting or internet-based participation would need to be developed.

It is important that the addressee of the ultimate account holder's right to be made a representative, to direct and authorise the exercise or to receive appropriate evidence defined. Since the ultimate account holder has access to the holding chain only through its own account provider, it should be up to this account provider to arrange for the ultimate account holder's right to be put in practice. This account provider maintains the securities for the ultimate account holder and should consequently ensure that it is legally and operationally in a position to satisfy the ultimate account holder's right to determine the exercise of and receive the rights attached to the securities under one of the three alternative methods. To this end, it must make appropriate arrangements with the remaining links of the holding chain. Market standards regarding the operational aspects of processing rights attached to securities timely and reliably through the holding chain should make possible and support such arrangements.

Following general principles this area is subject to contractual party autonomy. However, it should be made sure that dominant negotiating power of account providers *vis-à-vis* ultimate account holders, in particular retail investors, does not lead to a situation where cost structures effectively preclude the exercise of rights. It is therefore appropriate to address these aspects in some detail The various types of rights attached to securities should be taken into account. Allowing an opt-out from processing material rights (like dividend and interest payments) would only make sense in very limited cases, whereas there might be more room for contractual opt-out from participatory rights (like voting).

17.3 Questions

Q34: If you are an investor, do you think that a Principle along the lines described would make easier any cross-border exercise of rights attached to securities, provided that technical standardisation progresses simultaneously? If not, please explain why.

Q35: If you are an account provider, would you tend towards the opinion that your clients can exercise the rights attached to their cross-border holdings as efficiently as their domestic holdings? What would be the technical difficulties you would face in implementing mechanisms allowing for the fulfilment of the duties outlined above? What would be the cost involved?

18 Non-discriminatory charges

18.1 Principle

The national law should ensure that Charges levied by an account provider on its account holders for any service relating to the compliance with any of the duties established in Principles 16 and 17 in respect of cross-border holdings of securities should be the same as the charges levied by that account provider on its account holders in respect of comparable domestic holdings of securities.

18.2 Background

The implementation of Principles 16 and 17 may cause an increase of costs born by account providers, especially as concerns the costs related to crossborder holdings. The first public consultation on the securities law legislation held in 2009 reported a tendency for account providers to elevate fees or reduce the level of services concerning the passing up and down of information and the processing of corresponding rights.

Generally, such costs related to the processing of rights are shared on a contractual basis between account providers and issuers on the one hand, and between account providers and account holders on the other hand. But the creation by virtue of law of additional costs related to crossborder transactions bypasses ordinary contractual arrangements and should therefore be accompanied by provisions organising their fair allocation.

Therefore, the Commission services consider an alternative solution consisting, instead of a direct regulation of the allocation of costs, in the setting of a general principle governing the level of costs incurred by crossborder holding. As a matter of fact, since the major mandate of the contemplated securities law legislation is to ensure an efficient single market where crossborder holdings are as safe as domestic holdings, a parallel rule regarding costs should ensure that fees incurred by crossborder holdings of securities are the same fees charged for domestic holdings. A similar approach was followed in the payment area, where regulation 2560/2001 and regulation 924/2009 set a rule granting that fees charged for crossborder transfers of cash should not be higher than fees charged for domestic transfers of cash.

As a consequence and with a view to promoting investment throughout the entire EU and to protecting investors holding portfolios of securities from more than one EU jurisdiction, it is appropriate to prevent discrimination of cross-border holdings as opposed to purely domestic holdings in terms of cost structures. The principle above is inspired by Article 3 of Regulation 924/2009, especially the concept of 'corresponding national holding' referring to correspondences between domestic and national holdings, by class of assets or by description of securities. Contrary to Article 3 of Regulation 924/2009, it might not be necessary to set a threshold since the first consultation of 2009 has shown that the risk of discrimination due to a crossborder context concerns large holdings as well as small holdings.

18.3 Questions

Q36: If you are account holder, have you encountered differing prices for the domestic and the cross-border exercise of rights attached to securities? If yes, please specify.

Q37: If you are an account provider: do you price cross-border exercise of rights differently from domestic exercise? If yes: on what grounds are different pricing models necessary?

19 Holding in and through third countries

19.1 Principle

An account provider should make reasonable and appropriate arrangements with its account holder if the account holder maintains account-held securities for others and is not subject to the rules of this Directive, facilitating the effective exercise of rights attached to the securities which the account holder holds for others. Technical standards to be adopted by the Commission on this issue could be envisaged.

19.2 Background

As a considerable part of cross-jurisdictional holding situations involves third-country account providers, there needs to be a rule promoting the principles described above in exactly such a context. This is all the more important as sometimes holding chains 'exit and re-enter' the EU, i.e. in cases in which one of the account providers involved is located in a third country but its account holders are, again, located within the EU. The application of the proposed provisions themselves will be naturally confined to EUregulated entities. Therefore, any mechanism promoting the principles in a third-country context must in the first place connect to an EU-regulated entity that is the last entity before the holding chain 'exits' the EU. This entity has to comply with the envisaged legislation, also in relation to its third-country account holder. If this non-EU account holder is itself an account provider for a third party, the duties of the envisaged legislation cannot apply to this latter relationship. Therefore, an EU-initiative will be unable to *guarantee* the effective exercise of rights by clients of a non-EU account provider. In order to *promote the improvement* the effective exercise of rights in such cases, it is appropriate to introduce an extended duty of the EU regulated account provider which serves the non-EU account provider.

19.3 Questions

Q38: Have you encountered difficulties in using non-EU linkages as regards the exercise of rights attached to securities? If yes, please specify. If not, please explain why.

Q39: Admitting that non-EU account providers cannot be reached by the planned legislation, which steps could be undertaken on the side of EU account providers involved in the holding in order to improve the exercise of rights attached to securities through a holding chain involving non-EU account providers?

20 Exercise by account provider on the basis of contract

20.1 Principle

Where an ultimate account holder is able to exercise itself the rights flowing from securities but does not want to do so, its account provider exercises these rights upon its authorisation and instruction and in accordance with the contractually agreed level of services. There should be an EU-wide standard regarding the formal requirements to be met by such an agreement as far as it provides for general authorisation of the account provider to exercise the rights flowing from the securities.

20.2 Background

Where an ultimate account holder could exercise the rights attached to securities itself because it is at the same time legal holder of the securities but does not want to so, the account provider should be obliged to exercise on his behalf only within the framework of the level of service contractually agreed between both parties. Since this principle bears the risk that ultimate account holders transfer the right to receive and exercise the rights in too extensive a manner, again against the background of bargaining power and cost structures, detailed rules could define the limits of such transfer, in particular the formal requirements to be met by a general and permanent transfer of the right to exercise and receive the rights attached to the securities.

20.3 Questions

Q40: Do you think that a general authorisation to exercise and receive rights given by the account holder to the account provider should be made subject to certain formal requirements? Please specify.

21 Account provider status

21.1 Principle

All securities account providers should be regulated on a European level. To this end, 'safekeeping of securities [etc.]', Annex I Section B (1) of the MiFID, should be upgraded to become an investment service (under Section A(9) of Annex I) and those which provide this service should be authorised and supervised under MiFID.

21.2 Background

All jurisdictions aim at increasing the safety and soundness of holding through account providers as these entities are in a position to play a central role in the safeguarding of the integrity of a securities issue and the protection of investor's holdings. Therefore, account provider's activity is regularly put under the scrutiny of a competent authority. Providing the service of maintaining securities accounts is an 'ancillary service under Annex I Section B of the MIFID. The provision of ancillary services per se does not require an authorisation. However, if provided by an investment firm, the rules of the MIFID apply (cf. Articles 5(1) and 6(1) of the

MIFID). This means that if an account provider is not an investment firm in the sense of MIFID, its activity, though being an ancillary service, is not subject to the rules of the current possible legislative initiative. Hence, at the level of the EU, there is a regulatory 'gap' as there is no common rule on the question of whether or not such entities have to be subject to authorisation and regulation which might be filled by upcoming harmonised legislation.

21.3 Questions

Q41: Should the status of account provider be subject to a specific authorisation? If not, please explain why.

Q42: If yes, do you think that MIFID would be an appropriate instrument to cover the authorisation and supervision of account providers?

22 Glossary

(a) 22.1 Principles'securities' means financial instruments as listed in Annex I Section C of Directive 2004/39/EC, which are capable of being credited to a securities account;

(b) 'securities account' means an account between an account provider and an account holder allowing for the evidencing of securities holdings of that account holder with that account provider;

(c) 'account provider' means a person who:
- maintains securities accounts for account holders and is authorised in accordance with Article 5 of Directive 2004/39/EC to provide services listed in Annex I Section A indent (9) of Directive 2004/39/EC or is a Central Securities Depository as defined in [. . .] and, in either case, is acting in that capacity;
- *[in relation to Principles 3 to 13, if not subject to a national law, in the course of a business or other regular activity maintains securities accounts for others or both for others and for its own account and is acting in that capacity;]*

(d) 'account holder' means a person for whom an account provider maintains a securities account, whether that person is acting for its own account or for others, including in the capacity of account provider;

(e) 'ultimate account holder' means an account holder which is not acting in the capacity of account provider for another person;

(f) 'legal holder' means the shareholder, bondholder or holder of other financial instruments, as defined by the national law under which the relevant securities are constituted;

(g) 'insolvency proceeding' means any winding-up proceeding or reorganisation measure as defined in Article 2 (1)(j) and (k) of Directive 2002/47/EC;

(h) 'insolvency administrator means any person or body appointed by the administrative or judicial authorities whose task is to administer an insolvency proceeding;

(i) 'securities of the same description' means securities issued by the same issuer and being of the same class of shares or stock; or in the case of securities other than shares or stock, being of the same currency and denomination and treated as forming part of the same issue;

(j) 'securities settlement system' means a system as defined in Article 2(a) of Directive 98/26/EC for the processing of transfer orders referred to under the second indent of Article 2(i) of Directive 98/26/EC;

(k) 'acquisition' means the receiving of account-held securities or of a security interest or other limited interest therein;

(l) 'disposition' means
- to relinquish account-held securities (disposal), in particular for the purpose of a sale,
- to create security interests or other limited interests in account-held securities in favour of another person, or
- to relinquish security interests or other limited interests in accountheld securities.

(m) 'reversal' means that a crediting, debiting, earmarking or removal of an earmarking is undone by a converse act;

(n) 'crediting' means the adding of account-held securities to a securities account;

(o) 'debiting' means the subtracting of account-held securities from a securities account;

(p) 'earmarking' means an entry in a securities account made in favour of a person, including the account provider, other than the account holder in relation to account-held securities, which, under the account agreement, a control agreement, the rules of a securities settlement system or the applicable law, has either or both of the following effects:

- that the account provider is not permitted to comply with any instructions given by the account holder in relation to the accountheld securities as to which the entry is made without the consent of that person;
- that the relevant intermediary is obliged to comply with any instructions given by that person in relation to the account-held securities as to which the entry is made in such circumstances and as to such matters as may be provided by the account agreement, a control agreement or the rules of a securities settlement system, without any further consent of the account holder;

(q) 'control agreement' means an agreement in relation to account-held securities between an account holder, the account provider and another person or, if so provided by the applicable law, between an account holder and the account provider or between an account holder and another person of which the account provider receives notice, which includes either or both of the following provisions:
- that the account provider is not permitted to comply with any instructions given by the account holder in relation to the accountheld securities to which the agreement relates without the consent of that other person;
- that the account provider is obliged to comply with any instructions given by that other person in relation to the accountheld securities to which the agreement relates in such circumstances and as to such matters as may be provided by the agreement, without any further consent of the account holder;

(r) 'attachment of account-held securities of an account holder' means any judicial, administrative or other act or process to freeze, restrict or impound account-held securities of that account holder in order to enforce or satisfy a judgment, award or other judicial, arbitral, administrative or other decision or in order to ensure the availability of such account-held securities to enforce or satisfy any future judgement, award or decision.

22.2 Background

The terms contained in this glossary define the basic legal terms on which a possible legislation could be built. In the present context it is particularly important as the functional approach requires the use of neutral terms, in order to avoid confusion with traditional legal terms which might differ in detail in the various Member States' law.

For example, 'control agreement' refers to methods to create for example a pledge, charge, mortgage or other security interest. 'Control agreement' is used to encompass pledges, charges, etc. under national law which can be created by an arrangement where a person obtains control of the pledged asset and exercises that control to ensure the security takers right to enforce the security interest in case of default of the security provider.

The functional approach is therefore a descriptive one, helping to avoid the misunderstanding that identical words mean the same thing in different legal traditions.

On a number of defined terms more specific information is provided in the context of the material provisions presented in the previous sections.

Attention of stakeholders is drawn on the definition of 'Account provider', second paragraph, which seeks for global compatibility with non EU definitions, in the case of holding chains that cross EU borders. This second paragraph is at a very preliminary stage of drafting and presented only for the sake of consistency.

22.3 Questions

Q43: Do the terms used in this glossary facilitate the understanding of the further envisaged Principles ? If no, please explain why.

Q44: Would you add other definitions to this glossary ?

Answers to be sent to: markt-consultation-sld@ec.europa.eu

Specific questions can be asked to :

Marcel-Eric Terret: marcel-eric.terret@ec.europa.eu

Olga Tyton: olga.tyton@ec.europa.eu

* * *

Commission européenne, B-1049 Bruxelles / Europese Commissie, B-1049 Brussel – Belgium. Telephone: (32–2) 299 11 11. http://ec.europa.eu/internal_market/

INDEX